Athena Unbound

Also by Peter Baldwin

Command and Persuade: Crime, Law, and the State across History

Fighting the First Wave:
Why the Coronavirus Was Tackled So Differently across the Globe

The Copyright Wars: Three Centuries of Trans-Atlantic Battle

The Narcissism of Minor Differences: How America and Europe Are Alike

Disease and Democracy: The Industrialized World Faces AIDS

Contagion and the State in Europe, 1830–1930

The Politics of Social Solidarity:
Class Bases of the European Welfare State, 1875–1975

Athena Unbound

Why and How Scholarly Knowledge Should Be Free for All

Peter Baldwin

The MIT Press

Cambridge, Massachusetts | London, England

The MIT Press would like to thank the anonymous peer reviewers who provided comments on drafts of this book. The generous work of academic experts is essential for establishing the authority and quality of our publications. We acknowledge with gratitude the contributions of these otherwise uncredited readers.

This book was set in ITC Stone Serif Std and ITC Stone Sans Std by New Best-set Typesetters Ltd. Printed and bound in the United States of America.

Library of Congress Cataloging-in-Publication Data

Names: Baldwin, Peter, 1956– author.
Title: Athena unbound : why and how scholarly knowledge should be free for all / Peter Baldwin.
Description: Cambridge, Massachusetts : The MIT Press, [2023] | Includes bibliographical references and index.
Identifiers: LCCN 2022027103 (print) | LCCN 2022027104 (ebook) | ISBN 9780262048002 (hardcover) | ISBN 9780262373951 (epub) | ISBN 9780262373968 (pdf)
Subjects: LCSH: Open access publishing. | Scholarly electronic publishing.
Classification: LCC Z286.O63 B35 2023 (print) | LCC Z286.O63 (ebook) | DDC 070.5/7973—dc23/eng/20220628
LC record available at https://lccn.loc.gov/2022027103
LC ebook record available at https://lccn.loc.gov/2022027104

10 9 8 7 6 5 4 3 2 1

For

†Andrew Paulson
Therkel Stræde
Morten Vest
Cathy Watson

Half a century of friendship each

Contents

Contents

Introduction
Snatching the Good from the Jaws of the Best

"The best is the enemy of the good" is an aphorism purloined by Voltaire from an Italian source. Aiming for perfection, we ignore the achievable. Open access is a visionary quest whose ultimate ambition is an absolute: All knowledge should be freely available to anyone anywhere. From the Ptolemies on, humans have dreamed of an Alexandrian library housing all we know, a single unified source of all information, enlightenment's abode. In the era of parchment, paper, and binding, the closest we came were the great national and university libraries. These cathedrals of learning's reading rooms envelop visitors with a secular sense of the sacred. Knowledge is shuttled back and forth, readers bow their heads over the tables, and visitors murmur in hushed tones.

Digital technologies, with their almost costless reproducibility, and the internet, with its seamless global embrace, catapulted this vision skyward. Every laptop connected to the internet could now be Alexandria. Rarely had a potential utopia appeared to materialize so unexpectedly or quickly. Little wonder, then, that the ambitions inspired were fervent, the passions behind the cause, strong.

Yet aspiration and disappointment go hand in hand. As Bismarck, father of *Realpolitik*, reminded us, politicians exercise the art of the possible. A digital Alexandrian library was now theoretically and technically feasible. But did that mean we could achieve it? Realizing open access in practical terms faces many hurdles. Not all authors want their work made available to consumers at no cost. Many live by selling their content and see no reason for change. Their claims are what copyright was invented in the eighteenth century to protect. As instituted in some nations, moral rights give authors even stronger protections—not just to sell their work, but to guard it against misuse, reuse, and unauthorized change. None of that bodes well for open access.

To persuade such authors to surrender at least some of their rights, open accessors have argued the virtues of networking. The more information is available to others, drawn into linkages of association and affiliation, and thus put to use, the more fruitful and valuable it becomes. As science and creativity have become more collaborative, pursued by groups rather than solitary authors, access and availability have enhanced knowledge's worth. Knowledge embedded is knowledge multiplied.

Add in, that realistically, not many freelance authors make a living from their work, and it stands to reason that being used by others may be more important than slight mercenary rewards. Such considerations must be weighed by each author. Do we hope—however vainly—for a breakthrough into stardom with its attendant audience? Or do we cast our lot with the globe's collective creativity, each contributing a modest brick to building the tower of human knowledge? This decision has no moral import. Authors can be persuaded, but not obliged, to consider the collective good over their personal ambitions.

However, this is not true for those who are paid to labor for humanity, not just themselves. Work for hire is an offshoot of copyright that assigns rights in works to their commissioner, not the immediate author. The doctrine was first developed to deal with portraits, paid for by someone else, often the person rendered. In such cases of *Gebrauchskunst*, art that serves a practical purpose, the commissioner was thought to have a closer relationship to the work than the artist. The privacy right of controlling the portrait outweighed the moral rights of the artist who had accepted a fee for the commission. From here, work for hire expanded to include the collaborative arts, especially film. Since many toiled, not everyone could be the author or rights holder. The more collaborators, the less any one participant had the oversight to be an author in the Romantic sense.[1] Yet, someone had to assume ultimate responsibility, and that was usually the commissioner or employer of the others.

The bulk of scientific and academic work today is done by employees of universities, think tanks, museums, and research institutes. Corporate R&D—the biggest single bloc of all scientific work—is governed by work for hire. No one gives a second thought to the rights of Boeing engineers or Apple software programmers to their work. University professors and researchers, in contrast, are birds of a different feather—enjoying the security of civil servants and the intellectual freedom of bohemians, as Henry Rosovsky once put it to a cohort of newly hooded PhDs. They are considered to be much like Romantic artistes, individual creators whose work—emanations of their personalities—is their property. They are free to do with it as they please, even as salaries pay for their activities and research funds cover their labs, assistants, and travels.

Legally, work for hire does not apply to the American professoriate. But what about the ethical import of how its work is financed? Most research funding is paid from tax revenues or is at least subsidized by the deductibility of private donations. Academic researchers, in effect, work for the tax-paying public. Broad social benefits may arise from making academic work widely available. But the moral leverage exerted by open access rests on the implication that, having paid for the work, the public is entitled to use it. So long as access to publicly funded work involves no control or influence, and academic freedom remains inviolate, the ethical logic here is persuasive.

But this holds only for scholarly work. Most scientific articles are written by academic researchers, and it is here that the first battles over accessibility have been fought. For books, the case is less clear-cut. Only a small fraction of all volumes are authored by salaried researchers, published by university presses, or otherwise subject to the moral logic of open access. For obviously commercial media—film, music, art—there is no case to be made for open access. In the heat of debate, it is easy to miss the obvious point that only for a small fraction of works is the moral argument for opening it to the public—as opposed to the argument from social utility—convincing.

Yet, even where open access is justifiable, further obstacles loom. In the old analog system, readers paid for the pleasure of their consumption. Whether retail buyers or libraries settled the bills mattered less than that the funds came from the demand side. With digitality and especially the promise of collections that go beyond merely national institutions to approximate a global library of Alexandria, that has to change. After Alexandria under the Ptolemies in the first century BCE, no single library has again aspired to collect everything. Even national collections are not exhaustive for their own remits, although in theory, deposit libraries, where publishers are obliged to send a copy of everything they issue, should come close. The Library of Congress, for example, receives two copies of every book printed in the US but is not mandated to preserve even one.[2]

But for anything beyond the nation, barring unprecedented international cooperation, no single analog library could hope to be universal. The acquisition costs alone would be insurmountable, not to mention storage, preservation, and access. To collect globally, a new funding system is required. Financing has to shift from demand to the supply side. Only if those who produce content also pay to disseminate it can it all be made available. That was possible only once digitality had largely eliminated the expense of all copies after the first.

The idea that the author should pay to publish seems revolutionary when compared to the inherited system where eager readers or their library proxies bought works. In practical terms, however, the change is less far-reaching. Authors already bear the cost of producing content. For much scientific research, with its labs, field stations, telescopes, and colliders, the sums are huge. Of course, it is a big ask to demand that a poet or philosopher whose research infrastructure may amount to a notebook and pencil should underwrite dissemination. But for scientists with impressive research budgets, broadcasting the results costs a small fraction (2% perhaps) of the overall expense of their work. Authors already pay to produce content; why not also to disseminate it? Open access hinges on flipping the funding stream from consumer to producer. Whether the dissemination is paid for directly by authors, or indirectly by funders or some third party, including governments, is less important than shifting the cost away from consumers. This core tenet of open access is what allows us to envisage the global availability of all (scholarly) content.

The ease and perfection with which digitality allows work to be duplicated reduce, but do not eliminate, the cost of the first copy. The value added by legacy publishers has doubtless been exaggerated. Compared to analog precedents, digital efficiencies can be harvested, and of course, the final copy at the margin is practically free. Furthermore, tasks once gathered under the publisher's umbrella—copyediting, typesetting, proofreading, indexing—can be outsourced. Nonetheless, short of just posting typescripts to the web, dissemination costs money that must be found even for open-access works.

The good news is that enough money exists already in the world's current library systems to flip all academic content from the traditional reader-pays model to a new author-pays system. Whether libraries are financing journal subscriptions and the retail price of books, as before, or the fees required for open access publication does not much matter, so long as the sums are comparable. If 200 libraries pay $75 each for an academic monograph or band together to pay the $15,000 an open-access publisher needs to make the work freely available is a wash for their budgets.

But for the world, the difference is huge. In the old system, patrons could read a work if they chanced to live nearby and if they happened to be permitted access to the library of a university or other closed institution. In the new system, everyone can read the work at any internet connection. In effect, digitality allows the most efficient bulk-purchasing conceivable. The discount granted these libraries, united as a buyers' consortium, takes the form of universal access.

The bad news is that, just because the money exists, does not mean it can be used for such purposes. First, only part of library budgets is earmarked for academic content. Even if all scholarly output became open access, much work would still need to be bought in the usual fashion. Second, much of the part of library budgets used for academic content is already spoken for and is unlikely to be easily repurposed. Long before digitality and the first hints of open access, scientific periodical publishers had stitched up the library market to their own ends. Starting in the 1970s, they brought forth many new journals, published more articles than ever, and charged steeper subscription prices.

Part of this shift reflected the postwar boom in scientific output. More researchers were at work as universities hired women and once-excluded minorities. Research institutions in the Global South began to contribute to the swelling stream of content. Since all this deserved to see the light, the science publishers spotted an opportunity not only to do what was right and necessary but also to profit from it. The cost of journals skyrocketed, and library budgets were drained by paying subscriptions, while monographs and other scholarly output were neglected.

This serials crisis predated both digitality and open access. When these new possibilities appeared, the scientific publishers at first feared their lush markets would desiccate. They soon learned, however, that the new world was nothing to fear. Whether libraries paid subscriptions or article processing charges was a matter of indifference, so long as the monies remained comparable. The scientific publishers quickly adopted the new open-access mantra, chanting it all the way to the bank. As with subscriptions, they charge what the market will bear, not what it costs to issue online articles. The most prestigious publishers demand fees that are perhaps five times what their more modest competitors levy and what studies suggest are the actual costs. The serials crisis continues to afflict the post-paper era, as library budgets still cannot meet the scientific presses' prices and other media, such as monographs, are sidelined.

This is the landscape where battles over open access are fought. On the horizon, a Shangri-La of limitless available knowledge beckons, but to reach it, forbidding terrain must be traversed. Doubtless, humanity would profit if everyone could read everything, but important vested interests block such aspirations. Works with commercial ambitions constitute most output, and the bulk of content, susceptible to no moral argument for openness, remains closed

Scientists work directly on the natural world. When they write up their research, there is only reality's facticity and their conclusions. Copyright in others' work is not an issue. Nor do they entertain any hopes of reward other than the purely intellectual. They are indifferent to sales. For them, the open-access problem is easily resolved. Once the monies have been found to pay for scientific publications, they can be offered to the world.

For humanities scholars and many social scientists, in contrast, their subjects are often the copyrighted work of others. The problem of continued intellectual lock-up must be faced. And for all authors who aspire to audiences and royalties, open access has no appeal. Only two arguments could gain traction with them. First, those with no realistic chance of a large following or a lucrative career may be won over by the virtues of making their output more widely available—harvesting readers rather than rewards. Beyond this, most works lose their commercial appeal shortly after publication. Rare is the book that is bought even a few years out. Despite having no further monetary value, content still remains locked up by copyright for well over a century. Since little would be lost, both considerations favor the public good of making works freely available.

Though it falls short of true open access, one means of liberating works is known as controlled digital lending. Libraries have retooled for the digital age by making books available on-screen to any reader, one at a time, as with physical volumes. Digitality's conquering of distance and time is harnessed to library lending. Yet, copyright is preserved by not allowing more than the initial (digital) reproduction nor more than a one-to-one loan-to-own ratio. If controlled digital lending holds up against its current legal challenges, it might help free up content that would otherwise not be susceptible to open access. This would not meet the purist's standards of true accessibility, but it would at least allow on-screen reading anywhere by anyone.

The vested interests of rights-holders are open access's biggest hurdle. For scientists, this is not a pressing issue, and some non-academic authors may be persuaded to favor open access by the virtues of networking. Controlled digital lending may pry works from copyright's clammy grasp after a few years. Some rights-holders' objections can be overcome or sidestepped. But not all. Established scientific publishers are the most powerful interest impeding open access, and they are a tough nut. Their conquest of the journals in the postwar years and their subsequent discovery that publishing charges could be as lucrative as subscriptions persuaded them to dig in. More recently, they have begun moving up the research chain. They now stake claims to organizing, managing, and disseminating scientific data, not just the published results. That will make them even harder to dislodge.

Open access's vaulting ambitions thus slam head-on into powerful, entrenched, and widely popular interests supporting the existing copyright system. To achieve broad access via legal reform, two approaches are available, but unlikely to succeed. Scaling back copyright's duration for all content in order to make the prize less worth fighting over would antagonize almost all non-scholarly authors and many academics, too. Trying to distinguish legally between academic and non-academic content, allowing open access for the scholarly, would involve endless definitional hairsplitting and objections from academic authors with ambitions for an audience. Going down these roads, we are unlikely to achieve much success soon.

Expecting scientific publishers voluntarily to relinquish their gains is equally implausible. Reformers have spent the last 30 years seeking to regulate pharmaceutical prices in the US without much luck. Since every consumer prefers cheaper medicines and therefore sides with the reformers, that does not bode well for hopes of prying loose the publishers' grasp of scientific output—a dispute where the status quo has the backing of most authors. The most immediate beneficiaries of broad open access would be developed-world citizens without research library cards and the Global South. Neither is a constituency with much heft in the industrialized world's disputes over intellectual property.

Realistically, broad reform is unlikely soon. The sciences have largely solved the problem for themselves. Scientific research is on its way to becoming freely available. As university and research budgets are rejiggered to pay for publication fees rather than subscriptions, we are within sighting distance of that goal. But it comes at a steep price—the gutting of library budgets for purposes other than the scientific, leaving academic monographs and humanities journals adrift. Exploiting the efficiencies of digital dissemination on behalf of non-scientific publications and channeling funding in this direction remain the practical goals the open-access movement can set. This is less than what the most fervent open accessors aspire to, but it is likely to be what can be hoped for. And it remains a far cry better than what we have.

Where We Are Going

Torrents have been written about open access, but little comes from those who supply or consume knowledge: the scholars who produce the works that are to be accessible and their potential readers, whether colleagues or the general public. Instead, the drum is beaten by librarians, information- and data-science scholars, media professors, and others who populate a kind of second-order stratum of academia, scholars of scholarship.

A vast quantity of work has billowed forth, professionalizing the field by making it a full-time job just to keep up. Countless conferences, workshops, networks, study groups, Twitter feeds, journals, and blogs keep up a tireless outpouring. The caravan moves on, but where is it going? Founding and running open-access journals and publishers, organizing boycotts of the worst-offending academic presses, lobbying politicians to reform copyright laws, probing the boundaries of what counts as legal under current rules: such activities move us toward a freer exchange of information. What the theorizing and discussion contribute is less obvious. As so often in the academic world, noble intent does not necessarily produce tangible results. Process is often confused with progress.

Why, then, add another brick to the edifice? Because many participants come from a nimbus formed around the scholarly enterprise without being part of it, they often pay little attention to workaday academics' concerns. Especially in the humanities, arts, and social sciences, the professoriate is surprisingly ignorant of—and, if aware, often hostile to—open access. Because the well-funded sciences have been the first to warm to the cause, open access has been tailored to their specifications, with publishing fees paid out of generous research budgets. Including less well-endowed fields remains a hurdle.

This book seeks to flesh out debates that often remain focused on the sciences. It situates current discussions in a long history of information's progress toward greater openness. Despite the mantra that "information wants to be free," much does not. Corporate R&D makes up the majority of research and is not striving for release. Most writers of fiction and commercially viable nonfiction sell their wares in the marketplace, hope to live from the proceeds, and have no interest in opening up. That holds for most producers of visual and aural content, too. Nor are privacy and open access harmonious bunkmates. We naturally resist freeing up information about ourselves except as we choose.

The problem of too much information is a leitmotif. Even without copyright reform or open access, as the public domain inevitably expands, freely available content will eventually dwarf what any current cohort of creators issues. What effect will this have on future cultural producers' motivations to bring forth novel work? What does the common complaint that we disgorge too much information mean? Can more information ever be a bad thing, even if some is mediocre?

Enthused by the idea that openness must be an absolute, the debate often fails to situate the particular circumstances of academic knowledge in the broader domain of intellectual property. For most content, there is no moral case for accessibility. Yes, other arguments also speak for the virtues of opening up—the logic of knowledge as a commons and the turbocharging of its usefulness allowed by networks. These are claims of public utility. None packs an ethical punch. Most cultural producers do not (yet) want to make work freely available. Only for content that society has paid for can it also claim access. Work for hire is the logic of open access's moral leverage. But when applied to scholarship, it is often dismissed as a neoliberal encroachment on academic freedom and the sanctity of the university. Perhaps it could just as well be seen as an element in democratizing access to the ivory tower's knowledge.

The humanities and social sciences have been the stepchildren of these debates. For the hard sciences, existing funding only needs to be repurposed. The expense of disseminating results is a small fraction of research's total cost. But more than money separates the humanities from the sciences. Humanists cannot be as indifferent to aesthetic and presentational issues as their scientific colleagues. They claim a continued stake in how others use their works. Their data are not just nature's coalface, but often the copyrighted work of others to which they can lay no claims. Lack of funding has not only hamstrung their ability to adopt open access on the scientific model. The sciences' ability to solve the problem for themselves has drained library budgets that once were more equitably shared, compounding the issue for other scholars.

1

Some Knowledge Wants to Be Free

Senegal is among the world's poorest nations. At the law library of Cheikh Anta Diop University in Dakar, the stacks are full of photocopies of textbooks, not the books themselves. Eager for knowledge, obliged by their course syllabi to read, but unable to afford the texts, students vandalize the originals by tearing out the pages their professors assign. The library has countered by installing xerox machines—to make copies of the copies, rather than decimate what remains of the books.[1] Scarce resources thus prompt at least two offenses: destroying the books and then violating their authors' copyright with the library's tacit connivance.

How unfair that some parts of the world wallow in a surfeit of information while elsewhere a thirst for knowledge finds no slaking. What makes this crass disparity not just another instance of global maldistribution is that, in our era of astonishing intellectual flourishing, we also have the means to give all knowledge to every human at no significant new cost. Global redistribution of other resources—physical, costly, and rivalrous—remains expensive and politically fraught. Intellectual property has always been intangible. But in the past, it was embodied in physical media that cost money to make, reproduce, and distribute, which therefore were similar to other goods.

Digitality, however, has ephemeralized intellectual property. The first copy of a book or article is expensive, but every further digital copy costs almost nothing. Because intellectual property is non-rivalrous, many can use it simultaneously, with no one the worse off.[2] Distributing intellectual goods widely and freely has thus become possible in a way inconceivable for other resources. We live in a tantalizingly fecund moment when we see how knowledge can become a global public good but have not yet quite figured out how to achieve it.

Not everyone agrees that our era is a cultural cornucopia. Examples of decline abound—children stare at screens rather than read books, classical music is wasting away, modern figurative art is treated by collectors as a store of value, pornography has an oversized presence on the web, and tacky literary prizes proliferate to mark intellectual achievement—whatever one's favorite measure of postlapsarian degeneration.[3] Is what was once known as culture *tout court*, the genteel art forms, prospering? Opinions differ wildly.

But if we take a more expansive view of culture to include also scholarship and science, things look up. No matter what is true for the humanities, the social sciences, and especially the life and hard sciences, are flourishing. As measured by practitioners, students, output, and funding, things have never been better. Almost 7,000 scholarly articles are published every day, two and a half million annually.[4] As measured by the content in JSTOR, the main Anglophone social science repository, the output of scholarly articles has expanded tenfold, from one per 16,000 US residents in 1800 to one per 1,500 in 2000.[5] Research funding increased from 1% of GDP in the early twentieth century to almost thrice that in 2017.[6] Authors have published more books this past year than ever before, and that counts only conventional ones. Add in the self-published works now possible thanks to digital technologies and the number mushrooms.

Measuring our knowledge output is tricky, but it has rapidly expanded. It grew 1% annually into the mid-eighteenth century,

2% to 3% through the interwar years, and 8% or 9% in the post-war era. At the current rate, knowledge doubles every nine years.[7] Humanity now produces more information every year than during its entire span from civilization's beginning to the year 2000.[8] Granted, sudoku books make up a large slug of this. Nor is every field overfulfilling its five-year plans: Despite massive research funding, the number of approved drugs has fallen since the 1980s.[9] And suppose that by information we mean only *data*. In that case, such production numbers are multiplied by the ever-growing avalanche of bytes spat forth by the internet of things, as it tracks traffic, mail, passengers, customers, doorbell ringers, and the content of our fridges.[10] Quantity may not be everything, but it does indicate a certain rude health of our endeavors.

Knowledge's Inexorable Spread

A fundamental premise of modern society is that the more broadly knowledge is spread, the better. Priestly castes once monopolized access to the divine, to what counted as knowledge. So long as most people could not read, the literate derived power from mediating information. As literacy spread in the early modern period, new readers could forge their own immediate connection to the known. With the Bible translated into Europe's vernacular languages, the laity formed its own opinions of doctrine. Protestantism attacked the priesthood and its stranglehold on official truth. Its most fervent sects preached a universalist epistemology, giving each believer a direct connection to the godhead. With everyone equally knowledgeable, all followers, in effect, became priests, pursuing their interpretation of scripture regardless of doctrine.[11] The printing press fired the engines of the Reformation.

Knowledge's spread had both enlightened and nihilistic results. Giddy at the thought that everyone stood equidistant from the truth, many who were emancipated into the light felt released from social bonds and conventions. Convinced of their omniscience and infallibility, the illuminati sometimes ran amok. In the twelfth and thirteenth centuries, the Free Spirits of northern France and the Rhine Valley thought their immediate relation to God unfettered them from the Church and its sacraments. Sinless and unbound by conventional morality, they indulged in spectacular feats of sexual promiscuity, even incest. Intercourse with the illuminated, the men cunningly claimed, restored a woman's virginity.[12]

With the Scientific Revolution, starting in the sixteenth century, knowledge shifted its foundation from religious revelation to empirical observation informed by secular theory. The scientific method assumed that any rational, sentient human could understand and practice the technique. In its everyday aspect, the scientific process was broken into bite-size pieces, so that carrying out experiments became a technical task—as anyone who has worked in a lab can attest. Yet, the caste mentality of the initiated persisted. Knowledge did not arrive effortlessly but required discipline, training, and perseverance. Even as most were theoretically capable of attaining it, only a few did in practice.

The distinction between knowledgeable insiders and benighted masses persists today. While education and even universities eventually democratized, they remained based on a hierarchy of expertise, topped by a mandarin class. Once an inherited status, the professoriate was passed like the family silver to male offspring. Eventually, it became more meritocratic. Still, requiring cultural capital to access and years of training, the university mandarinate remains less open to raw talent than occupations where outcomes can be ruthlessly quantified, such as finance and some branches of industry. Untutored talent holds outsized sway also in activities where capability is distributed at random—music, acting, modeling. Yet, some aspects of academia became more meritocratic. Newcomers and outsiders, such as Jewish and working-class students, succeeded better in emerging fields than in venerable subjects—physics more than chemistry, sociology more than philology.

In its time, every expansion of education has been resisted, whether mandating schooling for youngsters or opening universities to women. Not everyone was cut out for study; trying to educate the lower classes would sour them to their lot in life; knowledge would be devalued if dumbed down for all to grasp: such were the arguments against an unfettered opening of enlightenment.[13] And yet, the spread of knowledge has been unstoppable. Compulsory secondary education, state-financed universities, night and professional schools, correspondence courses, continuing education, mass online university classes—all have served to breach the academy's palisades. Public expenditure on education in the developed world has risen tenfold, from 0.6% of GDP in 1870 to 6.1% in the 1990s.[14]

University attendance has not unstoppably increased. In the eighteenth century, university enrollments in England were lower than they had been in the seventeenth.[15] But over the past century, university attendance has shot up globally. In 1869, 1.3% of American 18- to 24-year-olds went to university; in 1991, 54% did.[16] The US was an outlier in how early it educated the mass of its population, but most Western nations followed suit over the twentieth century.[17] In the many countries where at least 40% have now completed a first university degree, probably almost everyone who can go to college, and wants to, does. The developed world has likely hit peak university. Higher education has therefore become an export industry, especially in the Anglophone nations. Recruits from abroad supplement a flat-lined domestic applicant pool. How long foreign-student enrollment survives the sticker shock from skyrocketing tuitions and ever-improving alternatives at home remains to be seen.

There is more knowledge to delight and enlighten us, and not only are we better equipped to appreciate, enjoy, and employ it, but also it is more available. We think of libraries as a great public good, an appurtenance of democracy, one of the palaces of the people.[18] But neither ancient Athens nor the Roman republic had public libraries. At first, the great collections were the work of rulers like the Ptolemies of Egypt or the absolutist monarchs of Europe. Their books were available to only a few favored scholars, whose presence buffed their masters' reputations for culture and sophistication. Only later did things change. In the eighteenth century, lending libraries began to rent books to their subscribers, allowing members access to many more than they could buy on their own, much less ever read. The state then took on that function, socializing membership costs for all. Public libraries now serve everyone in the developed world. In the US, their number has steadily increased from 1833, when Peterborough, New Hampshire, opened the first, to over 17,000 in 2012.[19] In Germany, borrowings from public libraries have increased a hundredfold over the twentieth century, from 3.8 million in 1901 to 377 million in 2010.[20]

Buying books has become more affordable. Publishers have delivered an ever-cheaper product. In the Middle Ages, books were produced by hand, often adorned, expensive, and the property of the wealthy—or at best chained to the shelves in monastery libraries to prevent theft. The shift from vellum and parchment to paper in Europe during the late Middle Ages reduced prices by five-sixths.[21] Gutenberg's printing press in 1439 made books an object of mass production, dropping costs perhaps 18-fold.[22] Wood-pulp paper and steam-driven presses continued the trend in the nineteenth century. Paperbacks and then e-books have accelerated the decrease. More books than ever are sold. In the US, expenditure has tripled from 0.11% of GDP in 1929 to 0.38% in 2000. Book sales have outpaced population growth twofold since 1982.[23]

Privileges were the monopolies monarchs granted publishers for their books, raising their prices. But pirates leavened this system by bringing out cheap knock-off editions. In 1710, copyright was first created in England to bolster publishers' claims against such now-unauthorized use of their intellectual property. Yet piracy satisfied a pressing need for popular enlightenment and was hard to squelch. Some nations entirely sidestepped the international spread of copyright in the nineteenth century. The US long remained a copyright outlaw, reaping the benefit of cheap enlightenment without paying rights-holders.

American publishers ripped off their European colleagues, bringing out affordable domestic editions for the masses in an era when Old World books remained leather-bound, multivolumed, and pricey. American print runs were often quadruple the British runs, with each American volume costing but a quarter of its European counterpart. Entire novels were printed in periodicals sold at a fraction of book prices. Charles Dickens and other popular authors were serialized on the back of railroad timetables.[24]

Digital technologies allowed another step toward widely available cheap content. Physical texts are what the economists call rivalrous. My use of a tablet, parchment, book, or newspaper means you cannot at the same time. This is not so with digital works. Once the costs of producing the initial digital edition have been met, the marginal last copy is essentially costless. Everyone can have their own simultaneous copy. For the first time in history, our nonrivalrous thoughts can be conveyed through nonrivalrous media.[25]

Works that have fallen out of copyright and into the public domain are increasingly available for free on the web or as inexpensive reprints. Thanks to the stultifying effect of works remaining in copyright while out of print, there are ten times more books published in 1910 than in 1950 available on Amazon today.[26] Electronic editions of current books are often more affordable than paper versions. Self-published books, in turn, are even less costly. Their numbers now dwarf conventional publications. Amazon—the biggest venue for self-publishers—encourages cheap books by staggering royalties inversely to retail prices.[27] Kindle Unlimited allows subscribers to choose ten e-books each month for a flat fee, having become, in effect, a digital lending library.

Today, everyone can speak directly to the digital public, skipping the book as an intermediary. Social media have become the biggest bullhorn ever. A global soapbox stands ready to be mounted at the digital Speaker's Corner. Dissemination has become even more democratized. Furthermore, fake news is not a modern invention. The *Malleus Maleficarum* appeared in 1486, shortly after Gutenberg's press. It encouraged the belief that witchcraft was widespread and pernicious, justifying the persecution of people accused of sorcery.[28] *The Protocols of the Elders of Zion* has been spreading its poison since the early twentieth century. But fake news thrives on new technologies. For example, the more scientific Covid vaccine information that was posted, the stronger the anti-vaccination movements became.[29] Those reliant on social media for information were also most likely to believe in conspiracy theories about the Covid pandemic.[30]

Despite our celebration of it, openness has a dark side. Printing was hailed in the sixteenth century as depriving physicians of their monopoly on medical expertise.[31] Today, physicians face patients bristling with Googled information and diagnoses.[32] Doubtless, the professionals' reactions are complex.[33] While some patients challenge received opinion, others are made anxious by confusing and ill-digested data.[34] Self-diagnosis and treatment liberate patients from professional overbearance, but they also saddle the newly empowered with responsibility for their fates.

A tsunami of information—good, bad, and indifferent—washes over us. Fake news and social media manipulations are the dark sides of the web's success. Filters or other hurdles to access no longer blend out the cranks, fabulists, and conspiracy theorists. Every voice insists on its points equally loudly. Many are broadcasting. How many are listening?

The Networked Ape

The secret of *Homo sapiens'* success—cultural anthropologists have argued—lies less with our primate line's intelligence than with our talent for transmitting knowledge among ourselves and across time. We receive guidance from our ancestors, preserving and embellishing it for descendants. Thus, we may be the cleverest ape, but that does not most saliently distinguish us from our primate cousins. More interesting is our ability to cooperate and to develop knowledge collectively. We have domesticated ourselves sufficiently that we can collaborate instead of ceaselessly quarreling.[35] Chimpanzees and even the more pacific bonobos fight among themselves incessantly. Chimps are a hundred times more violent than humans. We are not happy packed into long-haul flights, but three hundred chimps confined for hours in similar circumstances would likely tear each other apart.[36]

Self-domesticated, we cooperate and share knowledge. Human infants do not solve puzzles or tasks better than their primate peers, but they excel at discerning what others want and understanding nonverbal cues of intent. Marooned in inhospitable environments, Western explorers have starved, frozen, and perished even as the natives they called savages survived just fine. Bereft of local skills and knowledge, otherwise well-endowed outsiders failed to master their environment. Meanwhile, the locals drew on accumulated knowledge to harvest the right plants, to render them harmless and nourishing, to hunt where game was most plentiful, and to protect against the elements. The more extensive and ancient the knowledge network, the better they mastered the situation. Conversely, indigenous peoples have become deskilled when their numbers were decimated by attack or disease, their reduced populations no longer maintaining and transmitting a critical mass of know-how.[37]

The more humans there are, the deeper the pool of accumulated wisdom, the greater our knowledge, the more likely someone is to solve looming predicaments.[38] Yet sheer numbers do not automatically generate insight. Seventy thousand Florentines produced much of the Renaissance, fifty thousand Edinburghers, the Scottish Enlightenment. Those who would accomplish something must also be well educated and trained. Above all, they must be connected, learning from each other. The denser the networks, the bigger and more productive the collective brain.[39] Before the Industrial Revolution, technological advances arrived in brief spurts, rarely generating prolonged growth or development. Continuous and sustained progress became possible only as the pool of scientific knowledge deepened, sparking economically useful interventions into nature. As important as knowledge's specific content was, allowing inventors and entrepreneurs broad access was equally crucial. That became more common between the Scientific and Industrial Revolutions.[40] If it is not widely available, knowledge remains esoteric and useless.

Libraries are one embodiment of our collective minds. Though the web has surpassed them, in the analog era, they contained the largest accumulations of information possible. Alexandria's library under the Ptolemies sought to assemble all that was known. Its ambition was complete coverage of everything ever written. Often, it owned the originals, insofar as that was a concept when everything was embodied in manuscripts and copies of them. The Ptolemies ordered all works on ships passing through Alexandria's port to be copied, and they kept the one they had taken, returning the facsimile. By the first century BCE, the library had collected 700,000 rolls, some 100,000 works.[41] As its store accumulated, researchers who tasted its distilled essence knew more about the world without going into it than those who merely experienced reality in its diluted everyday form. Some of the ancient world's best cartography and ethnography was produced by scholars who never ventured outside the library's walls.[42]

A major research library contains undigested the potential answers to countless questions. The medievalist Michael McCormick once described squeezing from the otherwise mute 300 billion or so words within Harvard's Widener Library an answer to his question: was European trade with the Arab world in the eighth and ninth centuries—the murkiest of the Dark Ages—partly responsible for kindling the fires of later economic revival?[43] Within a week, he and his students had tracked down data on archaeological discoveries of coins from the Levant in Europe. Obscure numismatic journals demonstrated contact between the two regions.[44]

Networks, then, amplify the knowledge they connect. Thanks to the post office, Ramanujan, the brilliant Indian mathematical autodidact, was in touch with British colleagues before World War I. Yet, as an observant Brahmin, he long refused to leave India to study in England. His mentor, G. R. Hardy, wondered what Ramanujan could have accomplished had he encountered highly trained colleagues at age 16, rather than only a decade later.[45] Even his limited connections, in turn, stood in contrast to previous Indian mathematicians, such as Madhava in the fourteenth century, whose work was unknown just a few miles from his ancestral estate in Kerala.[46]

Stealing ideas is a form of networking, the inverted homage paid to knowledge worth pilfering. Nineteenth-century American industry was seeded by inventions and know-how purloined by entrepreneurs from their English competitors. The mills of Massachusetts began as rip-offs of those in Lancashire, just as English fiction amused nineteenth-century Americans without the cost of royalties.[47]

More recently, the power of networked knowledge was demonstrated by how rapidly researchers genetically sequenced the coronavirus in 2020. In 2002–2003, the SARS virus had taken several months, but the coronavirus just weeks. Earlier, data had been hamstered away, anticipating publication in prestigious paywalled journals. Even as recently as the Ebola and Zika epidemics, scientific information still flowed sluggishly. During the Covid pandemic, barriers fell. After a rocky start, as the Chinese sat on information, epidemiological data began to be posted rapidly on the web as preprints, permitting its efficient use.[48] Indeed, a torrent of submissions to scientific periodicals, not just about Covid, poured forth during the pandemic.[49]

The human mind has also gradually extended beyond the skull, joining up more broadly with the world. Our senses have long been amplified by technology. Vision is the most obvious example, expanded through lenses and later their electronic offspring. Hearing has been enhanced via telecommunication, tying us aurally into the globe. Through writing, our memory has been outsourced onto papyrus, parchment, and paper. In 1946, Vannevar Bush envisaged his memex machine as a means for gathering our books, records, and communications, allowing them to be immediately available and thus becoming an "enlarged, intimate supplement" to our memories.[50] The web now functions as our collective memory, allowing us to offload the burden of data storage externally. Our brains meld with our surroundings, as we incorporate enhanced stimuli and externalize our thought processes via ever-more-sophisticated devices, whether abacuses, sextants, slide rules, calculators, computers, or whatever implants are heading our way.[51] For most of history, we have been en route to becoming cyborgs.

Seen in this context, open access is but the latest instance of an evolutionary imperative. The momentary culmination of a venerable historical trend of increasingly available information, it supplements humanity's armamentarium of collaborative resources. But, more deeply, it adds functionalist heft to an evolutionary imperative, allowing us as a species to enhance our ability to cooperate and to develop collectively. This richness of motives spurring the pursuit of open access is joined by a moral imperative, too—social justice.

Information Wants to be Free?

Information freely shared and widely available may be humanity's greatest resource, giving us an evolutionary leg up as a species. But information that can be privatized and kept exclusively for a few has an inbuilt constituency for hamstering it. That "information wants to be free" is the mantra of open access, perhaps of digitality more generally. But is it true? Steward Brand, usually cited as the source of the claim, also said that information wants to be expensive because it is valuable, and this tension is irresolvable.[52] Broadly speaking, Brand was asking whether knowledge can, or should, be a public good. Should knowledge be like clean air or national defense, something we must underwrite collectively since none of us can, or should, be prevented from using it?

Posing the same question about education suggests some of the issue's ambiguities. As a good, education is both public and private. Individuals benefit from being trained, both intellectually and economically as their earning power rises. But society also prospers as its citizens improve themselves, becoming informed voters, considerate neighbors, and skilled employees. Financing and access to education reflect this dual nature. Primary and secondary schools are usually free for the immediate consumer, while universities often require some copayment from students, even in the most heavily state-financed systems.[53]

Are knowledge and the research that produces it also public goods? Not all—indeed, arguably only a small part—seems to be the answer. The bulk of R&D in industrialized economies (between two-thirds and three-quarters) is paid for by corporations and serves their interests.[54] Even within university research, a good slug is financed by the private sector—35% in the UK, reaching a high of 58% at Oxford.[55] Such knowledge is unlikely to be openly accessible. Nor are universities immune to the logic of proprietary information as they patent their research and partner with companies set up to commercialize their breakthroughs.

Similar to the corporate world's grip on its knowledge is the nation-state's. Nothing is as jealously guarded as national security data, nor as zealously plundered. Wernher von Braun and 1,600 other German rocket scientists were spirited off after the fall of the Third Reich to work in what became NASA. Sometimes knowledge relevant to corporate and national security are the same. Taiwan's lead in microchip technology, and the difficulty of reproducing its know-how elsewhere, help make the nation indispensable to all its customers, East and West. That safeguards it against takeover from the mainland.

Even if its owners allow it, can knowledge be freely transmitted? It depends on what sort. Formal learning fixed on paper can most easily be preserved and conveyed. But informal know-how is hard to transmit except in face-to-face encounters and is usually passed along on the job. It exists in practitioners' minds and muscle memory and is conveyed by word and deed to apprentices. Patents allow trade knowledge to be securely exploited, and their numbers have mushroomed. In fields such as pharmaceuticals and IT, large companies eagerly patent, but much other commercially valuable knowledge remains protected in more traditional ways. Secrecy is widely used, and first movers take advantage of their lead to exploit know-how ahead of the competition.[56]

Nor does academic knowledge inherently make itself available to the world. Researchers on the cusp of a breakthrough maintain secrecy so long as they can hope for priority and more publications.[57] Even academic work fixed on paper and widely accessible is not always easily digestible. Without the broad spread of literacy and then further education, research remains a closed book for most. Insiders have aggravated such obstacles by not always making their work easily penetrable. Scientists' technical vocabulary saves time when writing for each other, but it also excludes the uninitiated. That keeps science journalists in clover. Nor are the humanities and social sciences immune. Lay readers often complain about the esoteric and abstruse language favored in certain literary and philosophical fields—a linguistic version of the emperor's new clothes.

And primary among the many forms of information that explicitly does not want to be free is our own personal data. We guard our
privacy jealously. Nature serves as an apt analogy, most appreciated
as we begin to lose it. Those whose lives are dominated by wolves,
hunger, and cold are unlikely to wax lyrical about nature's beauty
and bounty. But once it has been trampled underfoot, we begin to
grasp the immensity of its destruction. So, too, with privacy. For
most of history, humans had neither privacy nor anonymity. We
lived in small communities, unable to keep secrets beyond those
that remained within our skulls. But as cities grew, especially as they
expanded to allow anonymity, privacy became possible.

"Stadtluft macht frei" (city air brings freedom) was the medieval
slogan that reflected the legal emancipation from feudal bonds
delivered by residence in a town for a certain time. Escaping their
feudal masters, city dwellers were now free of arbitrary imprison-
ment and could pursue whatever profession the guilds permitted.[58]
But the slogan could just as well have served as a reminder that
only in cities could humans disappear, shuffling off their ties to kin
and kith to become fully anonymous. What we today sometimes
consider the anomie of urban life must have felt like a delicious
liberation for escapees from restricted circumstances—as indeed
it still does for those whose habits, beliefs, or predicaments con-
demn them to oppression in their home communities. At the historical moment that media saturation, electronic surveillance, and
data accumulation have blanched most hopes of keeping personal
secrets, privacy becomes seen as a right.[59] Not all information wants
to be free.

What control do individuals have over their bodily tissues once
removed? May they be used for further scientific inquiry without
permission, as happened with Henrietta Lacks's cervical cancer
cells thanks to their ability to grow outside her body?[60] Groups also
guard their information. When pharmaceuticals or useful varietals
are derived from local plants, what claim do the indigenous peoples

whose knowledge pointed in that direction retain? Thediosgenin found in Mexican yams was instrumental in developing contraceptive pills during the 1970s, but once the ingredient could be synthesized, yams were no longer needed.[61] Without participating in downstream benefits, why would locals share their knowledge in the future? Native Americans have resisted genetic analysis of their ancestors' remains and whatever it might reveal of their ultimate origins or the current composition of their membership. In 2002, Navajos imposed a moratorium on genetically testing their members.[62]

Yet, despite some information resisting accessibility, a kernel of truth remains in the slogan that it wants to be free. At least scientific and academic knowledge should not be encumbered. The inquiry into fundamental processes of nature and society, the discoveries motivated by curiosity and the yearning to know—not only should their results be available to all interested consumers, but information is also improved through openness. The scientific method relies on transparency and free critique. Without that bracing tonic, the outcome would be impaired.

Knowledge production became open to competition in an intellectual market at the dawn of the Scientific Revolution. The lid was blown off three centuries during which secrecy had been prized.[63] The political and social elites were in no position to judge the merit of the scientific work they underwrote. Only when subjected to the harsh light of intellectual evaluation and competition from peers was its value revealed. After all, who knew what a science hidden away was worth? Especially if the work was formulated using mathematics, inscrutable to even the most cultivated patrons. Might one have sponsored a charlatan or even a heretic? Public scrutiny was required to vet and evaluate the work of natural philosophy.[64]

But once exposed to analysis, knowledge's value became primarily intellectual—the glory that redounded to breakthrough discoverers and, by association, to their patrons. Not that cultural credit and prestige were all that awaited scientists and their backers. Some knowledge could pay off and improve the world in practice. In the thirteenth century, the median began being used as an alternative to the mean to grasp the significance of lumpy data sets with extreme outliers. Two centuries later, the median was put to practical use, allowing navigators dealing with divergent instrument readings in stormy weather to chart more accurate courses. A breakthrough scientific concept allowed more useful data organization with real-world payoffs.

That meant making knowledge public. The patent system allowed discoveries or inventions to be monetized fairly. Yet to reap their benefits, disclosure was the price. In return for revealing their secrets, inventors were granted time-limited monopolies. Because their claims were to ideas—not just their expression, as in copyright—the terms had to be limited. Had inventors been allowed to lock up entire branches of applied science indefinitely, chaos would have ensued. Cultural stagnation was one possible outcome if monopolies reigned; widespread piracy was another, if monopolies were undermined willy-nilly. Either way, the patent system worked by granting terms sufficiently long to promise some reward, yet short enough that competitors agreed to wait their turn to exploit the innovation freely, perhaps licensing it in the meantime.

For knowledge with no immediate prospects of being exploited or put to patentable use, however, free access seemed the most desirable fate. What was gained by secreting away insight into nature's basic processes, society's workings, or the past's inheritance? Once opened, knowledge is nonrivalrous and non-excludable. No one can be kept from knowing, and no one is worse off when others know, too. Yet, given the difficulties and cost of dissemination, in practice, even academic knowledge has been kept from most people, either by publications requiring subscriptions or by institutions limiting access to their members.

What is the argument, much less the moral imperative, for sharing knowledge?[65] Some argue that everyone who can benefit from access to information already has it; therefore, little is gained by making knowledge universally available. Others point out that, given national disparities in research funding, not everyone contributes equally to pushing back the frontier. Of the $1.7 trillion spent annually on R&D, ten nations pony up 80%.[66] Nor does each country invest in the same areas. Asia favors the natural sciences and engineering, the West, life sciences and medicine.[67] Basic and applied research are funded variously among nations. So, even if one country's taxpayers deserve insight into research they have supported, does that also hold for the free riders?

Proponents of openness counter that, since the overwhelming majority of the world is excluded from conventional scholarly information, the likelihood that only a few would profit from access is tiny. National differences in scientific focus, in turn, serve equally well as an argument for opening access across borders to benefit from differential comparative advantages. A crabbed accounting of who pays for what, and who deserves to see it, thus falls away. When the virtues of networking are added, insights are disproportionately amplified as connectivity multiplies.

The argument for opening up then widens from altruism (imparting it even to those who have not contributed) to include self-interest as the whole expands to more than its parts. And if, as we shall see, the costs of dissemination remain much the same whether paid for by readers or by authors, whether closed or open, then even a mere Pascallian wager would favor open access. The costs being comparable, the upside of opening up is potentially great, the downside modest. For the first time, digitality permits disseminating information at a marginal cost approaching zero. With some goodwill, funding, and hard work, scholarly knowledge could become one of the first global public goods.

Social Justice

Agreed that at least scientific and academic knowledge should be a public good, we arrive at the most powerful argument for open access, social justice. Knowledge is unequally distributed. The developed nations' largest libraries are ten times as big as Africa's (the national libraries of Egypt and South Africa), and seven times Latin America's (Chile and Mexico).[68] Harvard's library subscribes to ten times as many periodicals as India's best-funded research institution, the Institute of Science.[69] Per capita, Americans buy four times as many books as Brazilians (South America's biggest market).[70] Including Asia, developed nations account for 97% of all patent applications, Latin America 1.7%, Africa 0.5%.[71] Scholars in the Global South find it hard to participate in the research, conference, and publication circuits of the US and Europe.

Inflated subscription prices are especially prohibitive for developing nations' libraries, and article processing charges, an even greater barrier. Networks of scholars have sprung up in Latin America and Africa to substitute for those in the West. While better than nothing, this further balkanizes what should be a global enterprise.[72] Such observations could be multiplied at will. They confirm a depressing reality evident to all—the precarious tilt of knowledge and its availability away from the developing world. Digitality, coupled to open access, promises to bridge such gulfs.

On rare occasions, the last are made first. The economic historian Alexander Gerschenkron gained immortality with his concept of the advantages of backwardness. Latecomer nations, he argued, could skip steps on the road to industrialization that early birds had to take.[73] With mobile phones, developing countries have leapfrogged the once-necessary infrastructure of cables, masts, and landlines. For those old enough to remember party lines in rural areas, with one phone per household, usually installed in the darkest, coldest nook, its use limited by cost and the need to share, not to mention callers connected by operators plugging into switchboards, the idea of everyone with their own phone seems miraculous.

Even in emerging nations, phone availability has outstripped what it was in the industrialized world within current lifetimes. On a list of the world's 216 countries, mobile phone penetration reaches one line per person already at Zimbabwe (rank 137). Even South Sudan and North Korea have fourteen lines per hundred people—statistically speaking, one for every seven users. In practical terms, that differs little from the 78% landline penetration rate per household achieved in the US in 1968, assuming five people per residence.[74]

Digitality holds out similar prospects. It permits the developing world to skip infrastructure once needed for dissemination: publishers, periodicals, libraries, and archives. As the world's libraries come online, anyone anywhere with an internet connection has the virtual equivalent of a global library card—with access at least to public-domain material.

Alas, technology and its possibilities are not the only drivers here. International law does not invariably encourage enlightenment's spread. Little could be done when the US pirated Europe's copyrighted works in the nineteenth century. America was not yet a major cultural exporter and taking revenge by inflicting the same on US works promised little. Only once the first American bestsellers (works by Harriet Beecher Stowe, Mark Twain, and Walt Whitman) were ripped off by European publishers in the mid-nineteenth century did the tide begin to turn.[75] When the US refused to join the international copyright system set up in Berne in 1886, Bismarck regretted the decision but realized he could do nothing. "Am I supposed to dispatch warships?" he wondered?[76] Nowadays, the rights-holding nations may not unleash the navy, but their armamentarium includes trade sanctions. The increasingly globalized world economy forces developing countries to play by the industrialized world's rules if they expect to trade.

Granted, this has not been a one-way street. During the 1970s and 1980s, Third World nations that insulated themselves from the global market did poorly as they inefficiently created second-rate substitutes for products otherwise available. Other developing countries, such as South Korea and Taiwan, profited from selling to the West, and their success highlighted the advantages of joining the world market and playing by its rules. Some nations had their own intellectual property to export and protect—India's software and films, for example.[77] In the meantime, China has become a major exporter and therefore seeks to protect its intellectual property.[78]

Yet, the poorest nations remain in a bind—unable to ignore global trade regulations yet keen for better access to knowledge. Some intellectual property regulations do consider developing nations' predicament. India has wrested the right to produce generic copies of medicines.[79] Others have been granted some leeway, allowing them to license books for educational use, to translate without permission, and to import cheaper foreign editions. But more should be possible. In Africa, copyright is still applied much as elsewhere, with little regard for local circumstances. Indeed, some nations here hobble themselves needlessly. They adopt more stringent copyright criteria than international treaties demand—longer durations and self-contradictory licensing requirements for public-domain works, for example.[80]

Open access is a rare example of a cause backed in theory by a global unity of interest. What is a convenience for the public in industrialized nations, sparing readers a trek to libraries, is a quantum leap for Third World citizens, who have limited access to the world's scholarly knowledge. When such information is treated as a global public good and everyone can read it, the taxpayers who finance research are deprived of nothing.

That it is a virtue to spread knowledge, both to First World citizens without access and to developing nations, presumes that this benefits humanity. Universities are not the only source of the knowledge whose access is disputed, but because they are among the main drivers, their role is unavoidable. Universities are certainly open to criticism. Higher education benefits the market. Industry profits from academia. Access to universities is not always universal, equitable, or fair. Academia itself is governed by internal markets whose criteria are both intellectual and mercenary. Academic credentialing supports hierarchies of status and salary in the broader economy. University-generated content supplies the bread-and-circus acts of commercialized entertainment empires. Like other large enterprises, universities use short-term and casual labor, not always justifiably. Among their main functions is training the mid-level worker bees of modern economies. In short, scholarship is one with contemporary capitalism.

One can, of course, attack academia as part of capitalism and open access as part of academia. Perhaps it is true that open access masks an underlying commodification of knowledge by pretending to make a gift of something that must still be paid for. Intellectual workers may be deprived of their labor's fruits by having to give them away. Open access could gloss over exploitative relations among the informalized ranks of university teachers or the publishing industry's casualized and ill-paid labor. Maybe when open access is granted to readers, it locks out authors who cannot afford publishing charges. Perhaps the data mining it permits by releasing information allows another intellectual land grab by media industries. And, possibly, open access helps pharmaceutical, medical, and computer businesses outsource their research functions to universities in return for creaming off the results of government-financed work.[81]

Open access also lends itself to neoliberal interpretations.[82] Such suspicions often attach to solutions claiming to be technologically and politically neutral. Defined thus, open access sees freedom as the centralized state's absence, leaving citizens free to choose among options.[83] It becomes part of the allegedly Californian evangelism of tech-based answers to information problems.[84]

Although this is arguable, attacking open access by lambasting modern industrial capitalism is akin to complaining about gravity when feeling weary. Both the problems and their solution emerge from modern technologies and their exploitation. Open access may put pressure on young scholars compared to their elders, who faced no demand to make work available. But it also gives today's rising academics an audience potentially vaster than that of their seniors, immured in the ivory tower. Publications financed by processing fees may be accessible to readers, while their cost excludes would-be authors in the Global South. Yet open access can make all knowledge available in even the most distant nook. And it could unleash flows of ideas and information not just from North to South, or even in reverse, but as a global Brownian motion of data and insights.[85] Opening the channels of data promises to level tilted playing fields. It allows a potentially worldwide intellectual exchange, permitting many who have been excluded to participate and raising the chance of reciprocal influence across the equator. Entirely erasing the inherited division between culture exporters and importers, producers and recipients, may still lie in the future, but using digitality on behalf of open access is the single most powerful tool we have.

Some Distinctions

Let us clarify a few terms that recur here. In practice, *open access* means being able at any internet connection to read content that earlier would have been available only to journal subscribers, book buyers, or library patrons. Whether it means more is hotly debated. Should readers also be able to download content, reproduce it, repurpose it, and publish it in new editions, translations, or other formats? Like other commercial enterprises, conventional publishing requires customers to pay for its products. Libraries breach the practice of treating content like other purchasable items. Readers can borrow or read in situ books or periodicals bought by librarians. No other commercial items are lent out in this sense. Rental car companies and airlines sell the temporary or partial use of what customers would otherwise need to purchase in toto. And agricultural machinery cooperatives are similar to private lending libraries, sharing the costs of common consumables. But for no other consumer items—except perhaps public transport, education, and medical care, insofar as they are considered commodities—does the state spend to grant citizens use.

Who pays to make content freely available? So far, consumers, including libraries, have underwritten conventional publishing. Thanks to digitality, open-access publishing could, in theory, be cheaper than paper and binding. Yet, however efficient digital production may be, costs remain to be met. Who should shoulder them? The obvious answer is authors, but this works only for some of them. Authors are motivated to write by the attention their work receives and the sales it generates. Intellectual property can be more easily pirated than material forms of ownership. Not until the state used copyright to give authors a legal monopoly on their content could they hope to make a living by selling it. Those who earn money from their work naturally have no interest in paying so that audiences may enjoy it. But not all content producers sell their wares, nor do most authors sell enough to make a living.

Spreading the word, advancing truth and enlightenment, enhancing their intellectual or aesthetic reputations—such motives have equally spurred authors on. Some are paid for their efforts by other means and do not need sales. Scholars, scientists, theologians, museum curators, think-tankers, and others with an institutional affiliation do not depend on selling content. They create to gain attention and to have their ideas heard. Many work for employers who have a say in what they write and pay them for it. Some have little control over the final product and are perhaps not authors in the conventional sense. But others, such as many of Hollywood's creative staff, are certainly *artistes*, if not authors, and see their work as expressing their personalities, even if they are paid salaries.

Open access is intended for authors who do not earn a living from selling their work, who are salaried or otherwise provided for, yet who control their rights. For them, readers trump buyers. Expanding their audiences by making works freely available might well tempt them. Why charge admission if your aim is attention? William Masters and Virginia Johnson's 1966 book, *Human Sexual Response*, was written in a deliberately obscure style to lower the topic's sizzle. Yet it sold well. Masters described it as "the most purchased, least read book in history."[86] Masters and Johnson were in the anomalous position of being academic entrepreneurs. Although their research started while they were faculty at Washington University in St. Louis, it continued at their independently financed research institute. Doubtless, the royalties were therefore welcome. But in terms of getting their message out, selling their book was counterproductive. Had it been issued as open access, it would have remained unread by even more people.

Open access flips the funding stream from consumers to producers. At the point of what used to be a sale, the product is free. Who, then, is to pay? The debates distinguish various forms of open access. Gold open access has authors or their research funders pay. Platinum and diamond open access differ from gold only in that someone other than authors pays. Sometimes libraries band together to pool dissemination costs, thus gaining access to works not just for themselves but for all readers. In effect, this is cooperative bulk purchasing for humanity. Other times, funders subsidize presses or periodicals, allowing them to issue works without cost to authors or, of course, to readers. Works—especially books—can be published both under open access in digital form and in print for a fee. Book buyers thus subsidize digital readers.

Green open access, in turn, makes public a copy that is less than the final version of record, whether a typescript, the page proofs, or another hobbled variant of the ultimate product. Green open access can thus coexist with conventional subscription or other reader-pays forms of publication since it does not compete head-on with the marketed edition of the work. To all this, we return below.

2

The Variety of Authors and Their Content

The open-access movement arose in reaction to rights-owners' overweening claims to their intellectual property. No one disputes authors' rights to their works, but at least two distinctions are necessary: which works, and which authors?

Start with the works. Public-domain works are those published so long ago their copyright has expired. Copyright's terms have lengthened over the past three hundred years. In the early eighteenth century, authors had rights for a scant 14 years. At the rights-holders' behest, copyright terms have continuously expanded, and today protection lasts for the author's life plus 50 or 70 years, depending on the jurisdiction. The public domain has correspondingly shrunk. In the US, works enter the public domain on a rolling-year basis. In 2020, the cut-off was 1925, and proceeds annually after that. Thanks to the vast explosion of publication starting in the mid-nineteenth century, combined with ever-lengthening copyright terms, the bulk of our cultural inheritance remains legally reserved. That was not so in the past, when copyright terms were shorter. Nor will it be true in the future, when the public domain will have swelled to fill the horizon.

Public-Domain Infinitude

Thousands of years from now, unless humanity expands or becomes more creative and productive than today, the bulk of all content will be in the public domain. Even if copyright does not change its terms, only the latest fringe of works from the past century or so will remain protected. How will that affect culture? Scientists want the latest cutting-edge work. Since they study external reality, past investigations are unimportant. Old science mainly concerns historians. But for artistic creators and for scholars whose subject is humanity and its doings, the growing accumulation of readily available material has implications. A few classics may attain relative immortality, but what counts as one varies by era. Though performed earlier by university students, Shakespeare was ignored by literary scholars until late in the seventeenth century. Jane Austen's reputation was created after her death.[1] *Moby Dick* was poorly received at first. Works once considered great also fade from view. Old Master paintings' market value has declined, and Renoir's reputation has tanked. Ever more past greats will compete for attention with the future's creators, although we cannot predict precisely who will have staying power and for how long. Parts of the public domain's cultural reservoir will fade in and out of fashion.

But once the bulk of human creation has entered the public domain, much of what can be said will have been uttered and will be freely available for reuse by anyone. Of course, new artforms and styles, entirely new genres, will be invented. Human creativity will hardly grind to a halt. And the scholars who study humanity will have a growing body of evidence to feast on. Mediocre and now-forgotten novels are a treasure trove for literary and cultural historians, psychologists, and anthropologists. Nonetheless, overwhelmingly immense cultural riches in the public domain will cast shadows over the creative landscape like a mountain looming over a valley.

How will that affect the hopes and abilities of future creators to innovate? Will we grow listless and bored? Become magpies and recyclers of past content? Become adept at variations on themes? Already, the role of reuse, sampling, imitation, and pastiche in modern culture puts paid to outdated Romantic conceptions of artists eternally creating anew. We may well end up having a new version of the seventeenth-century battle of the ancients and moderns, which pitted the greats of antiquity against contemporary pretenders to an equivalent stature.

An overwhelmingly vast public domain poses issues that are psychologically akin to the immortality problem. Granted eternal life, we would find our motivation to do anything in particular at any specific time undercut by knowing that other equally good moments will always arrive.[2] Excess memory has similar effects. Nietzsche warned against too much remembering. Without a cleansing forgetfulness, we become impotent and immobile.[3] The Struldbruggs, the immortals in *Gulliver's Travels*, are passive, slothful, and lethargic from having lived too long and seen too much. And in 1819 Washington Irving argued that only by forgetting once-prominent authors can we create without being overwhelmed by past works.[4]

The economists' notion of creative destruction amplifies fears that past encrustations hamper present action and therefore must be scoured away. Schumpeter, father of the idea, was heavily influenced by Nietzsche.[5] As a surfeit of time demotivates, subverting the value of any present moment, so an excess of freely available content may undermine what we today think of as creativity.

Something like this is already at work in serious music. Given certain restrictions on duration, variety, and what is considered a harmonious progression of notes, there are only a finite number of melodies—a sizable number, but not limitless.[6] At some point, all available melodies will have been worked into compositions— and thence may end up in the ultimate dustbin of music, as mobile phone ring tones. Indeed, one copyright skeptic is algorithmically generating all possible melodies, thus preventing any from being protected and putting all into the public domain.[7]

Realizing that melody is not an infinite pasture to be grazed forever has affected the development of classical music. After music's start as almost pure melody (plainsong, Gregorian chants), polyphony and counterpoint introduced juxtaposed themes. As composers strove for novelty, melody became increasingly striking and unprecedented.[8] They needed other means to make their works stand out. Harmony became important, supplementing and eventually almost supplanting melody, as music developed into its Romantic phase. Mozart was easy to whistle, Schubert still, Beethoven less so. Despite his leitmotifs, Wagner's lashings of harmony are even harder to hum.

Melody was then expressly forbidden in twelve-tone theory. In its purest form, it obliged composers such as Schönberg and Webern to use each note in the scale before any particular one could be trotted out again. Melody in the conventional sense was effectively outlawed. Eventually, John Cage's 4'33", a composition of silence, dispensed with music's content altogether. Like other art forms in high modernism, music walked up to the brink and jumped right in. Little wonder that here, too, the way forward has been through various forms of neotraditionalism.

To continue stimulating, art cannot just repeat itself. Habituation and the attendant fading of arousal drive a constant search for variety. If novelty is prized, no art form can remain standing. Striving for something new and original, it seeks ever-fresh sources of stimulation. Since the world is large but finite, any art genre is eventually condemned either to repeat itself or to exhaust itself and die.[9]

Melody's fate in serious music foreshadows the general effect that a vast treasure trove of public-domain content may have on future creators. What has been the case for melody holds for plot as well. Many stories exist, but not an infinitude.[10] High modernist literature's disdain for mere plot resembles the dodecaphonic approach to melody. There are only so many different ways to twist a doorknob. Once you have done them all, twisting itself becomes a bore. If novelty remains prized, a new approach to doorknobs is required. The copyright merger doctrine acknowledges such limits of the human imagination. It denies protection to the expression of ideas that can be formulated in only a limited number of ways—a drawing of a hand, explanations of simple business methods, or instructions and illustrations of how to hang drapes.[11] In the long run, all ideas are simple.

In popular music, the success of rap and hip hop, emphasizing rhythm, beat, and text, has downplayed the importance of melody, too. Nonetheless, a spate of recent copyright suits has claimed infringement of melody, rhythm, or other less tangible aspects of popular songs.[12] They suggest not only that rights-owners and their lawyers are running amok, but also that we may be approaching the outer limits of novelty in pop music, an art form that is especially hedged about by convention, expectations of genre, audience tolerance, and other aesthetic restrictions—not to mention perfectly legitimate reciprocal influencing.

Yet, as a culture, we are nowhere near public-domain surfeit. Thanks to the explosive growth of publishing beginning in the nineteenth century, public-domain works make up only a fraction of all books. Two-thirds of major US and UK libraries' holdings were published after the 1920s, and thus are still copyrighted.[13]

For open access, public-domain works are not the issue. Open access seeks to enlarge the public domain, rolling back copyright's ever-expanding encroachment on the cultural commons. It would prefer to scale copyright back to approximate its origins, with shorter terms and fewer works affected. But within the existing parameters of public-domain content, the main question is how technically to disseminate it.

Grey Literature

Thanks to the expansion of copyright terms over the past two centuries, a second category of works is now one of open access's primary targets. Sometimes referred to as grey literature, these are the books or periodicals that remain copyrighted but are no longer in print. Orphan works are a subcategory of grey literature whose rights-holders can no longer be found. Publishers have decided that grey literature's sales no longer justify printing and stocking copies. Except on shelves in libraries or for sale second-hand, such works are not available.

Books lose their commercial value quickly. Most copyrighted books are out of print. Of the 10,000 US books published in 1930, only 174 were still in print in 2001.[14] Of the 63 books that won Australia's Miles Franklin prize over the past half-century, ten are unavailable in any format.[15] Most sound recordings' value is used up within a decade and the sales of most fiction dissipate after a year.[16] In the era when copyright terms had to be renewed, very few authors bothered.[17] What was the point for works with no market? Sometimes, the original publisher has gone out of business or been absorbed by a competitor. The authors may have died, and their estates and heirs are often unaware of their rights. The resulting orphaned works are still technically protected, yet they usually have little commercial value.

The bulk of books in major research libraries are grey works. Assuming we can make new academic work accessible, time will eventually solve the problem of today's grey literature. As copyright's line retreats year by year, the public domain advances, gradually whittling down the number of grey works. The task is to accelerate an inevitable process. Whether we can also correct the absurdity of extensive copyright durations—protecting value that no longer exists and rights claimed by no one—is another matter.

We have, then, three different kinds of works: those in the public domain, over which there is no dispute; those in copyright, where the legal framework is clear; and works in copyright yet out of print (grey literature), some of which are orphaned, their rights-holders no longer identifiable. Although they are without economic value, grey works are prevented from joining the public domain until decades after their authors' deaths. They present the biggest challenge.

Romantic Copyright

Our second question, after which works, is, which authors? No one wants to deprive creators who live from their works of rightful recompense. Undeniably, piracy of books, music, film, and other content is theft. Open access does not seek to dispossess authors of their property nor to stint them of their rightful earnings. But authors are not all alike. Those whose creativity supplies their livelihood are entitled to the fruits of their labor. But most authors either do not make a living from their work or are already supported in other ways. In the latter case, having been paid once, their output arguably does not, in a narrow sense, belong to them, even though they may retain aesthetic and other claims.

Copyright was invented in the eighteenth century to give cultural producers property rights in their works, stimulating their creativity by rewarding them and permitting the most successful to earn a living from their efforts. But copyright also invented and legitimized the public domain, the trove of no-longer-protected work that belongs to all humanity. Had intellectual property been property in the conventional sense, creators and their heirs would have owned it forever. That natural law concept of eternal property rights was abbreviated for matters of the mind. Copyright thus benefits society by ensuring a steady stream of content into the public domain as (short) copyright terms expire.

Copyright specifically aimed to help those who worked independently, not for wages or salary. It reflected in law the Romantic ideal of the author. Romantic creators were thought to produce individually and independently, as single authors inspired by their muse, indebted to no one else, and solely responsible for the ensuing masterpiece. They lived primarily from selling their works directly to the public, much like shopkeepers or artisans their wares. If unsuccessful, they starved in their garrets. They were independent twice over—economically, working for themselves, and aesthetically, indebted only to their personal inspiration.

This Romantic ideal of the creator became dominant in the eighteenth century. It broke with earlier concepts of authors' social role in two respects. Aesthetically, creators now stood alone. Previously, they had often been part of larger groups working collaboratively. Some artforms lend themselves more easily to individual work, others are collective endeavors. Sonnets, sonatas, novels, and still lifes are perhaps best created by a single person. In contrast, sculpture, frescoes, architecture, theater, opera, and symphonic concerts, not to mention film, usually involve teams, although they are often supervised by one dominant influence. That painters like Rubens ran large workshops, churning out works attributed to the master, was not due to their product's scale or size, but to the insatiable market they sought to supply at their peak. In the Romantic era, even collaborative efforts were seen as ultimately the inspiration of a single creator.

Second, in the Romantic view, the work expressed its creator's individuality. Earlier, singular creativity had garnered less of a premium. Artists were seen as channeling eternal values, not creating their own vision. With artists indebted to forerunners, imitation was valued higher than novelty.[18] The great works were in the past; the goal was to reachieve something similar. The Greeks and

Romans considered authors discoverers more than creators, uncovering the timeless reality of nature's forms.[19] Augustine argued that philosophers' statements were like silver and gold, not created by them but dug from the mines. Truth and wisdom belonged to all and could not be private property.[20] Classical antiquity inspired Renaissance artists to imitate nature and to emulate past masters.[21] They were more mimetic than creative.

Romanticism flipped such aesthetic ideals on their ear. Rather than borrowing from the past, authors should seek to connect directly to the divine.[22] As with Protestant sects, an unmediated tapping into the godhead released the now-enlightened from convention and the commonplace. In the nineteenth century, bohemianism extended this Romantic pose into a kind of over-ripe decadence. Self-professed outcasts, presenting themselves as marginalized and impoverished, indeed with a dashing streak of self-destructiveness, bohemian artists nonetheless laid claim to be venerated cultural exemplars.[23] Like early medieval hermits and monastics, they both despised and implicitly expected social approbation.

Such liberation from inherited strictures aimed to free artists to express their inner being. Borrowing from others, admitting to their influence, copying past models—all undermined the purest claims to originality. Plagiarism became a cardinal sin. Since works emanated from the individual, authors owned them, both spiritually and economically. The work was an integral part of the author. The primal form of property, Balzac insisted in 1834, was the work, "that which man creates between heaven and earth, that which has no other roots than in his intelligence."[24]

Economically, creators moved from being patronage recipients to becoming entrepreneurs during this period. Music allowed various income streams—composing, performing, conducting, and teaching. Unlike writers (other than playwrights), composers created but also disseminated and performed their works. Having been employed by royal or aristocratic courts, they branched out to engage across the spectrum of their creations' life cycle. Patronage had once paid the rent; now, it was profit.

Haydn was a street musician before working for various aristocratic households, eventually as a court composer for the Esterhazys. Handel enjoyed the support of several noble English lineages even as he launched successive opera companies. Despite some success in producing concerts as a pianist playing his music, Mozart was happy for a part-time appointment cranking out dance music for the Austrian emperor.

Eventually, artists became entrepreneurs in their own right. In 1779, the Esterhazys permitted Haydn to write for their amusement, works that belonged to them, but also to hawk other compositions directly to publishers. When he cut ties to the Esterhazys and moved to London, Haydn was successful on his own. Beethoven enjoyed patronage from the Viennese aristocracy, but much of his income came from commissions, payment for work. Mahler's day job was as a conductor. For writers and painters, who could not promise wealthy families similar entertainment and whose output was physical objects, the practice of selling their wares had begun earlier and was more pronounced.

Abandoning support from wealthy patrons, creators turned instead to the public for sustenance. Insofar as authors had to please their benefactors, patronage had inhibited artistic freedom. By contrast, they were at liberty to do what they wanted in the marketplace—as long as it sold. Whether the tyranny of the patron or the tastes of the public limited artistic freedom more is a long-standing debate.

The distinction between scientific and artistic creativity was also significant. Scientists sought to understand something objectively out there. Thus, they were more discoverers than creators, or at least that was the view in the era when scientists were natural philosophers and were considered nature's bookkeepers.[25] But Romanticism also brought to science an emphasis on the individual researcher's creativity, the spark of genius that fired investigations.[26]

Copyright was developed in the eighteenth century to protect publishers' property in works they had bought from authors. It aimed to encourage and reward Romantic creators—whose work, as an emanation of their personality, belonged wholly to them and could be alienated as they pleased. During the twentieth century, however, such Romantic certainties eroded. Bohemian artistes pouring out their souls in garrets now seemed overwrought and outmoded. Postmodernism undercut the assumption that artistic inspiration was individual and asocial—bereft of context, history, and background. It focused on creation's collective and historical aspects, how authors were inspired by, borrowed from, and copied their colleagues, peers, and predecessors.

Works were no longer seen as monads in splendid self-isolation but as strands in a cultural fabric, woven together with common and inherited assumptions, sentiments, references, archetypes, and tropes. Even the most celebrated writers were now recognized as borrowing shamelessly from their peers: Shakespeare from Montaigne, Racine from Euripides, Coleridge from Schelling, Picasso from Manet, Joyce from Homer, Pound from Dante, T. S. Eliot from almost everyone. Nor was the meaning of their works thought to be decided by authors alone. The authors' intent may have been part of the story, but how the public received and interpreted works also determined their ultimate meaning.

The Rise of Collaboration

Authors no longer work as alone as Romanticism's tropes suggested. Collaboration has become more integral to artistic, scholarly, and scientific efforts. As knowledge grows and disciplines mature, individuals can hardly ever master their fields by themselves. The increase in knowledge made specialization less the dehumanizing outcome of modernity or capitalism, and more a necessary process for mastering some part of a discipline. But a fond nostalgia for the Renaissance's semi-divinities, such as Leonardo, who excelled at many endeavors, died hard. Even Marx succumbed to the illusion, with his idea of well-rounded communists of the future, generalists who hunted in the morning, spent the afternoons fishing, reared cattle in the evening, and were critics after dinner.[27] They bore more than a passing resemblance to the country squires and club drones of Marx's own time.

The result of knowledge's increase and the demise of the Renaissance's hyper-accomplished person is the need for collaboration. The solitary genius has retired, replaced by the lab team.[28] Even in the social sciences, articles are written by sizable groups. Assemblies of researchers now do the work, often spread across the globe. As measured by citation intensities, the results of such collaborations are superior to individuals' outputs.[29] Few significant accomplishments remain the outcome of one person's efforts. Planes, buildings, medicines, computer programs, games, and films are all the result of collaborations. Outside literature, the humanities, and some art forms, we would be hard-pressed to name a significant fruit of solitary endeavor.

Attribution has democratized in tandem. Collaboration occurred earlier, too, but it was often treated more like an apprenticeship relation than collegially. The seventeenth-century chemist Robert Boyle published his results without much mentioning his coworkers, except occasionally to blame them for mishaps.[30] Nineteenth-century German professors commanded small armies of *Assistenten*, their postdoctoral students. Appropriating their work shamelessly, the professors could be impressively productive on the backs of others. Even now, James Patterson, a best-selling author of some 150 books, publishes several volumes annually. His hired team of writers drafts chapters for his edit, approval, and appropriation.[31]

Today, such hierarchal relationships have given way to a percolation onto the title page of almost everyone involved. In the 1890s, 98% of articles published in what was to become the *New England Journal of Medicine* had single authors; a century later, fewer than 5%.[32] In the sciences, the ranks of coauthors swelled. Doubling between 1960 and 1980, they increased almost 50% again in the two decades after 1988.[33] At times, so many claim coauthorship that the point of listing them all is unclear. Two physics articles from the 1990s, presenting findings from work on particle accelerators, had 406 and 271 coauthors, respectively.[34] That was nothing in comparison to the 2012 publication announcing observation of the Higgs particle at the Large Hadron Collider. The work was written by almost 3,000 coauthors, of whom 22 had already died by the time it appeared.[35] Such hyper-authorship was bested in turn in 2015 by an article with well over 5,000 coauthors.[36]

The film industry has solved a similar problem of mass authorship—if solution it can be called—by an inscrutable hierarchy in its endless parade of attribution. Conventionally, the opening credits list many—sometimes dozens—of producers of various stripes. Counterintuitively, executive producers rank two notches below producers, much like an "ordinary" professor in Germany outstrips any kind of extraordinary appointment, and Super Mammoth olives are larger than merely Super Colossal, while they, in turn, dwarf the Extra Jumbo.[37]

The film *The Butler* required no less than five producers, seventeen executive producers, six co-executive producers, four co-producers, and seven associate producers. Ninety minutes later, when the action fades, comes a veritable phonebook of worker bees, from the dolly grip to the gaffer, not forgetting the clapper loader and the focus puller.[38] As many as 3,000 people can work on a film, with an average Hollywood crew of 500, including at times as many as 250 stunt actors and 140 costume people.[39]

Scholars, too, have their hierarchies. Coauthors who are equal participants are generally listed alphabetically, as in high-energy particle physics. Other sciences follow other conventions. The first author (of whom there can be several, although obviously not all can be first on the list) is the one who conceived the project, was its main mover, and did most of the empirical work. The last author is usually also the corresponding author and is similar to the producer of a film. Often, they head the host lab. Usually, they design the research strategy, worry about responding to peer review demands, and are blamed if problems arise. In between come the other participants. Also in the middle are gift authorships, which are often granted to distinguished figures in the field who may have had little to do with the project but are honored with ceremonial participation.[40]

To tame the circus that some disciplines have become, classificatory schemes detailing participants' roles have been worked out—something more akin to Hollywood's hierarchy. CrediT, the Contributor Roles Taxonomy, launched in 2014, distinguishes fourteen roles.[41] These run the gamut from the necessary (funding acquisition, project administration) through the sufficient (data curation, methodology, resources, software, supervision, validation), to the sublime (conceptualization, validation, writing—original draft).

Works are increasingly the outcome of collective efforts. Poems and novels may still be solitary undertakings, but almost everything else tends toward the collaborative. The Nobel prizes, hailing from a less collective era, are limited to three recipients, even though dozens may have been equal participants. Hollywood allows only three producers credit for a Best Picture Oscar. Conversely, the number of prizes celebrating cultural output has mushroomed along with the works they reward, leaving us with an embarrassment of riches. With awards for everyone, being singled out loses its value.[42]

Neo-Patronage

Since copyright was first institutionalized, two changes have fundamentally altered its legal landscape. First, most authors or content producers—their current more sober designation—are no longer independent workers. Few authors make a living exclusively from their works. How many is hard to gauge. Looking only at those who write, a 1976 study calculated that 300 US writers could live off their literary earnings (of ten million aspiring colleagues). Three years later, a survey of over 2,000 writers revealed that almost half held paid positions besides freelance writing.[43] More recently, the Authors Guild has discovered that half of all full-time authors earn less than the federal poverty limit ($12,488) and 64% of authors' income comes from sources other than writing. Only 57% of authors derive all their income from writing, and only 40% could be said to earn a livable income.[44] These figures are partial at best, but clearly, freelance writing is not a profession in the conventional sense.

To make ends meet, writers have long relied on other employment. Henry Wadsworth Longfellow and James Russell Lowell were professors, Nathaniel Hawthorne was the US consul in Liverpool. Washington Irving was a merchant, Ralph Waldo Emerson lectured and was a minister, Edgar Allan Poe was an editor, and Henry David Thoreau, a jack-of-all-trades. T. S. Eliot was a banker and editor; William Carlos Williams, a physician; and William Faulkner wrote *As I Lay Dying* while working in a power plant. Dashiell Hammett was employed by Pinkerton's and the railroads, and Nathanael West was a hotel night manager. An insurance executive, Wallace Stevens turned down a faculty position at Harvard to remain vice president of his Hartford firm. The composer Charles Ives, also an insurance executive, helped develop modern estate planning.

Today, many authors are employees of universities, think tanks, museums, magazines, other cultural institutions, or corporations.

Novelists and poets often have day jobs as creative writing teachers. Such authors are paid by salary, not necessarily precisely for their creative work, but usually for something sufficiently close and undemanding not to distract them from their primary mission. Their salaried duties not only are congruent, but also usually require only some time and energy, allowing leeway for creative work. And, of course, all authors who are full-time faculty are paid for their output. At research universities, faculty receive perhaps half their salary for classes, the rest for scientific work. Lab scientists are even better off, fusing teaching with research by enlisting students in their experiments. At liberal arts colleges, community colleges, and other teaching-intensive institutions, the deal is less favorable. But staff there still enjoy the three reasons that, as the old joke has it, motivate even schoolteachers to take up their unfavored profession: June, July, and August.

In the early nineteenth century, when copyright was still young, this was less true. Today, we lament the fate of the academic precariat, the adjunct faculty who are paid a pittance for each course, enjoying few benefits and less security. Things were once worse. Tenured professors, whom we now regard as among those most comfortably ensconced in salaried employment, used to be an even smaller minority. When the German universities expanded in the nineteenth century, most teaching fell to irregularly employed *Privatdozenten*, paid—if they could collect the money—by fees from students attending their courses. As late as the 1950s, professors made up only a quarter of the teaching staff.[45] Schopenhauer needed the wealth inherited from his father when—as a provocation—he scheduled his courses at the University of Berlin in 1820 at the same hour as his despised but popular colleague, Hegel, thereby dampening attendance and fees.[46]

Today, much content is produced by salaried authors. Our age is one of renewed patronage, but now from institutions, not the aristocracy. Compared to when Hegel died in the 1830s, Germany today has per capita a dozen times as many professors.[47] Similar trends hold elsewhere. Even during the early twenty-first century, when universities were commonly seen as in crisis, faculty numbers at US institutions continued a gradual climb.[48] Many authors are now salaried employees for whom—other than its promise of aesthetic control—copyright should be a matter of indifference.

The state has become the new Maecena. During the Cold War, officially favored authors enjoyed government support in the East Bloc nations. Sweden has a system of paying (modest) salaries directly to writers and artists.[49] The *New Yorker*'s staff writers benefit from a private variant of this. In Western Europe, ministries of culture support art forms, especially those with elaborate infrastructure, such as opera and film. From the BBC to the FilmFernsehFonds Bayern, they are the modern-day Medicis.

In the US, universities assume a similar function. Without them, classical music would scarcely exist, and many novelists and poets earn their keep teaching creative writing. Even the military has paid to underwrite academic skills and talent deemed geopolitically necessary, such as Russian fluency during the Cold War. Think tanks in the US are numerous and largely privately financed, while their European equivalents are funded by unions, business associations, or political parties.[50] They, too, are part of this ecosystem.

By whatever means, the government is by far the single biggest funder of scholarship and academic research. Direct state sponsorship is most evident. Other times, the subsidy comes indirectly when donations to universities and cultural institutions are tax-deductible. Either way, 80% of global academic research is paid for by government, thus by all of us as taxpayers.[51]

For the sciences, government funds a multi-billion-dollar global research complex. That follows long traditions of directly underwriting scientific research. The Royal Society of Britain, founded in 1660, claims to be the oldest institution supporting science. The Academia Secretorum Naturae was established in Naples a century earlier, the Accademia dei Lincei in Rome in 1603. Today, global expenditure on research and development is slightly above 2% of GDP.[52] Almost $2 trillion are at stake annually. In 2013, worldwide research costs were $1.48 trillion. Much was corporate R&D, but governments financed between 25% and 30%. Universities paid for a fifth or so ($296 billion).[53]

The government's role in producing knowledge can hardly be overstated. Curiosity is ultimately the psychological driver of the search for understanding. Yet, without the infrastructure behind curiosity's regular and continuous exercise, only the occasional enthusiast would be active. Like artists, the earliest scholars enjoyed either independent means or wealthy patrons. With the rise of universities in the Middle Ages, the pursuit of knowledge began to institutionalize. The first universities were more like professional schools than institutions selflessly uncovering new understanding. They trained priests and theologians for service in churches. Later, military academies supplied the absolutist state with officers to calculate projectile trajectories, plan fortifications, and otherwise master early-modern technologies of warfare. Universities trained lawyers and other civil servants for ever more bureaucratized government administrations.

Private patrons' leverage over their in-house authors is evident. Early universities, too, were in thrall to rulers. Theological faculties had to toe the doctrinal line espoused by the monarch. Henry VIII and Edward VI purged English universities in a Protestant direction. Mary I took them back to Catholicism. Only male Anglicans could be students at Oxbridge until the 1850s.[54] When the state began intervening in higher education, it took over existing institutions, as in Scotland and continental Europe, or created them directly, as in Berlin in 1810 or with the American land-grant institutions. Dispossessing the Church, the French Revolution nationalized universities throughout Europe, leaving them reliant on student fees and state financing. Elsewhere, endowments continued to be part of the mix; they were raised privately, as for the ancient English universities, or from the state, as in Sweden and the American land-grant establishments.[55]

The outcome was the modern university, pioneered in the early nineteenth century by the new University of Berlin, inspired by Alexander von Humboldt. Research and teaching were to inform each other, professors and students alike engaged in the mission of advancing knowledge while communicating their discoveries accessibly, and all financed by a combination of state monies and tuition payments. Self-administration was crucial. Where private institutions remained powerful, as in the UK and US, that was self-evident. But even state-financed universities in Europe asserted their claims to independence. Selecting mainly on scholarly merit, they decided whom to admit, hire, and promote, how to teach, and what to research.[56]

The Salaried Creator

What followed from this shift in the aesthetics and economics of creativity? With copyright tailored to the Romantic artists' predicament, who decided once they no longer set the tone? Nowadays, salaried authors working collaboratively are commonplace. Copyright has not entirely ignored such creators, but they have been something of an afterthought. Work for hire was how copyright dealt with employees who created at others' behest. It evolved in the mid-nineteenth century, but not equally in all nations.

Work for hire grants employers—not the immediate creators—most rights in works produced by their employees. It dates from the late eighteenth century, giving those who commissioned art the rights in the creation they paid for. Portraits were an early genre covered, with rights vested in either the subject or the work's commissioner. The artist was assumed to be doing their bidding.

(Ghostwriters will understand the logic.) For collective efforts, such as encyclopedias or periodicals, authorship was vested in the publisher.

Work for hire took off in the twentieth century, especially in the US, at the film industry's behest.[57] It is not hard to see why. Film is inherently collaborative, requiring cooperation among scores of creators, all with claims to be essential participants. To tame the many voices clamoring for recognition—from director to costume maker—someone had to be in charge. That holds equally for the software industry and gaming. The Romantic idiom of the single author failed to do justice to multiple creatorship. "Contributor" was one suggestion to designate collective authors.[58] More generally, this posed the question, what is the collaborative entity that creates or knows when authorship becomes collective? When the wisdom of crowds is invoked, who is being wise?[59] That, in turn, was a subset of the thorny idea of collective knowledge, the claim that groups, not just individuals, can be cognizant entities.[60]

The question we address in the conclusion is whether work for hire should provide the template for a broader approach to copyright in an era when most content is produced by creators who do not earn their living from selling their works.

3

The Open-Access Problem

From an artisanal Romanticism, culture has moved into a postmodern aesthetic of publicly-financed collaborative creativity. Against this background, open access raises specific and sometimes technical issues. The question of who pays for scholarship and science looms above it all. Still, differences also distinguish the various tribes of content producers in terms of their workflow, how collectively they labor, and the formats they present their findings in.

Digital technologies and their vast potential are to be thanked for our current dilemma—for both good and bad. In the analog era, we had broadly achieved the access to knowledge then possible. The most important research libraries, vast shrines of learning, had been built up over the eighteenth and nineteenth centuries, often nationalizing what had once been royal collections. Deliberately burning the Library of Congress in Washington during the War of 1812, the British targeted the hoard of knowledge that was recognized as crucial even then.

Libraries eventually dotted the landscape, but not every one was open to everyone. Only faculty and students could use university libraries, with occasional visiting scholars allowed in. A few public libraries could compete in size and holdings: the New York, Boston, and Chicago Public Libraries which were open to anyone crossing their thresholds. The British Library in London and the Bibliothèque Nationale in Paris were scholarly institutions requiring application and credentials for entry, but the determined and persistent could usually surmount such obstacles. Marx wrote much of his oeuvre at the British Library, although an impecunious, disheveled foreigner. To judge from the rules at the old Bibliothèque Nationale in the Rue de Richelieu, which forbade patrons to rest their heads on the tables, admission was sufficiently accommodating that not all visitors came intent on reading.

For the analog era, these great libraries were the state of the art. Microfilm and microfiche allowed newer institutions to copy otherwise unobtainable works. In the 1930s, American librarians sought to mass-microfilm European holdings, duplicating Old World repositories.[1] Interlibrary loans spared institutions the need to buy the long tail of rarely used materials—at the cost of transport and logistics. Beyond this, it was hard to see how the existing technology could have been much improved.

Digitality upended all this. It has spoiled us, raising the bar and leaving the old system woefully inadequate. That is what progress means—when we come to take a novelty for granted, indeed when we make it a necessity, and then drive down its cost to become a commodity and no longer a luxury. Combined with the internet, digitality expanded access in two directions: to sources beyond those available in the local library. At the same time, these sources were now usable not just in institutions but wherever readers could access the web.

There lay the rub. In the analog universe, a library could grant access to anyone it chose. Public and national libraries served a broad constituency—all readers, or at least all scholars. University libraries were generally restricted to faculty and students. The first-sale doctrine (copyright exhaustion) specifies that having bought a book, owners (such as a library) are at liberty to do what they please—read, destroy, resell, rent, or lend it. Some things are exempted: in many countries, sound recordings, films, and sometimes music scores may not be lent.[2] But on the whole, analog content was as available as it could be in libraries.

Publishers have always regarded libraries ambiguously, much as they do secondhand bookstores. Both cut into primary sales by creating secondary markets, either in lends or used copies. In a publisher-dominated world, both would be outlawed. But in the interests of education and the spread of knowledge, publishers were forced to tolerate them. Books borrowed from libraries were potential sales forgone. But, at least there were physical limits to how patrons could use works—one at a time. And after several lends, books in high demand fell apart, needing replacement. Libraries did not just compete with bookstores for readers but were also among publishers' biggest customers. A modus vivendi emerged: so long as libraries continued to buy books, publishers would not object to seeing them lent.

Digitality undermined this analog ecosystem of secondary uses —reusing and lending works. Digital works were unlike their analog predecessors. Copies were easy to make and perfect replicas, indistinguishable from the original. A single copy could spawn infinite new ones, none ever wearing out. Lending in the analog sense of passing on something that was then no longer possessed became impossible. Readers enjoyed the promise of digital copying, while publishers feared it. In the worst case, a single digital lend of an indiscriminately copiable work could end a publisher's sales altogether.

Some publishers therefore reneged entirely on the fundamental compact between publishers and libraries. Amazon, the largest issuer of self-published books, refused to allow library loans at all.[3] During the Covid epidemic, however, it was criticized for its apostasy.[4] In 2021, it struck a licensing agreement with the Digital Public Library of America.[5] But even less intransigent publishers made things difficult for libraries.

Digital works, either born that way or format-shifted from the analog, were a potential delight for consumers and a nightmare for disseminators. Only by clipping their wings, making them resemble their analog predecessors, could disseminators market works without fear of piracy. The legacy publishers embraced the digital revolution by seeking to undermine most of its advantages. Fearful of piracy, they hobbled digital works to make them more like their analog equivalents—hard or impossible to copy. From this sprang digital rights management (DRM) software, which hampered digital works' free distribution and copying, limiting who could consume the works and how.

Beyond such precautions for the retail market, libraries' rights to lend digital materials were further tailored to analog precedents. After a certain number of lends, paper books wore out, spines broke, and pages dog-eared, so that eventually they had to be replaced. When publishers agreed to permit libraries to lend digital works, they often charged more than for paper copies. They also insisted that they be paid repeatedly, even though digital works did not wear out. Unsurprisingly, publishers and libraries differed on how many lends physical books could withstand before degrading—twenty-six, according to HarperCollins, many thousands in the experience of most libraries.[6] This analogy was now carried into the digital age. With e-books, libraries have to license rights for a certain number of lends, then pay anew once that is reached.

If lending digital works was complicated, reselling them was worse. Secondary markets for digital content threw up problems. Unlike with analog items, sharing, selling, and copying digital works tend to be the same act. But copying digital works was not allowed, even under the first-sale doctrine. How, then, do you ensure that works are sold in the old-fashioned sense of a singular copy transferred between users and not in the digital sense of being copied? With resold digital works, how can you be certain that only one copy exists and that each sale does not just multiply copies?

Transferring a digital work from one hard disk to another was not like passing along a book, where the object indisputably changed hands. In digital transfer, a new copy was created while the initial one remained untouched at its source. To sidestep this problem, software was developed to ensure that the original was deleted upon transfer. The company behind a program intended to allow the sale of secondhand digital music recordings argued that as the files were transferred to its servers and then to the buyer's hard disk, they were deleted on the seller's. What appeared to be a series of copies was, in fact, a transfer or migration. That logic was rejected when challenged. The court found that, inasmuch as a digital transfer meant copying, it was not protected by first-sale.[7] First-sale limited the rights-holders' distribution rights, but not their reproduction rights.

In Chapter 2, we distinguished between different kinds of works and authors and how each kind raises particular problems. Works in the public domain present the fewest issues. Anyone who wants to pay can digitize them and open them to all. The Google Books project has already accomplished much, and its files are now stored with the HathiTrust.[8] It has digitized swaths of the world's largest libraries, some 25 million books, at a cost of $400 million.[9] Of works not yet in the public domain, only snippets can legally be viewed. But the others can be opened up. Ever more books and periodicals published through the mid-1920s are thus freely available on the web.

Yet the serpent's tail was visible even here. Some libraries have licensed companies to digitize public-domain collections, and then sell subscriptions to other research institutions for use by their patrons.[10] That creates two types of public domain. One is theoretically open to all readers, if they can find a copy they may look at.

Another is available only to those with access to paywalled databases. Of course, digitizing public-domain content is not costless and must be paid for. Privatizing the digitized copies for subscribers only is one less-than-ideal way of recouping costs.

Digitality has also allowed some publishers to discover gold where earlier they saw only dross. Even the public domain—once digitized—revealed an unanticipated value. JSTOR is a database of most Anglophone social science and humanities periodicals from their beginning, often in the nineteenth century.[11] Funded at first by the Mellon Foundation, it has been spun off into a separate organization. It is available by subscription to libraries and their patrons. For scholars, it is a lifesaver. Authors once spent countless hours tracking down old journal articles in the compact-shelving basements of the libraries they were lucky enough to access. Today, PDFs rain from the digital heavens like manna.

The journal backlists used to have nothing but academic value. Publishers themselves often did not own a complete run of their journals. Even the most devoted editor might not have realized that there was money to be made from yellowing copies of the *Journal of the County Louth Archaeological and Historical Society*, the *Fairy Tale Review*, *Norwegian American Studies*, the *Journal of Intersectionality*, *Jazz Education in Research and Practice*, *Pacific Coast Philology*, and so forth, in all their stultifying scholarly specificity.

JSTOR awoke publishers to the realization that some customers—research libraries—would pay for these scholarly Cinderellas in sack-cloth, rounding out their collections and sparing them the bother and cost of maintaining paper copies. By digitizing the backlist, JSTOR, in effect, created its value. Once this had been done, publishers moved to capture the value for themselves. To suggestions that subscriptions be opened to libraries unable to afford the going rate, or that discounts be offered poorer institutions, or even that JSTOR be thrown open to the public *tout court*, publishers objected, fearful of losing their new income stream. Only slowly and partially have institutions in the Global South been offered price reductions and sometimes free access.

Except for public-domain material, the digital paradise remains closed to readers without a library card for a major research library.[12] The JSTOR story is repeated for other databases that remain shut to nonsubscribers: HeinOnline, Proquest, EBSCOhost, and the like. Only occasionally have similar collections been opened up to everyone, as with Harvard Law School's Caselaw Access Project. That makes case law up to 2018 freely available, with some limitations that end in 2024 and not counting headnotes for cases after 1922.[13]

With JSTOR and its peers, no reader is worse off than in the analog era. The paper copies remain readable in the few university libraries they have always called home. But that is cold comfort to those without access to digital copies. They must still trek to the host institution, if they can gain admittance, while others read from anywhere. Digitality has thus opened up a divide. Nothing has been taken from those without digital access. But in an age when some gain wondrous new benefits, the excluded can hardly avoid feeling disadvantaged. The haves are now separated from the have-mores.[14] Sometimes, digitized materials are made freely available after a period of exclusive access for research library patrons. If that becomes the norm, the divide may prove to be less of an issue than feared.[15]

For in-copyright works, in turn, digital editions have been a boon for publishers and readers. The public can choose between e-books and conventional editions; periodical and newspaper readers can choose between online or app versions and the usual print ones. Whether and how open access can be offered for works in copyright, we take up again later. For works that are still in copyright but out of print, the situation has been ambiguous. Digitizing them remains illegal. But since the publishers and rights-holders for out-of-print works have ceased exploiting them, no one loses by their dissemination in new formats, while readers gain. This situation is explored further in Chapter 7.

One Size Does Not Fit All

For employed authors, especially university academics, variants in approach, medium, and format among fields have created distinct cultures with different means of disseminating work. These have consequences for open access.

First, scientists are not authors in the Romantic sense of people whose works express their personalities and are thus connected to them by ineffable ties of creativity. Not that scientists are not creative, too, but they stake professional recognition on channeling truth in statements that reflect an external reality. If one scientist does not deliver a particular insight, another will. A personal element is unavoidable in expressing their ideas, but it is not the point of the work. Insofar as the personal intrudes, it renders the work less worthwhile as a truth statement.[16]

More mundanely, works in the humanities and many social sciences are often published as books, while the hard sciences' primary medium is the article. Yet, the social sciences, too, are shifting toward articles.[17] The humanities, in turn, account for only 9% of scholarly articles.[18] Simplifying somewhat, articles in the humanities are often first or secondary versions of content that later appears in books. Equally often, they are review articles, surveying a field and its literature. Unlike in the sciences, humanities periodicals also publish book reviews, conference notes, letters to the editor, and other incidental work. For most humanities scholars, journals are a sideshow. Careers are not made via articles. A researcher will publish one perhaps every several years, if that. For scientists, in contrast, periodical publication is their lifeblood. A steady stream of output in the most prestigious journals, with its associated cascade of citations, grounds a successful career.

This distinction may seem peripheral to outsiders, but much hangs on it. A book is the consummation of long labor on a subject of considerable import, usually written by one author. Books tend to be magisterial pronouncements, a high-stakes throw of the dice by scholars who have spent years researching, developing, and refining an argument. They pursue a sustained narrative, arriving at what they intend to be definitive conclusions. At the margins of some humanities fields, mainly in literature, scholars have begun assembling their essays on similar topics, as though they collectively constitute a book.[19] But on the whole, humanities researchers seem content with the significant effort and in-depth scope that anchors the monograph as their medium of choice. Academia's orientation toward the sciences threatens books. In the UK, evaluations of university departments' productivity are used to allocate research monies. These massively discount books, considering them the equivalent of a mere two articles. The evaluating bodies apparently compensate for that unfairness in other ways.[20]

Once issued, a book may generate reviews in its first year or two. After that, if it resonates in its field, other scholars may respond to it as they, in turn, write their books, taking on board its arguments or disagreeing with its conclusions. The exchange among books takes place over decades. Even humanities articles differ from their scientific peers. Lengthier, more substantive, and written less frequently, they also have a longer shelf life. In contrast, citations of scientific articles peak three years after publication, trailing off after that. The faster a body of work grows, the quicker it ages.[21]

Scientific articles differ from books in several ways. First, they may be ongoing accounts of work as it unfolds. A lab reports on its findings frequently, sometimes weekly. It seeks to establish priority, ensuring that competing teams do not scoop it, and to keep peers up to speed. In many fields, algorithms and specialized software are involved in the writing. Sections are preformatted and literature reviews and citation compilations are partly automated. AI stands poised for authorship.[22]

Second, besides serving an informational role, articles may be part of an ongoing discussion among colleagues, rather than the definitive statement of years of reading, research, and reflection by one author found in a book. An article aimed at the interchange of ideas invites a response. It is a thrust or parry in a longer intellectual duel, one voice in a dialogue. Since the article is just one contribution in a rapidly moving exchange, its value is quickly exhausted, except as future historians of science later take an interest. In some fields, articles are much like blogs, a dialogue in text, where no one link is particularly interesting, well crafted, or well researched, and where the value lies in the act of participating.

Scientific articles have also become collective efforts, the report of many coauthors, not the fruit of solitary creators. At the start of the twentieth century, most articles had solo authors, but at its end, an average of two to seven collaborators.[23] That affects the concept of authorship. Not only do science articles often have multiple coauthors, but many scientists, with their collaborators' aid, are also wildly prolific by humanities standards. Some 8,000 physicists publish at least 72 papers annually—on average, one every five days. Life scientists are the next most fertile.[24] The Soviet chemist Yuri Struchkov churned out one article every three days in the 1980s.[25] Tasawar Hayat, professor of mathematics at Pakistan's Quaid-i-Azam University, was once the world's most fecund scholar, issuing almost 1,000 articles between 2016 and 2018. By contrast, Gregory Lip, professor of cardiovascular medicine at the University of Liverpool, coauthored a mere 548 articles during the same time.[26]

In these fields, the concepts *article* and *author* clearly differ from their definitions in the humanities. Of course, it may be that geniuses in other fields manage to achieve weekly what takes humanities scholars years. More likely, the standards of researching, conceiving, writing, and publishing vary widely. Scientific articles are more a constant trickle of reports from the research front than considered articulations of a summated conclusion. An experiment is performed, written up, and published. The equivalent for humanities scholars would be to issue field notes as they dig in the archives or read sources—something unlikely to happen, even if they kept such annotations.

What it takes to be an author in the sciences also differs from the humanities. In 1988, the International Committee of Medical Journal Editors set criteria for who counts as an author.[27] These expressly excluded merely supervising or mentoring other authors or ensuring funding for a study. In other words, scientists were known to have claimed authorship on such spindly bases. Now, according to the new criteria, to count as an author, a scientist should have done all of four things: participated in designing or conducting experiments or processing results, helped write or revise the manuscript, approved the published version, and taken responsibility for the article's contents. In no humanities field would such criteria need to be spelled out. Clinical cardiologists have miraculously become up to 80 times as prolific when promoted to full professor, department chair, or institute director—just when additional administrative burdens might have been expected to curtail their research. In medicine, one-quarter of purported authors admit to making no substantial contribution.[28] Clearly, the criteria of authorship in such fields are not those of others.[29]

Such differences between book- and article-driven fields are not water-tight. The distinction between articles and books is not always clear, least of all if length is the sole criterion. Articles in law journals routinely rival books in size. Many are hundreds of pages.[30] So acute is the problem that in 2005, major law reviews announced they would discourage submissions longer than 70 pages and then proceeded blithely to ignore their own strictures.[31] Book-length works in other fields are also sometimes published as articles.[32] Conversely, short books are becoming a genre in themselves.[33] In online publication, size does not matter, either way. Nonetheless, such distinctions influence how various scholarly communities approach open access.

If nothing else, books and articles differ as aesthetic outputs. A single-author book is a more personal product than a group-written article reporting the results of last week's experiment in the technical prose affected by the sciences. Humanities authors will have conceived and executed the project largely on their own. They will have revised each sentence multiple times, seeking to instill a distinct and personal voice in their prose. They will have strong opinions about seemingly trivial aesthetic choices, such as typography, page layout, margin size, and placement of the notes (end of the book or bottom of the page).

Let us linger briefly over footnotes. Social science citations are often minimal—in the text, a parenthetical author-date reference to entries in a bibliography at the end of the work, often without page numbers. The results can be cryptic and weirdly anachronistic: "Reality does not necessarily correspond to our image of it (Plato, 1978)." Conversely, law review articles fetishize the footnote. Law professors often take their footnoting obligations to extremes. Respected law school journals (*Harvard Law Review* and the like) are not peer-reviewed and are edited by second-year students, who evaluate and publish their teachers' manuscripts. There are few barriers to entry for a select group of authors, and contributors may feel pressured to demonstrate their scholarly credibility.

At most, half the average law journal article is text, while the rest consists of notes that reference each assertion, however trivial or obvious. The standard guide to legal footnoting insists that every statement outside the author's "reasoning process" be attributed. The author may not assert so much as "The sun rises in the east" without citing Copernicus, as one legal scholar puts it.[34] The implication is that, since legal scholars have no ideas themselves, everything they write must be attributed to its source.[35] In defense of legal footnoting, the convention of indicating each cited work's argument provides a useful running historiographical commentary.

In contrast to the humanities' preoccupation with presentation, aesthetic concerns are little evident in science articles. They are, in effect, bulletins, written in (at best) serviceable prose, with their technical vocabulary incomprehensible to outsiders, and printed in dense multicolumned pages to shoehorn in maximum content. In some disciplines, periodicals have taken a back seat to websites that post preprints, the manuscripts submitted by their authors. Mathematicians and physicists already work mainly through prepublication sites, such as arXiv.

The sciences and humanities also differ in citation intensities. This, too, may seem arcane, but prestige and visibility, therefore promotion and salary, hinge on how often work is referred to by scholarly peers. The life sciences are the most assiduous citers. Since each researcher publishes hundreds of articles, eagerly flagging each other, the outcome is a tangled morass of mutual reference. Books cite other tomes much as elephants lumber through the landscape—slowly, stately, and at a remove. The reciprocal citation of innumerable articles, in contrast, resembles Brownian motion. By the law of networks, the bigger the field, the more intense the overall citation rate.

Citation intensities vary accordingly. Unsurprisingly, they also fluctuate depending on who is counting. Web of Science, Thomson Reuters's citation index, tallies only articles cited in journals from its database, mostly Anglophone. Google Scholar, in contrast, also indexes books, chapters, dissertations, theses, working papers, reports, conference papers, and articles from non-Thomson journals. The effects can be dramatic, with Web of Science ignoring entire fields. One prominent computer scientist, whose work appears mainly in conference proceedings, had over 20,000 citations in Google Scholar, a mere 240 in Web of Science.[36]

The most influential writers have been cited over a million times. In Google Scholar, Michel Foucault ranks highest in this pantheon. Freud comes in at about half that. More unexpectedly, Marx clocks in well below, at about 300,000 citations. Sex and power now trump the means of production. Of the top ten cited scholars across all fields, ranked in this case by their h-index (an author-level metric of productivity discussed below) as well as total citations, seven are currently active medical researchers, while only three are long-departed luminaries from other fields (Foucault, Freud, and Pierre Bourdieu, the sociologist). After that, health and engineering professors dominate until we get to Heidegger at number 24 and then again to number 47, the economist Joseph Stiglitz, the next entry from outside the hard sciences.[37]

Citation intensities allegedly measure a work's influence. Those most referred to have had the greatest impact. A cynic might argue that scholars write less to be read than cited.[38] And doubtless, many logs roll as colleagues in allied fields cite each other. Why is a work cited? All publicity may be good publicity, but perhaps not all citation. The most direct route to heavy citation is to assert something plausible but wrong. Fellow scholars will be encouraged to note in order to refute, burnishing their reputation for eagle-eyed perspicacity while inadvertently boosting the vanquished offender's score.

Conversely, those with the most influential ideas may become victims of their own success. Their thoughts are channeled by others, who are then cited instead. Or they are incorporated into the common stock of knowledge without specific attribution.[39] What citation intensity measures is thus less the quality of the work than the attention it has garnered—whatever the motive—among other authors.[40] But in the academic world, as elsewhere, publicity is generally welcomed. As the Irish writer Brendan Behan once said, the only bad press is an obituary.

The h-index measures how many papers a scholar has published that have been cited that many times. Ten articles cited ten times each give an h-value of 10. But one article mentioned a thousand times is but a tenth of that. Authors who write one highly influential work fare worse than those with many of middling impact. The aim is to identify durable and compelling careers, not one-off flukes. Scholars in collaborative fields with multiple coauthors inherently outperform solitary worker bees.[41] And naturally, the results for book-driven disciplines, whose scholars enter the citation market only once every decade or so, are so modest that the h-index plays no role for them.[42] In 2019, the health sciences' total citations in a sample of journals were twelve million, for history, one-hundredth of that.[43]

Yet, such methodological and presentational differences separating the humanities from the sciences are pipsqueaks compared to the elephant in the room—funding. The sciences are underwritten by direct government or other agency and university monies. Of humanities papers in the US, under 4% receive government funding, in the UK, about 5%. For the social sciences, it is about 20%, for the life sciences, in the high 70s, and in the natural sciences, the high 60s.[44] Given ample financing, dissemination costs are but an afterthought for the sciences. Dividing total research funding by the number of articles published annually suggests that, on average, each is supported by $290,000.[45] Compared to that, an article processing charge (APC) of $3,000 or $4,000 is but a rounding error.

Some humanities and social science research is also government funded, but much less so. On the whole, humanities scholarship requires less infrastructure. As the story has it, a dean imposing budget cuts demands savings from the departmental chairs. First, the sciences explain how they would trim lab costs. Then the chair of mathematics points out that they are already frugal, needing only paper, pencils, and a wastebasket. Finally, comes the philosopher, who wonders, why the wastebasket?

Yet, even though the humanities seem like a bargain compared to high-energy particle physics, they still require costly investment. The Large Hadron Collider cost $4.75 billion. The Library of Congress's Jefferson building cost $6.5 million in 1897. Inflation-adjusted, that is a bit over $200 million. At $100 per volume to buy, catalog, and store its 32 million books, add another $3.2 billion. Globally, another half-dozen institutions have cost similar amounts. But on the whole, and in any given funding year, biologists, chemists, and physicists require more equipment than philosophers and philologists.

Humanities scholars enjoy sabbatical funding and, if lucky, research grants to pay for travel to archives and the like. Their salaries derive from some combination of student tuition (or its equivalent in state subsidy), university endowments, and the overhead charged on science funding that deans redistribute to other fields. Humanities research is largely self-funded, insofar as scholars spend the time on it that they are not preparing or teaching classes. Modest amounts of research monies sometimes can be included here. For those few able and lucky enough to tap into an audience, there may be additional income from royalties on books or from journalism.

Scientists, in contrast, live on the public's largesse. Their labs and staff require huge budgets, derived from government and other funders, and only secondarily from their universities. Scientists often teach less than their humanities colleagues, buying out their pedagogical duties through outside funding. In the US, where a Humboldtian belief in the unity of teaching and research remains strong, that is less true than elsewhere. Distinguished scientists can still be found teaching intro courses to undergraduates. In Europe, that is rarer, especially where, as in France and Germany, research has been broadly shifted from the universities to specialized institutions, such as the Max Planck Institute and the CNRS. Here, the pedagogical function is hived off to the universities while the institute researchers take on graduate training, integrating advanced students into their labs.

Such differences affect how the fruits of research are made public. Humanities scholars prove their academic credentials over decades by publishing monographs on specialized topics. Their audience is mainly colleagues, interested amateurs, and students. As they advance up the ranks, they are often tempted to write works of synthesis aimed at a broader public. If successful, they may end up with a bestseller, possibly even narrating a TV series. Popularizers can be found in the humanities, authors without academic positions or even credentials who write books of general interest. Many presidential biographies, indeed biographies in general, are written by such authors. That is not surprising since biographies are one of the few nonfiction genres that sell, where a diligent author can hope to make a living.[46]

But overall, the scholarly and popularizing functions tend to be filled by the same researchers, though at different points in their careers. Popularization is often a phase of the humanities scholar's professional life cycle. Besides monographs, professors sometimes write books aimed at a broad audience, hoping for popularity and royalties. A few scholarly authors, such as Andrew Roberts, Frances Fitzgerald, and Daniel Goldhagen, have even managed to live off their royalties or other income, including journalism or whatever their families have squirreled away. They follow the gentlemen scholars familiar from the nineteenth century and earlier.

Scientists resist such temptations. For them to publish a book, or more generally to write for a nonscholarly audience, usually marks a career's conclusion, not—as in the humanities—its pinnacle. Popularizing science typically falls to specialized journalists trained to make otherwise impenetrable research accessible to the public. *Haute vulgarisation* ("lofty popularization") the French call it. Rarely do top scientists write popular books. Stephen Hawking was an exception. Popularization has been baked into the university curriculum in the UK through professorial chairs intended for such writers. More a polemicist than a scholar, Richard Dawkins held one of the first such positions in the Public Understanding of Science at Oxford.

Publishing as a Profit Center

Digitality has accentuated the distinctions between science and humanities publishing. Research libraries are the biggest customers for scholarly work. In the analog era, their budgets paid for both humanities and science output. Until recently, the distribution of resources between fields was broadly equitable. The sciences broadcast mainly in periodicals, the humanities in both books and journals. Libraries bought them all. But during the 1980s, scientific publishers began putting the system under pressure. They jacked up the cost of existing journals and issued many new ones. Academic journals' prices increased more than eightfold in the quarter-century after 1984, while inflation merely doubled.[47] Some scholarly publishers expanded enormously.

In 2009, the world had 53,000 commercially licensed academic journals, some 24,000 from large scientific publishers and 28,000 from small ones. The large houses published hundreds of distinct titles, the biggest, thousands. By offering libraries expansive portfolios of standardized-format content in package deals, these publishers gained the upper hand.[48] The commercial publishers also took over journals from scholarly societies. Earlier, the societies had often published the main journals in their fields, sold inexpensively with subscriptions usually baked into membership fees. Now, as scientific publication became big business, the for-profit houses bought these journals for their own stables.[49] Today, commercial houses issue 64% of journals, societies 30%.[50]

In 1960, there were some 30 English-language economics journals, half published by nonprofit organizations. By 2000, of the 300 economics journals now in print, two-thirds were issued by commercial publishers.[51] The commercial publishers both multiplied and consolidated. Fewer and bigger houses dominated the field. The five largest academic publishing houses now bring out over half of all natural science and medical research: Reed-Elsevier, Wiley-Blackwell, Springer, Taylor & Francis, and, depending on the metric, either the American Chemical Society or SAGE Publishing. The social sciences are even worse off. In 1973, the big five published one in ten articles; now, it is more than half. They bring out 71% of all psychology papers.[52]

More and more specialized journals emerged, each becoming a must-have for libraries. Peer-reviewed periodicals increased by a third over the twentieth century's last decade.[53] Thanks to the academic market's peculiarities, having more journals did not lead to competition and lower prices. Quite the contrary. Rather than selecting among journals, libraries' clients insist they buy them all. Scientific publishers' goods are not substitutable. If readers cannot afford a specific article in one physics journal, they cannot just read another competing, cheaper one instead—or do without.

Yet, as an aside, in theory, academic publications are not wholly unsubstitutable. Where the subject is the invariable physical world, information not available from one source could potentially be found in reasonable approximation elsewhere. Studying *Drosophila* for a particular purpose in one lab will lead to conclusions—if the science is solid—similar to those drawn in another. But suppose the study involves others' interpretations of events, or specific content, as is often true in the humanities. Then those precise materials must be available to scholars interested in the subject. Studying Shakespeare's sonnets requires reading them and the associated secondary literature.

In any case, to avoid substitutability, scholars usually conduct exhaustive literature searches to ensure that no one else has already invented their particular wheel. That is becoming easier with digital search tools and as the scientific world adopts one lingua franca. Even so, Bradford's law of information scattering holds that searching for relevant literature outside a core of pertinent sources means trawling through exponentially growing numbers of unfamiliar journals.[54] A literature search that entirely eliminates the chance of replication may be more time-consuming than simply performing the work in the first place. Otherwise, scholars might end like Poincaré's would-be traveler, packing and repacking a suitcase for a journey never undertaken.

Nor is every kind of content unsubstitutable. No doubt, some romance novels are better than others. But readers looking for a

good cry will find that many do the trick. A similar effect probably holds for porn. Even something as seemingly academic as textbooks is substitutable. Textbooks for schools and universities are
by-products of the scholarly enterprise, thus tangential to our concerns, but they soak up professorial time and energy. With prices
rocketing, they, too, have become unaffordable, like scientific journals. Yet, because they are substitutable, they are subject to competition, and the market has begun providing alternatives.

When a scholar writes an article, anyone seriously studying the
subject must read it, however expensive it is. No other one on the
same or similar topics will do. Not so with textbooks. One decent
one will serve as nicely as another. Teachers will have preferences,
but their students will object when prices hit the pain threshold.
The rat race of producing ever-updated editions of existing textbooks, compelling successive cohorts of students to buy new ones,
can be derailed by competition from open-access or other cheaper
content. Rice University's OpenStax program has developed a suite
of textbooks that are free or cheap.[55] MIT has something similar,
and other programs exist elsewhere.[56] From a low base, open textbooks are becoming more widely adopted.[57] Two statistics are worth
noting. Overall expenditure on educational books rose from $8.5
billion in 1999 to $11.6 billion in 2019.[58] Meanwhile, students have
responded by reducing their spending on textbooks per capita from
$700 in 2007 to $415 in 2018.[59]

For most serious academic work, however, substitutability is not
an option. Journals multiply and cannot be interchanged. Nor is
there downward pressure on prices. Scholars are indifferent to costs.
They do not pay for subscriptions and care little how expensive
they become. Only exceptionally do authors bear costs. The *Proceedings of the National Academy of Sciences* levies both article charges
on writers and subscriptions on readers. As a quirk of the discipline,
economics journals often have submission fees, not refundable
even in case of rejection. But on the whole, the costs are shouldered

by the consumer, which is to say, by libraries. They have to buy ever more expensive journals.

Among the peculiarities of scholarly publishing is that presses receive their content largely free. Conventional periodicals are staffed by salaried writers and editors with their associated costs. Freelancers are paid. Scholarly journals' articles, in contrast, are researched, written, vetted, and largely edited by their academic authors, paid for by science funders.[60] The product is then delivered for free to the journals, ready for their finishing touches: organizing—but not paying for—peer review, some editorial work, and typesetting. In the pre-digital days, they had to print and distribute, but now they maintain sites and storage. Thanks to this lopsided division of labor, the scientific publishers' profit margins are substantial.

Other goods also enjoy a similar quasi-monopoly position, such as first-class postage or electricity. Hence they are carefully regulated.[61] Not the publishers. They have exploited their hammerlock—monopoly without regulation—by increasing the subscription costs of scientific periodicals at triple the consumer price index over recent decades.[62] As the commercial publishers tilled their newfound turf, prices skyrocketed. In the US, research library spending on periodicals during the 1980s and 1990s increased by over 200%, while it *decreased* by 21% for monographs.[63] In Australia, the cost of journals quintupled between 1986 and 1998, while monograph prices increased merely 50%.[64] As libraries shifted resources in their direction, buying fewer books, journals devoured the lion's share of budgets. In the mid-1980s, research collections spent half their money on books, but by 2011 three-quarters went to subscriptions.[65] In the UK, books cost 9% of research library budgets in 2008, but serials almost a quarter.[66]

Everyone has their favorite example of outrageous scientific journal prices. In Elsevier's stable, *Tetrahedron Letters* costs $20,960 per annum and the *Journal of Chromatography A*, $22,025.[67] Before we let indignation get the better of us, recall that these journals' prices reflect the patentable market value of their content—the chemical structure of new molecules of potential industrial use.[68] If *Harvard Business Review* published investment advice and stock tips, it, too, would charge more than its current subscription ($120), much as no one expects a Bloomberg terminal to be cheap ($24,000). But even apart from such outliers, average library subscription rates for chemistry journals were almost $5,000 in 2019. By comparison, the cost of humanities journals is modest, even touchingly cheap. History journals cost $472, and music periodicals are practically giveaways at $332.[69] For decades, libraries have patiently paid the scientific journals' charges, skimping on acquisitions in other fields and formats as their budgets drained into the pockets of the major academic publishers.

Some humanities journals are subsidized by the professional societies that publish them; others calibrate prices at the modest level their markets will bear. Institutional subscriptions for journals such as the *American Historical Review* and the *Proceedings of the Modern Language Association* almost never exceed three figures. Despite their lower prices, humanities journals are arguably more expensive to produce. They get more editorial attention and include material not found in their scientific counterparts, such as book reviews and conference proceedings.[70] They are often less specialized and receive more submissions per published article than scientific journals, thus requiring more sorting and filtering. Their average article is longer.[71]

Also worth noting is that until recently, few libraries paid retail. Such eye-wateringly expensive journals have been rolled into big-deal bundles bought by libraries for lump sums. The official sticker price of each subscription has been rising, but overall, the cost per journal and per article in these bundles has dropped.[72] Whether the price per read, download, or citation has also fallen is another question. More information may have been available, but was it used less? While the journals held by one group of US university libraries

in the 1980s and 1990s quadrupled, the number cited only doubled.[73] Large consumers seem to have done best from bundles. Their
cost per article download is below $1.[74] But the average was over $4,
and publishers formulating their business plans counted on libraries being willing to pay up to $25 per download.[75] Whether that
holds across the board is unclear.

Much-used journals are bundled together with obscure ones that
libraries might not subscribe to if left to their own devices. Like
music albums long ago, you must buy it all to get the hits you want.
The publishers load the smorgasbord ever higher with intellectual
herring and lutefisk. Even though libraries no longer pay à la carte,
the all-you-can-eat price has risen as the assortment has broadened.
Thanks to burgeoning content combined with ever-higher overall
costs, acquisitions budgets continue to be drained. Hence libraries
have recently sought to unbundle their big deals, a process to which
we return later.

This serials crisis of ever-increasing subscription prices predated
digitality and open access. Both could have helped alleviate the
problem, but the scientific publishers have not allowed that. True,
the costs of publishing are often underestimated and the promise
of digitality in delivering content cheaply has likely been exaggerated. Digitality does vaporize many of conventional publication's expenses: printing, warehousing, distributing. It also lowers
libraries' costs in receiving, cataloging, binding, storing, shelving,
reshelving, preserving, and replacing paper copies. And open access
eliminates expenses from the old system, such as managing copyright and subscriptions.

But even digital publishing is not gratis. The output can be
treated more or less thoroughly. But some degree of vetting, evaluating, copywriting, and editing makes it more presentable. Content
must be tagged and metadata entered to make it discoverable. PDFs
are serviceable, and not every text needs an e-book's bells and whistles. But optical character recognition to allow searchability is crucial and can be done at varying levels of accuracy and cost. Servers

need maintenance and software updating, and backward compatibility must be ensured after major upgrades.

We take the coddling required by paper media for granted—binding and rebinding, humidity and temperature control, not to mention intensive measures for ancient and priceless texts. And we often ignore how old texts survived only as they were upgraded to new media, copied into later works that in turn came into our hands. Papyrus lasts 200 years, parchment, many centuries.[76] Papyrus writings had to make it to parchment to survive for us. The equivalent problems for digital content are not unusually demanding. Nor are they peculiar to open access. They are an issue for any form of digital record-keeping, whether government or corporate, and must be solved by society as a whole. Digitality is marvelously efficient and scalable, but its content does not fall like manna from heaven.

Open access has brought some relief to library budgets, which no longer have to pay for certain publications. That has been counterbalanced by university administrations cutting acquisitions appropriations in tune with their new obligation to pay publication fees for their faculty's writings instead. Sometimes the trade-offs have been explicit. The Sponsoring Consortium for Open Access Publishing in Particle Physics (SCOAP³) channels funds released from library budgets by open access to pay instead for article charges.[77] In the same spirit, the Open Library of the Humanities uses contributions from libraries to sponsor open journals, thus lessening the burden of subscriptions.[78]

Varieties of Open Access

Open access comes in various colors. Strictly speaking, gold open access means journals (or books) that offer immediate access upon publication to the final, typeset iteration of the author's manuscript, usually known as the version of record. How this is paid for varies. Some journals rely on article processing charges or publishing fees paid by authors or funders. But other sources of finance are also possible. Presses that can waive publishing fees thanks to independent sources supply diamond open access, and this is technically speaking a subset of gold. Hybrid journals offer some content to subscribers while other articles have been paid for and are available to all. Read-and-publish agreements between publishers and research libraries combine payments for reading access and the cost of disseminating in a lump sum, allowing staff to publish without further charge and everyone to read the resulting articles. This, too, is a gold variant.

Green open access releases a version that is degraded and thus not in direct competition with conventional subscription publications or gold editions. This is a parallel form of green access that runs in tandem with an otherwise unreformed publication system. The degradation can be either in the quality of the version or in the delay before the version of record is available. In the latter case, access to the version of record is granted, but only after an embargo. In the first, inferior prepublication versions are offered freely when a subscription journal is issued. Immediately available variants are stunted to hobble competition with paid versions. They may convey the gist but are less polished and—lacking the typeset publications' pagination—can be cited only imprecisely. Access can be permitted on a journal's website or via aggregators like JSTOR or by authors' self-archiving.

Gold access aims to prevent readers being excluded by subscriptions or paywalls. Yet, in doing so, it solves one accessibility problem by creating a new one. Both gold and green permit anyone to read content. But the author-side fees required by gold keep out would-be contributors who cannot afford them. Paywalls become playwalls.[79] Only if other resources to allow diamond publishing are available or if largely costless green approaches via self-archiving are accepted can such authors participate. Of the two accessibility problems—for readers and authors—only one has been resolved. Not everyone can afford article charges, much less their heftier, although more intermittent, book equivalents.

The idea that digitality would make dissemination cheaper worked only if publishers charged for actual costs. That is what funders sought, but not what they got.[80] They miscalculated on two counts. First, publishers billed according to the price structure inherited from conventional subscriptions, thus high. Second, they charged what the market would bear.[81] The more prestigious the venue, the costlier. Publishing charges therefore vary widely. The Mellon Foundation calculated the sums required to sustain open journals, arriving at between $960 and $1,622 per article. Building in a reasonable profit, they concluded that charges for First World periodicals should lie between $1,103 and $2,566.[82]

In Latin America's well-developed open-access landscape, publishing charges are reasonable, between $200 and $600.[83] In the industrialized world, the average is $900, but top-ranked periodicals demand much more, from $2,500 to $5,000.[84] Squeezing its prestige and position until the pips squeak, *Nature* now charges over $11,000.[85] The price for issuing open books (which we return to) ranges from $5,000 to $15,000. Even though we are early in the transition to open publishing, the sums reaped are impressive. Publishing charges for open periodicals generated almost half a billion dollars in 2017, expected to grow steeply. The leading conventional journal publishers have established their command also of open access.[86]

From these publishers' vantage, whether expenses are recouped beforehand as publishing charges or afterward as subscriptions or books' wholesale prices is irrelevant so long as the overall sums remain comparable. If anything, book publishers benefit from upfront money, much as subscriptions pay journals before they deliver the product. True, when all the publisher gets for a book is the publishing charge, they miss the windfalls from unexpected bestsellers—unless many buyers splash out for physical editions rather than just downloading free e-versions. Indeed, the term *best-seller* becomes something of a misnomer in the open-access world. We need a new word—*best-read* or something to that effect. (Royalties for Amazon's e-books already depend on the number of Kindle pages read, rather than just downloads.[87])

But publishers reap the charges also for books that turn out to be turkeys and, in the conventional model, would lose money. Authors now bear the risks, while readers enjoy the rewards. There are few economic windfalls in open publishing, only fame and reputation for authors whose books go viral. Journals, in contrast, do not suffer the same volatility as books. Subscriptions gradually rise or fall, but runaway successes or abject failures are less common.

Gold open access is like reversing a river, as in 1900 when the Chicago River was re-engineered to flow into the Mississippi rather than Lake Michigan. The direction changes, but the river remains. Green open access, in contrast, poses a bigger threat to entrenched publishing interests. But that depends on what kind of green accessibility. In the usual formulation, it changes little. It patches up the existing subscription model, supplying an overlay of good-enough, freely available versions. That provides a work-around within a largely unchanged conventional system. Indeed, this variety of green arguably allows the old system to continue, preventing the emergence of fully open journals. Subscription periodicals remain, but various forms of access are permitted. The final version is opened up after an embargo period, allowing publishers to skim off most of its commercial value. In effect, this merely accelerates what copyright was originally intended to be—monopolies of short duration followed by the public domain's timeless embrace. It returns us to the original laws' abbreviated terms—but even briefer.

How long an embargo between publication and the freely available version of record should be is hotly debated. Subscription publishers favor lengthy embargos, extending their monopoly; readers and funders prefer shorter ones. Embargos affect the sciences most, where progress moves rapidly and oven-warm articles command a premium. The humanities and social sciences require less speed. Embargos hurt more when the topic is a promising new treatment for childhood leukemia than if a history of the dietary habits of French peasants in sixteenth-century Dordogne. The half-life of humanities and social science articles (the time to reach half an article's total downloads or citations) is much longer than in the hard sciences, especially medicine.[88] Longer embargos may therefore be justified for humanities subjects than some sciences.

Yet, green open access that relies on access to a hobbled version and/or embargos is not the only way. Rather than keeping subscription publishers in their accustomed position, depository green open access potentially undermines inherited procedures. If depositing content in the cloud is considered the equivalent of publication, new vistas open up. Digitality will then finally have contributed to making publishing affordable and widely available.

Green access usually means conventional subscription publication leavened by preprint dissemination. But if, instead, it disseminates content via online repositories, new possibilities arise. Imagine that the version posted is not just a typescript but approximates what once would have been published—copyedited, typeset, proofread, and otherwise like an e-pub. (We leave aside the selection, filtering, and attention-drawing functions of publication for later discussion.) That would increase costs compared to merely posting raw preprints. Yet, judging from the experience of preprint repositories, it would be much cheaper than open-access journals' fees. And for books, as we will see in discussing Amazon self-publication, the expenses could be a small fraction of what open-access houses demand.

Repository-based green access would not require the parallel realm of subscription journals or the existing scholarly book publishers. Indeed, it might well undermine both, though one could imagine a continued role for publishers-on-paper for trade books and works with sufficient appeal to percolate beyond the repository. A continued demand for books-as-our-ancestors-knew-them needs fulfillment. But for academic research, conventional publishers may be superfluous. We return to repository open access in Chapter 8.

Green access as currently practiced threatens little. Parking preprints or embargoed versions of record in repositories leaves conventional subscription and gold journals free to roam. This version of green continues the inherited system while giving those readers hindered by subscriptions or paywalls a slightly inferior but fundamentally equivalent substitute. That largely solves the access issue. But it does nothing for affordability. Indeed, it worsens that problem by adding the expense of repositories to exploding subscription costs. Gold access suits scientists well. Academic publishers also prefer gold, having learned to profit from the system. But the coexistence of gold and green generates friction.

Suppose some nations follow a gold route and others green. As readers, the latter free ride off the publishing charges paid by the first, while the gold players get no more than the preprints or embargoed versions allowed in green. The UK, a research-intensive nation, has worried that striking out along a gold route would leave it shouldering disproportionate costs as it paid for both its authors' publishing fees and subscriptions to foreign journals.[89] For research-intensive countries, the old subscription model (combined with green open access) is preferable because it spreads dissemination costs to those who do more reading than writing. The same holds for fields where corporations often take subscriptions, distributing publishing costs beyond the scholarly world. And for those, such as psychology or medicine, where practitioners subscribe, shifting burdens beyond academia.

The subscription model also redistributes costs between read-intensive and research-intensive academic institutions. Libraries in liberal arts colleges and teaching-intensive institutions help pay the costs generated by research universities. In contrast, with gold access, high-research nations and institutions bear the brunt of expenses alone.[90] With subscriptions, research-intensive libraries shoulder only an average burden, proportional to their purchasing but not to the publishing of their faculty. As these institutions now face publishing charges for their prolific scholars, they seek supplemental monies from elsewhere. Grant funding is sometimes used to pay publication costs.[91] Authors might also have to participate directly, giving them skin in the game and helping contain costs.

Such tensions threaten to split the world between green and gold approaches, with gold regions curbing access to the information they have paid for.[92] Jean-Claude Burgelman, the European Commission's open-access envoy, argued that a "geospecific access model" would twist arms in those areas not signed up for gold by locking them out.[93] A partially gold system threatens to treat research outputs not as public goods but as club goods—available only to the in-group that has underwritten them.[94] Such balkanized geo-walling of open access undermines hopes of solving the accessibility problem. Those outside the golden bubble would be no better off than in the days of subscriptions.

The Version of Record

Among the disputed issues between the humanities and sciences and gold and green approaches comes also the version of record. The version of record is the publishing equivalent to standard units of length and weight—meters, pounds, and so forth. Once, these were metal facsimiles housed in controlled circumstances, but they have since become linked to physical constants of the universe.[95] The version of record is the canonical variant of the work, inscribed on metaphorical stone, against which others are judged. Scientific publishers like to emphasize the importance of a version of record since that makes readers dependent on their edition. Elsevier, for example, uses Crossmark, a system to track variants and alert readers to changes made to published content.[96] Publishers appreciate how it uses their version as the benchmark to which readers are pointed.[97]

The version of record is a consequence of paper media, the idea of a singular, static, official rendition. Has that become outmoded in the digital age? Digitality introduces a certain fluidity to texts. They now permit variation, emendation, and revision. They can be linked to other web content that is not part of the text itself but forms a larger ecosystem of meaning and reference. Yet, digitality also tracks each change and variation and thus accounts for alterations. Wikipedia articles, for example, are often edited, sometimes with the changes hotly debated. Each modification can be identified, attributed, tracked, revised, and reversed if necessary. The text is both more malleable and more stable than the illusory singularity of paper print. Faculty of 1000 Research, for example, is a platform that encourages multiple, revised incarnations of articles, all linked and independently citable, thus blurring the line between versions of record and others.[98]

A version of record could instead be replaced, it has been suggested, by a record of versions—a trackable catalogue raisonné of the text as it is refined, edited, and revised.[99] There is something to this. Fetishizing a static version of record ignores possibilities raised by digitization. For one thing, thanks to repositories being constantly updated, the prepublication manuscript and the version of record are increasingly indistinguishable.[100] With an article revised, accepted, and published by a journal, the author re-deposits the updated manuscript in the depository so that it now contains an edition identical to the version of record. Some publishers specifically make authors promise not to update their preprints, however little cricket that may be.[101] But that is not all. As authors continue to revise and update works, depositing ever-newer editions in the repository, the version of record, supposedly etched in stone, begins to look more like yesterday's newspaper.[102] Given a choice between the canonical version of yore or the latest, which would you prefer?

Suggesting a move from a version of record to a record of versions is perhaps more than just clever wordplay. Nonetheless, it also ignores the role a stable edition still plays in some fields. It is sometimes claimed that the prepublication version, usually the author's accepted manuscript, is not inferior to the version of record.[103] That is whistling in the dark. In many ways, it obviously is. For one thing, it is not properly printed. For scientific journals, with their triple columns and minuscule typeface, that may be an advantage. Scientific articles are one of the few instances where publication diminishes readability compared to typescript.

But with their adjustable font sizes and correspondingly fluid—sometimes nonexistent—page numbers, e-publications have raised a relatively trivial problem. How does one quote a specific passage without a stable page number? The hard sciences, publishing brief articles, are not reliant on page numbers to indicate sources of information. The social sciences use in-line references to back-of-the-work bibliographies. They often do not give precise locations, even for quotations and even from lengthy books. The results, as noted, are often imprecise and weirdly anachronistic. But most humanities subjects, usually heavily text-based, must refer to a stable version of the source, accurately indicating the origin of a quotation, reference, or idea. For them, a version of record is indispensable. Digitality's ability to search text provides a solution only for precise quotations, not for paraphrases or references to ideas.

Both e-publications and preprints undercut scholars' reference to stable versions of record. If the freely available version is not identical to the published one, readers can still plumb the gist of the argument, even if quoting chapter and verse is impeded. We could also sidestep this problem by adopting a Wittgensteinian numbering of paragraphs rather than pages—stable across different editions. New editions of classic philosophy texts—like Kant's—usually provide the pagination of the original or canonical edition in addition to their own, facilitating citation across editions and translations. And of course, the Bible showed the way, organizing references layout-independent of its countless editions. Early church councils organized its division into books, but the numbering of chapters was standardized only by Stephen Langton in 1203 in the Dominican concordance. Verse numbering followed in the sixteenth century.[104]

More broadly, being able to cite specific pages (or paragraphs) raises the broader problem of needing a stable version to refer to. In fields that exhaustively parse subtleties of meaning and rely on precise quotation of locatable passages, versions of record remain necessary. The transcendental deduction is one paragraph in Kant's *Critique of Pure Reason* that answers Hume's problem of moving from correlation to causation. Without an agreed-upon text to parse, the scores of books written on the topic would have faced even knottier problems. Scholars of literature confront similar issues. However quaint, a stable referent is not entirely outmoded in the digital age.

Equally crucial: the digital record's fluidity invites retrospective fiddling, undermining faith in any stable referent. Digitality need not be indeterminate. Blockchain techniques or other less complicated means of establishing invariant records allow data to be chiseled in electronic stone.[105] But without some such assurance of invariance, digital texts may be suspect. Dominic Cummings, Boris Johnson's Rasputin-lite special advisor, sought to buff his foresightedness by altering past texts from 2019, making them appear to warn of a Covid-like pandemic soon to befall Britain.[106] He was outed when the original versions were excavated from the Internet Archive's Wayback Machine. Similarly, two historians responded to criticism of their claims that the discipline was losing its influence in the public arena by covertly doctoring their text in its open-access version to present less of a target. Only after sharp-eyed observers brought the alterations to the publisher's attention were they explicitly indicated and acknowledged.[107]

4
Information on Wings: The History of Open Access

"Information wants to be free" is the open-access movement's mantra. But does it? And can it be? If by free we mean gratis, then the expectation may be exaggerated. The Budapest Open Access Initiative's declaration from 2002 expected the costs to be "far lower" than for conventional publication.[1] That likely overestimated the possible savings. But the grain of truth here is that, with upfront expenses met, the last marginal copy of a digital work is almost costless. Yet getting to that point takes largely as much work as for an article or book on paper. Only by letting the standards slip or by achieving new efficiencies would digitality help bring down overall publication costs—and not just those of dissemination. Digitality has, in fact, accomplished much of that already. Everyone can produce what would earlier have counted as camera-ready copy on their laptops. The web allows us to post anything for the world to see. If we are willing to call that publishing, then we are all publishers now.

Whether information wants to be free, as in universally knowable, is another matter. As we have seen, knowledge can easily remain a secret so long as it is not imparted. A proper secret—one undivulged—remains with its knower. Even a dangerous, forbidden, or heretical thought does no harm if thus kept. Nor does it redound against its knower so long as they refrain from its utterance. Even when the Church vigorously pursued wrong thinking, it excepted heretics' unspoken cogitations. In 1484, the Spanish Inquisitor Tomás de Torquemada decreed that those who had never revealed their apostasy should be allowed to abjure and do penance in secret, thereby never being exposed as heretics.[2]

Some information wants to remain secret. Not just what we hope to keep from the authorities, but more generally, our private data. As the personal becomes harder to hide, splashed across social media, we self-contradictorily jealously seek to guard it. To this comes the value of turning our daily behavior into data. Acts whose documentation we scarcely realized served any purpose turn out to interest companies eager to parse our profiles as consumers.

The value of some information is enhanced by not being widely known. Whether medieval occultism or modern trade secrets, their worth lies in scarcity. The advantages of hiddenness are exploited, whether for mercenary gain or for the appearance of insight, wisdom, healing powers, sorcery, or technical expertise it gives its bearer. While the public is kept in the dark, the circle of initiates has to be large enough to keep the show running. At some point, the knowledge has to be transmitted or inherited. While the recipe for Coca-Cola is locked in an Atlanta bank vault, the formula for Chartreuse remains in the heads of only three Carthusian monks, who daily drive a jalopy together along a winding mountain road to the distillery.[3] How medieval glassmakers produced their stained windows' deep rich blue remains lost. The method the Saxons used to manufacture white porcelain was secreted in the Green Vault of the Dresden palace.[4]

Some information remains secret despite our best attempts to know it. Black box algorithms generate conclusions beyond what humans can yet follow. DeepMind's AlphaFold software predicts the structure of proteins with unexpected accuracy, based on insights into biological fundamentals that we still do not fathom.[5] Explainable Artificial Intelligence (XAI) seeks to pry open the black box, allowing humans to grasp the reasoning behind particular outcomes.[6] A new EU directive requires artificial intelligence's conclusions to be comprehensible to natural persons.[7] Without human oversight, algorithms may draw accurate results for reasons we do not understand but they may also jump to unjustifiable conclusions.

Deep learning neural networks can now locate abnormalities on medical scans as well as the average radiologist.[8] Other times, the gains in knowledge are less clear. An algorithm claims to discern people's sexuality from photographs on dating sites better than humans can.[9] The programmers focused on grooming choices and facial features, which may have reflected hormonal effects in utero. But when other studies achieved comparable predictions even when blurring the faces, it became unsettlingly unclear what the algorithms based their forecasts on—lighting, color, or other factors associated with sexuality in ways we do not yet understand?[10]

Beyond speech, writing has vastly expanded our ability to transmit knowledge, but not necessarily broadly. At first, so few people could read that the medium itself was restricted to insiders. As the spread of literacy expanded such limits, secret languages, codes, or encryption again allowed transmission to a select audience. Using Native Americans speaking their tongues for clandestine radio transmissions during the Second World War relied on rarity to keep secrets. Through the Middle Ages, science remained the preserve of the elect. Hippocrates wanted to retain holy things, such as nature's secrets, for the initiated.[11] Renaissance scholars reserved knowledge for themselves. Guilds hid craft techniques.[12] Before the law began protecting intellectual property, monetizing knowledge was often accomplished by keeping others in the dark.

Only with the Scientific Revolution in the seventeenth century did the idea emerge that science was something inherently public.

To the discoverer went the intellectual credit; to the inventor, eventually the patent. In both cases, the knowledge was public and could be elaborated and expanded by others. As a scarce commodity, hidden among the initiated, knowledge was a dead end. Barring some inscrutable source of occult insight, how much could any isolated person or small group ever hope to achieve? Breaking open nature's secrets was accomplished better when more participants were engaged. Science is, plainly, a social enterprise.

With the Scientific Revolution, openness and transmissibility were recognized as independently improving information's quality. Widely available knowledge had been tested by other minds. The larger the network it was broadcast across, the more eyes scrutinized it. An avalanche of print inundated the world. Universal compulsory schooling created a huge audience of readers. Newspapers and periodicals, along with cheap new books, sated their curiosity. Libraries supplied readers with costless content. The mail system ensured information's steady flow, with discounted postage subsidizing the spread of printed matter.

To encourage the exchange of news and ideas, newspaper editors could send their latest edition to colleagues across the US for free. By the 1840s, each editor received an average of 4,300 different exchange newspapers annually, a dozen every day.[13] Scissors ready, they cut and pasted text into their own periodicals—an analog foreshadowing of today's blogs. We now fret as the web effortlessly spreads bad information along with the good. True, but keep in mind that a similar explosion of ephemera rained down on readers in the eighteenth century as pamphlets, broadsheets, and newspapers.[14] The web has amplified but not created data surfeit. The difference is of degree, not kind.

Knowledge that is open and accessible has long been recognized as a virtue. Locked inside our skulls, information is worthless. As perishable as we are, uncommunicated knowledge is also uncorroborated, unchecked, and unverified by interaction with others.

Besides not being put to use, unshared knowledge is of lesser intellectual worth. Individual knowers cannot determine the quality of their insight without correlating it with others or testing it against the outside world. Only knowledge that passes intact through the crucible of verification can claim a truth recognizable to others. But once outside our heads, information can be no more than a social secret, guarded for a while among a few select knowers, yet ever-leakable to others.

The Royal Society of Arts, founded in England in 1754, regarded patents as an illegitimate monopoly of information that ought to be freely available. For a while, it refused its prizes to anyone with a patented invention.[15] That was somewhat unfair to patents. Their aim, after all, was to grant inventors means of profiting from discoveries without having to keep them secret. In exchange for revealing insights, rights-holders were rewarded with temporary monopolies. Everyone gained—inventors earned profits, society reaped new knowledge. However distant this may now seem, the concept of intellectual property was part of broadening access.

Intellectual property was a trade-off between creators and the community. The invention of printing turned ideas and their articulation into potential commodities. That allowed their theft. With writings and books worth something, their content became valuable. Kings and governments granted publishers monopolies on their works. Booksellers had contracts with their authors for exclusive printing rights. But neither grants nor agreements kept competition at bay. Piracy ensued, with works reprinted, repackaged, and repurposed at will by rogue publishers outside the net of enforcement.

That problem was addressed by inventing property rights in works, starting with copyright in the English Statute of Anne in 1710. Law now granted authors a claim to something so intangible that enforceable ownership would otherwise have been impossible. Along with patents and eventually trademarks, this made intellectual matters property. Creators could briefly exploit their works. Ideas were no longer kept secret or limited to a few initiates. Still, they were restricted to those who paid the price of admission by buying a legitimate copy or joining a lending library.

Independent of intellectual property, the university's prestige economy made secret knowledge a self-defeating ambition. Submitting truth claims to the scrutiny of peers honed their accuracy. Equally important as any profits, publication established priority and credit. To the first discoverer, inventor, or formulator went the spoils. Keeping knowledge under wraps was for alchemists, druids, and other mystifiers.

If secret knowledge was largely worthless, it also became increasingly clear that what an individual could achieve alone was uncompelling. It stands to reason that big projects and some forms of intellectual activity must be collaborative: encyclopedias, massive particle accelerators, opera, film, and the like. Turning collaboration from a necessity into a virtue takes the insight a step further. Open software enjoyed the benefits of many participants, all working toward common goals. Such advantages were revealed by open software projects such as the operating system Linux. With that apparent, corporations often unblocked projects that had begun closed. Microsoft opened its once-proprietary software in 2014 to reap the benefits of Linus's law: "Given enough eyeballs, all bugs are shallow."[16]

Broadcast television and radio, paperbacks, subscription periodicals, and public libraries: that was state of the art for spreading enlightenment in the analog era. Compared to the year before Gutenberg's invention, an unimaginable cornucopia of content has long awaited any willing reader able to access media. The progress toward more information and better availability was steady, interrupted only rarely. Under totalitarianism, things took a step backward. The East Bloc nations had functioning publishing industries, but their output was official rubbish, read by no one.[17] The

"Classics" sections of East German bookstores were well stocked with Marx and Engels and little else.

Dissident writers, their voices muffled, had to wield rudimentary tools. Mimeograph duplicators and plain old carbon paper, banged ragged and faint by reuse, allowed dissidents' manuscripts to circulate clandestinely. Getting to publishers involved perilous smuggling by Western allies—the negatives of Aleksandr Solzhenitsyn's Nobel speech were carried inside a transistor radio.[18] Even so, the porosity of borders to modern technologies leavened the worst effects. East Germans watched West German TV, except in a few areas too remote for analog signals. Today, the internet firewalls imposed in China and the Middle East have a ferocious bark, but proxy servers and virtual private networks mitigate their bite.

Digitality then expanded the analog universe enormously in two directions. It made producing something worth watching, reading, or hearing less technically demanding. Cinema-ready film could be shot on smartphones, with a bit of postproduction software to sand the rough edges. Laptops became both an orchestra of instruments and their recording studio. Every writer could edit, typeset, and print copy that might not reach the standards of Aldine editions but certainly put to shame 1970s mass-market paperbacks. Dissemination was even more important than this revolution in production. The web allowed any content to be posted on a global bulletin board, readable by anyone, anywhere, anytime. Authors could now be their own agents, publishers, marketers, and distributors. With the work ready, the cost of delivering it to a potentially global audience was negligible, baked into the web's running costs.

That upped the stakes. In the analog era, cheap media had made works broadly affordable, although not costless. Public libraries had plugged the gap, giving everyone access to most legible content so long as they could make it to a reading room. Libraries did not ignore music and film, but they were not as adequately covered as print for technical and copyright reasons. Museums achieved something similar for the plastic arts, although dealing with singular objects, their ability to facilitate access was necessarily less ambitious than for reproducible content. Digitality made truly open access technically possible. Content could be available to anyone. The hurdles were no longer how to do this, but at what cost and to whom.

With their material costs, analog media could no more have been given away than food or housing. But with digitality's radical dematerialization, content could now be imagined as something akin to municipal water. Though not free, it could still be provided through taxes, fees, and other means of paying for something accepted as a basic necessity of civilized life, supplied largely at cost to all residents.

The Causes of Open Access

Open access must overcome three hurdles: technical, financial, and legal. Without digitality, global access is unthinkable. Digital editions cost money to set up, but the last marginal copy is practically costless. And finally, copyright gives authors and publishers stakes in content that must be waived or surmounted.

Copyright was invented to give authors who lived from their work a chance to harvest its fruits. That original idea was admirable, and how it was executed, reasonable. After short initial terms, works joined the public domain. Meanwhile, extending copyright's terms has hijacked that intent, leaving the bulk of content in legal limbo. It remains protected, but because most is no longer read, no one benefits—neither authors nor the public. Authors have a stake in protecting their rights, but not in walling off work long after it has lost commercial value.

Intellectual property has also been attacked as socially unjust and contrary to public enlightenment. Some inventors have forgone patenting their inventions to benefit the public: John Walker, the friction match; Jonas Salk, his polio vaccine; Stanley Dudrick, the technique of direct intestinal feeding of hospital patients; and Tim Berners-Lee, the underpinnings of the web.[19] Authors have released works into the public domain without seeking profit. In contrast to Erasmus, Luther refused all royalties on his massively well-selling works. Tolstoy annoyed his wife by treating his rights carelessly. He hoped to allow anyone to read him after his death.[20] Influenced by Tolstoy, Gandhi regarded copyright as hindering the free circulation of ideas. But he also acknowledged its value in attributing works to authors and used it for his own purposes, to curtail exploitation of his writings.[21] The title page of the 1910 English translation of his *Hind Swaraj* (*Indian Home Rule*), issued by Gandhi's International Printing Press, clearly states "No Rights Reserved."[22]

Beyond a few high-minded creators, ready to share their work, open access has also become an imperative. Open access was made possible by digitality, but it has become necessary because we now have more scientific research and content than conventional publishers and libraries can handle. Without digitality and its costless marginal copies, growing content could not be made freely available. With paper publication, the costs of each physical copy need to be met. As scientific research expands, it becomes ever less feasible for any one collector to own all content in a system where the reader pays. Not even a large country can shoulder that expanding global load. The dissemination costs must be borne by humanity as a whole—an unlikely prospect barring a global government—or they have to be paid by authors, thus making content free for readers. We return to this basic point in more detail below.

The driving forces behind open access have been several. Without digitality, it would be impossible. In the analog world, the closest approximation would have been a global deposit library, something like the Library of Congress or France's Bibliothèque Nationale, but for the world. Every nation's publishers would have sent their works, and scholars and readers could then assemble in one place to find everything. Even with costs shared, they would have been insurmountable. And, as with Mecca or other mass pilgrimage destinations, the logistics would have been daunting.

But that moment has passed. Digitality and the potential availability of everything everywhere have changed the game. The global paper deposit library would have brought all the world's scholarly Mohammeds to the mountain, but now the mountain can be everywhere. The initial costs of preparing a work for dissemination remain much the same, although technology has trimmed some charges. Yet, digitality has also added new expenses, such as the bells and whistles of e-editions. Once such up-front costs have been met, however, the coast is clear. In the paper era, there still remained the physical printing, binding, shipping, distributing, displaying, selling, cataloging, and shelving. Much of that has now vanished, replaced in some measure by digital-specific costs, such as tagging with metadata, storing, updating, and maintaining availability.

Digitality was open access's necessary but not sufficient cause. What then prompted the need for it? Foremost, there was copyright's needlessly extended duration. Having been 14 years in the eighteenth century, today it guarantees prolonged rights in works—usually 70 years after the author's death. Even that fails to satisfy the most table-thumping fundamentalists for authors' rights. Why can we not keep our works forever, as we do our houses, they lament? Eternity minus a day was the solution slyly proposed by Jack Valenti, Hollywood's long-time shill in Washington. That would have allowed movie makers to sidestep the Constitution's insistence that copyright was for "limited times."[23]

But, in fact, intellectual property was treated more favorably than real estate. Most jurisdictions tax houses, whether they generate income or not. The state thus captures their value every certain number of years. How many depends on the rates, but it is often less than the life-plus-70 guaranteed for intellectual property. Authors in California, for example, would have to die at age 30 to find their intellectual property treated as badly as their houses.[24]

Had not nineteenth-century reforms endlessly prolonged copyright terms, this appendix might never have ruptured. Imagine five- or even ten-year copyrights. Few books or articles are still read or bought after a decade, except perhaps by historians. Of the 11,000 US books published in 1950, only 400 were still in print half a century later.[25] Shorter copyright terms would have allowed authors and publishers to capture the economic value of academic works. With digitality permitting easy distribution, the swift onset of the public domain would then have released them quickly. Some arrangements would still have been necessary for archiving and updating digital records. A role perhaps for libraries? But that would have been it. Had copyright law been reformed to return it to something like its eighteenth-century origins, we would probably not be having this discussion in the first place. Open access is in large measure a justified reaction to rights-holders' overweening claims.

To copyright elephantiasis then came the challenge of scientific demography, which threw up financing issues. The amount of research now produced globally is simply too much for the inherited system where readers pay. Digitality's efficiencies can alleviate the problem but not solve it. Ultimately, content can no longer be financed by readers and will have to be underwritten either by governments or authors and their funders.

The research establishment has grown continuously, but rarely as fast as in the postwar decades. In the US, the 1944 GI Bill diverted millions of returning soldiers to higher education. At its peak in 1947, recipients made up about half of all college students. Almost eight million new state-funded students sluiced through the massively expanding system.[26] As universities multiplied, so did the faculties teaching students and the researchers supplying knowledge to fill their lectures and textbooks. This held equally in the developing world. No nation has stamped universities out of the ground more rapidly than China. During the first decade of the twenty-first century, its institutions of higher learning doubled.[27] Eager to participate both as consumers and contributors, scholars in the Global South have published ever more actively. China issued 21 scholarly journals in 1970, but over 11,000 by 2019.[28]

Mushrooming in size and number, universities improved in quality, too. Undoubtedly, mindless credentialism, overly specialized research, and a myopic fixation on publication have occasionally been overvalued at the expense of teaching. Much more striking is the overall improvement in the quality of academic institutions, their faculty, and their output. There are more good universities than ever, producing ever-better research. The Ivy League has become the Ivy Plus, and institutions outside its hallowed halls best it at its own game—Berkeley, Chicago, and Stanford, with Duke, UCLA, and Hopkins in the wings. Oxbridge has become the 24 members of the Russell Group. At the top, the best jostle for position in the myriad rankings, whose metrics and their gaming have become university administrators' fervid preoccupation.

Fighting for a handhold at the pinnacle of the greasy pole brings out the worst, and it is easy to mock deans and chancellors endlessly spouting the rhetoric of excellence.[29] Higher education inhabits its own Lake Wobegon, where every institution is both above average and in someone's Top Ten. The metrics higher education evaluates itself by often have house-of-mirrors qualities. As always, the measure by which the outcome is judged quickly becomes the goal. If selectivity is prized, the solution is to solicit more applicants to reject.

Still, it seems churlish to lament a fundamentally desirable process. Universities compete to be good, better, or at least improving at their mission: delivering well-educated and well-socialized young adults, shedding light on social problems, and probing what science documentaries portentously call the mysteries of the universe. The patronizing idea that newcomer institutions will never join today's elite universities ignores strivers from the lower ranks and especially the developing world's aspirants.[30] There is plenty of room at the top.

The number of students mushroomed as more 18-year-olds entered tertiary education. As a matter of simple arithmetic, a burgeoning denominator has dropped the overall averages of many outcome metrics, compared to the era when only a few of an already select elite's offspring attended university. It has led to more stratified systems, with specialized institutions aiming at various clienteles—polytechnics, ag schools, liberal arts colleges, research universities, junior and community colleges, *Gesamthochschulen*, and the like. But in fact, more well-prepared and thriving students attend higher education than ever.

Grade inflation may be a problem. But at least it testifies to the urgent desire of Stakhanovite undergraduates for recognition of their hard work and the world's acknowledgment that university study is desirable. Compare that to yesterday's gentlemen's C tradition, which exemplified the indifference to education among well-heeled students. We have gone from *Brideshead Revisited* (Oxford undergraduates do everything but study) to *The Paper Chase* (Harvard law students work too hard).

As well-trained PhDs flooded the market, institutions that earlier had not presumed to demand advanced training or independent research from their faculty now had their pick of young scholars with reputations, publications, and ambitions. Franklin Ford, Harvard history professor and dean, once received an honorary degree at a small southern college. During the ceremony, almost everyone was addressed as Professor; he, however, as Dr. At some point, one of the locals on the stage leaned over and explained: We have lots of professors here, but not many PhDs.

This has changed in the meantime. A massive leveling-up has raised many ships in academe's flotilla. Universities have bootstrapped themselves up the league tables. Barriers that had once kept outsiders from the gentlemanly club of self-financing amateur scholars fell away as the universities expanded. The obstacles were gradually cleared that had excluded women, Jews, ethnic minorities, and working-class students. They now made careers of what had earlier been reserved for those who could take it up as a hobby or a calling.

Added to this expansion in the West was the growth of science in the developing world over the past half-century. America once sent its scholars to Europe for training. In the twentieth century, American institutions overtook the motherland's, reversing the brain drain. That is happening again. Chinese and Indian students who once flocked to the US and Europe are now returning as mature scholars to institutions at home with first-rate facilities and infrastructure.[31] Their students will soon no longer need to make an intellectual pilgrimage abroad. These recent arrivals to scholarship now find their place in the pantheon of publication, reception, and recognition. The scientific world has doubled if not tripled over the last half-century.

In step with the massing of faculty and researcher ranks has come an explosion in productivity and publishing. Professionalizing criteria for advancement and promotion, universities have emphasized scholarly output, painstakingly measuring quantity and quality.

Readers of David Lodge's *Changing Places*, set in the late 1960s, remember his description of the literature don, Philip Swallow. Mildly interested in many things, Swallow had no academic specialty, had published no more than a few book reviews and an occasional article. His main function seems to have been emotionally holding the hands of troubled undergraduates in his seminars. Publish or perish was the new hurdle that caught the Philip Swallows of his generation's university dons by surprise. Although an American invention, it spread widely. Swallow was Lodge's representative of British universities, anno 1969—the foil to hard-charging Morris Zapp from Euphoric State University on America's West Coast.

Zapp's ambition was a series of exhaustive commentaries on classic authors, starting with Jane Austen. Having covered every conceivable critical angle, he intended to shut down the need for future works on these subjects, putting his fellow literary scholars out of business. Meanwhile, having once dallied like amateur scholars, British academics are now held to more stringent publishing requirements than in the US. Britain's repeatedly renamed research assessment system has unleashed publish or perish to new ferocity. University departments' financing now depends on faculty productivity—submitted to labor-intensive assessments by government funders—in a way the decentralized US system could never enforce.

Intellectual productivity has accelerated. Far more books have been issued in the past century than ever before. Three-quarters of the titles in Google Books were published after the Second World War, half after 1974.[32] Total global book production as of 1911 was slightly over 10 million, as of 1940, about 15 million.[33] That leaves the remaining 165 million books in existence today, some 92% of all, having been issued in the subsequent 75 years.

Eviscerating the Libraries

So much for the quantum of intellectual output, increasing as more researchers notch up their productivity. To that comes the cost of acquiring it. In the paper era, university libraries were largely the only customer for academic periodicals and the main one for monographs. Occasionally, a wealthy collector—Aby Warburg—could be a player, and a few private libraries remain: the London Library and the Mechanics' Institute in San Francisco. Some scholars and professionals may take periodicals in their fields, and corporations with research departments subscribe, but for scholarly journals and monographs, the locomotive is the university library.

For academic monographs, libraries account for about half of sales. They buy one-quarter of university press books more generally, which today include many titles marketed to a broader audience.[34] Late in the twentieth century, before the worst of the library budget cuts, a university press could count on selling out an edition of 1,500 to research libraries alone, recouping its expenses. Today, average sales of a humanities monograph (half perhaps to libraries) are 600 or 700 five years after release.[35]

Libraries once footed the cost of academic publishing. Scholars may have been the main readers but not the primary customers. Little did they care how expensive a journal or book was, so long as they could expect to find it on the library shelf. Nor would they accept substitutes. Each article or monograph is unique and equally necessary for scholars hoping to write authoritatively and exhaustively.

Few criticisms are more damning than suggesting that a scholar has missed or neglected a crucial source. The defense that the local library could not afford it would be laughed out of court. One way or another, the presumption is that serious scholars have access to everything in the field. Only laziness or ignorance could explain not consulting a source. Librarians are thus mandated by their primary clientele to buy whatever the publishers issue. No matter that the vast majority of works in any given library sit unread for decades, usually forever. In a medium-size US university library, only 20% of books are checked out even once.[36] On the off chance that someday a scholar may amble the stacks looking for this obscure article or that dusty tome, it must be ready for its Cinderella moment. For research libraries, tails are very, very long.

The need to be comprehensive left academic libraries vulnerable. The scientific publishers identified a captive clientele required to buy their offerings at whatever price. Committed to exhaustive coverage, librarians could not be discerning consumers. Media entrepreneurs found themselves in a business fantasy. There were no market failures, no misjudging customer wishes, no New-Coke-style fumbles: their products were guaranteed a market at the price they chose. Not since Soviet tractor monopolies did producers have it so cushy, and even the machinery manufacturers had to scramble for raw materials and energy. With academic publishing, the materials delivered themselves for free in ever-growing quantities to the receiving bays. All that was required was sorting it a bit, slapping on a fresh coat of paint, and deciding at what price to push it out the door.

The potential for exploiting this situation was not new. Academic libraries and publishers had long danced a pas de deux. But their interactions had worked because the scholarly offerings had not yet exploded and the suppliers were self-restrained by a courteous gentlemanly understanding that publishers and librarians were in the same business of providing for scholars. Publishers neither oversupplied nor overcharged, and librarians bought most of their goods. The new media entrepreneurs, in contrast, were prepared first to fatten up, then eviscerate the system.

Starting in the seventeenth century with the first scientific academies and their meetings, papers, proceedings, and reports, scientists worked for free, motivated by truth and recognition. Their output was not regarded as their intellectual property, except to vouchsafe their moral claims to attribution and recognition. If they discovered something that could be patented, that was one thing, but for basic research and scholarship, there was little market. Scholarship rested on an economy of symbolic exchange of prestige and recognition.

That did not change until science assumed geopolitical implications and governments began underwriting research. States had long supported technologies of warfare, mining, exploration, and other endeavors, allowing them a leg up. Early academies and universities had received government funding for such pursuits.

The increasing cost of labor and the difficulty of sacrificing citizen-soldiers, whose families voted, made warfare even more expensive as democracy spread. Medieval armor had been the preserve of the aristocracy. Military technologies that both attacked and protected even common soldiers, such as tanks, did not come cheap, nor did those allowing combatants to fight at arm's length, sparing personnel—bombers, rockets, missiles, drones. Most expensive of all were those—atomic—armaments whose logic was that they never be used at all. Warfare without killing costs more than the deadly kind. Nor did state-funded explorations come cheap. Columbus received the equivalent of one million dollars in royal support for his voyages.[37] By modern standards, that was a pittance. At $160 billion and counting, the International Space Station is the most expensive object ever built.[38] The pyramids were a bargain by comparison—perhaps a billion dollars in construction costs each.[39]

The Second World War accelerated government funding of useful R&D, which continued into the Cold War, with the arms race and competition in space. With big science came big universities and big collaborative projects: the Manhattan Project, Sputnik, Collider Detector experiments at Fermilab, the Hubble space telescope, CERN, the Human Genome Project, the National Nanotechnology Initiative, and the like. Government funding went to universities and other research institutions, such as Bell Labs (13 Nobel laureates). The universities' growth undermined their own monopoly, producing numerous graduates who went to work for new competing institutions.[40] As the supercharged engines of research began spitting out results, the inherited system of scholarly dissemination faltered.

Among the first publishers to scent blood was Robert Maxwell and his Pergamon Press. In the immediate postwar years, Maxwell worked for the press control division of the British occupying army in Berlin. In command of paper supplies, he was lobbied by publishers and struck up a relationship with Ferdinand Springer, owner of a once-powerful scientific house. As with so many other German intellectual and cultural achievements, the Nazis also vaporized academic publishing. Learning the ropes from Springer, Maxwell was astounded to discover a unique business model. Unlike other content industries, scientific publishers did not need to create the product or pay others for it. Academics delivered it for free, libraries paid to take it off publishers' hands. Only a bit of sprucing up was needed before the finished output could be sold.

Maxwell returned to Britain, having acquired worldwide distribution rights to Springer's huge backlog of journals and other scientific output. In addition to trainloads of periodicals and books came seven rail carriages of manuscripts awaiting the light.[41] Maxwell had worked as a commodities broker, selling a Noah's ark of products. If commodities are goods distinguished primarily by price (pork bellies, iron ore, wheat), scientific articles were the opposite— something whose provenance was determinative, that one could charge almost any price for without killing the market. Maxwell had spotted the opportunity nestled where increasing scientific output outstripped the conventional channels' ability to keep up.[42]

In the early 1950s, Maxwell entered publishing directly, founding Pergamon to repeat Springer's prewar success.[43] With a keen eye for developing new academic fields, he positioned Pergamon as the premier English-language supplier of scientific content in an era when the research world was becoming Anglophone. He recognized the allure of slapping "International Journal of" before almost any field or discipline, from "Solids and Structures" to "Parasitology," from "Educational Research" to "Applied Radiation and Isotopes."

Maxwell and his competitors identified a value in academic publishing distinct from any marketable discoveries it might contain. As state financing for research increased, disseminating it became a juicy prize. Even if it cost only a few percent of total research funding to issue the results, the sums were impressive. As citations began to be tracked and journal impact factors measured, the market became less elastic. Certain highly cited journals became the core of collections, must-have acquisitions for librarians. Maxwell and other scientific publishers raised the price of journals libraries could not forgo.[44] The postwar university boom produced thousands of new researchers itching to publish and hundreds of new libraries to fill. By itself, Pergamon issued 700 new journals.[45]

The commercial scientific publishers did not cause the demographic revolution in science, the thousands of new scholars and their output, but they did exploit its opportunities. Expanding the number of journals was necessary, jacking up their prices less so. The explosion of scientific research would eventually have posed an unsustainable expense for libraries even had it not been exacerbated by rent-seeking publishers driving up costs as well. Their greed merely brought forward the moment of reckoning. Independent of price, the research explosion tolled an end to the old system of subscription journals (and retail books, to a lesser extent).

The Serials Crisis

Something as seemingly mundane as the increasing price of scientific periodicals precipitated the open-access movement. This crisis of serials subscriptions sprang from the postwar divergence between supply and outlet for scientific research. Researchers writing articles multiplied, yet publication venues failed to expand in tandem. Into the breach stepped the commercial houses. Before the war, professional societies and their journals had issued most scientific research. Their prices were reasonable, the pace sedate, the volume adequate. But when government research funding continued into peacetime, the old system failed to keep up. The new commercial journals took up the slack. At first, library budgets increased along with general research financing, and subscriptions to new journals were part of a rising tide.

All was well until late in the century.[46] University library budgets could accommodate the increased volume, and prices remained reasonable even as quantity increased. But as of the 1980s, the shoe began pinching. Cutbacks in university financing left libraries unable to keep pace. Worse, the publishers got greedy. Vast new numbers of specialty journals proliferated, their subscription prices arching ever skyward, far beyond inflation or costs. Libraries' expenditure on serials now escalated at triple the consumer price index.[47]

At the same time, the big commercial publishers consolidated into a handful of giant firms running huge stables of titles. In 1991, for almost half a billion pounds, Maxwell sold Pergamon and its four hundred titles to Elsevier, then a small Dutch publisher of technical journals.[48] From the 1980s onward, three publishers (Reed Elsevier, Springer, and Wiley) enjoyed the lion's share (42%) of the 25,000 leading English-language scientific periodicals. No other house controlled more than 3% of the market.[49] When the libraries' shrieks of despair could no longer be ignored in the late 1990s, the publishers switched tactics.

Eyeing the burgeoning internet and its threat of easy and low-cost dissemination, they realized that the libraries' golden geese had perhaps been pushed to the limit. Rather than having to order à la carte, libraries would now be offered all-you-can-eat buffets. Big-deal packages gave them access to a publisher's entire list for flat-rate prices. Smaller presses lacking sufficient content to stock bundles on their own joined aggregators, such as Aggregagent, BioOne, or Project MUSE.[50] Eventually, book publishers extended similar deals for their monograph lists.

The big-deal packages dropped the per-article or per-read costs but imposed new expenses on libraries. It locked them into multi-million-dollar annual contracts for content they neither chose nor controlled. If they balked, large fractions of their collections would go dark. Prices were calculated not on publishers' costs but on the libraries' purchasing history. Rates were set slightly above what libraries had earlier paid for all their individual subscriptions. That increased the publishers' intake and cemented in the libraries at already prohibitive expenditure levels. The now locked-in prices ratcheted up at rates set by the publishers.

Big deals did nothing to alleviate costs and froze the status quo of funneling library budgets to the publishers' bottom line. They did supply the full range of publishers' output for those institutions able to keep pace on the big-deal treadmill. Above all, they made the publishers indispensable. By 2015, Elsevier, now one of the largest, owned a quarter of scientific journals. Anyone who dared monkey with its big deals—as a few libraries valiantly tried—had to be prepared to ask faculty to do without (or find other access to) a quarter of all content.[51]

Despite the Covid pandemic and numerous boycotts of its journals, Elsevier posted robust results for 2020—down from 2019, but still with profits of over £2 billion on revenues of £7 billion.[52] Big deals also undermined small publishers and scholarly societies, with their few or sometimes single journals. With their budgets locked up by big deals, libraries had little money left for anyone but the major players. To survive, small journals often sold themselves to larger publishers and were folded into their bundles.

Scientific publishers have also played hardball with libraries in at least two other ways. TV viewers will recognize the first strategy from how cable companies package channels. Since no one wants more than a few in each bundle, customers are encouraged to pay for several. Publishers also sell collections of journals, insisting that each be bought in toto and making it hard for libraries to pick and choose. In desperation, libraries have begun unbundling their subscriptions. They pay à la carte for the journals that faculty demand most, relying on interlibrary loans or individual purchases to plug gaps.

Second, confidentiality agreements forbid disclosure of publishers' arrangements with each library. Pricing is thus what the market can bear, with richer institutions and nations generally paying more than others. Grotesquely, sometimes developing countries, such as South Africa, have been billed more than rich ones, such as Germany.[53] Ignorant of what others are charged, libraries cannot strike cooperative purchasing agreements and the publishers are spared competition.[54]

From all this flowed enviable profit margins, an astounding 35% to 40%. Few other businesses outside software and pharmaceuticals could promise anything close. Besides banknotes, the *Frankfurter Allgemeine Zeitung* said in 2012, scientific papers were the most lucrative item you could print.[55]

Open Access Takes Off

Against this background, open access seemed like a solution not only to the serials crisis and squeezed library budgets but also to broader problems of scholarly publishing. Digitality promised to trim dissemination costs in general. If control of content could be wrested from commercial publishers, exorbitant profit margins could perhaps be pared back. Yet, while digitality broached the opportunity of making everything available, it did not specify how to meet costs.

There were two aspects to open access, embodied respectively in each of its terms. *Open* came from the open-source software and free culture movements of the 1980s. Emphasizing a do-it-yourself and anticorporate ethos, this strain sought not just access, but for productive and creative processes to be reclaimed from the institutions thought to have monopolized them—libraries, think tanks, journals. Those attracted by the openness of the new technologies expected them to unleash new possibilities. Anyone could create near-perfect output on ubiquitous devices. Cutting out the middle people, creators could speak directly to their audiences. The web linked to everyone and all but eliminated connection costs, allowing new collaborations to emerge spontaneously. Unprecedented information resources could be assembled—vast collections of photographs or the miracle that is Wikipedia.[56]

For the *access* enthusiasts, in contrast, the issue was less whence and how content emerged but that it was available to consumers without unreasonable impediment.[57] The inherited institutions did not necessarily have to change so long as end consumers could freely use their output. Over what that meant, opinions could differ. Two decades ago, during the web's cowboy days, Pirate Bay, Napster, MegaUpload, and similar sites posted bootlegged copyrighted content that could be downloaded or viewed without payment. Differing in the technicalities, they all claimed to allow private file-sharing among users without centralized storage or reproduction of content, therefore not in breach of copyright law.

However, such claims were ruled disingenuous, and the sites were pursued and curbed. In their place, a regularized ecosystem of legal streaming services—Spotify, Apple Music, Hulu, Netflix—now offers much the same at reasonable prices. An Amazon Prime subscription at $13 per month is not open access in the strict sense of content available costlessly. But the opportunity to watch some 13,000 films for the price of one trip to the cinema monthly is a good deal as lending libraries go. Does that count?

Today, open access is dominated by scientists. Initially, however, the humanities and social sciences sparked the initiative. As with Tolstoy and Gandhi, copyright has long been feared as stifling the free use of ideas. Nor is the celebration of reusing content for new creations an exclusive hallmark of contemporary culture. Modernity threw off the Romantics' exalted view of individual creativity. Mutual indebtedness and influence, use of others' works in unabashed bricolage and pastiche, have become commonplace. As early as 1819, Washington Irving had argued that literary creation was parasitical. Like birds, who served nature's intent by excreting fruit seed, authors were but a means of conveyance, passing along ideas from old works into the present.[58]

Creativity seen as a collective effort was the soil that nourished more mundane ambitions for bypassing the publishing establishment to open up content. The old regime of paper and ink had limited information's spread, but once digitality sprang the technical barriers, new vistas opened up. In the university world, an online journal appeared for the first time in 1987, with the perhaps less-than-pulse-quickening first issue of *New Horizons in Adult Education*, hosted by Syracuse University.[59] The 1980s and 1990s brought other journals dedicated to accessible content: *Surfaces, CTheory, Postmodern Culture, Music Theory Online, EJournal, Journal of Political Ecology, Electronic Journal of Differential Equations*, and the *Bryn Mawr Classical Review*.[60]

Meanwhile, a series of foundational meetings elaborated the emerging view of open access. As activists formulated their ideas during the first years of the new millennium, ambitions expanded. In 2002, George Soros's Open Society Foundation hosted a meeting in Budapest. Of its 16 participants, most had been trained in the humanities or social sciences, only four in the hard sciences. Its declaration is commonly taken to be the starting gun of the movement, but as we will see, it was pipped to the gate by developments in Latin America.

The Budapest declaration took the conventional format of peer-reviewed scientific articles as its primary concern.[61] It defined *open* as the right to read, download, copy, distribute, print, search, or link the articles, to crawl them for indexing, and to pass them as data to software, or any other lawful use. The only restrictive author's rights it recognized were to be acknowledged and cited and to control the work's integrity. It accepted digital self-archiving of (refereed journal) articles as a way of disseminating them. With a shopping list of "many alternative sources of funds," it foresaw the founding of new journals that charge neither subscriptions nor publishing fees. In its bootstrapping vision, these were solutions that scholars themselves could effect, without relying on changes in legislation or the existing publishing industry.

The humanities' influence quickly evaporated, however. The following year, in April 2003, a meeting was held in Chevy Chase, Maryland, but its declaration was named after neighboring Bethesda. Attendance was heavily from medicine and focused on the "biomedical research community" and its "primary scientific literature."[62] The Bethesda Statement expanded the Budapest principles. It required that for content to be considered open, its reuse for derivative works must also be allowed. Curiously, despite its expansive definition of *open*, it required only digital uses; therefore, the statement had to tack on a separate right to make limited numbers of printed copies for personal use. The statement also demanded immediate deposit of works upon publication in repositories run by academic institutions, scholarly societies, government agencies, or other well-established organizations engaged in open access. If the work was not published openly, it had to be simultaneously made freely available, with no embargo. Nor would works be considered open unless they were put in a suitable noncommercial repository. Publication in a commercial open-access journal was insufficient.

In the autumn of 2003, a further meeting at the Max Planck Society in Berlin—Germany's largest and most prestigious network of scientific research institutes—brought together over a hundred organizations from far and wide. It defined open access as "a comprehensive source of human knowledge and cultural heritage that has been approved by the scientific community."[63] Oddly, that shifted the focus from the work's content to its origins. Stranger still, it restricted open access to material evaluated by the scientific community, even though the concept of cultural heritage surely went beyond that. It also expanded the scope of the openly available from scientific articles to include raw data and metadata, source materials, digital representations of pictorial and graphic works, and scholarly multimedia material. It loosened requirements for the attribution right by leaving it to "community standards" for enforcement.

The Publishers Capture Open Access

Early plans for open access seemed to threaten the scientific publishers. Demands that content be available for free did not sound encouraging. Nor the expectation that digitality would trim costs. For scholars to begin disseminating their work threatened publishers' business. Advocates for open access did not just want the commercial houses to take on the enterprise. They hoped that hitching digitality to open access would allow a refounding of the business altogether. "It is time to return control of scholarly publishing to the scholars," the Max Planck Society announced 10 years after the Berlin Declaration.[64] New noncommercial journals were launched in this spirit. *BioMed Central*, begun in 2000, was a for-profit venture, while the *Public Library of Science* (PLOS) from 2003 was not. To cover costs, *BioMed Central* pioneered article processing charges, paid by authors or their funders. In 2002, these were a modest $500 per accepted article, with waivers for hardship and for authors from developing countries.

But expecting the commercial houses not to crowd in was unrealistic. Libraries had financed subscription journals. The publishers had learned how to turn acquisitions budgets to their ends. Was that now to evaporate? Open accessors eyed library budgets as a potential funding source for new scholar-led journals. If the commercial publishers could also tap such sources for open access, would their exorbitant profit margins from the subscription days go unchallenged?

The shift from reader- to author-side financing is a story in progress, and its ultimate outcome is still unknown. So far, the commercial publishers appear to have turned it to their advantage. Despite a decade of protest, boycotts, funder grumbling, threats of legislation, investor pull-back, and other obstacles, their profit margins remain substantial. In-copyright digitized content can either be opened up or closed down. Digitality allows both liberation and control.[65] Just being online does not mean it is freely available. That is among the considerations that have helped commercial publishers make their peace with open access.

In 1991, Elsevier launched The University Licensing Program (TULIP). After digitizing back issues of some 40 science journals, Elsevier made available to university libraries online versions of content most of them already owned on paper. Elsevier did not charge fees, but participating libraries had to invest in hard and software and log in via various then-novel security mechanisms to ensure a walled-garden approach to access.[66] A similar project launched the following year by Springer, the Red Sage Digital Journal Library, reinforced the publishers' conclusion that digitized content was useful and had a market, and that academic libraries were willing to cooperate by keeping it squirreled behind authentication walls.[67]

As born-open journals issued forth, how did existing subscription periodicals manage the transition? The scholarly societies, publishers of many traditional journals, were in a difficult position. Unlike the commercial rivals, their prices were not extravagant. Many, especially in the humanities, would have found it hard to flip to open since their members could not pay publishing charges.[68] Their earnings (over £100 million in the UK, much of it from foreign subscribers) were plowed back into their scholarly mission.[69] They had not been part of the serials crisis aggravated by their commercial rivals. Many felt unfairly burdened by the new demands for access to which they had never presented more than modest barriers. Yet, to be fair, nor had they done much to help disseminate the increasing content from the postwar research explosion. They had allowed the vacuum that commercial publishers rushed to fill.

In turn, commercial publishers quickly learned to live with open access. With the green version, they made their peace by insisting on long embargo periods and that repositories not post the version of record. Gold open access, in turn, opened new vistas.

Cleverly, some publishers turned their journals hybrid. They included some paid-for articles, freely available, while others were reserved for subscribers only. The most prestigious outlets were still the venerable subscription journals. Scientists with sufficient funding who wanted the best of both worlds sought broad access to their writings together with the prestige of the respected venues. The hybrid journals accommodated both. Articles for which publishing fees were paid appeared for the world to read; others remained behind paywalls or were restricted to subscribers. To supply readers with everything, libraries had no choice but to continue paying subscriptions, even as some content was open. The publishers double-dipped, the libraries were double-charged. Hybrid journals should have offered discounts in proportion to the content already paid for via fees, but the overall cost of subscriptions showed no signs of declining.

Hybrid publishing had begun in 1998 at the *Florida Journal of Entomology*. In 2004, Springer began experimenting with the idea, collecting fees in addition to subscriptions.[70] What was there not to like? To be fair, hybrid had been accepted from the start in the open access declarations and was not just a cynical publisher's ploy to have it both ways. The Bethesda Statement specified that open access was a property of individual works, not necessarily journals or publishers. And it allowed for an "open access option" for articles published within conventional journals.[71] The Open Knowledge Foundation's definition forbade restrictions (such as requiring accessibility) on other works published together with open ones.[72]

From hybrid, it was only a small step for publishers to plunge fully into the open-access stream. Springer bought *BioMed Central* in 2008. Other commercial publishers followed.[73] Springer, owner of the venerable subscription journal *Nature*, now publishes *Nature Communications* and *Scientific Reports*, charging several thousand dollars for each article, somewhat less for reports. One calculation estimated the total income for both journals in 2016 at $50 million.[74] Gold access spares publishers some expenses (sales, licensing, marketing, copyright, and subscription management), which once accounted for about a third of total costs. Investment bankers have concluded that, with article charges of $3,000 per article, publishers are unlikely to lose revenue.[75]

Fully open-access publishers like Biomed Central and Hindawi enjoy juicy profit margins (27% and 43% in 2008 and 2011, respectively), comparable to their conventional competitors.[76] Hindawi cashed in when Wiley bought it for almost $300 million in January 2021. Elsevier has bought Mendeley, an academic social network, and the Social Science Research Network (SSRN), a prepublication repository. The latter allows it to guide readers to its open-access versions of papers that may later appear paywalled with competing houses.[77] Gold access has increasingly become the preserve of the dominant conventional publishers, able to afford such acquisitions: Springer, Wiley, and Elsevier. In November 2020, Springer announced that *Nature* would flip to open. Tooting its own horn as a "progressive publisher and innovator in open access," it also announced that the fees for each article would be over $11,000 (€9,500).[78] The gift of open access kept on giving—to the publishers.

The journals realized that it made little difference whether you called their monies subscriptions or article charges. It was merely a question of flipping the funding stream from consumer to producer, from reader to author. The source was ultimately the same, the government or private science funders. And for them, the costs were so small that reversing the current meant little.

Nor did publishers meet much resistance from scientists. As publishers and funders learned not to be fussed by gold access, the scientists climbed aboard. Keen to preserve the inherited ecosystem of prestige, few minded continuing the subscription model or the emergence of hybrid publications. The Bethesda Statement had been issued by a group of researchers mainly from biomedicine. Their meeting was held at the Howard Hughes Medical Institute, the second biggest US philanthropy and the second richest medical research institution globally. It had blithely stated that since publication was an essential part of science, such costs were part of research expenses, and it promised to help meet them.[79]

The monies were already in the system. It mattered little precisely how they were deployed. For scientists, gold or diamond access left inherited methods of communication and credentialing largely untouched. That was the attitude given voice by the Max Planck Society in 2015. The monies were already present, they argued, locked into library subscriptions. Only repurposing them was needed.

In their doubtless well-intentioned approach, the scientists were oblivious to how the serials crisis had already allowed their journals to devour the bulk of library budgets, undercutting humanities publications. Maintaining "the established service levels" scientists had become accustomed to was the goal, plundering library budgets as "the ultimate reservoir for enabling the transformation without financial or other risks," the means.[80] Had such discussions been held before the serials crisis, not in its bleak aftermath, it may have been better received among other scholars. As things stood, to flip the funding stream from subscriptions to publishing charges while leaving library budgets to bear the brunt meant locking in a status quo that was unacceptable to all but the hard sciences.

Many governments aligned themselves with gold access. In the UK, the Finch report in 2012 embraced this route forward.[81] Ignoring Britain's well-developed green repositories, it plumped for gold.[82] Whether fully open access or hybrid did not concern it, but publication charges should fund the transition. Embargo periods should not be overly shortened since that endangered traditional subscription journals. The report recognized that during the transition period, funding would be duplicated, with both subscriptions and publishing charges, not to mention the cost of repositories. It therefore called for more government money and savings from "other features of the research process" as well as efficiencies in publishing. Boats were not to be rocked. The Finch committee had been instructed not to endanger the British publishing industry.[83] Its report followed through, insisting that "the underpinning of high-quality publishing channels" should not be put at risk.[84] In effect, the Finch report sought to preserve the commercial publishing model, not change it.[85]

On this march toward gold access in the sciences, Plan S has been the latest installment. Using the tortured acronyming popular in open-access circles, a group of European private and governmental funding agencies named "cOAlition S" launched Plan S in 2018. As of 2021, it required all scholarly work they underwrote to be published in open journals or to have the accepted version of the manuscript made available in repositories without embargo.[86] This undercut green access, which relied on the accessible version being handicapped compared to the published edition. Plan S thus suffered the faults of gold access without solving any of them except by demanding compliance. The affordability problem for under-funded researchers hoping to publish remained untouched.[87] Nor did the concerns of humanities and social science scholars without funds receive attention.

By pushing a narrow view of open access, Plan S also alienated conventional scientists, who were unhappy that anyone accepting such funding was barred from subscription journals. Eighteen hundred chemists harrumphed that this was an attack on their academic freedom.[88] Nor has the Global South been impressed. Plan S struck them as merely restating gold access. It allowed readers in, while doing little to help scholars in developing nations to publish.[89]

In response to objections, Plan S adjusted course. It introduced a Rights Retention Strategy that allowed authors to be compliant by self-archiving the final version of their manuscript.[90] Those who published in subscription periodicals could thus remain within the pale so long as journals accepted that authors posted competing versions of papers. Only the journals that flatly refused to accept work that had also been self-archived would not be compliant.

The success of this attempt to swing the guiding assumptions of science toward gold open access remains unclear. As of 2021, Plan S mandates extended only to those who accept research monies from a limited set of European funders. Outside of Europe, only three funders had signed on: Howard Hughes, the Templeton World Charity Foundation, and the Gates Foundation.[91] Some European funders had exited: Sweden's National Bank Jubilee Fund and the European Research Council. German and Swiss funders had also jumped ship; the Spanish and Belgians never joined. So far, the outcome has been a two-tier system, obliging some European researchers to publish in compliant journals while their colleagues elsewhere remain free to go where they can. By dropping its initial price cap on article publishing charges, Plan S did nothing to restrain costs.[92]

Financing beyond Gold

The analog world's most far-reaching ambition could not be more than national deposit libraries. Once digitality broached the opportunity for all content to be available everywhere, a new financing model was required. Making readers pay, whether directly or through libraries, no longer sufficed. No consumer could afford the world's output. But if content's dissemination costs were prepaid, then everyone could have access.

So much for the theory. In practice, the developed world's scientists have hijacked the existing system via gold access. For this to change requires at least one of two scenarios: either the science funders revolt or copyright has its terms shortened by legislation to make the prize less worth fighting over.

Many funders have long insisted that results of their support appear openly. Governments were first off the mark. As of 2005, the US National Institutes of Health demanded that its sponsored research be made publicly available within a year after publication.[93] The Research Councils UK and the European Research Council followed suit.[94] In the US, private funders, such as the Gates Foundation and Howard Hughes, insist on it.[95] In the UK, the Wellcome Trust requires articles to be open access (tolerating no more than a six-month embargo) and offers to pay fees.[96] Other European funders have similar requirements.[97]

State authorities have been especially likely to insist on open access. As stewards of taxpayer monies, their conclusion that public funding should entail public availability is direct and obvious. Where research funding is centralized, compliance can be more easily extracted. The National Institutes of Health requires open access. But its remit is more limited in federalized America than for its equivalents in Europe or China's more centralized system, where the state funds most research. Discussions have therefore gone further in the UK than in the US. Even Britain's humanities and social sciences are now being squeezed into the open-access mold. Universities' research funding in the UK hinges on their faculties' openly available productivity. Monographs, not just articles, are being brought under the umbrella. Austrian, Dutch, and Swiss science agencies have also recently begun requiring accessible monographs.[98]

Universities, too, enforce open access, although without the same leverage. In 2008, Harvard's faculty agreed to require posting articles in a university repository, while granting a nonexclusive copyright license to archive and distribute them.[99] Even that, however, allowed faculty to request exceptions. Enforcement is reputed to be indifferent at best. Other American universities' policies appear to be similar.[100] Comparable conditions also hold in Europe.[101] British universities, in contrast, have put more muscle into deposit requirements. Thanks to centralized research funding, the government exerts leverage over faculty.[102] Because textbooks do not count as research for the assessments, scholars are now discouraged from writing them.[103] The threat to withhold monies has concentrated the professoriate's mind. Cambridge's Apollo website, for example, is a model of organization and clarity.[104]

Yet, enforcement is not easy. In the humanities, most research is self-financed by scholars, and outside funding rarely covers more than some costs. Should a grant for a summer archive visit entail that the ensuing book appear with an open publisher a decade later? Could an author repay the grant with royalties from a trade edition? What if, later on, the scholar writes a popular trade book using some of the research funded with an open-access requirement? Other researchers can refer to and use their colleagues' open-access-mandated results without themselves being similarly obligated. Why not the original author? Does a statute of limitations eventually release authors from funders' strictures?

UK Research and Innovation, the body responsible for government research strategy and funding in Britain, tied itself into knots in 2021 when trying to formulate a policy for books. Trade books it defined as ones that appeal to a broader audience. Had the research been funded with its monies, they fell under its requirement to be open. But then it turned on a dime and declared that trade books need not be compliant, leaving that decision to author and publisher discretion. Also excepted were textbooks, fiction, and books resulting from dissertations.[105]

As things stand, requiring open access in the humanities accomplishes little other than putting scholars in a bind if their work does not, or cannot, appear freely available. Even in the sciences, which are much more heavily dependent on outside financing, enforcement is lax. Short of threatening never again to underwrite those who ignore instructions, funders have little leverage. The Wellcome's generous policy is complied with only a bit more than half the time. The National Institutes of Health has achieved only 60% compliance with its deposit requirement.[106]

All this leaves unaddressed the elephant in the room, the cost of dissemination. UNESCO estimated global gross expenditure on R&D at almost $1.5 trillion in 2013. Most of that was corporate spending, but about a third came from government and a fifth from universities, $800 billion in sum. The expense of disseminating that research is difficult to pin down. Annual revenues from English-language science journal publishing are thought to have been $10 billion in 2017, with a global market estimated at $25.7 billion for all forms of scientific, technical, and medical information.[107] If so, then dissemination costs some 3% of government and university research spending, which tallies with other estimates of between 1% and 2%.[108] Disseminating thus swallows only a small fraction of research outlays. With little skin in this game, funders are unlikely to press publishers to trim their profit margins or to cut costs. Scientists themselves resist change to their inherited ecosystem of prestige and reward. The existing commercial system works well for them.

Reforming copyright legislation, in turn, means limiting not just the rights to academic content but to all works. Either that, or it requires making distinctions between scientific and other content that will be difficult to define and police. Only a fraction of all content is tax-funded academic work, for which open access is justifiable. How to distinguish between it and other nonfiction that may be equally serious and valuable? Reforms that shorten copyright terms for all content would face fierce opposition from rights-holders. If, instead, reforms aimed only at academic content, endless disputes over which side of the line particular works fell on would result. Thoroughgoing copyright reform therefore seems a distant possibility.

The most likely outcome is that, having won the battle, the science publishers will not be dislodged from their position astraddle the main funding channels. Other disciplines and the developing world will have to exploit digitality's efficiencies to establish new forms of dissemination and seek other financing. How the landscape of alternative models may evolve is only dimly perceptible now. But we can point to current experiments that may turn out to have shown the way.

Someone other than consumers must pay if content is to be freely available. Gold open access can be only a partial solution, as shown by its success in the sciences. Having authors shoulder the burden excludes creators who cannot afford fees. To rectify that, governments could finance dissemination costs, as they do for much research. As we see below, that approach has been taken in Latin America. Even without state funds, other groups can achieve similar results.

Readers can band together to underwrite the price of opening work, bootstrapping it for the world. The brilliance of digitality is that bulk cooperative purchasing not only gives immediate buyers a discount but also provides the goods gratis for all consumers. The analog era knew such paying in advance, too. Books were subscribed to and published only once the requisite sums were collected. *Festschriften* were volumes of essays issued to celebrate a distinguished colleague on retirement or a round-number birthday. They were often financed by collecting monies from the contributors, who would receive a copy in return. Weighted down by paper and binding, such volumes naturally had to be conventionally bought by others who wanted one.

Digitality has simplified such techniques. Knowledge Unlatched, for example, organizes university libraries to subscribe to books.[109] Once sufficient funds have been collected, works are released to the participating institutions and thus to the world. In 2014, 28 new books were unlatched, at an average cost to pledging libraries of $43.[110] The Knowledge Unlatched website claims a total of over 2,700 such works. In the meantime, however, Knowledge Unlatched became a commercial enterprise incorporated in Germany. It charged libraries for its amalgamation of open books, which largely duplicated what is available for free at the Directory of Open Access Books.[111] Then, in 2021, Knowledge Unlatched was bought by Wiley.[112] Toward an Open Monograph Ecosystem is similar.[113] Other publishers, too, have joined in such subscribe-to-open ventures.[114] Having assembled 160 participating libraries, MIT Press published much of its Spring 2022 list as open access.[115] Such funding experiments collaborate with existing open publishers, providing the fees normally collected from authors.

Unglue.it crowdfunds books.[116] With the necessary sums in hand, the volumes are released. This works retrospectively, too, allowing publishers another bite of the apple. In 2013, De Gruyter applied crowdfunding to previously published monographs. Once $2,100 had been collected, the title was released under a Creative Commons noncommercial, no-derivatives license. Only if the campaign was successful were pledgers charged and the book opened.[117]

The tactic works with journals, too.[118] PeerJ offers plans allowing authors to publish one article a year for $99, or as many as wanted for $299.[119] In 2020, the Public Library of Science (PLOS), a prominent series of open journals, scaled up this logic. It issues some of its titles by collecting annual flat fees from institutions.[120] Affiliated researchers can publish without separate charges in three journals. Those without an institutional association pay fees per article, almost double the current ones. The goal is to lower expenses, to collect no more than necessary (fees beyond what is needed are returned), and to distribute costs equitably among institutions by staggering payments according to their research intensiveness. Third World institutions would automatically be members without fees.

Open journals do not need payments from authors if they have other financing. Many scholarly societies and other organizations sponsor diamond journals that impose no author payments. Most open periodicals charge no fees—some 12,000 out of 17,000 in the 2021 Directory of Open Access Journals.[121] But counting journals paints a rosier picture than articles. Of scholarly articles published annually, some 8% to 9% are diamond and 10% to 11% are gold.[122] And, as seen, prestigious journals charge the most eye-watering fees.

Resistance

The march of open access has not gone unchallenged. Sadly, the movement has gained a martyr, Aaron Swartz. He saw the fight in moral terms, taking from greedy corporations and giving to the dataless.[123] As a 24-year-old, he was arrested in 2011, charged with electronic and computer fraud for having downloaded almost five million documents from JSTOR via the MIT library.[124] However well-intentioned, his downloading violated MIT's license terms, prompting the supplier to shut down campus access for several days.[125] Had he released the 80% of its archive he had downloaded, none of which was JSTOR's property, the damage would have been significant. Nor was JSTOR, as a nonprofit digital distributor of social science periodicals to libraries, an obvious villain. To set an example, the authorities sought a long sentence but also offered Swartz a zero-to-six-month plea bargain, substantially discounting the seven years he could expect if convicted. Tragically, he found his predicament so intolerable that he committed suicide.[126]

Swartz's solution was much like Sci-Hub, Z-Library, and other pirate sites—a calculated violation of copyright law. In his case, within the law's reach, he would have suffered the consequences. The extraterritorial pirate sites, in contrast, continue in rude health, useful for the cause in pressuring publishers to temper their demands. Yet, such approaches are no long-term solution. Offshore tax havens are being pressed into the corners by international fiscal regulation. Eventually, a similar fate will overtake pirate sites, as has already happened for those that dared challenge the music and film industries.

The 1960s and 1970s were the golden era of European national radio systems. A handful of government stations in each nation, sometimes only one or two, offered a restricted menu of listening options to captive audiences of tax- and fee-paying customers. Pirate radio stations flourished in this stifling atmosphere, operating from ships in international waters or renegade jurisdictions, such as Luxembourg. Dangerous content—more than an hour of jazz or even rock music—thus leached into the European soundscape. Today, such breaches of official channels seem merely quaint. Very little content cannot be found somewhere on the web. In an age of surfeit, pirate stations have little use. They are likely to offer the most telling historical analogy to the pirate sites' eventual fate.

Beyond the pirates and Swartz's sadly quixotic attempt to right the wrongs, others have resisted the commercial publishers. A "Cost of Knowledge" boycott of Elsevier was launched in February 2012.[127] To date, it has been joined by 19,000 researchers from many disciplines and institutions around the world. Its leader, the Cambridge mathematician Timothy Gowers, cited the exorbitant subscriptions and big-deal bundles that libraries have to swallow whole.

Large consumers of journals have also boycotted publishers. Among the notable is the University of California (UC), one of the largest research institutions, with a huge collective acquisitions budget. Starting in 2019, UC boycotted Elsevier for two years.[128] In the interim, faculty and students made do with alternative sources of articles and interlibrary loans. UC announced its aim to make its research immediately available at no cost to readers. Elsevier was holding out for a double-dip, both publishing charges and subscriptions. UC wanted the sums paid at either end in effect to count as publishing charges, eliminating subscriptions.[129]

The outcome of the UC boycott testified again to the publishers' clout. In March 2021, the parties signed a four-year agreement. UC researchers' articles in Elsevier journals would be gold access. The UC libraries paid the first $1,000 of the fee. Authors would be responsible for the rest if they had funds, otherwise the libraries would pay. Elsevier extended a 10% or 15% discount on the usual charges.[130] For journals whose fees often amounted to $8,000 or $9,000, the main novelty was a modest discount, with publishers still charging as usual, and those costs now shared—for UC members—between libraries and authors. In any case, authors could opt out if they wanted to or could not afford the fee despite the $1,000 library contribution.

UC-authored articles now appeared freely readable by anyone. That was a clear advantage. But the journals issuing them remained as before, often hybrid, and therefore still substantially locked behind paywalls. Nor did it lessen the subscription burden of hybrid journals for the UC libraries. While this outcome may have worked for a reasonably flush and research-intensive institution like UC, the signal sent to those unable to negotiate with publishers was discouraging.

The UC deal with Elsevier was an example of read-and-publish or so-called transformative agreements. These were yet another variant on gold. Sometimes subdivided into read-and-publish and publish-and-read variants, their divergent details need not detain us. They sought to grapple with the obvious unfairness imposed on libraries by hybrid journals. Libraries were required to pay twice, both publishing charges for open articles and subscriptions for the rest. In some nations, mainly European, payment streams were split. Libraries continued to pay for read access via subscriptions while funders underwrote write access. Either way, publishers cashed in at both ends, increasing overall costs.

Read-and-publish agreements sought to alleviate this imbalance, consolidating charges. University libraries would pay a lump sum allowing faculty to read a given press's content and publish a certain number of articles in its journals without separate charges.[131] Renewed every so often, read-and-publish agreements were a new form of subscription that libraries were locked into—déjà vu all over again.[132] Their faculty could read all they wanted, as in the days of subscription journals, and they could publish all they wanted, as in the subscription era. What had changed, other than a smattering of articles now free for outsiders to read? Because only works authored by the pertinent faculty were flipped, not entire journals, the overall effect was modest, even for readers outside the university bubble.

In theory, if every institution did this for every publisher, all content would be both free to read for everyone and every scholar free to publish. Except that researchers without institutions, publishers without agreements, and countries whose authors remained outside would still be excluded. And read-and-publish agreements left publishers where they wanted to be, in much the same position as with subscription journals. Valid for a few years at a time, with built-in price increases, such agreements nailed fast the dominance of the gold approach and incentivized researchers to publish with the journals in question.

Nor did the agreements solve skyrocketing subscription prices. They also loaded research-intensive institutions with most of the burden in a kind of reverse Matthew effect—from those who have, much shall be demanded. British universities signed such an agreement with Wiley in 2020. Its claim that the proportion of open articles by UK researchers would increase from 28% to 85% in year one, potentially going to 100% thereafter, made sense only if all British researchers published in Wiley periodicals.[133]

Read-and-publish agreements fit the trend of publishers directing the open-access impulse to their ends. The agreements did nothing for overstretched library budgets or the prestige hierarchy that allows sought-after journals to charge above the going rate. They have undercut whatever competition might have been hoped for if authors had taken their publishing funds to where they got most value.[134] In theory, gold access might have unleashed competition, driving down costs. Subscription models leave authors price-insensitive, since they do not pay. But with gold access, they are price-insensitive as well, since their funders pay.[135]

One suggested solution has been to make authors pay directly to publish, prompting them to consider costs, select cheaper venues and press prices.[136] Giving authors skin in the game promised to make them skinflints. The UC multipayer model described above called on grants to help cover charges, not just library budgets—or national research monies, as in Europe.[137] But insofar as third-party payers still pick up the tab, scholars remain indifferent. Since the libraries signing transformative agreements have sought only to shift funding from readers to authors without using the leverage of their boycotts to drive down overall costs, this failed to address the serials crisis.[138] But at least such agreements implicitly acknowledged the unreasonableness of publishers' double-dipping. Whatever the final amounts, the monies paid them were now to be conceptually amalgamated as one sum for both reading and publishing.[139]

Latin American Success

The scientific publishers' entrenched position has hindered open access's spread. Creative destruction removes past encrustations, allowing the new to emerge. In Gerschenkron's formulation, the advantages of backwardness meant not needing to destroy before creating headroom for change. This applies to Latin America's publishing industry, which has been less developed than in Europe and the US. Many of the editions sold are imported from its colonial homelands, Spain and Portugal.[140] Even today, authors take publication by a Spanish press as a mark of having arrived.[141] And many Latin American markets are dominated by Global North trade houses. Penguin Random House is the largest or second-largest venue in several markets—Chile, Argentina, Colombia, and Mexico.[142] Whatever that implies for Latin cultural development, the absence of dominant scientific publishers left a blanker slate with room for new experiments.

Although Global North academics are often unaware of it, an entire parallel universe of Hispanophone scholarship has established its own networks and institutions. Journals in the Latin world are usually brought forth by university departments rather than scholarly societies or commercial publishers. The Guadalajara International Book Fair plays a role like Frankfurt's as the largest Spanish-language market. Latindex, created in Mexico in 1997, indexes South American scientific articles.[143]

Diamond open publishing, paid for by governments, has become the customary route for Latin scholarship. In 2011, gold journals made up 74% of all outlets here, compared to 7% in Europe and 5% in North America.[144] Almost a quarter of venues listed in the Directory of Open Access Journals is Latin. Of these, most are diamond, charging no fees.[145] Over 70% of academic output in Latin America is open, while no other region exceeds 20%.[146]

Credit for this happy state of affairs goes largely to SciELO, an open publishing and indexing platform started in Brazil in 1998.[147] That put it four years ahead of the Budapest Initiative, which has been conventionally taken as the movement's opening salvo.[148] Latin America's gambit arose not from the Northern movement, but directly from the continent's own hopes of lowering dissemination barriers. With no well-resourced research library system to pay their subscriptions, conventional journals found it hard to take root.[149] Without library budgets pulling the scholarly communication train, commercial publishers had no reason to hijack this mode of locomotion. Like Africa skipping landlines and going straight to mobile phones, Latin America avoided the circuitous detour where libraries financed journals. They cut out the middle person, with governments directly underwriting open periodicals.

SciELO garnered government support in Brazil and expanded first to Chile, then to most other Ibero-American countries as well as South Africa.[150] Intent on helping compensate for the weak representation of Latin journals in international indexes, it is now the major provider of entries in the Directory of Open Access Journals.[151] Similar platforms emulated its success, including RedALyC, CLACSO, AmeliCA, Latindex, and LA Referencia.[152]

However, being theoretically accessible on the web does not also mean being findable. A posted work may hide in plain sight, invisible to all but the most dedicated pursuers. SciELO has tackled such problems, too, seeking to supply the metadata and indexing required to make its content readily apparent to researchers worldwide.[153] It is now indexed in its own citation index, partnered with Clarivate's Web of Science, and most of its content is in SCOPUS as well.[154] And on Google Scholar, a more ecumenical index, it ranks among the top ten most accessed sites.[155] In terms of indexing, SciELO is no worse off than arXiv, the physics preprint repository. That is also unindexed by the major commercial services, yet is one of the most popular open sites globally.[156] SciELO is not limited to Latin America and includes the Hispanophone world more generally.[157] Brazil provides over five times as many articles as its closest rivals, Colombia, Mexico, and Chile. But, even so, that is only 45% of the total.[158]

Despite its flourishing open-access repertoire, Latin America has not escaped arguments like those in the Global North. From the start, SciELO has functioned as an indexer with similar impact metrics as the developed world's.[159] RedALyC, more focused on the social sciences, has, in contrast, signed on to the DORA declaration, discussed in Chapter 5, to downplay the importance of numerical metrics in appointments, promotions, and funding.[160] It sees itself as more aligned with the predicament faced by researchers in the Global South to win recognition for their work.[161]

5

The Professoriate and Open Access

Let us assume that university scholars are paid to uncover new knowledge and apply their training to dispel ignorance, hoping to arrive at what we once—in a more innocent age—called truth. How, then, would we expect them to approach open access? Add to the mix that open access permits anyone easily and costlessly to read, comment, cite, use, and criticize, but also admire, work, opening authors to a potentially larger audience. And that, insofar as their professional standing depends on influence in their fields and sometimes more broadly in public debates, their ideas would be amplified by an expanded reach. Naively, we might anticipate that the professoriate would be in the battle's vanguard, delighted by the prospect of being widely read. Alas, disappointment would be our lot.

The professoriate is surprisingly uninterested in open access. A survey of French researchers revealed that, in principle, they had no objections to making their work accessible—so long as it required no significant change to their routines. Unrealistically, most considered that the cost to authors should be less than €500. And some were furious at the effrontery of making authors pay. A return to slavery, fumed one computer scientist.[1]

The professoriate's attitude stems from a combination of indifference, snobbery, and otherworldliness. University researchers do not recognize the problem of exclusion from knowledge because they do not suffer it. As a fish does not ponder water, the professoriate is insouciant about access because it knows only surfeit. University scholars routinely fail to realize that the overwhelming majority of humanity in the developed world, and even more in the Global South, has no access to JSTOR or HeinOnline, nor any of the wondrous scientific databases that populate their laptops. In the analog era, authors bought offprints of their articles to send would-be readers without subscriptions. In the sciences, requests for offprints from developing nations often arrived on preprinted cards with heartfelt pleas, pointing out that the senders had no other hope of reading the work. Today, such constant reminders of the information divide no longer prick the professoriate's conscience.

In 2019, 217,000 Britons worked as academic staff.[2] Thus only about a third of 1% of all British could, even generously, be classified as academics. Do any other groups have access to the scholarly databases, except perhaps by talking their way into the nearest research library or during their brief and happy years as undergraduates? If not, then 99.7% of the UK has no access to the cornucopia of material available within universities. The figures are similar elsewhere.

Only a few nations, including Egypt and Uruguay, have negotiated licensing deals with some publishers, allowing all their citizens access.[3] India has announced plans for something similar.[4] Adding injury to insult, the scholarly goodies are wildly mis-distributed. Most faculty within the digital bubble will use only a tiny fraction of the abundance on tap. The vast majority of big-deal journal articles, like most library books, remain unread by the patrons of any given institution.[5] Meanwhile, talented amateurs and interested citizens outside remain excluded.

The professoriate alone is well-served by the existing system. Consider Wikipedia's footnotes. Wikipedia is the greatest assemblage of human knowledge ever, the closest we have come to the Enlighten-ment ideal of a universal encyclopedia. Yet, however open Wikipe-dia's text, the sources indicated in the footnotes are often locked down. The Internet Archive is trying to "blue" Wikipedia's foot-notes. If it owns the work in question, it allows click-through to the page referenced. But, with over six million entries in the English-language Wikipedia alone and multiple footnotes for many, the task remains Herculean. For "Holocaust," for example, there are ref-erences to about 150 books and articles. Of these, a dozen appear to be clickable, but only two or three go to the source without some sort of subscription or affiliation with paywalled databases. The average reader who wants to check a reference cannot, except by going to the nearest research library, wherever that may be.

Many academics seem unaware of this brutal imbalance. They inhabit the university bubble without even realizing it. In a 2010 survey, 93% of university and college researchers considered access-ing journal articles easy.[6] Naturally, they would, given that the system exists to supply their needs. The historian Jill Lepore—a force of nature and an enviable scholarly talent—gave voice to such academic obtuseness when she wrote that "most of what aca-demics produce can be found, by anyone who wants to find it, by searching Google."[7] That is simply not true, except in the plushly feathered nest of a university proxy server or perhaps on the illegal pirate sites.

Add to otherworldliness a dash of snobbery. Regularly employed academics have no pressing reasons to expand their audience. Even scholars deeply involved in open access, such as Paul Ginsparg, founder of arXiv, worry about a poor signal-to-noise ratio if just anyone can comment.[8]

In academe, the readers who count most are the colleagues who decide hiring, promotion, and research grants. And they reside within the bubble, too. Some professors go beyond this personal lack of engagement to claim that those excluded from the scholarly riches do not want to be, nor should be, admitted in the first place. The argument is dished up with variations. Most unpleasant are those for whom scholarly knowledge is akin to the esoteric secrets of druids, alchemists, and others whose status derived from hamstering occult wisdom. Robin Osborne, a Cambridge ancient history don, exemplifies the species.

Because universities teach how to conduct academic research, others uninitiated into these dark arts cannot—Osborne insists—understand what professors produce.[9] Even if true, that would still leave all university graduates who—once exmatriculated—are deprived of access.[10] Since a third of British 18-year-olds pursue higher education, graduates are a nontrivial, and growing, part of the population.

Most readers cannot understand what professors write, Osborne insists, therefore, nothing is lost when they are excluded. Perhaps the good don intended a sly academic self-parody. Every year, JSTOR alone registers 150 million fruitless attempts to breach its paywalls and access the cream of Anglophone social science.[11] In 2010, 16% of document supply requests at the British Library came from researchers with no university affiliation.[12] DeepDyve is a commercial service providing access to academic literature for unaffiliated researchers.[13] What libraries could supply, its clients are willing to pay for. The Latin American purveyors of open scholarship, SciELO and RedALyC, are used only to a quarter by university staff, of which a mere 5%–6% are professors. The remainder of its clientele is students (50%) and interested lay readers (20%).[14]

Who are these deluded fools seeking information they cannot understand? Any biographer, author of popular science, nonfiction freelancer, and writer of historical fiction or other imaginative literature requiring research—unless they happen to be university faculty—will have to make do with the web, their local public library, or the pirate sites. The same holds for citizen scientists, such as data collectors in ecological studies.[15] And for journalists, civil servants, and social activists.[16]

A corollary of this attitude is the oft-heard remark from professors that only fellow academics are actually interested in reading their output. The implication is that since academics already reach their intended audience, restricting access causes no harm.[17] Before a House of Commons committee, the Royal Society of Chemistry testified that most academics care more about who, than about how many, see their work.[18]

Professor Osborne's words are those of what the Germans call a *Giftzwerg*, a venomous ankle biter. Others of this ilk are more harmlessly dreamy and otherworldly. They do not expect a large audience nor seek its accolades. Some point out that academia's specialization renders its output incomprehensible. That was also Osborne's argument. Ridiculous as it may be for ancient history, it rings more plausible for the sciences. Rather than just ejecting would-be readers into the cold, as Osborne did, solutions can be found.

Open access sidesteps the comprehensibility problem by offering up the scholarly coalface in all its impenetrable glory to anyone willing to shoulder a pick.[19] Others propose a concerted effort to make academic content broadly understandable.[20] Still, most such approaches suffer from faux humility, snobbery, or both. Why should authors be entitled to pronounce on the quality of their audience, much less restrict it? At publication, they lose control. Surely, it is up to the public to decide whether to read or not. Those keen to limit their audience to the select should join the Rosicrucians.

Some parts of the scholarly world have solved the access problem, at least for themselves. Fields that disseminate via online preprints, such as computer science, physics, and mathematics, have lost interest in the subscription journals that still issue the final fruits of their labors. Their published articles are interesting mainly to future historians, not today's practitioners. Yet, the journal subscriptions remain as charges to libraries, hogging resources beyond their value as historical documentation.

Humanities and social science scholars, in turn, present their own problems. That they write books as well as articles is the main issue. Large and intermittent, books are the pig in open access's python. The cost of opening access to books is daunting. Unlike journals, their sales are unpredictable. Even the driest academic book still nurtures faint hopes of royalties. Scientists entertain no such pretensions for their articles. From their start in the seventeenth century, journals have never paid for content.[21] But many humanities scholars fancy themselves independent creators in the Romantic mode. In their minds, they are authors, publishing works as they want, collecting royalties if they can.

Academic freedom is often understood to include scholars' right to publish their findings wherever they please.[22] It includes, say some, "full freedom in publication" or "the freedom to publish research results in venues of the researcher's choosing."[23] Requiring them to publish openly —or in any other particular venue—violates this. The logic is uncompelling. Academic freedom promises unconstrained dissemination of research findings, but not wherever it pleases researchers, only where they can convince the pertinent editors. Naturally, we would all like our books to appear as Borzoi editions from Knopf or Belknap from Harvard, preferably followed by swift and favorable reviews in the *New York Times* and the *TLS*. Alas, those institutions have their own opinions, as do the editors of *Nature* and *Science*. That hardly limits academic freedom.

Editors cannot be compelled to issue any particular work. Academic freedom promises scholars the right to publish if and where they can find a willing venue. Unless they are deliberately boycotted, authors who can persuade no editor have not necessarily had their academic freedom violated. Nor does open access do more than make it a condition of funding that the results be available. Wishing to retain full control, scholars can spurn conditional research monies. Admittedly, some funders require wholly unrestricted availability of content, a controversial issue we discuss below with Creative Commons licenses.

In any case, requiring access is no more constraining of scholars' freedom than the expectation that they publish in prestigious, high-impact venues. That, too, narrows their choice. Open-access mandates constrain scholars only because the universities' promotion and tenure committees have drunk the prestige Kool-Aid of the high-impact-factor journals. If funders required specific accessible venues, that might be a freedom issue.[24] But so long as they only say, open access wherever you can find it, there is no compulsion. And as the number of open journals grows, offering more choice, any hint of compulsion evaporates.

Dreaming of Reward

In *Swimming to Cambodia*, his one-person show, Spalding Grey accounts for his time on the set of the movie *The Killing Fields*, where he played a small role. Each time the cast and crew had to be mustered, their poker-faced minders would address them in the Romantic idiom, as in "Will the artistes please line up for the bus." University deans could learn something here. The humanities professoriate, too, longs to be treated as beret-wearing bohemian fops. Paul Fussell once observed that the surest way to humiliate university professors was to address them as "educators," lumping them together with grade school teachers, rather than treating them as high-minded servants of Athena.[25] Their sense of having a calling complicates the humanities professoriate's acceptance of open access, which many regard as a giveaway of the crown jewels. They feel a personal stake in their output beyond its content. And they quietly nourish hopes of writing something that will sell and return royalties.

Other fields also have aspirations beyond mere truth-finding, though not in the Romantic mode. Medical and engineering professors, not to mention chemists and computer scientists, often generate knowledge, breakthroughs, and discoveries with market potential. That has long been true. Alexander Graham Bell did the work behind his supremely valuable 1876 patents for the telephone as a professor at Boston University, but he owned them outright.[26] Fritz Haber won ammonia from the air, creating artificial fertilizer. Although Haber was a professor at the Kaiser Wilhelm Institute in Imperial Germany, he happily sold his rights to corporations, such as BASF. He also worked directly for companies and took out patents in his own name.[27] The University of Wisconsin set up a foundation in 1925 to administer patents resulting from Harry Steenbock's research on vitamin D.[28]

With the postwar flow of funds to universities, accommodations among research, funding, and commercialization followed. That increased in the late twentieth century as government financing diminished and universities sought new income. Initial hesitations that commercialized research threatened to sully the disinterested pursuit of knowledge were assuaged by the fruits promised.[29] Marshaling the computer and medical technologies founded on university research, ecosystems of corporate spin-offs and start-ups haloed around the academic cores. Transferring knowledge beyond the ivy-covered walls has become regularized, with universities themselves taking stakes in companies. Start-up firms in IT, pharmaceuticals, and engineering have opened in the shadows of the research nodes—in Boston's Route 120, Silicon Valley, and all the other Silicon spin-offs—Glens, Shires, Savannahs, Hollars, Fens, Saxonies, and Capes.

Given promising payoffs, US universities have long asserted ownership of patents worked up by their faculty, unlike in Bell's day. Harvard requires faculty and staff using university funds or facilities, including outside monies it administers, to report all inventions. Harvard takes ownership of patentable inventions, although it grants researchers those that only incidentally use university infrastructure. The university then decides whether to patent and exploit, promising only reasonable efforts to keep inventors involved and informed. Eventual royalties are shared. The inventor receives 35% personally, with another 15% for research, and the rest is divided among department, school, and central administration.[30]

Similarly, the professional schools whose faculty also labor outside the academy have guidelines to ensure a reasonable coexistence. A day per week of salaried outside employment is a rule of thumb, intended for doctors, lawyers, and others who can make serious money consulting or practicing on the side. While regular civil servants in the US may not earn outside their jobs, noncareer employees and presidential appointees can receive up to 15% of their basic pay in additional compensation.[31]

Distance learning has drawn even humanities and social science faculty into the logic of profit-sharing with their universities. A few decades ago, average humanities professors needed little more than chalk and a blackboard to teach. Now, the sizzle of digital technology has seduced them. Online courses require infrastructure, training, and backup, leaving faculty dependent on their institutions' IT offices. Online courses have advantages: larger audiences drawn from anywhere, new pedagogical tools to dazzle and enlighten, and an opportunity to focus on the qualitative aspects of pedagogy (discussions) rather than mere information transfer (lectures). Both faculty and university gain, whether from teaching remotely, asynchronously, and with less repetition, or by profiting from more backsides on seats. But, because teachers of online classes are reliant on university know-how and resources, they have had to concede their exclusive claims to content.[32] The professoriate's inability to project its message unaided has made the medium of transmission as important as the substance.

Yet, in other respects, the humanities professoriate resists the imputation that its output is not wholly its property. The sums at stake in the occasional bestselling book written by tenured faculty are small. One possible exception is Erich Segal's *Love Story*. That brought him renown and riches but also deep-sixed his academic career when Yale denied him tenure. Isaac Asimov posed the dilemma more starkly. While he was teaching biochemistry at Boston University's medical school, his prolific writing soon undermined his research. Sticking to lecturing only, he was dismissed for having abandoned lab work. He was allowed to keep his title of Associate Professor, and, eventually, BU gave him full professor status, recognizing his literary achievements. Both sides stuck to their guns and found an accommodation.

Who is to say precisely on whose dime such works are produced? When a bestseller is in the professor's field of expertise, the presumption may be that it is part of their salaried work. In other instances, matters are less clear. Bernhard Schlink wrote *The Reader* and other fiction while professing law at the Humboldt University and serving as a judge. Stephen Carter has written mystery novels and conservative cultural criticism as a Yale Law professor. Deborah Harkness writes vampiric Cinderella fantasies for the over-educated while a historian of science at USC. Bruce Holsinger puts out novels while teaching English literature at Virginia. We assume they are doing this in their spare time, those moments when they would otherwise be bicycling through Provence, cooking homemade pasta, listening to opera, or whatever the professoriate does when left to its own devices.

But when the popular works are in the author's field or when they are college textbooks written on company time, the situation changes. Professors would be outraged were their institutions to demand a share. And they would resist the idea of open access for such works as stealing their lottery ticket to possible royalties. The argument that popular books spread enlightenment and that academics perform a public service by getting the word out is undercut by considering how superior open works would be at the same goal.

Textbooks raise the problem most starkly. Yes, every field needs two or three to assign in introductory courses. But the current state of affairs is indefensible. Publishers issue a huge oversupply of texts. To undercut the second-hand market, the books are sometimes accompanied by websites or other ancillary media that can be accessed only with codes supplied to the initial buyer but not transferable to subsequent users. The books are revised on tight schedules—every two or three years now, no longer four or five.[33] That allows them to remain state of the art. In the sciences, being up to date has some justification. But in the humanities and social sciences, developments worth an undergraduate's attention occur over decades, not years. Again, the publishers' goal is to undermine the secondary market, as supposedly outmoded editions are rendered worthless by new ones.

Add to that the relentless price increases foisted on students who are harnessed by their professors to particular texts in specific editions for their required classes. Economics textbooks can cost over $300 once stranglehold extras are added, such as codes for homework assignments. Textbook prices have escalated over 1,000% since the 1970s.[34] Their authors whistle all the way to the bank. A Harvard economics professor, Gregory Mankiw, has sold more than two million copies of his *Principles of Economics* (Cengage Learning), pocketing over $42 million in royalties.[35]

More Than Reading

Unlike article-driven fields, whose practitioners nurture no illusions of authoring bestsellers or being paid for their writerly efforts, humanities scholars fondly imagine themselves as old-fashioned creators in the Romantic mold. Paying attention to form, style, and presentation, not just content, they stand on their moral rights more than scientists do. Moral rights protect the authors' claims to be recognized as such, their reputations, and their control over the work's aesthetic aspects. Historians may be among the worst offenders, writing in a field that still has a broader readership than, say, literary theory or analytic philosophy. To judge from the holdings of major US research libraries, history is the subject where most books (58%) are aimed at a general, not a specifically scholarly, audience (36%).[36] Ambitious for a general readership, humanities scholars are often allergic to open access. They regard it as giving their stuff away while also letting just anyone paw through it for their own purposes.

Text mining and topic modeling are big-data analyses of content. Text mining allows tracking of word usage and prevalence of concepts. Google's Ngram is an example.[37] Topic modeling produces conceptual maps, revealing networks and connections to highlight unexpected emphases. Both are examples of "distant reading" (as opposed to the humanities' traditional method of close reading), seeking big patterns in large aggregations of data.[38] Because they leave the text untouched, neither has raised the humanities' hackles. They use works for their factual or other nuggets without changing the original. The same holds for the possibility that the ability to search across texts will decompose them into their constituent parts, whether facts, ideas, assertions, or memes.[39] While this process may disregard the work, it does not change it.

Data mining, in contrast, again divides the humanities from the sciences. Scientists routinely generate massive quantities of data, which they often post along with the resulting articles, allowing others to test their conclusions or use it independently. More than the text that derives from it, the underlying data would seem to belong not just to the scientist who generated it. The data are an ordered version of the external reality under study, thus not self-evidently the scholar's property. In any case, they must be made available to verify the work.

Humanities scholars, who rely more on qualitative sources, rarely work with data in this sense. As mentioned, legal scholars footnote every assertion. Historians and literary academics reference the sources that ground their claims. Some of those sources are themselves copyrighted and cannot be delivered to new readers. Others are archives open to any who want to consult them. It is hard to know what material analytic philosophers would reference, much less what data they would present. Humanities scholars' research sources are indicated in their footnotes, allowing others to double-check them. But they could rarely provide them as data packages separate from the holdings of the libraries and archives they have consulted. Data mining thus seems largely irrelevant for them.

Yet, a database may be the fruit of endless labor and the result a boon to others. Scientists who thus organize reality, giving colleagues material to work with, deserve credit for that, even beyond their own published results. Here science and the humanities are alike. A historian or literary scholar who establishes an important text or an art scholar who develops a catalogue raisonné serve similar ends. Enormous effort parses variations, explicates obscure passages and vocabulary, presents a definitive text, or tracks down all of an artist's works. Much like databases, such work deserves more credit than is customarily granted.

Nonetheless, data mining is but one aspect of a broader question—whether uses beyond just reading should be permitted of open texts. Entirely unrestricted use of works would include quoting, misquoting, translating, parodying, abbreviating, paraphrasing, plagiarizing, excerpting, reprinting, filming or other media shifting, changing, reading aloud, setting to music, republishing, and indeed republishing under another name. This is the aspect of open access referred to as *libre*, free to use, as opposed to *gratis*, available at no cost.[40] Only the most ardent open-access activist is likely to countenance all possible uses. But many are willing to grant considerably more than most humanities scholars tolerate.

How much control do authors retain over works once released? Copyright law prohibits many uses without permission: republishing, translating, filming, or excerpting more than short quotations. Reproducing passages or ideas without attribution—plagiarism—is a moral, not a legal, transgression.[41] Only if it goes beyond the limits of fair use does it become actionable. The moral rights granted authors in some nations outlaw other uses, such as changing works, excerpting them at any length, sometimes setting them to music, or parodying them. At their most extreme, some countries, such as France, permit withdrawal, allowing authors to remove a published work from circulation—insofar as that can be accomplished at all.[42]

Humanities scholars have been more eager than scientists to assert moral rights of aesthetic control. In 2002, Creative Commons developed a suite of legal licenses for releasing works to the public. These are, in effect, the open-access equivalents of copyright, allowing authors to make their content available to varying degrees in a legally binding manner. Their great advance is to permit more uses than traditional copyright.

That alone does not address the problem of works that remain protected by copyright. Nor have Creative Commons licenses been uncontroversial. In debates over how to structure open access, a neuralgic point is how much control to guarantee authors. Funding agencies often require, and scientists, on the whole, have accepted, licensing (CC BY) that allows any use so long as new versions credit the authors and note if changes have been made.[43] Others can thus copy and redistribute works in any medium or format; they can remix, transform, edit, translate, and build on them. Such conditions seem in part curiously tailored to specific art forms—popular music—and it is unclear what remixing a book or article would mean, much less mashups.

Humanities scholars find agreeing to such conditions difficult. They may welcome works being read widely, but they are unlikely to be happy with derivative content boiled off them. Transposing works into foreign languages, braille, or audio to make them more available may be good. Many other derivative uses are also unobjectionable, even desirable. But not all. Reprinting an article in an anthology with a specific political slant or commercial ambitions might strike authors as illegitimate. "Building on" a work raises the possibility of plagiarism or unjustified appropriation, even if the original is credited.

Merely indicating that a piece has been changed, without specifying how, while crediting the author, raises the specter of mischaracterizing it.[44] At the extreme, a work on a controversial subject could be selectively edited to suggest a different meaning and then disseminated with the author prominently credited—all while remaining within the confines of CC BY.[45] The anodyne idea that this is not permissible or that moral rights will spare us is unconvincing, especially in Anglo-Saxon nations where moral rights have little purchase.[46]

Meanwhile, CC BY allows anyone to do as they please. Having paid fees for their work to be issued at no cost to users, some authors have been surprised to find it reprinted in for-sale editions—something legally possible under CC BY.[47] The new pay editions compete with the print versions that earn money for the initial open-access publishers, helping offset costs.[48] CC BY allows anyone, including commercial publishers, free rein with works, much as with public domain content. Such largesse would be eliminated by licensing open books as CC BY-NC, forbidding commercial use. Yet, a CC BY-NC license prohibits uses that authors might favor. Such works could not appear in free knowledge databases, such as Wikipedia, nor blogs if either had ever developed commercial uses to help defray the cost of open access.[49]

In nations that grant authors extensive moral rights, including attribution and integrity, how could others be allowed to do what they wish with content, such as changing and repurposing it? But even in more permissive legal regimes and among authors sympathetic to spreading knowledge, misgiving is the likely reaction to wholly unfettered reuse of work.

Examples of legitimate uses often include excerpting whole articles or portions of books—larger amounts than fair use tolerates—for inclusion in course readers/packs or anthologies. While this would seem harmless, it is also trivial when the work is already freely accessible. Course readers are a product of the analog era, spawn of the photocopier. Back then, it was difficult to ask large groups of students to read the same ten pages of a book or an article, even when the materials were held on reserve in libraries and lent for only a few hours at a time. Course packs were the solution to analog scarcity.

Today, a syllabus needs only to indicate the web location and page numbers of an otherwise freely available work. It is a very lazy undergraduate who cannot be bothered to click through to the original work, scrolling to the requisite passage. But even the professoriate finds the concept difficult. In the UK, 38% of journal articles copied under the licensing allowed for course material apparently come from content that is, in fact, already freely available.[50] Anthologies are similar. They, too, continue outmoded analog thinking from a time when articles could usefully be collected, united around a common theme in a new volume. A list of the relevant web addresses suffices to achieve the same effect today. For a generation that streams its music from cloud servers, why reproduce freely available content in yet another format?

Insofar as they agree to use of their works, humanities scholars generally insist that licenses forbid derivatives (CC BY-ND) and sometimes commercial use, too (CC BY-NC-ND). They also face the problem of third-party content. A scientist typically generates data directly from the coalface, trampling on no other rights, so long as they respect the protocols for experimenting on humans and animals. In contrast, humanities scholars' "data" typically consist of quotations or references to others' works, often with their own copyrights.

Such third-party rights are particularly thorny for art historians, historians of dance, and musicologists, among others.[51] If they buy reproduction rights to artworks discussed, they cannot promise future users of their text the same. Worse, since licensing fees vary depending on anticipated uses (print run of a book), open editions, with their unpredictable and potentially limitless readers, are hard to price. Open editions of books with illustrations often have blank spaces instead, with supremely unhelpful notes suggesting that the original edition be consulted. Literary scholars reliant on extensive quotation suffer similar problems, while historians can better make do with paraphrases or work with materials more likely to be in the public domain. Overall, humanities scholars are rarely masters of their "data" in the same way as scientists.

The insistence by gold open-access advocates on CC BY licensing also sticks in the craw of developing nations.[52] Allowing commercial reuse of content permits the dominant scientific publishers to scoop up, repackage, and sell content otherwise made freely available in the South.[53] Latin American universities have long paid the cost of diamond journals, allowing scholars anywhere to read. A fifth of their articles come from Northern scholars, but are published at the South's expense. If gold initiatives in the North were to set the standard everywhere, developing nations would suffer most.[54]

The Perils of Prestige

Academic prestige also complicates any move to open access. Prestige is the currency of the scholarly realm. Money is important but less crucial than elsewhere. Prestige, salary, and research funding go hand in hand. The material rewards scholars can win are sufficiently lackluster that they are not the primary motive. The most successful ones are paid upper-middle-class salaries. They can earn well into the bottom half of six figures, although varying widely by specialization. Yet, nothing here will excite a lawyer or doctor, much less any finance or business person.

Instead, scholars seek to be celebrated for their discoveries and insights. They covet the respect of their peers, though they do not spurn the trappings of worldly success if proffered—to pen an op-ed piece, appear as a talking head, lecture, or consult. Nor will they refuse an award, a gong, or other honor dangling from a ribbon, pinned to a lapel, suitable for framing, or perfect for a mantlepiece. That respect goes hand in hand with decent salaries and professional success is a given, but money is the least of it. Renown is what scholars strive for. Hence the attribution right is the core of their demands, that authors be named when their work is used. "Citing is paying," as David Nimmer puts it.[55]

Scholars' discoveries, knowledge, and talents can be parlayed into success in other fields. Investment banks snap up quants with math and physics PhDs. Some may be sought for political advice. But on the whole, the validation scholars aspire to is quite hermetically limited to their own world. Not for nothing is it the ivory tower. So self-referential is academia that too much success in other realms risks ostracization. A large readership or audience stokes suspicions of pandering. Worldly profit or attention and the pursuit of truth align only mistrustfully. Not long ago, publishing with commercial presses threatened budding academic careers. In the early 1980s, Thomas Kuhn, the revered philosopher of science, cautioned Sherry Turkle, then his junior colleague at MIT, that a second book with Simon & Schuster would put a pox on her hopes of tenure.[56]

Prestige is won by selectivity and exclusivity. The most discerning journals and publishers are the most respected. Hotly sought after are those rejecting most manuscripts, whose editorial standards are the hardest to meet, whose pages, the most difficult to breach. The more authors aspire to contribute to a journal, the more it limits the input it publishes, the more selective it is. Prestige is scarcity rewarded. It reverses the logic of Yogi Berra's quip: Nobody goes there anymore, it's too crowded.

Prestige must be patiently earned, not just stamped out of the ground. The publishing establishment is a tough nut to crack. Its product's unsubstitutability protects it from competition. As does the slow accretion of prestige and other signs of academic worth. A rival cannot just set up shop to offer better or cheaper products. The barriers to entry are imposing. The field is moderately concentrated. Its products are unique and the venue where they appear itself enhances their luster. Moreover, suppliers (scholars) are in a weak bargaining position, needing to sell and eager to land with the most prestigious disseminators.

Nor are the consumers (libraries and readers) negotiating from strength. They must buy most of what is on offer and cannot bargain. Worse, they are at odds—the readers are price-insensitive, while the libraries' budgets are strained by rising costs.[57] In theory, digitality should allow new journals to issue cheaply and efficiently, and many do. But the barriers to competitiveness at the food chain's apex impede a liquid market. To start with, newcomer journals have to convince the indexing services to include them so that their articles appear on consumers' radars. While digitality has disrupted other industries, it has served to reinforce inherited positions in academic publishing.

Prestige and quality are correlated, but not invariably. As a relational good, prestige is zero-sum. Only a few journals or publishers can occupy its pinnacle simultaneously. But nothing prevents many from being good in the sense of high quality.[58] Nor does prestige necessarily guarantee quality. Prestige is taken as a proxy for quality by departments deciding on hires, tenures, and promotions and funding agencies distributing their largesse.[59] Busy scholars seeking a steer on what to read opt first for works from renowned presses.

The most prestigious venues receive the most submissions. At the extreme, one could imagine the top publisher receiving every manuscript completed each year, aspiringly submitted to it first. Yet, some sense of self-selection convinces hopeful authors that they waste their time waiting for the detour via a rejection letter from their top choice. Nonetheless, having to wade through more submissions, the most desirable presses face the steepest selection tasks. Prestigious journals incur costs as they staff up to vet manuscripts.

High-status periodicals can charge hefty subscriptions and publishing fees. But for books, if anything, prices are inversely correlated to prestige. The bigger the names of authors publishing with the most prestigious presses, the lower a book's price. The more obscure the press, the higher the price. A Palgrave book invariably costs more than one from Princeton. Oxford and Cambridge are perhaps exceptions to this rule. Their scholarly monographs are priced significantly above—easily double—their US university press competition. In effect, they gouge the captive research library market. In return, they deliver profits to their host universities, while the American outfits require subsidies. Since 80% of UK print monograph sales are abroad, foreign libraries help keep Oxbridge afloat.[60]

Unlike books, journals do not enter the market with each publication. Their prices are locked in for years, with little ability to fluctuate with demand. Also, it is only with books that digital publishing's cost savings have been reaped. While digital journal prices have been steadily ratcheting up, e-books sell for less than their paper counterparts. In 2007, at their launch, when Jeff Bezos announced that Kindle editions of bestsellers would go for $9.99, he shocked conventional publishers with the realization that he was benchmarking prices down.[61] Add in self-published volumes, and the book market's reverse movement compared to journals becomes even starker—at least for works other than scholarly monographs.

For books, another consequence of the prestige arms race is the role of literary agents. As of the 1990s, authors in the Anglophone world could no longer approach trade book publishers unaccompanied by an agent.[62] That is less true for university presses. Trade houses are not necessarily those that scholars favor, though they have gained a certain caché in recent decades—largely for their more generous advances, publicity, and distribution. Against this speaks that they work largely without the imprimatur of peer review, sometimes publishing books no scholarly press would touch. Their printed volumes are often mediocre specimens—with miserly margins, shoddy paper, and flimsy bindings.

Acquisitions at trade houses are handled by staff with little expertise in their books' subjects. They work from 20- or 30-page proposals, not the manuscript, nor even sample chapters. The author's previous sales history and the market potential of the current project are among their primary considerations. Trade publishers, approached by scholars and freelancers alike, stagger under more submissions than university presses. Agents have become the first line of defense, running interference for the in-house staff.

All readers will have had the experience of being disappointed by books from first-rank presses despite their sizzling blurbs. Less frequent than such false positives are the works that surprise even their editors by taking off like rockets or achieving widely cited classic status—the false negatives. Fiction sees this often, since subjective taste bears heavily on decisions, and peer review plays no role. J. K. Rowling's Harry Potter books, rejected by several publishers, ultimately made the fortunes of then-fledgling Bloomsbury. Hedging its bets, the press had paid Rowling a £1,000 advance, printing five hundred copies.[63] *Shuggie Bain*, Douglas Stuart's Booker-winning novel about growing up poor in Glasgow, was rejected by 32 houses before Picador took it up.

Some of the most influential social science books were published by lesser-ranked presses lucky enough to spot a gem. Norbert Elias's

The Civilizing Process was originally issued by a now-defunct press in Basel. Among the LSE's list of most cited and influential social science works, Gert Hofstede's *Culture's Consequences* was published by SAGE, Erving Goffman's *The Presentation of Self in Everyday Life* by the University of Edinburgh's Social Sciences Research Centre, and Richard Lazarus and Susan Folkman's *Stress, Appraisal, and Coping* by Springer, which is a prominent publisher of journals but no one's first choice for a book.[64] Alfred Crosby's *The Columbian Exchange* was issued by Greenwood, the English-language edition of Ulrich Beck's *Risk Society* by SAGE, and Richard E. Nisbett and Dov Cohen's widely cited *Honor Society* by Routledge. Having been rejected by Columbia, Princeton, and other presses, Raul Hilberg's monumental *Destruction of the European Jews* finally found an outlet with Quadrangle.

On the whole, size and prestige are inversely correlated. The smallest press imaginable—proud outlet of one book—is not necessarily the most prestigious. Yet, the mill that churns out thousands annually will shine dimmer than a publisher whose several dozen volumes spill into the bookstores glossy with meticulous curation, editing, and marketing.[65] Prestige is also a quality earned by a track record. The older the press or journal, the more likely it is to have won its spurs. Because age and prestige go hand in hand, open journals will take time to build up patina. Many of the most respected science periodicals remain subscription-based. *Nature* and *Science* are still among the most tensile jumping-off points for career advancement. Open journals face a hard slog against such established competitors. That would be true for any newcomer journal no matter how it paid the bills. Open-access presses sometimes marshal prestigious editorial boards to compensate for their lack of accreted gravitas.[66]

But open-access competitors face additional hurdles. With an author-pays model, they are incentivized to accept as many submissions as possible without undermining the brand. In China, where even subscription journals often levy publication fees, some publish up to 36 issues annually, with dozens or even hundreds of articles in each.[67] Certain gold periodicals have fought battles with their editorial boards when they resisted demands to accept more and worse submissions.[68] Conversely, the more prestigious and selective journals justify higher fees because of their heightened sorting obligations and to compensate for their lower throughput.

As discussed below, so-called "predatory" journals accept almost everything that crosses the transom, collecting the fees. The most selective conventional journals reject 95% of manuscripts submitted. *PLOS Medicine*, one of the most prestigious open journals in its field, accepts only 15% of submissions.[69] To build prestige, such serials must keep rejection rates high. That, in turn, requires high publication fees to pay for the winnowing, which impedes would-be authors. Many open journals therefore rely on support from parent institutions or other sources. They sometimes cross-subsidize from less-discriminating affiliated journals where acceptance rates are kept high to reap publication fees for use elsewhere. *PLOS One*, for example, is treated as a cash cow, accepting 70% of submissions. Its publication charges (ca. $1,350) underwrite fellow PLOS journals.[70] Other journals have followed this example, including *Scientific Reports*, *BMJ Open*, and *PeerJ*.

Striving for prestige, humanities and social science scholars are blinded to how they effectively extinguish their books by sticking with traditional publishers. To issue an academic monograph with a conventional university press or one of the commercial scholarly houses often means dropping your work into a black hole. The only readers who will see it are those who can afford the three-figure price of a Routledge or Oxford University Press book or who enjoy lending privileges at major research libraries. Monograph publication is effectively privatization. Here are some examples of Oxford works that no one other than research libraries will buy. From the reading public's vantage, these books might as well have been buried in their authors' back gardens.

W. E. Vaughan, *Ireland Under the Union, I: 1801–1870*, $480.00

N. G. L. Hammond and F. W. Walbank, *A History of Macedonia*, v. 3, $440.00

W. Bernard Carlson, *Technology in World History*, $400.00

Edward M. Spiers and Jeremy A. Crang, *A Military History of Scotland*, $250.00

Stuart Carroll, *Blood and Violence in Early Modern France*, $213.00

Prestige's hammerlock also has wider pernicious effects on the scholarly world. Academia outsources what should be one of its primary tasks to publishers. Publication by the most prestigious houses is considered a proxy for quality. When hiring, tenuring, promoting, or allocating funds, academia relies on publishers' pronouncement of worth. Where content is published matters more than it should. Publishers become part of academia's credentialing process.[71] It is not uncommon for tenure to be granted once a book is accepted by a well-regarded press.[72] Articles forthcoming in the most renowned journals play a similar role. The trend for dissertations to become collections of published articles shifts the evaluation function from faculty-as-teachers to faculty-as-peer-reviewers. The same people do the same work, but journals now effectively credential PhDs, not the universities.

For journals, rejection rates give some sense of their exclusivity, but no comparable data exist for book publishers. Their metric of prestige is an anecdotal pastiche of other authors in the stable and how well their works have been reviewed and sold. Academic presses often specialize, upping the ante for books in their fields— Princeton for economic history, MIT for linguistics and architecture, Oxford for philosophy, Duke and Texas for South America,

Minnesota for literary theory, Hopkins for the history of medicine, and so forth.[73]

When dissemination was difficult and expensive, it may have made sense to incorporate publishers into the credentialing process. With resources at stake, theirs was the decision to publish or not. And as their reputations were built up by a track record of consistent choices, perhaps there was some logic to making the press a proxy for quality. But once dissemination has become the least of it, once works can be posted on the web and read by anyone, the issue shifts from getting it out to getting it noticed. Evaluation, not publication, becomes the goal, as is discussed in Chapter 9.[74]

The irony is that the vetting undertaken by publishers is done by scholars anyway. Rather than organizing evaluation on its own, academia allows publishers to enlist its own members and then accepts the results unquestioningly.

Pursuing prestige may itself also distort the truth value of the most sought-after content. The winner's curse is a concept economists use to analyze auctions where the value of what is bid for is unclear. Bidders who expect oil reserves to be plentiful—likely overestimating them—are motivated to go highest and overpay. Analogously, journals keen to publish articles making the most striking, novel, or unexpected claims—whose results are least likely to withstand future scrutiny without regression toward the mean—are most likely to issue corrections and errata notices.[75] Selectivity and its attendant prestige do not invariably lead to quality.[76]

Peer Review

Peer review is scholarly publishing's gold standard. Scientific presses submit works to experts who write reports recommending publication or not. Even thumbs up, they often suggest extensive revision. If and when their concerns are met, publication follows. Books and articles are often significantly altered and—one hopes—improved in the process. Some do not make the cut at all. They either wander off to other presses or journals with different criteria or back into the author's bottom drawer.

Publishers have normally organized, but not directly paid for, peer review. Needing its imprimatur to accept manuscripts, they keep a Rolodex of scholars to call on for their specialty. Publishers are right to point out that peer review has to be organized and administered even when staffed by volunteers. Vetting submissions takes time and effort. Scholars and their universities are bad at recognizing the implicit costs of labor time, which they regard as sunk and therefore negligible.[77]

Yet, publishers bear few of the true costs of peer review. The scientific dissemination industry employs 125,000 editors who maintain a network of 2.5 million reviewers.[78] In 2016, they undertook some 14 million evaluations to publish 2.9 million articles.[79] Reviewers work largely for free. For journal articles, they normally receive nothing. For books, they are customarily offered $100 or $200 in cash, or sometimes double that amount in books from the publisher's list. The workload varies, but even a cursory book report clocks in far below minimum wage if calculated as an hourly fee. The collective value of peer reviewers' work has been estimated at £200 million in the UK alone and £1.9 billion globally, 23% of total publishing costs.[80] That works out to some $250 annually for each of the world's scientists or each manuscript reviewed, depending on who does the calculation— perhaps not an unreasonable contribution to the cause.[81]

But are publishers the best venue for peer review? It's hard to see why. First and foremost, some of the most prestigious outlets undertake none. The content of the most venerable US law reviews is selected by the drones of the legal world, students. They often judge the work of faculty who grade them and recommend them, or not, for their first positions. Hardly a recipe for disinterested expert evaluation.

Nor do trade presses undertake much peer review. They decide to publish based on anticipated sales. Whether the arguments made are convincing or well-grounded is less pressing. Publication may be agreed upon without expert blessing. Worth noting, too, is how fluid distinctions among publishers are. University presses publish not just scholarly monographs but also trade books on light and popular subjects. Conversely, some trade houses publish works with intellectual heft, though mainly those with a broader appeal, too. Some compete prestige-wise on equal footing with the major university presses: Norton, Basic, and the Free Press in the US. In addition there are the commercial scholarly presses, which feed on the second and third tiers of manuscripts to supply research libraries with expensive works: Palgrave Macmillan, Blackwell's, Routledge, Duckworth, Bloomsbury, Polity, and the like.

That is the Anglophone world. Without a long-established university press system, European scholarly publishing happens in commercial houses specializing in serious nonfiction. Publishers here tend to keep decision-making in house. Peer review is a fairly novel Anglo-Saxon import. Austrian publishers (admittedly a hardscrabble lot faced with their larger and glossier German competitors) scarcely have peer review.[82] The French lack even a word for the process.[83] Sometimes European publishers are advised by scholarly editors or boards, acting, in effect, as outsider readers. Editors at such presses may have advanced degrees in the fields where they judge manuscripts, but they are rarely practicing specialists.

In Germany and the Netherlands, presses such as Springer, De Gruyter, C.H. Beck, Vandenhoeck & Ruprecht, Campus, and Brill are commercial scholarly presses. They have long plowed the same furrow as the new university presses that have recently sprung up: Amsterdam University Press, Central European University Press, and so forth. Despite its name, PUF (Presses universitaires de France) was not a university press but a commercial issuer of serious nonfiction.

Such diversity of venue affects peer review. For the university world to allocate its resources based on books from Farrar, Straus and Giroux, Knopf, Penguin, or other trade houses means—not to put too fine a point on it—to accept evaluations by agents and editors with no more than undergraduate training in vaguely related fields, whose foremost concern is sales potential. While peer-reviewed publishers may supply useful proxy evaluations of scholarly merit, trade houses do not.

Even where a university press or scientific publisher organizes peer review, it does not necessarily tap into the best advice. Specialized journals with editorial boards of experts are adept at sending manuscripts to the most pertinent evaluators. But will the in-house editors at university presses, who are not themselves specialists, know whom to ask? And will they reliably convince the best experts to promptly read and report on 600-page manuscripts in exchange for $200 worth of press books (one or two volumes at current list prices)? The hotter the topic, the better-known the major figures in the field, the less likely a manuscript is to get a reading from them. Other scholars are also capable of careful evaluation. Indeed, often the academics at lesser institutions with greater teaching responsibilities and fewer ambitions to publish are most conversant in their fields, most up to date in the literature, and best able to judge new works. They could play invaluable roles. But are they the ones familiar to harried editors in New York, Berkeley, Madison, or either of the Cambridges?

Even when it is well organized, peer review has faults.[84] Does anyone still quaintly believe that it ranks works based on their correspondence to some external reality?[85] The autobiographical reflections on slavery by Joel Williamson in the *Journal of American History* jolted the complacency of assuming peer review to be objective. With the author's agreement, the six referees' reports were published, too. The four reviews from White historians recommended publication, while the two Blacks rejected it.[86] Every reader has favorite examples of shoddy work that passed muster. Though harder to quantify, excellent pieces have doubtless also been rejected by peer reviewers.[87] Even work that eventually went on to win a Nobel prize has been spurned at first.[88]

Trusting peer review means being guided by the opinions of two—max three—scholars who pronounce the work fit for consumption. That is not nothing. Nor is it a guarantee of much. Depending on how peer review is structured (blind or not), decisions may be influenced by the prestige of the authors' home institutions or other irrelevant factors. Editors aiming to publish a manuscript, or not, can select reviewers to achieve their goal.[89] New techniques have sought to avoid such problems. Without much success, some scientific journals have opened up the process to a broader pool of reviewers. Others, however, claim better results. Since authors fear being widely shamed, public peer review may discourage them from submitting low-quality work.[90]

Either way, when their submission is rejected, authors generally ignore an initial slight and move on to other journals or presses until they find one willing to recognize their merits. Most economics papers are submitted between three and six times before finding a home.[91] Peer review imposes costs and soaks up time, sometimes needlessly. If an initially rejected article is repeatedly resubmitted en route to its eventual resting place, efforts are duplicated and resources wasted. Multiple, repetitive peer review consumes up to 15 million hours annually.[92]

It would be better to evaluate work once, with competing outlets then vying to publish it. Something like this is already in place among the mega-journals, large aggregations of open content that we return to in Chapter 8. They avoid needless duplication of review by pooling efforts, producing cascading evaluations. Reviews are done once, with the work then resubmitted until it finds its proper niche in the publication hierarchy. The mega-journals have also instituted portable reviews that can be taken along until a welcoming venue is identified.[93] Publishers even cooperate on sharing evaluations.[94]

In effect, mega-journals allow publishers to capture the output and (more modest) publishing charges for submissions rejected by their prestigious flagship organs.[95] *PLOS One* receives manuscripts rejected by the other PLOS titles. Authors submitting to BMJ journals can have their manuscript automatically considered by *BMJ Open* if it is not accepted by their first choice.[96] What does not make it into (the highly selective conventional subscription journal) *Nature* may instead appear in (the open access) *Nature Communications* or, if not that, its mega-journal, *Scientific Reports*. At the very least, such one-off assessment helps solve peer reviewer burn-out, curtailing repetitive efforts.[97]

Peer review suffers other problems, too. There is no need to rehearse the debate over whether it works at all. The alleged crisis of scientific reproducibility is part of this. Unreplicable work should be spottable by functioning peer review—though how, short of re-running experiments, is unclear. Such weaknesses are not specific to open access. They affect subscription journals just as much and plague all scientific evaluation. Peer review's critics are harsher than it deserves. Yes, work is evaluated within a preexisting conceptual framework. Truly revolutionary accomplishments are unmeasurable by the inherited standards they reject.[98] Dialogue across Kuhnian paradigm shifts is impossible. Some researchers appreciate preprint depositories precisely for their lack of peer review, which tends to reward conventional wisdom.[99] Yet, like all skeptical positions, the grain of truth in such arguments is undermined by the irrelevance of the corner they maneuver their adherents into. If true, despair is the only plausible reaction.

The practical advice offered by peer-review skeptics dodges the fundamental problem. Let us say that, thanks to such criticism, resources are apportioned according to new criteria, not the self-referential and socially exclusive ones that existing peer review solidifies. Instead, publication is decided by soundness, adequacy, capacity, or the like in ways that undermine the current system's Matthew effect and bring more scholars into the fold. Even so, the basic problem persists: which among the thousands of works should readers take up first? If evaluation does not occur before publication, it will have to come after. But since there is more content than mortals can ever consume, judgment cannot be dodged. Even if we lived forever, we could not read everything.

Metrics

Recognizing the interrelated problems of peer review and the prestige hierarchy has spawned attempts at solutions. One is to quantify postpublication review, searching for metrics that indicate if not merit outright, then at least some other desirable quality: readership, citations, or—more nebulously—impact. For fields like biomedicine that publish countless articles, quantification promises relief. The brute amount of each scholar's output is the easiest indicator, but it is also crude, almost meaningless, except as a measure of diligence. The Journal Impact Factor (JIF), compiled by Thomson Reuters starting in 1964, was originally intended to guide librarians seeking the most-read periodicals, not to be a measure of their value. But citation density was quickly confused with quality, and the result put a premium on journals that were often referred to. Libraries knew they had to have those, and were willing to pay the going rate.

Quantifying citations allowed evaluators to skip reading colleagues' works by delivering a number that supposedly indicated their influence. Although it was an improvement on just counting articles, totting up citations still raised problems.[100] The system could be gamed. Institutions stuffed with clever people in fierce pursuit of choice morsels can expect to be hotbeds of manipulation.[101]

Universities themselves fiddle the metrics by which they are ranked; why not their faculty? Once a particular indicator has been announced as the measure of quality, it quickly becomes the goal all strive for. If citation intensity is the gold standard, then everyone will seek to maximize citations, all else be damned.

Editors encourage authors to submit, thus inflating their journal's rejection rate and prestige, much as universities bask in the glow of the many applicants they spurn.[102] Some journals stoop to heavily suggesting that authors cite other articles published in their venue, thus inflating their impact factor.[103] Self-citation, automated citation, log-rolling mutual citation, review articles that themselves are oft-cited as they free-ride on others' work—all are means of artificially inflating references to an author's work. Some fields practice self-citation more prolifically than others—engineering at twice the rate of medicine and the life sciences.[104]

Didier Raoult, an off-piste French microbiologist notorious for promoting hydroxychloroquine as a remedy for Covid, touts an h-index inflated by 25% through reference to his own work.[105] But that is just bush-league self-promotion. At least 250 scientists have received over 50% of their citations either from themselves or coauthors. One researcher can thank this method for 94% of his citations: Sundarapandian Vaidyanathan, a computer scientist at the Vel Tech R&D Institute of Technology in Chennai.[106] Why do they bother? Whether h-index or journal impact factor, the algorithms have long since been tuned to filter out self-citation.

Citation intensity measures whether a work has been referenced elsewhere. Why it is cited is ignored—whether as log-rolling by others, whether in review works surveying the field without adding to it, or whether to refute its deficient ideas. A much-cited work has not necessarily had a positive or profound influence. Citation frequency increases with the number of coauthors, each marshaling a cluster of colleagues, coworkers, friends, and other potential citers.[107] The more works an article cites, the more likely it is to be referenced in return by those who now owe it a favor in academia's gift-exchange economy. Some disciplines, such as medicine, often begin an article with a comprehensive overview of the field, citing the literature in a way foreign to the humanities and social sciences.[108]

And, as noted, citation density says less about the quality of work than the publicity it has generated, possibly its notoriety. Citation intensity measures attention more than quality. A mediocre article on a hot topic will be more cited than an excellent one on a theme of less pulsating interest.[109] Obscurity is punished, pandering rewarded. Attention and quality are not the same.

Some quantitative measures, like impact factors, pertain to journals, not their articles. Treating them as a proxy for the quality of articles merely reproduces on a smaller scale the same problem of the parasol of prestige that a renowned press unfolds over even its mediocre volumes.[110] And in any case, some metrics vary so widely across fields as to be meaningless except within them. Impact factors for top-rated mathematics journals are one-tenth of cell biology.[111] The citation rate is eight times as high in medicine as in law or the humanities.[112]

Alternative metrics (altmetrics) try to sidestep such problems by aiming beyond the journal to quantify article-level measures, using factors other than citations.[113] They track interest in the work and its qualities, refusing to accept the publication outlet as a meaningful proxy. Some measure immediate usage, as downloads or page views, rather than waiting for eventual citations.[114] Others analyze social media and venues other than journals to gauge the broader impact of abstruse research.[115]

Besides altmetrics, the antidote—so far very partial—has been to encourage evaluators to ignore shorthand indicators of prestige, seeking instead to determine quality independently. The Bethesda Statement insisted that a work's intrinsic merit was what counted, not where it appeared.[116] The San Francisco Declaration on Research

Assessment (DORA) from 2012 is the most prominent attempt to follow this lead. It commits signatory institutions to assess the quality of research on its own merits, not those of its venue.[117] Some universities, such as Utrecht, have followed this lead, explicitly doing away with impact factors in hiring and promotion.[118] Most major Western universities no longer consider numerical impact factors when hiring. Instead, they ask candidates to submit their five best articles, which are then read and evaluated.

But the problem extends beyond open access to a larger question thrown up as dissemination democratizes: How can we ensure that the best work in a swelling wave of content is recognized independently of the conventional signals of prestige? Some fields' hyper-publication habits impede hopes of qualitatively evaluating output. Specialization forces researchers who feel unqualified pronouncing outside their turf to rely on others' opinions, ideally quantified and easily digestible. Bias and prejudice can easily sneak back in. The qualitative assessments urged by DORA are, in principle, no different from the peer reviews performed for journals and publishers.[119] Why should they be better in one instance than another?

The university world's thralldom to the prestige hierarchy of the established publishing venues impedes open access. New presses and periodicals face an uphill battle for recognition. Even new conventional outlets would confront similar issues. Tackling the prestige dilemma is not specific to open access, but it has become especially acute as digitality promises to change the nature of dissemination.

Faux Open Access

The interface between analog and digital media is not the only source of friction. By itself, open access has also created problems. The gold version has partly misaligned the incentives. It flips the inherited business model on its ear. Libraries had been the main customers. Now authors are. Content suppliers and customers are identical in the new model—authors, supported by their funding agencies.

In the developed world, authors are largely price-insensitive—at least the scientists. Earlier, librarians paid for subscriptions to journals and bought books whose quality they judged and whose usefulness they could monitor by tracking circulation. They were part of overall quality control. With gold open access, that watchful eye has now clouded. Authors are willing to ask funders to pay the going rate for the most prestigious journals, and, as individual buyers, they have little collective bargaining power.[120]

True, funding agencies may come to play a moderating role similar to the one librarians once had. They have little interest in a journal's reputation so long as the work is read. Their concerns may set an upper limit to exorbitant charges. If so, that effect has yet to kick in.[121] But if it does, funders will be in a better position to negotiate than libraries since there are fewer of them. On the other hand, the cost of journals is a much smaller percentage of funders' budgets (1% or 2%) than libraries' (20%), which may inure them to high charges.[122]

Either way, having authors as the primary customers for gold content, no longer readers and libraries, may tempt publishers to lower quality and to maximize output. Authors and publishers are united in a vicious collusive circle.[123] Authors are keen to force-feed the dissemination channels, and the presses happy to oblige if paid. The system has no inherent brakes or controls other than scholarly shame, perhaps. At its worst, it generates intellectual moral hazard, with publishers printing all the content they can charge for while authors aim to place all they churn out.

What are sometimes called predatory journals reveal this spiraling logic at its most expansionary. Predatory journals are low-prestige gold periodicals. At their worst, they print anything sent to them, sometimes obvious rubbish submitted by muckrakers seeking to expose the scam. A paper consisting only of the repeated phrase "Take me off your fucking mailing list" was apparently accepted by the *International Journal of Advanced Computer Technology* in 2014, but it was not published when the authors failed to pay the charge.[124] *MAD* magazine used to mock the *New York Times'* venerable slogan with a variant, "All the News that Fits." In the digital age, everything fits. Yet another article generates only few additional costs even as a new publication charge is rung up. Some online journals are therefore open-ended size-wise. Format obesity ensues, and gargantuan journals waddle the digital landscape. Yet, just because big does not mean they are bad.

Lapses in quality control are not new, nor are they created by digitality or open access. Indeed, whether a slip has occurred is sometimes unclear. Parody would be impossible without texts pretending to be straightforward while actually blustering. Jonathan Swift's anonymous *A Modest Proposal* (1729), suggesting the sale of poor Irish children as food for rich Englishmen, was recognizably ironic. But Daniel Defoe got into trouble in 1702 for his *The Shortest Way with the Dissenters*, which proposed their execution or exile. Too subtle, his satirical intent was taken straight by readers, and he landed in the stocks for sedition.[125]

Angry Penguins was an Australian modernist literary periodical. In 1944 it eagerly published a nonsensical pastiche of words submitted as poems by a nonexistent author, Ern Malley, and it was eventually exposed to general ridicule.[126] In 1996, Alan Sokal, a physics professor, managed to place a rubbish submission, arguing the socially constructed quality of nature's fundamental laws, in *Social Text*, a postmodern cultural studies journal.[127] In fields like computer science, generating plausible nonsense has been automated.[128] Thanks to such labor-saving inventions, Ike Antkare, a nonexistent figment of a devilish imagination, was the most-cited computer scientist in Google Scholar around 2010 and the 21st highest cited in any field.[129] Whatever the reputational consequences of publishing nonsense, in the analog era, each worthless work occupied space that could have been better used. But gold access has lit the fires of self-interest under publishers to cash in and put out.

Gold access tempts to mischief. Predatory publishers solicit submissions, especially from graduate students, junior faculty, and scholars from poorer institutions and nations who may not know better. They accept them with little fuss and even less peer review or other editorial interference, cash in the charges, and slap up the results on a website. While at it, they run entire stables of journals. Academic predation has become big business. OMICS, one of the worst offenders—incorporated in Nevada but operating out of Hyderabad—"publishes" some 700 journals. Of the 69,000 manuscripts submitted to them between 2011 and 2017, only about half were peer-reviewed. The journals generated their own impact scores, and many of their allegedly associated experts had never even been asked if they wanted to participate. In 2019, the publisher was fined over $50 million in the US for deceptive practices.[130]

Yet, what distinguishes a truly predatory journal, intent on deceit, from a run-of-the-mill journal positioned low on the academic food chain? Not everyone can be *Nature* or *Science* or the *Proceedings of the Royal Society*. Insofar as predatory journals are remiss in imposing much quality control, they are more like digital repositories than conventional journals. That is not in itself a sin, though pretending to arrange and charging for nonexistent peer review is indisputably fraudulent. In 2008, Jeffrey Beall began compiling a list of journals classified as predatory. To recognize these supposedly rotten apples, he identified suspicious features: lacking an editorial board or sharing one with other journals from the same publisher, being issued by houses that ran large stables of similar journals, lacking procedures for archiving, skimping on peer review, and accepting many submissions, sometimes all.[131]

In 2017, Beall's List included almost 1,300 journals.[132] Some studies have identified 8,000 such periodicals, others 10,000.[133] By comparison, Thomson Reuters's Web of Science, among the most prestigious listings, indexed 9,300 journals in 2018.[134] How do such lists distinguish the predatory from the merely mediocre? Toward the bottom of the pile, even otherwise well-intentioned journals may assume some of Beall's characteristics. Yet, many supposedly predatory periodicals function well and, in any case, indistinguishably from their more conventional peers. One survey of Third World scholars who had published in supposedly predatory periodicals revealed that less than one-fifth found the journals' standards of peer review poor or nonexistent, and 70% had gotten good feedback. Most of the scholars were attracted by the journals' speed of delivery and low cost.[135]

How can predatory journals publish so much? One study in 2014 identified 8,000 such journals publishing some 420,000 articles. By comparison, Web of Science periodicals issued 1.85 million articles in 2018.[136] In the developed world, predatory publishers are often seen as motivated by ill will and greed, while their authors fall for the ruse out of ignorance. "The fact that so many of these 'journals' exist and publish so many articles is a testament to either the startling credulity or the distressing dishonesty of scholars and scientists the world over—or, perhaps, both," remarks one observer.[137] However comforting it is to find a villain, such conclusions gloss over how the problem is amplified, if not created, by First World publishers, both conventional and open access.

Predatory journals respond to broader problems. Some spring from difficulties Global South scholars face in accessing First World journals. These authors publish more often in open-access periodicals than their developed-world peers.[138] And they often contribute to mega-journals, with their less-burdensome review process and cheaper fees. Chinese scholars are coauthors in up to 40% of articles in *Medicine*, *AIP Advances*, and *Scientific Reports*. Mainland and Taiwanese authors proliferated in *Medicine* (from 1% to 40%) once it had transitioned to mega-journal status. In *Scientific Reports*,

Chinese scholars were responsible for 18 articles in 2011, 4,159 in 2015.[139]

While the brand-name open journals have eliminated barriers for readers, they have created new ones for authors. Publishing charges are perhaps not an obstacle at prominent Western universities, but they are a new hurdle for others. Global South authors publish more in gold journals than their North colleagues, happily paying at least some charges.[140] Indeed, some open journals waive or discount charges for developing nations, but discounts are often forfeited if any coauthors are from more prosperous places.[141] And even countries such as Nigeria and India do not qualify. Surveys reveal that more than half of authors in the Global South still end up paying publishing charges.[142] That is comparable to the 50% of authors globally who publish in open-access journals and pay fees.[143] So, how effective are waivers?

Publishing charges bite differently around the world. A typical Western fee of $3,000 is 50% more than an average annual income in Pakistan, a bit lower than one in Vietnam.[144] Even if academics are better paid, such charges are unaffordable. Given salary levels in Africa, a publication charge can be several months' wages.[145] One survey found that 11% of fees were paid out of pocket by rich-world scholars, but almost four times as many in developing nations.[146] Not for nothing is the average publishing charge in the low three figures for predatory journals. That is a small fraction of the low to mid four figures charged by conventional gold periodicals.[147]

Other factors driving scholars in the Global South toward predatory journals are homegrown. In certain nations, such as Iran, Nigeria, and sometimes China, universities insist that scholars have published work in order to receive advanced degrees. Articles in nonlocal journals also carry greater weight in hiring and promotion.[148] In China, some conventional subscription journals levy fees, which lessens the disincentive to publish in periodicals with author's charges.[149] Not to mention—a problem everywhere—how long it takes leading journals to vet and publish. That adds to the attraction of the quick turnaround promised by low-barrier predatory competitors.[150]

Predatory journals cater mainly to developing-nation scientists, daunted by the hurdles to established outlets.[151] Their authors are primarily doctors and engineers from India, the rest of Asia, and Africa. With its well-functioning infrastructure of open journals, South America needs predatory journals less and is underrepresented. The discrepancy is revealed by the per capita ratio of articles published in predatory journals compared to conventional serials indexed in the Web of Science. While it is only 6% in the US, it rises to 80% for Iran, 277% for India, and a staggering 1,580% for Nigeria.[152]

Predatory periodicals are, in effect, the poor world's open-access journals. They are to academia what junk bonds were to investment: despised, scorned, and reviled, yet a vehicle for democratization in their fields. The First World's open journals may have allowed free reading, but not writing. Predatory journals at least cut the price of admission for authors. They are to geographic diversity what self-published books are to gender parity. Two-thirds of top-ranked self-published books are by women, but only 40% of conventional books.[153]

6

The Digital Disseminators

Ephemeralization, a law of human progress formulated by Buckminster Fuller, is the progressive tendency to do more with less. Satellites transmitting phone calls, replacing tons of seabed copper wire, was an example. Digitization would have delighted Fuller. We have downloads, not bookstores. Rather than the libraries' vast cathedrals, information now hangs ethereally in the cloud. The cloud is not as ephemeral as its name suggests—quite the contrary. The countless server farms that form its leaden feet swallow electricity voraciously, although they are becoming more abstemious.[1] Yet, the cloud's ubiquity, expandability, and speed are little short of miraculous.

Distributed globally, cloud storage will not go up in flames simultaneously, but it depends wholly on maintaining the voltage. We must fear solar flares or other electromagnetic disasters wiping our cultural memory. And we should ponder how to transmit into the deep future. It is sobering to consider how briefly Homo sapiens have been able to communicate culture so far. Clay tokens used for accounting purposes have been dated to 8000 BCE.[2] Beyond that, artifacts from the Blombos Cave contain markings that appear symbolic, going back 70,000 to 100,000 years.[3] But that is it.

How can we pass what we know forward over the edge of our current event horizon? Digitality is still too fiddly and dependent on electricity to be reliable, especially to bridge possible disasters. "Digital documents last forever," in Rothenberg's dictum, "or five years, whichever comes first."[4] Our most prescient catastrophists are therefore sensibly wedded to analog technologies. The Arch Mission, for example, aims to print the core of human knowledge microscopically on durable media, placed strategically around the globe and possibly extra-planetarily.[5] To read it, resurgent post-catastrophe humans would need to have advanced technologically no further than the seventeenth-century optics of Huygens. More mundanely, though PDFs may not have vellum's durability, they are versatile and enjoy a hybrid status, being present in both digital and analog worlds, at home on paper and screen.[6]

What does digitality mean for the three main avenues of dissemination: bookstores, libraries, and publishers? Digitality fulfills the promise latent in the first printing presses of making authors their own disseminators. Will that undermine the intermediaries? Acting as a global bulletin board, where all are welcome to post, the internet threatens to swallow up the once distinct acts of publishing, disseminating, and storing.

Bookstores

Bookstores in their current incarnation as purveyors of physical tomes will likely continue to disappear. Some works will remain in tangible form. The book as an aesthetic object is no more apt to disappear than lithography was to end oil painting. A durable market for the bibliographic craft is revealed by the success of Taschen books. Its output is less books than works of art with pages. And its aesthetic *Gesamtgestalt* continues back up the distribution chain to its stores, each an architectural temple of nacre, dispensing pearls.

Whether conventional books are bought in physical locations or online depends on consumer preference. As their dissemination function diminishes, bookstores will increasingly become coffee shops with more elaborate inventory. The survival of independent bookstores, exemplified by the franchising of Shakespeare & Co., suggests a fate akin to coffee shops, with small one-off outlets in city centers coexisting with serviceable chains everywhere. Despite gnashing of teeth, the number of independent bookstores in the US grew from 1,600 in 2009 to 2,500 in 2019.[7] The Covid pandemic will not likely have increased that number. And having peaked in 2007, sales in bookstores slumped by 40% to 2019.[8]

Used bookstores as physical retail destinations are probably doomed, victims of the internet's ability to match long-tail consumers with wildly various and dispersed products. Few used bookstores have bothered to offer consumers temptations other than browsing. Browsing in a conventional bookstore is one thing. Customers select among the latest products, some recently reviewed in newspapers, mentioned online, or even TV. Serendipity may bring them into contact with books they had not heard of. The experience of a used bookstore is quite different. They are graveyards of the human spirit. Only a tiny fraction of what is published each year remains of interest a short while later. Knowing the labor invested in even incidental works, all authors turn glum when entering a used bookstore to survey the endless ranks of books-no-longer-read.

Before the internet, the thrill of the hunt remained. Customers rarely located a specific volume, but intellectual omnivores stood at least a chance of devouring some prey. Browsing the shelves, they stumbled across an occasional nugget at a bargain price. But today, with inventory digitized, the long tail is searchable. We know instantly where to find the work we seek. Since the market is transparent to both sellers and buyers, arbitrage is seldom possible. Prices cluster around what the market will bear, and bargains are rare. Scholars may derive some solace from knowing that the cheapest used books are the flash-in-the-pan bestsellers of a few years ago. They often cost less than to ship them, just a few cents. In contrast, scholarly tomes, published in modest print runs, are harder to find but often hold their value. Indeed, the most expensive used books tend to be still-read but out-of-print university press monographs— solid bricks in the wall of scholarship.

Thanks to digitality, the secondhand book business has consolidated. Mega-operations, such as Better World Books, with inventory deep into seven figures, outcompete mom-and-pop operations. Such secondhand bookstores on steroids have, in effect, become adjuncts to libraries as they deaccession little-used holdings. Often, they rival even the largest collections in size.

Libraries

Digitality has undermined libraries, too. Like bookstores, libraries have no rights to content to exploit and defend. They are better positioned in the dissemination process than bookstores only because they also house our collective patrimony even after publishers have lost track of their backlist or vanished altogether. Only thanks to the first-sale principle do libraries exist at all—along with used bookstores, video rental institutions in their day, musical score services, and the like. Once the physical object has been sold, rights-holders can forbid its copying but cannot prevent lending or renting. But that is all libraries may do—lend, store, and preserve works that otherwise, outside the public domain, belong to others.

Some countries, starting with Denmark in 1946, introduced public lending rights. These mediate relations between rights-holders and libraries, taking the edge off sales forgone by paying authors fees proportional to how often their works are lent. No such compensation has been attempted for loss of sales through secondhand bookstores. Since books almost invariably depreciate on the secondary market, losses here are less than from pirated works. For successful artworks, in contrast, subsequent prices sometimes dwarf initial sales, but artists do not profit from their burgeoning reputations. That unfairness helped persuade many nations—eventually the EU—to introduce a *droit de suite,* or resale right, that gives artists a cut of profits on the secondary market.[9]

Digital media change this landscape. For in-copyright trade print books, libraries will continue to play much their current role. There is no moral argument why such works should be opened up, and readers will have to negotiate access via libraries if they do not buy copies. Once books lose their commercial value, publishers may be willing to allow controlled digital lending, as discussed in Chapter 7, permitting patrons anywhere to read works on screen.

For e-books, however, the terrain has changed. The first-sale principle does not apply to digital media. They remain the property of publishers or intermediary vendors (such as OverDrive, the largest) even as they are licensed for reading in libraries. Rather than selling them, publishers lease their e-books to libraries for a specified time and/or a limited number of uses. The prices for e-books are generally higher than for the paper versions, and they vary depending on the kind of access allowed—one, many, or unlimited readers for few, many, or unrestricted uses, either time-limited or perpetual. While publishers cannot prevent libraries from buying their paper books at the same price as other customers, they can set library prices for e-books. Publishers have feared that leasing e-books to libraries would cannibalize print sales. Some, such as Macmillan, therefore embargoed new e-titles to exploit the retail market before allowing library lends.[10]

The situation is especially dire in the UK. Libraries there may lend only e-books licensed by their publishers, not scanned versions of paper books.[11] Worse, research libraries may not buy retail e-books, only versions specially licensed for university use.[12] Publishers can thus charge more for e-editions of works also published on paper—as much as ten times.[13] They sometimes force libraries to buy an entire list of their e-books, rather than selecting them individually.[14] To counter such issues, Maryland and New York have recently attempted to pass laws requiring publishers to offer e-books to libraries on similar terms as for retail customers.[15] In return, the Association of American Publishers has sued to defend their right to charge what they please.[16] Congress has taken an interest in the problem.[17] A Dutch case has insisted on treating library acquisition of books equally, regardless of the precise format.[18]

On the other hand, variable licensing gives libraries some control over costs, unlike the one-book-forever pricing of physical volumes. An Australian study found the cost of lends for e-book licenses premised on an ongoing one-copy-one-user model was often cheaper than for physical copies. In contrast, the price per lend of metered use (X number of lends before the license had to be renewed) depended on the work's popularity and on assumptions of how many lends physical copies can withstand before needing replacement. But, where licenses were time-limited, the library no longer had the work in its collection once they expired.[19] That, of course, was not true with physical copies unless they were deaccessioned.

With time-limited licenses, libraries are cut out of curating their collections. True, flexible licensing permits libraries to tailor their offerings to demand: a few permanent copies of enduring classics, many cheaper time-limited ones of flash-in-the-pan bestsellers.[20] While this may make sense for neighborhood public libraries, it wreaks havoc on major research collections and their preservation function. Penguin Random House claims that time-limited licenses at lower prices are what librarians want, given the short shelf life of many new works, especially fiction. For academic libraries, it offers perpetual e-books at a much higher cost.[21] In British university collections, the price of the most requested e-books on an unlimited-use license is two and a half times that of a one-user-at-a-time plan.[22]

Digital books are fiddly. Unlike robust cellulose products—foldable, droppable, shippable—e-content is finicky, corruptible, and subject to mishaps, and it works only on specific devices and platforms. E-books are not housed in libraries and are read with proprietary apps and software that belong to others. The curatorial, lending, preservation, and storage functions that libraries once served are leached away. Library budgets increasingly go not to buying curated content, then lending and preserving it, but to paying publishers for use of collections assembled and stored elsewhere. Access, not control, is the new mantra.[23] If things continue in this direction, libraries may end up serving only as the conduit for payments from funding agencies to e-book publishers.[24]

Digitality will change libraries. As content migrates to the cloud, it seems quaint to think it must be collected physically, sitting in a particular place awaiting readers. Eventually, Google Books and similar projects will have digitized the public-domain and grey literature. Increasingly, the most recent, in-copyright scholarly literature will be published via open access of one stripe or another. What role, then, will libraries play? For content unlikely to become open—recent in-copyright fiction and trade nonfiction—both bookstores and libraries will continue to be disseminators. Small public libraries will therefore least notice this shift. Their patrons will continue to demand books that are still sold and lent.

Large research collections, in contrast, will become almost redundant. Their vast precopyright holdings are rapidly being digitized, and their grey works will eventually follow suit. Their current scholarly work will increasingly be born digital and open, whether green or gold.

Google Books has already scanned 25 million books. As a collection, that brings it abreast of the British Library, with about the same number. Only the Library of Congress, with its 39 million books, is still bigger. In 2013, five years after its founding, the HathiTrust, which holds the Google Books, had more works on marine biology than the Library of Congress and 60% more Russian periodicals than its nearest competitor, the University of Chicago library.[25] Inventory, as logistics experts put it, is being consolidated. Digitality ends the need for physical libraries to store and lend content. We used to go to the village well to draw water, now we open the tap at home. So, too, will the digital flows be managed.

Nor will we need the research libraries' duplication of works. The dirty little secret of analog libraries is that they broadly replicate each other, at least within nations and cultures. They were, after all, created to solve a topographical problem by depositing content at reasonable distances. From the librarian's vantage, a simpler solution would have been one central, national library in each country. In smaller nations, that is broadly the outcome. When they organize into consortia to pool resources and expand holdings, libraries duplicate even more.[26]

Having said that, it is also true that individual volumes are often rare. Three-quarters of the titles of the Big Ten Academic Alliance's collections are held by three or fewer of its libraries.[27] In other words, on average, every one of these ten institutions has a core collection duplicated in the others that is 25% of total holdings. In turn, each library then holds another 25% of the entire collection, shared with only a few of its peer institutions, and would have to borrow a volume from the other half of total holdings via interlibrary loan. Similarly, 88% of the Research Libraries UK's collection is held by fewer than five of its constituent partners.[28] Sixty percent of the aggregate Google 5 (Harvard, Michigan, Stanford, Oxford, and the New York Public Library) library collection is held by only one institution. Among any two of these libraries, common holdings account for only 20% of their collections.[29]

Major research collections thus consist of a substantial common core, trailing thick and very long tails of rare works. Fully a quarter of holdings (in the case of the Big Ten) are duplicates everywhere, with a researcher pursuing a particular volume outside that core having a 30% chance of finding it in their home institution. Interlibrary loans make up less than 5% of all circulation in major research institutions (1.7% among all libraries).[30] That indicates the relative rarity of scholars reaching beyond the core duplicative collection at their home institutions (though it could, in theory, reveal a lot of travel by scholars to other institutions, sidestepping interlibrary loan). Put differently, 95% of scholarly work is accomplished within the duplicative core collection of the local research library.

Some 10% of all books at major US research libraries account for 90% of all circulation (this figure does not measure books consulted but not checked out).[31] As research libraries come online, the underconsulted bulk of their physical holdings will become superfluous. The core collection may remain present, absorbing scholars' energies. Meanwhile, the marginal interlibrary loan aspect of their function can readily be turned over to common digital storage of little-used books. Increasingly, interlibrary loan materials are digitized and sent over the internet rather than entrusted to the tender mercies of the postal system. Once the long tail has been digitized, even that will no longer be necessary.

Major research libraries in North America hold almost a billion physical volumes, but only 59 million distinct titles.[32] That is an average duplication ratio of 17:1. In 2011, WorldCat libraries across the globe had 1.238 billion books, but 128 million separate print book publications, a duplication ratio broadly the same.[33] A single institution approximately twice the Library of Congress's size could thus hold a single copy of every book in the US. A global library would have to be at least triple that.

Conversely, the extension of the long tail in major research collections, the commonness of rarity, suggests two other implications for digitality. The corncrake is considered an exotic and endangered species in Britain, with enthusiastic birders lying in wait on its remaining redoubts, the Western Isles. In Russia and Kazakhstan,

in contrast, it is common. Seen globally and sought in its customary habitat, the corncrake is neither rare nor endangered. So, too, a
book that is rare in the collections of one city, region, or nation may
not be when the world is surveyed. Approached broadly, there may
be no reason to fuss over an allegedly rare volume.[34]

Only 34% of the University of Chicago's books are also in Ohio
State's library. But three-quarters of them are duplicated across the
broader CIC library consortium in the upper Midwest.[35] Similarly,
88% of books in the UK's research libraries are held by fewer than
five libraries, but across the whole WorldCat system, that drops to
56%.[36] Once works are digitized, available anywhere, and geography's artificial scarcity has been eliminated, rarity will emerge only
in its proper worldwide context. Much that today appears exotic
will prove to be common. And in any case, it will not matter, since
even the rarest tomes will be readable anywhere.

Second, using the many works held in only a few collections
involves much friction. Among the Google 5 libraries, almost 40%
of works are owned by one institution only.[37] A third of the holdings of libraries in the BosWash corridor can be found in no other
US region.[38] Even if the long-tail books are rarely in demand, once
sought, they are unlikely to be nearby. To be useful, they must then
be shipped via interlibrary loan, or the patron must travel to them.
Digitization costs money, of course, but only once. Indeed, as libraries have discovered, the expense of digitizing a book is usually less
than sending it off for a singular use via interlibrary loan. Once
the long tail has been digitized, the price of using any particular
volume in the global holdings approaches zero, and the cost distinction between core and peripheral collections vanishes. If works
are digitized as they are requested via interlibrary loan, current
budgets—now wasted on postage and packing—will, over time, pay
for digitizing the long tail of holdings.

Once the 60 million distinct titles in the major North American libraries have been digitized and put online, existing scholarly

content will have been made accessible. Conventional libraries have been needed less for the diversity of their holdings than for their geographical dispersion. When geography and distance have been eliminated, what is left? Some items that each collection alone might possess will remain, motivating the occasional visit. But in that sense, libraries will have become like archives. And ultimately, the same fate awaits archives as will overtake libraries—their content in the cloud, their earthly purpose unclear.

The emergence of collective collections testifies to the forces behind such changes. Collective catalogs have long been assembled, allowing single searches among multiple holdings—WorldCat, the British Union Catalog, UC's Melvyl catalog. Institutions have long been fusing and coordinating their physical collections—the University of California's Northern and Southern Regional Library Facilities, those of the Five College Consortium in western Massachusetts, or the UK Research Reserve. Large collections are amalgamating their long tails, assembling least-used items in joint storage and deaccessioning duplicates. ReCAP (Research Collections Access and Preservation consortium) unites the Columbia, New York Public, Princeton, and Harvard libraries. Why not do this nationally or globally? Once digitized, the physical holdings will be merely for backup. HathiTrust's collection of Google Books and other digitization efforts are far down this road. By 2011, HathiTrust held in digital form about one-third of the books physically present in the Association of Research Libraries' collections.[39]

Libraries will continue to play roles. But they will be less needed for what was once their primary activity: lending or reading in situ. Publishers have taken over many of the functions once theirs. Digital publishing leaves libraries no longer owning physical copies of journals and books. Storage is left to the publishers. Big-deal bundles mean that librarians no longer select which content to acquire. Cataloging, metadata management, search services, and the like are also increasingly supplied by publishers.[40]

Libraries may still add value through curation: selecting, organizing, sorting, presenting, contextualizing, and the like. And they
may become social centers, as on university campuses, assuming
some of the functions that once belonged to bookstores. Conversely, today's internet café, with every patron busy at a laptop
and the sound level at what Amtrak mandates in its quiet cars as
a "library-like atmosphere," have taken on functions akin to study
halls. That would make libraries into pedagogical facilities more like
schools or adult education centers than content repositories. We
hear much about libraries' new functions as social centers. Sites of
connection, not collection, says Frances Pinter.[41]

When Stanford redesigned its engineering library in 2010, only
10,000 of its 80,000 books were not consigned to off-site storage.
Half as big as its predecessor, much of the new library's space was
given over to private and collaborative study areas.[42] All well and
good, but deep down, are libraries part of the hospitality industry?
Other than perhaps undergraduates, most patrons go there not to
socialize but for reasons analogous to why Willie Sutton robbed
banks, because that is where the content is. And when it isn't,
they won't.

As publishers become repositories of their own content and
libraries merely funnel revenues in one direction and content in the
other, issues arise. Libraries were once curated collections, differing as they served various clienteles. But increasingly, the content
rests with the publishers, as the libraries cut deals for large swaths of
their lists. Where eager readers once used the library catalog as the
main integrated source of knowledge, multiple search engines now
take researchers to the publishers' individual content silos.

No single library can own everything, but at least librarians
thought about what to acquire using criteria other than what motivates the presses. Thanks to digital balkanization, we now need
bridges to span a fragmented content landscape.[43] Kopernio is one
example. It is now owned by Clarivate, one of the main science

indexers. A browser extension, Kopernio provides access to articles via various routes—primarily through the publisher for content licensed to the user's library, but otherwise to an open version, so long as it is legal.[44]

Research libraries might find useful roles as dependable storage, at least for our predigital cultural patrimony. They could become more akin to symphony orchestras and museums: preservers of a canon. But they are also well-positioned to serve a crucial backup function for digital content. Although magical, digitizing does not solve all problems. To insure against catastrophe, paper copies of predigital works must be kept, and our cultural inheritance would be more secure if we had a printout of born-digital materials. Perhaps not every last e-mail or utility bill, but of content whose loss would be painful.

The Internet Archive stores its books in containers in the Bay Area and elsewhere. Nicholson Baker once crusaded to preserve decommissioned periodicals.[45] As Google Books has shown, kinks remain to be worked out in scanning content before copies become wholly satisfactory. Some readers will still need paper or original versions for reasons of their own. Content remains partly artifact.[46] Sometimes copies reveal their information more easily than originals, other times less so. Physical editions of past publications will not vanish altogether. But these are comparatively minor issues.

More important, someone has to be the long-term archivist. When libraries license e-books, they are stored on the publishers' servers. What happens when they go bankrupt, cease issuing a periodical, or otherwise stop being responsible stewards of their content? The materials in the cloud need to be preserved, kept up to date, made compatible with new software, and otherwise usable in perpetuity. No more than we could rely on conventional publishers to caretake their output forever can we with the digital. Amazon keeps its library of self-published works online for as long as authors wish. But, although ubiquitous, is Amazon forever?

One failure is on the supply side, the disappearance of publishers or their output. The other is on the demand side, the cancellation of subscriptions. What happens if a library ends a subscription to a digital journal? Can its patrons still read back issues, as in the paper days? Or is the new model akin to a lease, where all access is lost once the subscription lapses? The question also applies to publishers' bundled collections of monographs.

Preserving born-digital work becomes complicated the further it moves from a simple electronic mirror-copy of print version. With more bells and whistles, greater embeddedness in the web, connections to other materials, ongoing updating, fluidity of content, and multiple formats, e-books are tricky to preserve. The publishers know and control their software better than any would-be archivist. How likely are others, such as libraries acting as archives, to reproduce the original look and feel? Will they have what it takes to keep proprietary digital content up to date and retroactively compatible? Archiving digital materials is more complicated than the fairly rudimentary storage of the paper era. Yes, the fiddliness of keeping paper copies intact over centuries is often underestimated. Even so, heating, cooling, and moisture control have been the most technically challenging aspects, apart perhaps from the intricacies of compact shelving. Digital storage and preservation require more attention.

For digital content, libraries retain many of the virtues as institutions of storage and preservation that they had for paper. They are numerous, functional, solvent, long-lived, popular, and motivated by public service and the greater good. All these factors make them excellent stewards of our inheritance. The big difference now is that instead of maintaining hundreds of thousands of collections, we will have just a few, with suitably robust and durable backups. Another looming question is whether, as content is made available at the expense of the producers, taxpayers will as readily pay for libraries whose main function no longer is access, but storage and preservation.

Digital backups already exist, at least for some periodicals. Most (68%) diamond open-access journals have no preservation policy.[47] But other institutions help plug such gaps. The felicitously acronymed LOCKSS (Lots Of Copies Keeps Stuff Safe), its variant, CLOCKSS (Controlled LOCKSS), and Portico are examples. These enterprises synchronize digital journals with data from publishers, updating content and migrating it when software changes. As dark archives, they are not normally accessible. But with certain trigger events—if a publisher does not respond to information requests or fails altogether—the backup supplies the data instead.[48]

All well and good, and libraries, including the New York Public Library (NYPL) and Indiana, are involved. But how exhaustive is the digital archives' coverage? In 2007, only some 50 journals participated in LOCKSS, and 30 in Portico.[49] In 2011, Columbia and Cornell's libraries discovered that LOCKSS and Portico preserved only 15% of their e-journals.[50] But a decade is an eternity in the digital world. By 2021, that had mushroomed to almost 15,000 journals for LOCKSS, 26,000 for CLOCKSS, and 35,000 for Portico.[51] Nonetheless, however worthy these institutions, they do not have the heft, likely duration, and reliability of something like the Library of Congress or the NYPL.

So far, we have ignored most of what an institution to preserve our digital patrimony must include. As born-digital content becomes the bulk of human output, protecting it is urgent. Start with the elephant in the room, the internet itself. The Internet Archive's Wayback Machine has been archiving web pages since the 1990s and now contains half a trillion. But even it cannot be omnivorous. Sites can opt out, and it provides only episodic snapshots.

Other agencies also preserve the web, but they are often country-specific in accord with national electronic legal deposit laws, and often bizarrely restricted in terms of who may access, where, and how, all while imposing restrictions that outlive copyright itself.[52] As legal deposit institutions, libraries do not do digital materials justice. Hemmed about with regulatory limits modeled on print-on-paper, they are prevented, for example, from allowing viewers to access content from anywhere other than reading rooms or from having more than one person use material simultaneously. Based on fair use, private organizations, such as the Wayback Machine, have proven more capacious. But, they are also more impermanent than government institutions.[53] More is needed.

Further down the ranks of what must be archived come the predatory journals. In the most flagrant cases, having collected fees, predatory publishers have no interest in incurring further expenses, and minimal concern with durable archiving. Some other entity must shoulder that task, as it must also for well-intentioned journals whose long-term survival is questionable.

The same holds for the vast ocean of self-published books washing in via Amazon and other outlets. (We touch on the quantities shortly.) As with the predatory journals, it is easy to be snobbish and dismiss self-published tomes as rubbish whose loss means little. Granted, the value of some self-published books can be hard to spot. Many are personal testimonies to transformative events, whether religion, war, or encounters with aliens. They often unmask nefarious occult conspiracies. Others deal with topics dear to the author's heart, ranging from manuals on peripheral technologies to histories of localities and their sports teams.[54]

For historians, such ephemeral material often delivers fruitful insights. Speaking from the *Volksmund*, giving voice to the collective id, plodding novels, sentimental poems, pedestrian memoirs, and confessional autobiographies tap directly into rich historical veins. Historians are less interested in those who supposedly transcend their era than in those who exemplify it.

Norbert Elias based his influential idea of the civilizing process, the behavioral self-domestication underpinning much of early modern history, on etiquette manuals housed at the British Museum.[55] *The Other Victorians*, Steven Marcus's classic account of

the far-from-prudish sexual habits of our much-maligned predecessors, took evidence from a treasure trove of pornography, carefully amassed by Alfred Kinsey at his Indiana University institute.[56]
Robert Darnton's studies of pamphlet literature during Old Regime
France were possible thanks to the fortuitous preservation of the
papers of the Société typographique de Neuchâtel in the municipal
library.[57] To the past's nitty-gritty, ephemera are a well-paved route.

Future historians, cultural sociologists, evolutionary psychologists, and literary theorists will have a field day mining the unmediated outpouring of digital self-publication. In the past, when
storage was expensive, selecting what to keep was undertaken at the
time by people steeped in the culture given voice by the material
they were judging. Culturally blinkered by the conventional preju-
dices of their era, the archivists of any given moment are never the
best to know what to save or discard.

In digitality, storage is all but costless. Everything can be saved,
and no selection needs to be made now. That can be left to future
scholars, who will have a more clear-eyed vantage to judge from.
Yes, they will suffer an embarrassment of riches. But they will also
enjoy search and filtering tools unavailable to us. They will be sav-
vier in navigating the data cornucopia dumped in their laps. Much
better to leave decisions of what is important about today to our
descendants.

Already now, with vast and growing research output, complaints
are heard that the average article is uncited, with the implication
that it is also unread.[58] That follows from the power-law distribution of attention—a few hog it, most receive none. Ever since we
have had more content than could be consumed in one lifetime,
that has been true. A small fraction of library holdings makes up
the most circulated works.[59] Pop songs as well as scholarly articles
follow such distributions. It is inherent in how culture is consumed.
We would not have bestsellers without leastsellers. Our increased
storage capacity then multiplies the effects of surfeit. With free and

unlimited storage, everything can be saved. From that, it follows that the average content will never be seen by anyone except its author and a typical bit of information never by anyone at all.[60]

Publishers

Digitality has weakened all disseminators. Publishers, the recording industry, and film studios have been sidestepped—by illegal downloading, but more broadly by the leaching-away of their once-exclusive role as content purveyors. Yet, what looked dire just a few years ago has become a shift in their roles, not the end. With Pirate Bay, Megaupload, Napster, and other pirate sites shuttered, rights-holders have cut deals with new disseminators willing to license and pay royalties—Spotify, Apple Music, Netflix, Amazon Prime, and the like, some of which also produce content themselves.

Corporate rights-holders have tamed the frontier conditions that prevailed two decades ago. Clunky, overpriced physical media (VHS, Betamax, DVDs, CDs) have given way to streaming's seamless cornucopia. Rather than paying $20 for a CD with a couple of listenable tracks or for a movie DVD, customers sign up for a celestial gorge-yourself buffet—unlimited streaming of tens of millions of songs and thousands of films and shows, all for the price of a couple of lattés monthly. Who would have expected bingeing to have become something good? If there is one annoyance in this cornucopia, it is the music streamers' insistence that every chunk of every musical form is a song—whether the latest K-pop ditty or the last movement of Beethoven's Opus 111.

We finally come to the publishers. One might have expected them to suffer like bookstores and libraries. But they are doing better than expected. Indeed, as seen, scientific journals' juicy profits have exacerbated the libraries' affordability problem. Some distinctions are needed, first and foremost between books and journals. We start with books.

For conventional books by established publishers, the industry has flatlined rather than nosediving. In music and film, new competitors (Spotify, Netflix) operating in novel media have eaten the established industries' lunch. For books, in contrast, the publishers have managed to keep control over e- and audiobooks, exploiting the efficiencies of digitality. Overall, their revenues have remained stable, while profits increased.[61] Inveterate complainers, publishers are less badly off than they claim. Having shuttered bookstores and libraries, the Covid pandemic left publishers' mail-order departments and the online sellers an uncontested field.[62] Sales spiked as readers huddled at home, occasionally tiring of television. Educational sales were down, digital up, and print slumped, then rebounded. In Sweden, where no lockdown shut bookstores, Bonnier did so well that it decided to pay back government pandemic assistance.[63] University presses that opened their lists to online reading for free were gratified to discover that this sparked increased printed book sales.[64]

Even though other media have become fiercer competitors for the average eyeball, never have more titles been published. In France, while the number of books sold declined, titles increased from 63,000 to 68,000.[65] Italian titles grew 18% from 2010 to 2017.[66] In the Spanish-reading world, new titles climbed steadily during the millennium's first decade, plateauing thereafter.[67] Even the oft-forecast demise of the academic monograph appears to have been exaggerated. The numbers of US humanities monographs have either slightly declined or slightly increased, depending on whom one asks.[68] Among the four largest British academic presses, the trend was steadily upward for the twenty-first century's first decade.[69]

Scientific publishing has done very well, and that includes above all the academic journals. Among the top ten publishing conglomerates globally, seven are either scientific or educational, only three trade. In 2019, these seven houses' revenues were thrice those of the trade presses in the top ten. Put another way, of the 55 largest publishing conglomerates globally, almost 60% of their revenue came from professional and academic content, with trade books contributing only about 20%.[70]

Taking a step back to encompass the entire publishing universe, new vistas open up. As digitality has unleashed an outpouring of creativity beyond the conventional arenas, the legacy publishers no longer dominate. While the number of traditional books has remained steady, self-published editions—mostly print, but also e-books—have avalanched. These are the kind of works brought out by Amazon (CreateSpace and Kindle Direct, amalgamated in 2018), Smashwords, Author Solutions, Lulu Press, Blurb, and similar ventures.

Though tricky to pin down, the numbers of self-published works are huge. The US publishes slightly more than 300,000 conventional new titles annually, but over four million nontraditional works were issued in 2010. This quieted somewhat after 2010, but the number has remained well over a million annually.[71] Self-published works surpassed conventional output first in 2008.[72] They then more than tripled, from 461,000 in 2013 to 1.6 million in 2018, and that is counting only those issued ISBN numbers.[73] Since one title may have several IBSNs, one for each format, this may overcount new books, but not every work receives an ISBN.[74] In 2018, the US had 1.55 million print self-published books and 130,000 e-books, a total of 1.68 million.[75] CreateSpace was the largest venue, with 1.4 million works in 2018, almost 20 times the next, Smashwords.[76] E-book growth has been similar. In the first five years of digital self-publishing, up to 2015, that sector went from zero to one-third of all American e-book sales.[77]

Yet many such works are not new. Some self-publishing houses specialize in bringing forth reproductions of public-domain works as print on demand.[78] In 2010, BiblioBazaar issued 1.4 million such items. Together with General Books and Kessinger Publishing, they dominated the nontraditional market in 2010 with 2.7 million works.[79] The supposed mystery of why more books from 1850 are available on Amazon than books from 1950 turns on this.[80] Without these cheap and cheerful reprints, a trek to the nearest research library would be the only way to read obscure nineteenth-century works.

Whatever the precise figures, the point is that self-publishing continues to dwarf its conventional peers, with well over triple its output. This describes the US situation. Equivalent outpourings are not found elsewhere, or possibly non-American output is channeled via Amazon regardless of its origin, showing up in the US figures. The disparity is evident in the volume of ISBNs issued. For 2018, this was 3.4 million in the US, but only 186,000 in the UK, 140,000 in Germany, and even fewer elsewhere.[81] Other nations have also been less inundated by the self-publishing tsunami. In Chile recently, no more than 13% of books have been *autoediciones*.[82] In Latin America more generally, 12%.[83]

Under totalitarian censorship, authors wrote privately for their desk drawer—works that might one day be issued after a regime change or perhaps smuggled abroad. The self-publishing wave shows that everyone, not just dissidents in autocracies, has manuscripts squirreled away, awaiting new outlets to channel their creative urges. Who is writing, for whom, about what? Such questions remain largely unexplored. And how will these works be preserved for posterity?

Most self-published original works are fiction. More precisely, they are what the industry calls genre fiction, output that can be classified into easily identifiable categories so that consumers know what to expect—romance, mystery, horror, science fiction, and fantasy. Such genres dominate self-published books. Of Smashwords' works, 87% are fiction. By some measures, erotica alone makes up almost a third of e-books, with no less than one in ten dealing with specialized tastes, such as bestiality or incest, not to mention sex with billionaires and adult diaper eroticism.[84]

And erotica is to be distinguished from romance, another elephant in the room. On Smashwords, 11% is erotica, another 49% romance,[85] while 40% of Kindle books are romance.[86] One segment of the genre market where conventional publishers still hold the upper hand is thrillers—home of well-established brands such as James Patterson, John Grisham, Dan Brown, John Connolly, and their ilk.[87]

Conventional publishers' output, in contrast, is less fiction, either literary or genre. In 2018, fiction accounted for 27% of UK publishers' works, 25% of the French, 19% of the Italian, and 25% in Latin America.[88] Self-publishing's output is even more at odds with the libraries that collect conventional works. In North American major research libraries, of post-1923 holdings, only 8% are fiction.[89] Whether that reflects publishers' output or library collecting habits is unknown. Very few scholarly books are self-published.[90] The lack of peer review casts a pall over ambitious academics' hopes of clawing their way up the hierarchy. But on the other hand, blogs, tweets, and other auto-productions—self-publishing by the day or minute—are becoming ever more common among scholars. So possibly the trend will accelerate and broaden to new media.

7
Alexandria in the Cloud: Promises and Pitfalls of Global Access

How do we bring home the promise of universal access to ever-increasing academic knowledge for everyone? Scholars in the best-funded universities enjoy largely all-encompassing access already. Yet, they are only a tiny fraction of humanity. And even in wealthy universities, when library budgets are cut, digital holdings are, too. Nor can every collection afford every database. The ongoing battle between journals and monographs for the discretionary acquisitions dollar shows that hard-pressed library budgets can no longer solve even the professors' problem.

The pirates have held open a back door to the digital paradise. Sci-Hub, Z-Library, Library Genesis, and other off-piste sites violate copyright laws but deliver a tantalizingly attractive black or grey market product that reveals the possibilities if only we could do it legitimately.[1] Pirates pilfer the publishers' lists, undermining the existing system, but provide no solution. Amid Covid's lockdowns, when even those with library cards to major research collections were shut out, it became evident how crucial digital access is. Online usage of available materials skyrocketed as readers self-isolated.[2] Besides the pirate sites, the only major source of serious reading for average locked-down citizens was the Internet Archive's

National Emergency Library (discussed below). Publishers sued the Internet Archive for its efforts. The digital collections of otherwise exemplary institutions such as the New York Public Library were open for patrons, but for non-New Yorkers the offerings included only public-domain material.

It is technically and physically possible to make all scholarly literature available. As we will see, the money required is already sloshing around in the system. Even copyright's legal obstacles are not insurmountable. How, then, should we proceed?

Transubstantiating the Libraries

Digitality allows content to be consumed anywhere. Works can be seen by readers unable to reach libraries, whether due to distance, disability, or disinclination. As the internet has democratized, becoming a basic necessity akin to running water, so too has the content it can deliver. Yet, from the rights-holder's perspective, digitality has the disadvantage of making content infinitely reproducible. Once xeroxing became common, paper books also could be copied. That was illegal but, more important, expensive and inconvenient. The final product was but a rough approximation of the original. Though widescale xeroxing of classroom materials did become an issue for publishers in the 1970s, on the whole, analog copying was not a major threat. Digitality upended the analog era's stalemate between rights-owners and consumers by making copying frictionless, cheap, and perfect.

We must again distinguish among the various sorts of content at stake. For the public domain, nothing prevents posting everything on the web. Scanning the originals and making the text searchable costs something, but that is it. For grey and orphan works, out of print but still in copyright, the situation is murkier. These are the texts produced between that moment when copyright expires—which advances annually from its current position in the mid-1920s—and the more recent date when in-copyright works lose their commercial value and publishers let them slip out of print.

Digitality has, in the meantime, changed the quality of being out of print. Publishers once printed as many books as they thought would sell. Once sales dropped off, having to warehouse stock encouraged them to remainder leftover volumes at deep discounts. Readers of a certain age will remember the remainder tables at bookstores and the catalogs of such books—offered at cheap prices that signaled the end of their active lives. A bargain for readers, remaindering was a death knell for authors. It marked works' crossing the Styx to the realm where books dwell in twilight, awaiting their final extinction as intellectual property. In some small nations, such as Denmark in the 1970s, remaindering was organized nationally. The country's bookstores were flooded for several weeks annually with a wave of cut-rate reading—much as clothing sales used to be seasonal.

Today, with content digitized and print on demand spitting out one copy as efficiently as a thousand, the costs of maintaining a backlist have plummeted. Books are no longer binarily in or out of print. Still, for most works whose sales fall to zero shortly after publication, the economic effect for publishers remains much the same. Having had their day, they no longer promise a return. Such grey works make up the bulk of research libraries' holdings. Google estimates 70% of published works are grey.[3] A quarter of US and UK library holdings may be orphan works whose rights-holders can no longer be identified.[4] Other estimates put the figure as high as half of still-copyrighted works.[5] In theory, these works remain protected by copyright. In practice, they no longer promise rights-holders much economic value. Disseminating them and allowing derivative uses harms no one, while benefitting all. The problem particularly afflicts twentieth-century works, swallowed up by copyright's black hole.[6]

Of such works, the orphaned are the simplest to address. Since no one is hurt by digitizing and disseminating them, and many gain by being able to read them, why not? Given Europe's traditional insistence on authors' rights, one might have expected the first steps to digitize orphaned works from the Anglo-Saxon world. And indeed, true to form, one European blue-ribbon committee did insist that authors be paid when even their grey works were made accessible online.[7] In comparison, both the US Copyright Office and the Gowers Review in the UK backed removing obstacles for current authors using orphan works for new creations.[8] But, in fact, the EU pipped others to the starting post by passing a narrowly phrased orphan works directive in 2012 that permitted cultural institutions to digitize works whose rights-holders could not be found after diligent search. One proviso ensured that rights-holders who did emerge would be fairly compensated.[9] The UK now also has an orphan works registry.[10]

Bereft of clear legislation in the US to allow digitizing orphan works, workarounds have been needed. Controlled Digital Lending (CDL) has been developed to deal with this. CDL was first broached by Michelle Wu at Georgetown University Law School.[11] Institutionally, it was pioneered by the Internet Archive starting in 2010.

CDL allows patrons anywhere to view digitized works on screen but not to download or copy them. Only works the library owns a physical copy of can be read, and only one patron sees each digitized version at a time—the own-to-loan ratio. Others have to wait their turn. While a work is being used digitally, it is not available for physical loan, preventing any overall increase in use. In effect, CDL seeks to expand conventional library lending into the digital realm.

CDL solves the orphan works problem, but it also enables the use of works that are not orphaned although still in copyright. Like all library lending, CDL rests on the first-sale doctrine that allows owners to lend or resell works.[12] The wrinkle is that, while physical lending merely transports the work to other hands for a limited time, digital lending copies a work originally published on paper, thus format-shifting it. In theory, lending means fewer sales for publishers and bookstores. However, most library patrons probably would not have been buyers. Some may be inspired to acquire what they borrow, spurring sales. In any case, libraries are themselves major purchasers, thus compensating for some of the lost business they inflict.

CDL is not perfect open access. Reading is on-screen only, and works cannot be annotated or otherwise used. Yet, allowing anyone anywhere to read online is a major step. CDL, in effect, combines libraries' circulation and interlibrary loan functions. But it does not expand them, only making them more efficient. Libraries are already entitled to lend physical works to patrons and, through interlibrary loan, to other institutions. With CDL, except that the work is being lent in digital format, nothing has changed.[13]

For such lending to happen, however, involves the primal copyright sin of making a digital copy. Since most grey works have been printed on paper, scanning them enhances their usefulness. In a narrow interpretation, that violates copyright. Yet advocates insist that CDL passes legal muster. Fair use permits, and is intended to facilitate, noncompeting uses not otherwise possible. Format-shifting books does not add more lendable copies or deprive authors of anything they have not already lost to physical library circulation. Combined with the first-sale doctrine, CDL is therefore legally unobjectionable.[14]

Unsurprisingly, publishers have a different view. Amid Covid's first wave in March 2020, boundaries were pushed during lockdowns. HathiTrust member libraries were permitted to open scans of in-copyright books to patrons for on-screen reading.[15] The Internet Archive went further. It launched a National Emergency Library that stayed open until June.[16] Since conventional libraries were closed, the only means of borrowing was digital. The National Emergency Library broke CDL conventions by allowing on-screen reading by more than one patron at a time for books in high demand during lockdown.

That straw overtaxed the camel's back. CDL had been running for a decade without legal objection, but now permitting simultaneous reading sparked a reaction. Very few libraries were competing with publishers for readers during lockdown, and book sales were up during the pandemic. The University of North Carolina Press opened much of its list across various platforms, including the Internet Archive. Rather than tanking, its print sales increased. Nor does it seem that Amazon sales of books suffered during the time they were made available in the National Emergency Library.[17] Nonetheless, this was the moment the publishers decided to strike. In June 2020, a coalition of trade houses sued the Internet Archive for infringement.[18] With the suit ongoing, its effect on CDL remains unclear.

Following in the wind shadow of the Internet Archive, the New York Public Library has begun tailoring a similar approach to suit a large, well-established institution. NYPL combines the vast holdings of one of the world's preeminent research libraries with the street cred and civic spiritedness of the nation's largest public library system. It, too, aims to make out-of-print works available at least on-screen. First, it seeks permission from rights-holders. Only if they cannot be identified does it go ahead nonetheless. And it includes a promise to publishers: works that prove to be popular will be identified, allowing them to bring out new editions. In September 2021, the Boston Library Consortium began something similar, at least for books shared via interlibrary loan.[19] In Europe, CDL was tentatively allowed by the European Court of Justice in 2016, permitting Dutch libraries to lend on a one-view-at-a-time basis any e-book, including self-scanned ones.[20] In the UK, as noted, libraries are expressly forbidden to lend self-scanned works.[21]

As seen with JSTOR, publishers' backlists, once considered largely worthless, have been monetized by digitality. The long tail is valuable, but only the discovery and marketing allowed by digitality can identify which parts. In the early 2000s, e-readers became widespread, allowing easy consumption of digital content—had there been any. To supply this need, upstart publishers produced and marketed new digital editions of books with a continued readership whose print publishers' claims to the e-rights (unforeseen in the original contracts) proved to be shaky. Books with potential, by authors such as Kurt Vonnegut, Agatha Christie, and George Orwell, were reissued in new e-formats.

Yet, beyond such obvious works, publishers have little idea how appealing any of their backlist volumes are. The sales records of used bookstores might help identify which titles still have legs, but no one seems to be putting that data to use. More telling would be library patrons' demands for digital lends of grey works. With goodwill, libraries and publishers could develop a mutually beneficial relationship. Allowing libraries to scan and lend all out-of-print books would be the publishers' chit. Identifying which books still have commercial value and surrendering them back to the publishers for further exploitation would be the libraries' end of the bargain. As of this writing, and the start of the lawsuit against the Internet Archive, the auguries for a mutual understanding benefitting readers are not encouraging.

Though it might have this welcome effect, the point of controlled digital lending was not to help publishers extract chestnuts from the embers of our cultural patrimony. Most books lose their market value soon after publication. Much as a new car's price collapses as it is driven off the lot, books, too, quickly depreciate. Their commercial life is typically exhausted between a year and a half and five from publication. Some 90% become unavailable within just two years.[22] Yet, in the aggregate, their cultural value far transcends the few titles destined to become tomorrow's classics. They are the bulk of our cultural inheritance, of immense importance as evidence of what humans once thought, believed, and took for granted. CDL seeks to sidestep the hammerlock copyright imposes on still-protected out-of-print works, allowing them to be used.

Worth noting is that, if legally accepted, CDL would also allow access to work beyond the scholarly. Not just those works it is morally justified to open because taxpayers underwrite them, but all content would fall under CDL. That would not permit the full usability that open access conventionally demands, but expanding even just on-screen reading to much more content would be a major victory.

The Cost of Levitation

However the disputes over controlled digital lending resolve, let us assume good intentions on both sides and deal with both public-domain and grey content together. Making grey literature and orphan works available on-screen and public-domain content fully downloadable will not be costless. Compared to the value of having at our fingertips the entire corpus of printed human creativity up to, say, 2010, it would still be a small price to pay. But what is the cost?

For that calculation, the number of distinct books and periodicals is needed. The best guess comes from a software engineer at Google Books in 2010. He reckoned that there were 130 million books in the conventional sense and 146 million if we include bound volumes of periodicals and government documents.[23] The uplift for journals (12%) is high compared to an analysis of the UK's research libraries, where books make up 88% of the collection and serials only 5%.[24] A European survey, in turn, analyzing only holdings in libraries there, estimated 77 million book titles.[25]

Based in Ohio, WorldCat amalgamates the records of some 15,000 libraries in over 100 countries.[26] Although not exhaustive, it is the closest we have to a global library catalog. WorldCat's tally of "distinct print book publications" in 2015 was 180 million for the globe.[27] But what proportion of worldwide book output is collected by its libraries? By one estimate, WorldCat has been collecting the bibliographic records of between 44% and 48% of all books up to 1940.[28] Three-quarters of all books in the Google 5 libraries were published after World War II. Suppose that similar proportions hold for WorldCat's collections (and this also assumes that every book published has been collected by a library somewhere). In that case, 25% of the 180 million books in 2015 will have been published before the 1940s, or 45 million. If these then represent some 46% of total global book production, that means about 70 million books globally stem from the pre-1940s.

For the proportion of more recent books WorldCat registers, the figures become vaguer. For 2000, UNESCO estimated global book production at one million titles, while WorldCat collected 689,000 catalog records that year, or about two-thirds of global output.[29] For the most recent year available, however, global book production has been estimated at 2.2 million.[30] In 2019, WorldCat recorded 2.048 million new titles, in 2020, 1.439 million.[31] The average of these two figures' coverage rates is about 80% of global publication that WorldCat's records account for in recent years. If we conservatively estimate WorldCat's hit rate in the post-1940s era at 75%, then the 135 million post-1940 books in WorldCat scale to a total post-1940 book output up through 2015 of about 170 million. The total number of books that have been produced globally up to 2015, adding pre- and post-1940s books, would thus be ca. 240 million. If 2.2 million books are produced annually, we add another 13 million to get us to the present day, or a total of 253 million in 2021. That is higher than the Google estimate.

How many of these are in the public domain? The share of books in WorldCat published before 1923, a rough measure of out-of-copyright titles, is 18%.[32] To this in the US one would add works published between 1923 and 1964 whose copyrights were not renewed after the normal term. Estimates suggest that as many as three-quarters of these reverted to the public domain.[33] All told, it has been estimated that perhaps 20% of all books are in the public domain, so that would be 50 million of the 253 million, with 203 million still in copyright.[34] Then we need to know how many are out of print but still in copyright. Let us assume that books published more than 10 years ago have largely lost their commercial value and that some 2.2 million books have been published annually in the past decade. Lopping off 22 million from the 203 million that remain in copyright, we arrive at 181 million grey works that are in copyright but out of print or without commercial value.

Assume 181 million as the number of grey works in need of scanning. Add to that the 50 million in the public domain. A good chunk has already been digitized via the HathiTrust, JSTOR, Google Books, and the like. Google alone is said to have scanned 25 million books. So, if we do not duplicate, that leaves 206 million in need of scanning. At an average of 250 pages per book, that is some 51 billion pages. The Internet Archive charges 5¢ per page to scan and run optical character recognition for searchability, thus, a total cost of $2.575 billion.

That leaves scientific articles, of which 50 million existed in 2010.[35] Let us assume that three million have been published annually in the meantime.[36] Let us also assume that articles lose their intellectual and commercial value after five years (peak citations come at year three for scientific publications). To the 50 million, we thus add another 18 million, bringing a grand total of 68 million in 2016.[37] Estimating the average length of scientific articles is tricky. Salami-slicing research into ever more articles may have reduced each unit's size. The use of graphs, panels, and other data items has doubled in the life sciences over the past decade, complicating attempts to measure. The growing number of references has a similar effect. In 2013, the average length of life sciences articles was 10 pages.[38] That yields 680 million pages to be scanned, for a total (at 5¢ per page) of $34 million.

In other words, for slightly more than $2.6 billion, all public-domain and out-of-print or at least out-of-use books and scientific articles could be scanned. How much journalistic content is included here depends on what percentage of WorldCat material is of this ilk.

A report for the EU in 2011 estimated the costs of digitizing Europe's libraries at €19.77 billion, or $27.5 billion at the exchange rate then. Given that this was for digitizing 77 million books, the cost per book was an eye-watering $357, or more than a dollar per page. How these costs were arrived at is unclear from the underlying report. That document inexplicably assumed the total number of pages to be digitized as only 1.92 billion. In fact, it made an arithmetic error, multiplying the number of books by 25 pages each, rather than the 250 it took as an average length. As a result, it reported what would be a truly extravagant per-page digitization cost of between €2.5 and €6.

This total did not count rare or fragile books, of which there were estimated to be 7 million, costing €7 to €11 billion, depending on assumptions, to digitize.[39] Multiplication errors aside, the report used what appears to be a sophisticated and differentiated methodology. Advances in digitization over the past decade will have lowered costs. Also true is that digitization can be done to different standards. Preservation digitization is more painstaking than merely giving reading access. For the bulk of library content, the latter will suffice. Rare and nonstandard-format works require special handling. Yet, the costs per book assumed in this report of between €124 and €170 remain remarkably high. Recall that the Internet Archive budgets 5¢ per page, so $12.50 for a 250-page volume. Reports on the Google Book project have estimated costs at about the same level.[40]

Returning to our estimate of the cost of digitizing the entire global corpus at Internet Archive rates, this is a one-off expense and covers every no-longer commercially viable book and scientific article in the world. By way of comparison, $2.6 billion is about 15% more than the inflation-adjusted cost of constructing the Getty Center in Los Angeles, one-fifth the going rate for a new aircraft carrier, or the price of 10 Boeing 747s. In the grand scheme of things, to get the global library of Alexandria universally available would be a bargain at twice, thrice, or even ten times the cost. For the results, this is a fire sale: the entirety of published human creativity up through the last decade, open to anyone anywhere.

But this price gets us universal access only to content in the public domain and CDL-style admission to that which has lost its commercial value. Since few works exist only on paper any longer, scanning costs will fall away. If we soon solve the problem of opening current content, thus eliminating the issue henceforth, the inexorable advance of the public domain will take about 80 years to resolve the issue of material currently in copyright yet commercially valueless. In the meantime, barring the unlikely event of major copyright reform, the legality of allowing access, even just on-screen for one reader at a time, to in-copyright material hinges on CDL withstanding the suit brought by publishers against the Internet Archive.

Copyright and Property

Property rights are the foundation of capitalist democracy. They make ownership legally defensible, rewarding those whose efforts and ingenuity provide what buyers are keen to acquire. Even the most fervent social democrats recognize that the East Bloc socialisms were undermined above all by communalizing ownership. All owned everything, and no one took responsibility for anything.

"We pretend to work, and they pretend to pay us"—the Soviet joke summed up the logic. Crumbling housing, antiquated technology, moribund factories, and barren collective farms were the outcome. No one old enough to have visited the East Bloc before 1989, remembering its irremediable dreariness, gloom, filth, and decrepitude, can have remained unmoved by market economies' siren song. For all their sins and pressing need for regulation, they allocate resources more efficiently and motivate effort by rewarding it better than central planning ever could. We threaten property rights at our peril. Every nation has the legal means for eminent domain. They can take property—normally real estate—required for communal purposes, where the owner's claims must bow to society's. But such interventions happen rarely, for good cause, and only with caution.

Occasionally, an entire class of property is ended. For moral reasons, something earlier considered property and subject to its owner's will is emancipated. From object, it becomes a subject. Often this occurs without compensation. When the ancient Greek state forbade infanticide, when children were liberated from their fathers' control at a certain age, attaining legal majority, when they were allowed to choose their spouses, when their births were registered, when their parents had to school them—all these reforms chipped away at parents' property rights in their children. They curtailed fathers' absolute control and imposed obligations to meet minimum standards of care. For such loss of property rights in their offspring, parents were not compensated—unless one counts family allowances, public schooling, and other social policies to defray the cost of obligations now made a condition of parenthood.

Much the same holds for husbands' loss of full property rights in wives. At some point, the property a woman brought into marriage no longer automatically belonged to her husband. If women worked, or otherwise earned or were propertied, their income became reserved for them. Eventually, husbands could no longer physically chastise wives, nor did married women owe them obedience and submission. Nor, at long last, could a man treat his wife's sexual services as his to demand.

When slaves were emancipated into legal personhood—often just partial to begin with—compensation varied. In the US, the moral stain was regarded as so absolute that no recompense was offered owners, and the bloodiest war thus far was fought. In Britain, where slaves were owned far from the homeland, compensation for owners was the largest payout by the British state until the banking rescue package of 2008. Owners received £20 million, £2.4 billion in today's money or £150 billion if measured as the 5% of GDP slavery was then. The emancipation of enslaved Americans was the largest expropriation of what then counted as property since the Reformation's taking of Church lands and the French Revolution's of aristocratic real estate. Slaves constituted 40% to 60% of the South's total wealth, while the Revolution's appropriations affected 20% of all French land.[41] Only the expropriations in Eastern Europe under Communism were greater.

Is intellectual property something analogous to the unwarranted ownership of what was once considered legitimate property? An obvious difference is that property in ideas and their expression was created recently, not inherited as an ancient moral blemish from deep antiquity, as with property in humans. In debating intellectual property, each side has felt it commanded the moral high ground, with legitimate arguments, not just hoary convention, as with slavery or women's subjugation.

Slavery was an analogy enlisted on both sides of arguments over intellectual property. In the nineteenth century, reformers who sought to endow creators with stronger rights to their works in the US, akin to those enjoyed by Europeans at home, portrayed authors as slaves. Unprotected by international copyright, authors, like slaves, were deprived of natural rights to property—whether in their bodies or the products of their minds. "An English writer is treated by America," the English magazine *Punch* complained in 1847, "as America treats her Negroes: he is turned into ready money for the benefit of the smart dealer who robs him. . . . America sells the bodies of blacks, and steals the brains of the whites."[42]

Others turned this logic on its head. Both slavery and copyright were artificial limitations on natural freedoms. No more than one human could own another should they have property rights in ideas and their expression. Neither slaves nor works were natural forms of property. They were merely conventional forms of ownership created by human law that, once recognized as immoral, could and should be abolished. Authors were like slaveholders. They unethically subjected what they illegitimately regarded as their property to their wishes rather than freeing it.[43]

The debates over open access echo such positions. Is academic knowledge intellectual property like any other, legitimately owned by its creators? Or is it that part of intellectual property on which conventional ownership has least purchase? The positions span the gamut. At one end, publishers and authors demand perpetual inviolable rights. At the other, reformers call for nationalizing, or at least heavily regulating, scholarly publishing.[44]

Publishing Open Access

Though scientific articles have attracted most attention, scholarly books present their own problems. They fall into at least two categories. Those with commercial potential are often sold to trade houses that treat them like other books. University presses, in turn, are nonprofit and often subsidized by their parent institutions. Their mission has traditionally been to publish scholarly works with only marginal market appeal, purchased mainly by university libraries and a few researchers. Library budgets have financed university press books. To make up for cutbacks, these presses have also established trade divisions, eager to spot works that sell beyond the academy and fatten the bottom line. Occasionally, they strike gold. Thomas Piketty's *Capital in the Twenty-First Century* turned into a nice little earner for Harvard University Press in 2014, selling millions. Harry Frankfurt's *On Bullshit* worked similar magic for Princeton.

Who will pay for scholarly books, if not the research libraries? As budgets suffered under rising subscriptions, monograph purchases declined. The library sales in four figures that university presses relied on in the 1980s have shrunk. In 1980, 2,000 copies of a history monograph might sell, by 2005, only 200.[45] The average scholarly monograph these days sells 60 copies.[46] Who will pay to publish humanities research? Specialized open publishers and the open-access divisions of existing academic presses stand ready to deliver, but their expenses must be met.

For a sense of the cost of making scholarly books accessible, consider what publishers currently bill authors. Among the Anglophone publishers, Palgrave charges $17,500, Brill $12,200, Ubiquity between $5,000 and $12,000, Cambridge $10,000, Bloomsbury £6,500 to £12,000, the University of California Press's Luminos series $15,000, and MIT Press the same. Open Book Publishers, a nonprofit open-access house, charges about $8,000.[47] These are the sums announced on the publishers' websites. Some charge higher fees for works under CC BY, the less restrictive form of licensing that allows competing editions, than for CC BY-NC.[48] Other sources show that the mean book publishing charge in recent years has been somewhat lower than list prices suggest, namely $5,205.[49] Another study indicates that UK publishers average £7,500, or $9,700 at the going rate in 2017.[50] Dutch monographs cost €12,000.[51] Swiss monographs cost 13,800 francs in 2018, or almost $15,000.[52]

To put this in perspective, a recent study of the actual expense of publishing conventional academic monographs by American university presses arrived at per title costs for producing the final finished copy (but not its physical printing) that varied from $15,000 to $130,000.[53] That suggests much higher expenses for open editions, too. Are the open-access presses delusional, cross-subsidized from other sources, or wondrously efficient? The study also revealed that the single biggest cost for academic publishers was staff time. Acquisitions make up the largest share of staff costs, around half, depending on the size of the press. That is unexpected, since university presses primarily sort through manuscripts sent them by eager scholars.

Staff interviewed insisted of course that they were more engaged than that. But one of the activities driving up costs included acquisitions editors "immersing themselves in the fields in which they specialize"—in other words, reading around on company time. Nice work if you can get it, but unclear what value it adds to dissemination. The editorial process is more about weeding out the inappropriate than actively seeking the best—as it has been from the moment peer review began.[54] Even during the Covid pandemic, the rate of manuscript submissions at US university presses ticked over nicely.[55]

By providing a forum for work of a certain sort, editors may influence a field's direction. Journals make that most evident: *Annales* for big-scale history, *Past & Present* in its heyday for early modern social history, *Comparative Studies in Society and History* for historical sociology, and so forth. Even for monographs, such influence is not absent. Presses sometimes specialize. That in itself does not lure authors to enter those fields, though it does funnel existing work to specific houses. Occasionally, an editor may encourage scholars in directions they would not otherwise have taken, shaping a field— William Germano at Routledge helping birth cultural studies in the 1980s and 1990s.[56] But we would not want to go far down this road of confusing medium and message, nor underestimate the more fecund influence of *Doktoreltern* and above all scholarly peers.

The idea of a "commissioning editor" is something of a fiction, compounded since the term is an Anglicism for what in the US is more accurately known as an "acquisitions editor."[57] Sure, editors hang at the bar during big conferences, sweet-talking scholars into giving them a first look at their latest manuscript. But the idea that academic books are meaningfully commissioned seems something of a *Lebenslüge* in the business. Those rare occasions when trade presses pay large enough advances for authors to undertake projects could perhaps be construed as commissioning. With academic books, that never happens.

Add to that the editors' schtick of presenting a balanced list for each season, publishing some books on subject A and others on B, and never too many on any given topic—as though they were florists arranging a bouquet. A publisher's list is a transient assemblage of a smattering of titles in a sales catalog sent to a few thousand addresses twice a year. No one pays attention to its balance except perhaps other editors. Neither authors nor the reading public could care less. If three Lincoln biographies arrive in one season, buyers will not react differently if they are issued by one press or three. Why would they even notice the difference?

Striving for a pointless balance in publishers' lists may not be a major driver of costs, but it exemplifies the current system's crabbed inefficiencies. And it undermines a press's attempts to develop expertise in particular fields, a comparative advantage. But even that is a questionable ambition. Like the journal-level impact factor metrics that quantify a periodical's reputation, then assume it embellishes individual articles, so books published by certain presses renowned in specific fields may gain more attention. Yet the logic of such borrowed prestige is no more convincing for books than for journals.

As the variability of costs for open-access books suggests, the economics of publishing is akin to pharmaceuticals or Hollywood, with room for creative bookkeeping. One of the main drivers of expenses for established academic presses is their sales structure, which accounts for up to 60% of revenues.[58] Given that paper editions at conventional prices are published alongside open versions and that the open edition sometimes spurs sales of physical volumes, why are authors charged anything at all? Or, at least, why are charges not refunded if physical book sales earn their keep? A pilot project sponsoring open monographs followed this logic, with low publishing fees in return for allowing three years of print sales before open release.[59]

Let us take as a conservative estimate $10,000 to issue an open-access volume. How many books are in question? The US produces a bit more than 300,000 distinct titles annually, the world perhaps 2.2 million.[60] Such figures harbor some overlap. Many new UK titles are merely British reprints of US books and, conversely, a smaller slice of US titles. The trade agreements that still mandate separate US and UK editions produce duplication. Elsewhere, this is less likely. Austria and Germany do not require distinct editions of the same works for their respective markets. Overall, such overlap will be smallish and affect trade books more than academic monographs.

How many books are monographs produced as part of their professional work by salaried scholars? The figures are imprecise. They do not exist for the major Anglophone markets where university presses are best developed and most clearly distinguished from trade houses. For other countries where figures are available, they are low (3% in Italy). What is labeled educational publishing covers textbooks for schools and universities, which are not comparable to academic or scientific books. But even educational publishing's percentage of units is small: 4% in the US, 13% in France, 22% in the UK. Its share of publishing revenues is higher: 30% in the US and 41% in the UK, but only 13% in France.[61] In Chile, educational books are about 10% of total output; in Latin America, more generally, 8%.[62] Other sources suggest that, of total US publishing revenue ($26 billion), only 1% is generated by university presses ($260 million).[63]

In 2016, the UK's four largest scholarly publishers, responsible for two-thirds of academic press output, issued 6,650 titles.[64] The Association of University Presses unites 154 houses across 17 countries. Its members publish some 12,000 titles annually, 9,600 from the US in 2020.[65] To be conservative, let us double the US number to account for nonmember presses. If the US publishes 20,000 academic titles annually, then 6% of American books are scholarly. On the other hand, estimates of academic and professional titles published in the UK are half of total book output.[66] That seems unrealistically high and hard to reconcile anecdotally with bookstores bursting with nonscholarly content. Nor does it jive with the 15,000 or so books submitted in the UK for the 2014 research evaluation, covering the previous five years, i.e., some 3,000 works annually.[67] Unless, that is, the vast majority of academic books issued in the UK is authored by scholars employed elsewhere and therefore not submitted for local evaluation. In any case, only some of these figures account for serious nonfiction published by trade houses.

If the US proportion that 6% of total publishing is scholarly holds globally, 132,000 titles each year are academic works. At $10,000 each in publishing fees, the total annual cost would be $200 million in the US and $1.3 billion globally. This is broadly in line with the £19 million annually estimated as necessary to issue in accessible editions those books submitted to the British research evaluations.[68]

Where will we find the money for the world to read these works freely? The bad news is that these are large sums to stump up, especially for the humanities and social sciences. For the hard sciences, publication costs amount to 1% or 2% of total research funding. Somewhere around a third of scientific articles are now open.[69] 28% is a popular figure, but imprecise. Open access also varies markedly among disciplines. At 88%, astronomy and astrophysics have the most available content, while literature is the caboose, with only 14%. And it varies across countries. Up to half of scientific literature is said to be freely available in research-intensive nations, but that is hard to verify.[70] 40% of Swiss articles are open, but only 15% of Russian.[71] This does not take into account illegal content leakage onto the web via private postings or repositories, nor Sci-Hub or other pirate sites.[72]

If freely available scientific articles increase to 100%, we can expect costs perhaps to triple. Whether the expense will go beyond that is unclear. Only a fraction of open articles is published as gold, with the author or funder paying charges. Diamond access is financed from other sources but must show up somewhere in the overall cost of scientific publication even if the exact sums are unknown. Insofar as green access becomes regarded as insufficient and shifts to gold, that will also increase costs. On the other hand, the 1% to 2% figure mentioned above accounts for the total current expense of publishing as a fraction of research costs, not article processing fees. If so, it already captures the total cost of dissemination, and expenses will not increase even as more articles are opened up.

The good news is that existing library budgets are large and that sufficient money exists already in the system to cover costs. It merely needs to be rechanneled. There are almost 120,000 libraries in America. Their combined acquisitions budgets—not operational costs or staffing or the like, but the cost of buying content—is $4.7 billion for the most recent year available.[73] Globally, libraries spent $30 billion on content in 2018.[74] Such sums are not, of course, available for repurposing as a whole. These libraries include local public, school, and college libraries, not just research collections. They must buy nonacademic books, even as some of their holdings will also be works of scholarship that they no longer need to pay for in an open-access future. More narrowly, the 3,800 US research libraries' expenditure for all information sources in 2012 was $2.8 billion: $720 million was for conventional books and $180 million for electronic versions, about one-third of total outlays.[75] In 2018, the global academic library spend for content was $6 billion.[76] If the US ratio of books to content holds worldwide, then the amount available to pay for books in some other way is about $2 billion. Nevertheless, the data from other nations may not be equally encouraging. In the UK, for example, annual research library spending on books is only $16 million, over an order of magnitude smaller than the US figures.[77]

As we have seen, the theoretical cost of publishing all American academic books openly would be $200 million annually, an amount easily handled by the sums available (at least $720 million) in the research library budgets. But that amount must also pay for non-scholarly books and trade nonfiction. Moreover, 60% of holdings in US research libraries are in languages other than English. Assuming that each nation pays charges for its authors, foreign scholarly works become someone else's responsibility. The US library system already disburses sums greater than necessary to flip American academic monograph publishing to open access. With other nations doing their share, the problem would be solved globally.

For periodicals, much the same holds. US libraries spent almost $2 billion on journals in 2012 ($1.9 billion, of which $1.4 billion went for electronic editions).[78] Using rudimentary and low-ball calculations in 2015, the Max Planck Gesellschaft calculated that library budgets already had the funds needed to flip all scientific journals to open access.[79] Journals present different issues than books. They are a larger expense but also more centralized. The monies spent by American libraries alone are likely to free up a larger fraction of total global content than is true for books. Assigning scientific periodicals to their national origins is not as simple as for books, which remain a more local project. The scientific publishing industry is overwhelmingly Anglophone, the language of the trade. Most of the big publishers are European. Only Wiley is based in the US. But publishers work globally, and to saddle a nation like the Netherlands with the access charges for Elsevier makes little sense.

Also at issue with journals is whether the current state of affairs should be locked in as the new normal. The expense figures represent the situation at the end of a period of sustained escalating subscription and then article charges—the serials crisis. Suppose that an overall repurposing of library budgets is to be used for open access rather than to pay subscriptions and buy conventional books. A fair division of the spoils among academic fields and the media they employ is then required. Otherwise, what looks like a simple switching operation from the scientists' vantage means cementing in place an imbalanced status quo for other fields that have been pushed aside.

Whatever the decision on tolerable profit margins for the scientific publishers, flipping to open will likely bring other savings to the overall cost of scholarly dissemination. Physical libraries are inherently expensive. As content is digitized, resident in the cloud, that will cost storage, maintenance, discoverability, upgrading, and the like. But it will save what are likely the larger sums for acquisition, storage, shelving, preservation, and care of paper content. It is the nature of physical books and libraries that they duplicate—that is their purpose. The cost of several hundred copies of each monograph for the 3,700 US research libraries is saved when publishing flips to open. Instead, we spend $10,000 for each book to make it available not only at libraries but everywhere. Other savings accrue, too.

In 2019, North American research collections held almost a billion physical volumes and 59 million distinct titles. Of the billion, some 94% were thus duplicates.[80] Storage costs in open stacks (heating, cooling, reshelving, real estate) are estimated at $4.26 per volume per year.[81] If so, then the mere physical presence of those 941 million duplicates costs libraries over $4 billion annually. That sum is certainly exaggerated, given that other—compact—storage options are cheaper and that operating expenditures for US research libraries in 2012 were only $778 million.[82] Nonetheless, with digitization, the sheer physicality of content will no longer weigh as heavily. Much library space can be repurposed. It can be downsized as duplicates are deaccessioned and as the physical copies of now-digitized works that need to be kept are moved off-site from pricey downtown or midcampus locations.

US research libraries spent $32 million in 2012 on interlibrary loans. In the open-access future, that need evaporates. Preservation costs were $27 million, much of which will not be required or can be repurposed for software upgrading, backward compatibility, migrating, and the like.[83] No one wants to make librarians redundant. But again, some savings are likely. The need for cataloging, preserving, acquiring, managing subscriptions, shelving, and reshelving will diminish. US research libraries had 86,000 staff in 2012, paid $3.4 billion. Much of that will no longer be necessary, especially as we need fewer separate institutions.

Worth repeating is the caution that just because the monies are already there, it does not make them available for new purposes. In modernity, famines are caused not by an absolute lack of food but by its misdistribution. Existing library budgets could fund open access. For that to happen, the scientific houses would have to relinquish dictating subscription prices and article fees. Despite protests, boycotts, and funder mandates, their revenues have not been much dented. Nor would we be concerned with new venues for accessible publication were it not for the suspicion that the current players are unlikely to release their grip. The monies are there to publish every academic book openly, even at the top-dollar price of $15,000 per volume. The various new means of open publication, explored in the conclusion, bring efficiencies and trim costs. They are needed precisely because it is unlikely that the existing and available monies match.

Publishers and Open Access

Green and gold open access pose different scenarios for established publishers. Parallel green, where open repositories overlie existing subscription journals, does not much trouble them. That also holds for books, so long as accessible versions do not compete head-on with paid-for ones. Some presses allow authors to post prepublication versions of manuscripts even as the finished book is conventionally marketed.[84] Some, such as Leiden University Press, make published versions accessible after an embargo. Others discount publishing charges if books are made freely available only after a delay. That allows houses such as Amsterdam University Press a temporary monopoly for paper editions.[85] So too, some nations have enshrined in law authors' right to self-post articles and book chapters (not books) after embargos of six or twelve months, at least for publicly funded work.[86]

So long as they are not responsible for the green repositories, publishers are asked only to tolerate whatever competition prepublication versions pose to the finished editions. Their interest then becomes hobbling the open versions—keeping them distinct and inferior to the version of record and ensuring that embargos are lengthy.

Gold access, in turn, poses both threats and promises. If digitality is used as an excuse to trim publishers' expenses and cut their profits, dangers lurk. However, suppose the implications of switching to open dissemination are to pare now-unnecessary costs of conventional editions (printing, storage, shipping, subscriptions) but not the value publishers claim they add (reviewing, editing, typesetting, promoting). In that case, enough fat remains to keep them happy. Publishers have done well from open access. After some initial stumbles, they have nimbly repurposed as publishing charges most of the funds that once were earmarked for subscriptions and acquisitions.

Established publishers worry more about green access. Investment bankers have welcomed the gold route as delivering the same money in another guise but fear that green could undermine conventional outlets. If authors post work to repositories and all research is immediately available for free, who will subscribe to journals?[87] Publishers can live with gold and have negotiated an accommodation. So, too, they can tolerate parallel green, which in effect leaves them untouched. What most troubles them is the prospect of a green repository-style system that would slash the unit costs of dissemination and eviscerate their claims to a crucial role in the process. We return to this in Chapter 8.

We glimpse publishers' mixed motives in the tussle over the so-called rights retention strategy. Rights retention is part of Plan S, the policy of some European funders to require immediate access to work they support. It obliges authors who publish in conventional subscription journals also to deposit at least the final accepted manuscript in an open repository with no embargo period.[88] It thus insists on an immediate form of green access that competes with gold. The rights retention strategy seeks to accommodate authors who cannot pay article charges or who publish with small scholarly societies unable to afford the cost of flipping to gold.[89] The well-heeled scientific periodicals, finally at ease with the gold strategy, naturally oppose such poaching on what they regard as their turf.[90]

Publishers' preferences vary by historical tradition, too. European law has long upheld rights-holders' interests over the audience's. It has anchored moral rights, giving authors extensive powers over their works. It has extended authors' claims far beyond the score of years originally granted. The Anglophone nations, in contrast, have traditionally tended to emphasize copyright's social utility—how it rewards authors merely to stimulate their creativity, and then only briefly. As a content-importing nation for its first two centuries, the US had Robin Hood instincts: take what you need and claim you are motivated by the good of your people. By the early twentieth century, however, America had become the single largest exporter of intellectual property. Then its interests—or at least its major content-producing sectors—pivoted to align with the European penchant for strong rights.[91]

Echoes of such earlier debates resound in current positionings over green and gold. European companies dominate scientific publishing. All but one of the five largest (Thomson Reuters, dual-listed in Canada and the UK) are European conglomerates.[92] Scientific publishing has become a lucrative export earner. Of total publishing revenues, the scientific make up 15% in Spain, 16% in France, 27% in Norway, 46% in Belgium, and a whopping half in the UK— but only 8% in China and 1% in the US.[93] EU politicians bemoan California companies' hammerlock on search engines and social media, but their own monopoly on scientific information appears unobjectionable. They are keen to protect the home team. They often lard an economically nationalist argument with appeals to preserve the high-cultural European tradition against Anglo-Saxon predation. And yet, if anything, the lines of attack run in the opposite direction. European trade houses have been swallowing Anglophone publishers. Bertelsmann owns Penguin Random House, the largest trade book publisher, and it wants to add Simon & Schuster. Hachette has bought Time Warner and now Workman.

British publishing has been especially caught in the cross fire because of its peculiar nesting in the Anglophone world. Britain is a medium-sized nation fortunate to share a common language with a large country as well as several others, including the vast and partly Anglophone Indian subcontinent. Correctly positioned and protected, British publishing has been an important export industry. Its domestic market was cushioned by an agreement with US publishers that other countries' books could not be issued in the UK or the Commonwealth nations except by British publishers.[94] That cozy arrangement was ended in the 1970s by threats of antitrust suits in the US. The English-language market was no longer carved up between British and US houses, but UK outlets retained exclusive rights to their home market.

In subsequent decades, however, publishers from both sides of the Atlantic set up shop or bought subsidiaries on the other shore to flog their wares directly in the new market. Given their nations' respective sizes, UK publishers especially have sought an American beachhead. The large British scholarly publishers (Oxford and Cambridge), as well as those of the second (Routledge) and third (Palgrave) ranks, have positioned themselves on both sides to exploit the Anglophone market.

Publishing interests aside, a nation's research intensity also influences its take on open access. Research-intensive countries, such as the US, Japan, and China, are skeptical of gold since it saddles them with high dissemination costs. China seems less enamored of gold than the Europeans, more in favor of green, which suits its position as it expands its research output. China's university libraries have been hard-pressed to afford Western subscriptions, but as the nation's scholars supply a growing fraction of the world's content, it would find paying gold charges equally difficult.

In 2018, at an average fee of $2,323, the cost to issue China's articles as gold would have been almost $1.4 billion. Better then to go for green, with its lower costs.[95] The third-largest producer of scientific papers, India, also rejects Plan S, the European funders' attempt to cement gold as the preferred route. The Indians hope to negotiate a national bulk rate with publishers, allowing their citizens to read for one flat fee paid by the government. Their researchers, meanwhile, will publish in open repositories.[96] That would be the best of both worlds, cheap reading and inexpensive publishing—but it is based on the unlikely assumption that publishers will be willing to discount a countrywide subscription.

Research-lite countries, in contrast, stand to benefit from gold as readers who no longer have to pay subscriptions. But if they also entertain ambitions to produce content, they may anticipate problems with publishing costs. Several European nations are both research-intensive and—as home to major scientific publishers—content exporters. For them, the balance is likely neutral, whether collecting article processing charges or subscriptions.[97] They must pay subscriptions or publishing fees. But their publishers profit from selling their products, financed either way, in the great abroad.

Plan S, based on gold, is primarily a European phenomenon. True, the Swedes have bailed, and the Germans have not signed up. But neither have the Chinese, and only two US funders are on board. Similarly, transformative read-and-publish agreements, discussed in Chapter 4, are favored in Europe. In effect, they switch subscription payments to publishing charges for gold access.[98] The publishers are paid similar amounts as before, even as the terminology changes. Plan S institutionalizes such agreements, insisting that funders not pay for publication in subscription journals unless they are in the process of flipping to open. The University of California's 2021 agreement with Elsevier was a rare US version of such deals.[99]

More commonly, US institutions have tackled the problem by unpicking their big-deal agreements with publishers.[100] Research libraries subscribe to the journals most used by faculty and students. Rather than buffet-style, all-you-can-read contracts, they are reining in costs by ordering à la carte. Some report savings of up to half of big-deal prices.[101] Means of accessing articles in journals no longer on the menu have been worked out.[102] Search engines scour the internet for prepublication, privately-posted, or other accessible versions. If all else fails, individual articles can be summoned for a fee via interlibrary loan, although too many of those and the savings from canceling big deals evaporate.

Data and Content

A final observation on the growing role legacy publishers continue to play in open access requires a distinction between data and content. We have more content than ever, but even more data. Raw data pour out of huge scientific projects, such as CERN's supercollider, and from our everyday world. English-language Wikipedia is

90 times as large as the *Encylopedia Britannica*. But CERN's data output is much larger than anything from the analog world. It collects a petabyte of data daily (one million gigabytes, each a thousand times an expensive laptop's hard disk), which itself is only about one-thousandth of what it generates.[103] That, in turn, is dwarfed by the internet of things' byte torrent as every manner of device communicates with each other and us—five hundred zettabytes annually, each a million times the aforementioned petabyte.[104]

New tools will eventually help temper this flow, turning it to our purpose. More data often means less work and greater mastery. Fluorescent light sheet microscopes image at high resolution, producing large data files.[105] That increases the amount of data needing attention, but alleviates our tasks, allowing sharper images and more accurate diagnoses. In our daily lives, too, salvation often arrives through more data. Shifting from analog to digital photography, supercharged by omnipresent cameras in our pockets, has vastly increased the number of images. Digital photos dwarf yesteryear's Kodak Instamatic snaps or Polaroids. Yet, the output is more easily storable, shareable, findable, and usable. Gone are millions of family albums, their dried-up adhesive mechanisms spilling out the photos on those rare occasions they are pulled off the shelf. Not to mention billions of slides in plastic cases, piled high in closets and never looked at again.

The legacy publishers have positioned themselves to capture the market for taming data. Now that disseminating content is contested and no longer an unchallenged source of profit, they are poised to go backstage into the bowels of the scientific enterprise to manage data as well. Accumulating, storing, organizing, analyzing, packaging, and otherwise mastering the data on which content is based is the new growth area for many publishers. Formerly a content provider, Elsevier has rebranded itself as an information analytics company.[106] With vast content already in house, it is now moving back up the information chain to the headwaters of the scholarly undertaking, vertically integrating the entire enterprise.

Here, too, debate rages. Shall data be captured by the commercial houses, as content was? With storage practically costless, should not the data behind the results also be made public, allowing others to scrutinize and verify? The European Open Science Cloud, begun in 2018, is a forum where researchers can store data and make it accessible.[107]

In tandem, open-access activists have sought to rebrand the movement as open science, to indicate their expanding ambition. Open science includes not just research's final output but also its raw materials, data, field notes, lab journals, blog posts, and the rest of it.[108] Sometimes this is referred to as open scholarship, to embrace the humanities and social sciences as well. As we have seen, however, in these fields, data have different meanings and implications.

Early days, it is difficult to say much about open scholarship. Who are its main actors, and their interests? Scientists and their institutions are clearly players. But what about publishers?[109] Whether the public has a practicable interest in scholarship's backstage apparatus remains to be seen.

8
An Intellectual Aquifer: The Bulletin Board Goes Global

However well endowed, no library can pretend to collect all the world's output if journal subscriptions and books must be paid for. Yet, once scholarly publication has shifted to open, every laptop will access the new Alexandria in the cloud. Digitality and open access amalgamate the dissemination, collection, and storage that used to be divided among publishers, bookstores, and libraries.

With the subscription model of journal financing, problems arise if the quantity or price of periodicals increases out of line with library budgets. If both do, as has been true over the past half-century, then the scissors open widely. Something similar holds for books. Even the largest libraries serve national catchment areas. Besides being deposit institutions, preserving copies that domestic publishers must deliver, they are national collections—the Bibliothèque Nationale, the British Library, the Library of Congress among the largest, with equivalents in every country.

National libraries naturally have books from elsewhere, but they focus domestically. Few have aimed beyond their nation to collect globally or even regionally. Among only a few peers, the biggest US university libraries have explicitly collected transnationally. Of books in the major East Coast libraries (the Library of Congress,

Widener, and the NYPL are among the largest), more than 60% were published outside the US and Canada, and almost half are in languages other than English.[1] In the holdings of the US Association of Research Libraries, 48% are in English.[2] Such global collectors are the exception. A similar proportion of foreign books is found nowhere else. Of the British Library's 16 million volumes, only 16% to 27% are not in English.[3] That also holds for the 30 million distinct titles in the 32 libraries of the UK Research Libraries consortium, where 70% are in English.[4] Of the Bibliothèque Nationale's 13.5 million books, 25% are not in French.[5]

There are more books from Sweden in Harvard's Widener library than in the Royal Library of Denmark in Copenhagen, 30 miles from Sweden. Doubtless, the favor is returned at Stockholm's national library—surprisingly, a much smaller institution for a country twice as big. There are twice as many German books in Widener (1.6 million) than in the Bibliothèque Nationale in Paris (833,000).[6] To state the obvious: even massive research libraries cannot hope for every book or periodical. Most have not even bothered to try.

As scholarly output increased in volume and price, the inherited system felt the strain. Library budgets barely kept pace with the growth of domestic books and periodicals. Casting their nets wider became less realistic. A global library of Alexandria was unfeasible in the analog, paper-based, reader-pays model.

Imagine a global deposit library in the analog era, a single place where all nations send a copy of every book and journal published. It would be massive. If the US represents one-seventh of global publishing output annually (300,000 out of 2.1 million volumes) and if the Library of Congress's collections are 40% domestic works, then an institution holding the world's output would be at least thrice its size.[7] That implies an acquisitions budget for past content of $21 billion (253 million books in existence minus the 39 million already owned at $100/book) and operational costs of $2.25 billion annually, or triple the Library of Congress's current budget of almost three-quarters of a billion.[8] And let's not forget a reading room able to seat at least 5,000 readers.[9]

Even if we assume that this is a global deposit library with the world's book production delivered gratis into its hands every year, that knocks only about $220 million (2.2 million times $100) off its running costs, leaving $2 billion. That is still far above UNESCO's annual budget ($1.3 billion for 2020 and 2021 together), the closest we have come to global cultural cooperation.[10] Even if spread over the world's nations, it remains a hefty sum. And that is for a single library to which scholars and researchers must pilgrimage.

Duplicating such institutions in each country is even less realistic. It is a stiff cost to saddle publishers with delivering their books to each of some 200 national libraries. Historically, presses have bristled at having to provide just one or two copies to their own national institutions.[11] If not the publishers, then libraries' acquisitions budgets must pay—a weightier burden the smaller the nation and the more foreign content it must buy. And, of course, none of this makes the system open access, even for the scholarly literature. With reader-pays publishing, a global library is impossible. Only by flipping to author-pays or other means of making content gratis for the reader can we achieve such ambitions.

We live in a happy world where ever more researchers produce ever more knowledge. In developed countries, women and other formerly excluded groups now participate in research. Developing nations are joining the club, too. Scientific output has been welling up from China and other nations not previously in the international research community. In absolute numbers, China now publishes more scientific and technical articles than the US.[12] How do libraries deal with such waves of new content? In subscription or other reader-pays systems, there is no good answer. Acquisitions budgets are drained, and some form of rationing follows.

The dirty little secret of the reader-pays system was that it spread costs beyond the research-intensive nations and institutions. Books and periodicals bought by countries that produced little content and institutions that consumed more than they issued subsidized publication. In the Association for Computing Machinery's journals (global revenue $20 million annually), 80% of articles are provided by the top thousand subscribing institutions, but they supply only 32% of subscription revenue. Conversely, the long tail of 1,700 institutions publishes only one-fifth of content but pays 68% of revenue.[13]

As content production globalizes, such subsidies cancel each other out. China and India used to just buy Western output. Now they also produce their own. They cannot afford to buy it all, nor can the West. A reader-pays model is inherently unworkable when production grows and its sources are distributed more evenly worldwide. Libraries can collect globally only by reversing the funding flow, making authors pay. Paradoxically, recipient libraries do not even collect, catalog, store, or otherwise deal with works in this model. They reside on the publishers' servers, freely available to anyone once paid for. Put another way, the global library is possible insofar as conventional libraries vanish.

A similar logic holds for gold access. Gold relies on reciprocity of production and payment. If authors pay to have their work disseminated, readers everywhere benefit. But if authorship is geographically, nationally, or institutionally skewed, then some players pay so that others can read. Gold works only within a closed loop of mutuality. A nation that flips its publishing model, using monies earlier earmarked for subscriptions to pay publication charges, makes its research free for the world. Only if others do likewise does that function. Otherwise, it has to pay twice—to make its own work available and to buy foreign non-open work. Unreciprocity was the risk feared by the Finch Report in the UK and the top British research universities united in the Russell Group.[14] And by the Europeans who sought to restrict their gold material, making it readable only in regions that were doing the same.[15]

A similar logic holds for the PLOS's Community Action Publishing model, inaugurated in 2021. That seeks to relieve burdens on research-intensive institutions while keeping their read-intensive peers within the financing loop. High-read institutions' annual fees are lower, reflecting their lesser publication rates. Thus, they are encouraged not to exit altogether and free-ride on others' efforts. Those with no publishing history at all can participate at the lowest tier, which is only 1% or 2% of that paid by the most prolific.[16] Conversely, the same logic motivates Latin America's rejection of gold access. Latin nations have long issued most scientific work in government-sponsored open journals, that include many articles by foreign authors, who are unlikely to be taxpayers.[17] Having already made public goods of its scholarship, Latin America resented Plan S and similar developed-world attempts to exclude it by geolimiting access to gold journals.[18]

Gold works only if applied globally. If gold nations must pay both to publish their own work and buy other countries' subscription content, then the deal is off. As content production globalizes, however, the prospects of gold access's reciprocity being fulfilled increase. The payoff is handsome for everyone. At the cost of openly publishing its own content, each nation receives the rest of the world's in return. Small and poor countries must carry only their own burden to receive the entirety of the world's output.

The only remaining issue is ensuring that developing nations' scholars can afford publishing charges. They are in much the same predicament as the industrialized world's humanities and social science researchers. And the affordability problem is exacerbated by heftier book publishing charges for fields using that medium. Discounts and subsidies for publishing fees are partial solutions. Some journals offer them for humanities scholars.[19] The so-called predatory journals have flourished by providing gold access at a discount. Insofar as the gold route remains unaffordable for many scholars, other fixes are needed.

Having started to solve the problem for themselves via gold access, the sciences of the developed world have slammed the door on others. Gold might be globalizable, but not if scientific publishers insist on inflated profit margins. Only by unleashing digitality's potential to lower dissemination costs would gold be possible as a universal solution. If not, another form of open access is needed that cuts publication costs and provides a refuge for those locked out of the current science-oriented approach.

What Value Do Publishers Add?

Some publishers have done well out of gold access. And for non-scholarly content, the legacy industry remains fit for purpose. For academic work that seeks openness but finds publishing fees unaffordable, new solutions are needed. Before getting to them, let us ponder what publishers bring to the table. The question Ronald Coase famously posed to corporations can profitably be asked of publishers: Why do they exist? Could not the activities they unite under one roof equally well be sourced individually on the market? Publishers are arguably the least important of the participants helping to transfer work from an author's mind to its public. Most of the functions they have bundled together can be split off and outsourced. They are not among the irreplaceable actors—the authors above all, but also the reviewers, and for science, the funders. The journals need the scholars much more than the scholars, the journals.[20] And yet, the publishers make the most strident demands, not just for their cut, but often the rights, too.

From an author's vantage, the point is not to be published but to be read. From the reader's, the aim is not to buy a book but to be put in useful contact with new ideas. Can this be achieved otherwise? Whether a tree falling unheard in a forest makes a noise depends on how we define sound—as mere vibrations in air or their perception as well. But a book issued to no readership might as well never have been published. "Stillborn from the press," was Hume's sardonic description of the impact of his *Treatise of Human Nature* in his own lifetime.[21] Publication aims to make the work read, known, and impactful. Otherwise, it is pointless. Hume's comment implies that a work's readership may also await it later. Still, until it finds that audience, no one except author and publisher will even know it exists.

But works can have an effect even without being published in the conventional sense. During the Cold War, samizdat writings circulated the East Bloc in typescript, and carbon paper was the technology of enlightenment. The Odessa copy of Mikhail Bulgakov's *Heart of a Dog* was handled to shreds.[22] As homebrew can inebriate, so typescript can enlighten. Many samizdat works eventually made their way to the West for proper publication, both in their original tongue and translation. Pasternak's *Doctor Zhivago* and Solzhenitsyn's *Gulag Archipelago* were among the best known. And in today's autocratic regimes, turbocharged only by the advance from carbon paper to xeroxing, such clandestine dissemination continues—Nabokov's *Lolita* in puritanical Iran, for example.[23]

Even in the West, works not actually published have had a huge impact. Saul Kripke's foundational *Naming and Necessity* circulated for a decade as a typescript of three lectures given at Princeton in 1970. In 1972, a version emerged in an 800-page conference proceedings.[24] Because that was a pricey Springer edition, the underground typescript enjoyed a prolonged half-life, re-xeroxed among philosophy students and faculty, until a version was published as a stand-alone by Harvard in 1980. Faced with the difficulty of breaking publishers' monopoly, some have proposed a neo-samizdat system of homemade publishing.[25]

Admittedly, published books are more efficient than underground typescripts, and digital downloads, even more so. As disseminators, publishers therefore add value. What else? Digital dissemination eliminates the cost of the last marginal copy, which in the paper world still entailed the expense of its materiality. But it does not remove the cost of producing the first copy. Indeed, it adds new expenses, such as metadata needed for discoverability, storage, and software upgrading. What of such expenses?

Some of them have decreased. Digitality has democratized sound recording and film. Much of what used to require professional sound stages, mixers, cameras, and editing equipment is today available on laptops. Many of what were once the book trade's technical skills are now a mouse click away. Indexing is sometimes listed as a publisher contribution to the process, but presses foist that cost or effort onto authors, and journals are rarely indexed.[26] With text digitally searchable, what value does an index add? Supplying the metadata needed for discoverability remains a cost as well, although again, as with indexing, providing the search terms is a task expected of authors.

Publishers have also traditionally supplied copyediting, seeking to issue a crisp flawless work. But that can be done by others. Most copyeditors today are freelancers, roped in by the task, and their services are available to anyone willing to pay. Much of what they do has, in any case, been automated. Spell-checking and grammar software catches many of the mistakes copyeditors once earned their keep by correcting. It would be unfair to say that being a copyeditor these days is akin to being an elevator operator in a push-button lift, but much of the task has been accomplished before submission. In any case, presses have no monopoly on this function. As any published author can attest, copyediting varies from inspired and improving to an actual downgrade in quality.

That leaves layout as a publisher's contribution. This is largely an aesthetic question. Science journals are usually two or three columns of text, cramming much on a single page, with margins reduced to an afterthought. As an aside, scientific journals have not pondered the transition from paper to screen enough. While fine for reading a paper page, multiple columns of text are almost impossible to peruse on screen without an annoyingly constant scrolling up, down, and sideways. On screen, space is free. Only on paper does it have to be saved. The sooner publishers figure this out, the happier readers will be. Humanities and social science scholars are more interested in the aesthetic aspects of publication.

Still, any laptop can now produce almost publishable text. For those who sweat the details of book-level output, a little more effort and software are required. But broadly, anyone can do their own layout, producing pages that withstand bibliophilic scrutiny. For readers, this is a historic reversal of entropy. Those of a certain age will remember the nadir of scholarly publishing in the early 1980s, just before widespread word processing. Presses such as SAGE and Croom Helm then issued books that were little more than xeroxed typescripts—complete with Tipp-Exed corrections—in hardcovers at eye-watering prices. That was the worst of all worlds, bound volumes that looked like first-draft manuscripts. Today, everyone can produce camera-ready copy. Indeed, some publishers, such as Palgrave, charge three-figure prices for books that look suspiciously like what the authors submitted.

We have already examined the publisher's contribution to providing a version of record and found it to be less important in the digital era. Authors bring the final manuscript to the table. After that follows the publishers' value add: peer review, copyediting, and typesetting. Is the difference between the author's accepted manuscript and the version of record sufficient to justify the massive increase in cost from zero to list?

The publishers' main functions can all be outsourced or done by any author with patience and modest resources. Even peer review can be hired in.[27] Publishers' experiments with expedited peer review for an extra fee suggest how separable from their workflow it is.[28] Whether outsourced peer review is affordable is another matter. Peer review is normally done for free or nominal payment, but

only within the mutual scholarly self-evaluation that publishers
piggyback on. Once commercialized and extracted from the academic gift economy, reviewers will likely demand a living wage,
and its cost will approach market rates. Research Square's rates in
2013 were $500 to $700 per article.[29] One hates to imagine what a
book costs.

As publishers' various functions can all be decoupled and
assigned other players, they need not be united in one hand,[30] Self-
publication on Amazon reveals how dissemination without bells
and whistles can be streamlined and economized. A perfectly adequate physical book, adorned with a cover design and ISBN, can
be produced for a high three-figure sum.[31] A modest sales price can
recoup such expenses. For an average-sized paperback of 300 pages,
Amazon calculates a price of perhaps $5.00 per copy—less than
the cost of xeroxing.[32] For digital editions, readable with Kindle
software, Amazon requires a minimum price of 99¢.[33] But slightly
surreptitious ways also allow authors to make their works perma-
nently free.[34]

Other self-publishing enterprises, such as AuthorHouse, iUni-
verse, and Xlibris, offer publishing services for prices that span the
gamut of three figures.[35] Smashwords, which publishes only digitally, charges authors nothing, taking 15% of the proceeds if there
are any.[36] Assuming modest sales of physical editions, entrepreneur-
ial authors could publish books so as to cost them nothing while
providing anyone willing to read digitally with gratis access

Besides producing the physical book and providing peer review,
publishers' crucial function in the analog era was dissemination.
Delivering it to stores was the first step, but making the world aware
of the book's existence was also important. This meant submitting
copies for press review, advertising it, and positioning authors to
call attention to their work—with talks, lectures, conferences, chat
shows, and so forth. Websites, blogs, e-mail footers, and the like

have been added in the digital era. For academic works, publicity is not a publisher's major concern. Mostly, they submit copies to prominent journals in the field and, if ambitious, to some popular periodicals and newspapers. Yet the disparity between supply and demand is so stark that the likelihood of any given book receiving attention outside the scholarly organs is minuscule.

In the major Anglophone outlets, at best around 3,000 books are reviewed annually, out of 500,000 total published in the US and UK.[37] If we adjust to eliminate duplicates, let us assume the total is some 350,000. Thus, scarcely 1% are reviewed in the major press. Even if we doubled this figure to include the second rank of reviewing, the problem remains.

Of more interest to scholars are reviews in specialized journals. These provide blurbs for eventual paperback editions and evidence for the promotion file. The likelihood of sales being driven by colleagues' reviews is small, but some accretion of scholarly readers is possible. Oprah may be able singlehandedly to make a bestseller by including a book on her program, but little of that nature exists in the scholarly world. Charlie Rose was the closest approximation American TV had to French programs such as *Apostrophes* and *Bouillon de culture*, or *Bookmark* on the BBC, where serious authors were taken seriously, but he has not been replaced after his fall from grace.

Other forms of publicity barely concern scholarly books. What academic publishers mean by advertising is not much. At best, a book's dust cover gets a grainy thumbnail image, the title scarcely visible, the author's name often not at all. These are usually strung out in a kind of literary police line-up with half a dozen other culprits on a quarter-page ad at the back of a professional journal or—if lucky—in a book review outlet. Getting works noticed is important. Yet, academic publishers would be ill advised to claim this as one of their strong points.

Cosmic Postings

Publishers launch books with a few desultory attempts to make their presence known and some fond wishes for Godspeed en route to finding readers. We might call this the hunter-and-prey model. A hare is set running, and perhaps some foxes will notice and set out in pursuit. But what if, to stick with animal feeding analogies, content is a meadow, seeded with various plants among which herbivores graze, picking what appeals to them, ignoring the rest?

Imagine content uploaded to a vast site, host to every work. Authors could post in any format, from barebones typescripts as found on arXiv to the output of elaborate typesetting programs rivaling the timeless elegance of Clarendon volumes.[38] With works in the ether, authors can then seek to draw attention. But success connecting with readers is more likely to come from the demand side, as improved search engines alert audiences to the presence of new material. Precisely how the work is consumed would then be the reader's choice. A proper paper version of books or articles could be produced and mailed for a fee. Otherwise, PDFs or e-books could download to devices, or the work be read on-screen.

Such ideas have been with us for years. Stevan Harnad anticipated the possibility of a global bulletin board in 1990, early days of the internet. With authors' newfound ability to e-mail manuscripts to colleagues, they could hope for comments, suggestions, and revisions. Others would be drawn into an expansive process of bringing ideas to fruition—what Harnad termed scholarly skywriting.[39] Later, as the web matured, he imagined posting manuscripts in the ether, accessible to anyone and thus disseminated, if not published in the conventional sense.[40] Digital archives hosting e-prints allowed researchers to sidestep publishers altogether, posting their work individually and immediately. In 1994, Paul Ginsparg suggested that repositories could apply different levels of filtering, with both refereed and unvetted content.[41] A few years later, Robert Cameron imagined a vast cloud repository, connecting texts to all their references in a seamless whole.[42] The Budapest Open Access Initiative in 2002 pointed out that if individuals posting manuscripts followed standardized protocols, search engines would treat each independent archive as one undifferentiated mass of content.[43]

A global bulletin board of content would be but the first step in a differentiated dissemination process. Some works would never leave it. Databases, document collections, archives, letters, memoirs, and, more generally, the material that is not often read but is now available to all could simply remain in the cloud. Other content could descend from the cloud to assume physical form, should there prove to be interest or even a market.

In effect, we have something like this already in place for doctoral dissertations. In analog days, dissertations reposed in their university's libraries or archives, largely inaccessible except to those who could gain admission. Some nations, such as Germany, require dissertations to be published. That has spawned a strange mutant industry specializing in issuing dissertations in the few copies demanded by university regulations. Before digitality, these publishers were, in effect, glorified xeroxers and binders.[44] But they did manage to distribute a few copies among research libraries. In the meantime, the end product has improved. Digitality has made dissertations more widely available. Nonetheless, the publication requirement for Germany's 30,000 annual dissertations puts an upper limit on quality. KIT Scientific Publishing from the Karlsruher Institut für Technologie is the largest German open-access press, and 70% of its list is unrevised dissertations.[45]

In the Anglophone world, dissertations remain typescripts. As of 1938, University Microfilms International began microfilming most US dissertations. Subsequently, it was bought by ProQuest, which now supplies copies of digitized dissertations for a fee.[46] Something similar is the case in the UK.[47]

In the meantime, the issue has become whether recently minted PhDs should be allowed to embargo their dissertations. If they are revising the dissertation for publication, authors may prefer to keep it private until the book has appeared.[48] But the public may be keen to read new research findings. How long should an embargo last? Should the fact that doctoral students may have received scholarships influence the decision? The majority of ProQuest's electronic dissertations are not embargoed. That is less true in France and Germany.[49]

Whatever the outcome of this dispute, the dissertation ecosystem foreshadows what might hold for works more generally. Most dissertations remain typescripts, posted and available in their original state. Some are revised and recombined into other formats. They may have been, or become, articles. That holds especially in the sciences and harder social sciences, where a dissertation increasingly consists of a few published articles. Finally, some dissertations are turned into books, properly speaking

All dissertations are thus available in the cloud and in various other formats for those that are revised and subsequently published. Why could something similar not apply to all content on the global bulletin board? Everything should be readable, but not everything must be an article or book, any more than every book must be a printed volume, or every printed volume a leather-bound artifact. With the long tail of content coiled in the cloud, the fat end, commanding larger audiences, descends to assume earthly form. As on-screen reading becomes ubiquitous and typesetting software more user-friendly and sophisticated, the distinction between outcomes will blur, whether in the cloud or on paper. On the Kindle or its future flat, foldable, stick-in-your-pocket, digital-paper versions, the just-filed dissertation will increasingly resemble Belknap's output.

Once content migrates to our still-imaginary global bulletin board, the consequences will be profound. Bookstores will remain as outlets for trade books. Libraries will be relieved of most processing and storage functions, except for the trade books that, still sold, require a lending institution. Publishers will issue content that has been test-run in its cloud versions. Like farmers watering their fields, they will draw from the global intellectual aquifer. Editions will likely be smaller and their sales more predictable. Best of all, information will be equally available everywhere.

What would a global bulletin board cost? ArXiv merely hosts works that are posted, without reviewing, curating, or otherwise incurring costs. It has an annual budget of $2 million, and uploading an article costs $7 to $10.[50] At three million articles globally a year, that is $30 million. Since size matters little in the cloud, let us assume that books are only fractionally more expensive and go with $20 for each of the globe's 2.2 million annual books, or another $40 million. Even if costs for what would now be the world's content came to $100 million annually, this would be about 2% of the US library system's total acquisitions budgets. If the US's fraction of library spending is proportionate to its role in global publishing (about 14%), the cost of our celestial bulletin board would be a vanishing part of current acquisitions expenditure.

That would be just the start. Posting a typescript would be practically costless, and anyone could read that version for free. Authors interested in more bells and whistles would seek or supply the resources for improvement. Readers, too, could upgrade matters, much as sports fans bring cushions to stadium seats, airline travelers, neck pillows, and opera buffs, binocs. A hardscrabble typescript could be upgraded at will. Auto-typesetting programs will housetrain raw manuscripts. Readers themselves can improve content they read. In the eighteenth century, books were sold sheathed only in paper, since wealthy buyers bound them to match their libraries. Today, the average listener jacks up the bass on a song.

If the old model was supply-side publishing, this will be on-demand. Readers will be like shoppers at a farmers market choosing their vegetables. Rather than grabbing canned soup off the supermarket shelf, consumers will home cook their content. The global bulletin board will supply the intellectual raw materials readers consume—as, when, and how they please.

For works that prove to have public appeal, publishers could team up with authors to offer premium editions for a fee, much as cars upgraded with the fanciest options are perhaps a third more expensive than basic models. Analog foreshadowings already exist. Dan Brown's blockbuster novels are issued in higher-priced editions with illustrations of the artworks and scientific apparatus mentioned in them. Annotated versions of classic works—*Alice in Wonderland, Huckleberry Finn, Sherlock Holmes*—add interesting background detail for a price.[51] Digitality expands the realm of value-add. Literary agents would earn their keep by reading widely on the web, searching for nuggets not yet mined.

Mega-Journals

Scientific mega-journals are a first approximation of such a global bulletin board. They raise the question: What is the need for 53,000 different scientific journals?[52] Why reproduce the editorial machinery over and over? Journals specialized by subject or theme are, after all, but a first approximation of an index of their content. And that is assuming that journals are specialized rather than generalist. How much wider can you get, after all, than *Science*, unless it is *Nature*?

Following the logic of the old joke about searching for our car keys under the streetlight's illumination regardless of where we actually lost them, we go to where the title of a periodical suggests something interesting. Journals of entomology and etymology promise different fare. Why duplicate all that effort? A few mega-journals could serve the same function. In the end, one global bulletin board would do so even better—the ultimate mega-journal.[53]

We appreciate the quaintness of discrete establishments selling different wares or foodstuffs when at leisure on vacation, but in our daily lives, we head for the supermarket or department store.

Analogously, we have been liberated from the tyranny of the music album, with one or two good songs packaged along with the dross. The cornucopia of Spotify and Apple Music are the mega-journals of music. Worse than the subscription journals, with only a few articles of interest, are the edited volumes. At eye-watering prices, they contain only a chapter or two pertinent to any given reader. Often they are not available even to scholars through their university collections. Why not just bury your work in the garden?[54] Fortunately, that is slowly changing, as publishers unbundle books to sell chapters individually, and libraries subscribe to publishers' packages of volumes.

The effects of selecting precisely what we want are yet unclear. Some songs, articles, or chapters appeal to some people, others not. Insofar as each one is consumed by someone, everything is fine. But inevitably, some content will simply never be touched. Furthermore, we will be able to identify which content has resonance. The B sides of singles and the academic wallflowers among articles will slide down the long tail. Yet, thanks to costless storage, they will remain findable. As tastes change and tomorrow's scholars research currently unexpected topics, everything can hope for a future Cinderella moment.

Starting in 2000, mega-journals have become established features of digital publishing. In 2012, they issued some 47,000 articles annually. *PLOS One* was the first, but now an entire ecosystem has sprung up: *Scientific Reports, BMJ Open, PeerJ*, the BioMed Central Series, *Nature's "Frontiers in. . . ," AIP Advances*, the *Open Library of the Humanities, SAGE Open, F1000*, and about one-third of Hindawi's output.[55] For most of their content, they are the last step on dissemination's road. A few articles are sometimes poached for inclusion in overlay journals (something we touch on below). Latin America's SciElo functions much like a mega-journal, aggregating 1,500 journals and making their content available through its portal.[56]

Many mega-journals are perfectly reputable scholarly outlets, heralding a change in format but not quality. Their ample size testifies not to lowered standards but to a more capacious embrace. Mega-journals accept a broad range of submissions, unconcerned with limiting individual issues to a certain size or focusing on particular topics. In contrast, subscription journals, with their income fixed and already collected, have no incentive to expand capacity if submissions increase. They adjust to enhanced supply by dialing up selectivity or lengthening waiting times. But in the digital world, a journal can appear whenever it wants, however many submissions it has accepted. Slim or plus-sized, it matters not. The concepts of volumes and issues are inheritances from the paper era that have little meaning in digitality. Indeed, appearing as they please, mega-journals are less *periodicals*, in the technical sense of publishing to a schedule, than they are *sporadics*.

Nor do digital journals have to be picky about their subject matter. In the analog world with its space constraints, specialization served an editorial and filtering function. Postwar scientific publishers produced niche journals, supplying micromarkets.[57] Anyone for a subscription to the *Nordic Wittgenstein Review*, the *Latin American Journal of Aquatic Mammals,* or the *Indonesian Journal of Accounting Research*? With such laser focus, specialization became part of the editorial process. Regardless of quality, submissions could be rejected for not fitting in. Conversely, how fierce was the competition for attention in such circumscribed niches?

Early open journals were also specialized. But gradually, it became clear that the new medium did not require arbitrary boundaries. Since digital journals had no physical constraints—no size limits imposed by the cost of paper, binding, and postage—they could expand like a gentleman wearing Sansabelt trousers. Mega-journals can accommodate any number of articles. Nor is there reason to prissily police subject matter borders.[58] Hence they grow ever larger. *BMJ Open*, for example, published 97 papers in its first year and 1,143 four years later. In the print era, few journals have ever published more than 1,000 articles annually.[59] *PLOS One*, probably the largest mega-journal, published almost 32,000 articles in 2013, its peak so far. In 2014, *Medicine* transitioned from being a conventional selective journal to mega status. The 1,694 articles it published in 2015 were more than its total output for the previous half-century.[60]

Mega-journals are much like digital repositories, and drawing clear lines between the two is difficult. Both are cheaper than regular open journals. Repositories generally cost little, some $7 to $10 per hosted article for arXiv. Assuming that posted articles will eventually be published in journals, they typically impose no review. Mega-journals charge publishing fees, but usually much lower than for other open journals—often slightly more than $1,000.

Content undergoes only abbreviated peer review. Checking for basic coherence, logic, argument, presentation, soundness, and sense, they do not evaluate the work's broader significance, estimate what impact it might have, judge its novelty, or determine other subjective qualities.[61] All that is assumed to be the task of future postpublication reviewers. "Soundness not significance" is their criterion of acceptance.[62]

Setting few hurdles to dissemination, mega-journals are useful for the kind of work that rarely found accommodation in more rationed outlets. Journals with space constraints shy away from content that does not lay claim to new contributions. Yet, much of science is—or ought to be—kicking the tires, testing claims. Though it lacks sizzling novelty, reporting negative outcomes at least spares others from pursuing dead ends. Arguably, science's grunt-work is double-checking striking but improbable first results.[63] In mega-journals, such useful but uncelebrated work finds an outlet.[64] The same holds for work that used to be published preliminarily to establish precedence and then again—often with few changes—when completed. Such redundant publication no longer needs to clog the airwaves of more formal outlets.

So-called overlay journals select and curate previously posted articles, sorting and improving them in new venues. They anticipate a potential merger of gold and green access.[65] All content could be posted in the author's version of the manuscript. Overlay journals interested in curating, improving, promoting, or otherwise amplifying extracts poached from the content commons then work their magic with extra funding. Reviewed work—before or after—could be so indicated, possibly attracting more eyes. From the reader's vantage, overlay journals draw attention to curated and enhanced versions. From the author's standpoint, they serve the credentialing functions currently performed by selective subscription or gold journals. We return to them in the next chapter.

9
Finding What We Need: Searching and Filtering

How would authors or publishers know which works had market potential for snazzier editions? And how readers which were most worth their attention? Search engines present would-be readers with everything found on a subject. Depending on the topic, that could be an overwhelming amount. For those interested in much-discussed issues, where to start? In conventional publishing, prestige was the guide. Readers began with articles in the most selective journals, books from the most reputable presses. Here, peer review had worked its astringent magic, sorting wheat from chaff.

That still left a mountainous oversupply of content for weary eyes. Reviews in the press then did some postpublication sorting, alerting readers to the pitfalls and promises of recent output. The relationship between conventional peer review and postpublication review is akin to that between public health expert and emergency room medic. The former seeks to keep populations healthy and away from physicians in the first place. The latter deals with the mess afterward. Ideally, flawless peer review would leave postpublication review unnecessary, but of course that is rarely the case. And it raises the question: in a digital world, what is the point of prepublication review?

Peer Review Redux

In the analog era, prepublication peer review sought to reserve scarce resources for works deserving dissemination. But if the cost of posting content on the global bulletin board is negligible, why bother with upfront vetting? To continue with medical analogies, in theory, prevention would not matter if we had perfect and painless cures. Prevention makes most sense for diseases without remedies or that subject victims to avoidable suffering.

Yet, prevention also imposes costs of its own: restrictions on our behavior, pleasures forgone, travels or experiences shunned. A cure after the fact is often preferable to the abnegation of prevention. Our culture is saturated with the alleged virtue of prevention and its attendant moralizing. Prevention is premised on individual responsibility, and guilt when it fails. We are culturally blinded to the advantages of cures. Historically, treatments for venereal diseases have been attacked as promoting sin through sexual libertinage by sparing the promiscuous their ravages.[1] A pill to dodge obesity, permitting us the costless pleasures of gluttony: were that on offer, imagine the ensuing shriek of moralizing censure.

The issues are similar in debates about preventive pre-facto review versus curative post-facto review. Prepublication peer review assumes that the experts know best and can be trusted to weed out unsuitable content. Besides resting on a paternalist attitude toward readers, it works only when properly implemented. The experts can weigh in just as well after publication. By not limiting it to a small group of initiates, a more thorough review may follow. Once resources no longer have to be husbanded, with content posted to the global bulletin board, what is the advantage of reviewing before dissemination? In the old system, works whose qualities were overlooked or misunderstood by reviewers may never have seen the light. In any case, given a constant quantity of content, the weeding effort is the same, whether before or after publication. Why not instead throw all content against the wall and see what sticks?

Peer review's weaknesses have been minutely scrutinized. It often fails to spot problems, and few published authors have been spared the annoyance of a querulous commentator with pointless nits to pick. Academic presses in the US did not undertake peer review until the 1960s.[2] Trade houses usually do not bother even today. Even at serious European publishers, review is informal at best. In digitality, does conventional peer review still serve a purpose? We have looked at whether publishers are best placed to manage review, since they merely muster the author's scholarly colleagues to pronounce judgment. Even more pertinent: why demand prepublication review at all? Review is needed. It is one way the ocean of content is channeled into rivulets of enlightenment. But when should it be done, and by whom?

In the analog world, peer review had to occur before publication. Once issued, the work was locked in place, barring those rare occasions when demand spoke for updated editions. The manuscript had to be as perfect as possible before printing. Digitality has upended that finality. Texts have become more fluid, protean, and revisable. Posted on the web, not locked onto the page, they can be updated. Suggestions for revision are useful whenever delivered. Evaluation at various stages of a text's life cycle is already common in the hard sciences, part of what is known as open peer review.[3] Open review, with many participating and the author responding, was tried out already in the 1960s and 1970s by journals such as *Current Anthropology* and *Behavioral and Brain Sciences*.[4] Kathleen Fitzpatrick's *Planned Obsolescence: Publishing, Technology, and the Future of the Academy* was posted for comment before being issued on paper.[5]

In the sciences, peer review has evolved from a judgment akin to a jury's pronouncement and is now more like a conversation among colleagues. Instead of submitting a manuscript to reviewers, taking on board one round of comments, and then publishing once and for all, digitality permits flexibility. A preliminary version is posted on the web, commented on by colleagues. Revisions follow. By this point, almost everyone interested has seen the manuscript, and dissemination has effectually occurred. But only now does publication in a technical sense take place.

In the hard sciences, formal publication increasingly matters only to future historians, not today's practitioners. The point of traditional prepublication review was to spare the cost of issuing works not worth it. Now that such expenses have diminished, this falls away. Assessment can occur before publication, as part of it, or afterward. Articles have been criticized after publication, then modified or taken down.[6] In 2010, an article claimed to have discovered bacteria that used arsenic rather than phosphorus in their DNA. After skeptical blogs and tweets, further articles disputing it were published.[7]

The new model of review, in turn, questions the very nature of publication. In the digital age, does prepublication differ meaningfully from publication? Mathematicians, physicists, and computer scientists already work largely through prepublication texts posted online. This was their custom even before digitality made it easy. Since the mid-1970s, theoretical physicists have sent around preprints via ordinary mail, racking up large photocopying and postage bills.[8] Digitality merely turbocharged existing habits. Now content is posted to the web. As mentioned, arXiv is one of the most successful of such sites, with costs of less than $10 per article to host.[9] Since arXiv does not technically publish articles, a better comparison is Scipost.[10] It provides journal certification as well, but still at a fraction of the cost of traditional subscriptions or conventional gold periodicals.

Computer scientists are yet further along this route. They consider even articles passé and too cumbersome to keep pace. Instead, conference papers are the currency of the realm—posted, commented, and revised at a rapid clip. Their promotion and tenure procedures have adjusted accordingly.[11] Other fields have prepublication sites, too. For social scientists, the Social Science Research Network.[12] For economists, Research Papers in Economics.[13] For medical research, PubMedCentral.[14]

Even more impressive is how urgent knowledge can now be thrown up on the web for use globally. Gene sequencing of the Covid virus was posted early in 2020 on preprint sites before peer review, available for immediate use. Getting information out quickly via preprints had begun already with previous epidemics. Between the Ebola epidemic (2015–2016) and Zika (2016–2017), the proportion of articles with important data appearing as preprints (most then issued as conventional articles, but only several months later) increased significantly.[15] Nonetheless, the number of articles on Zika and Ebola that had first seen the light as preprints was small, less than 4% in each case. In part, they were hampered because only some journals accept submissions that have already appeared as preprints.[16]

During the Covid pandemic, matters improved. Research output grew even faster, whether appearing openly or not.[17] More information than ever was posted on preprint sites as scientists raced against the clock.[18] By February 2020, early in the pandemic, more articles on Covid had appeared as preprints than in journals. The venerable *New England Journal of Medicine* posted one paper within 48 hours of submission. Preprint servers, some researchers finally realized, promised them credit for discoveries, regardless of where they eventually were published, even as they contributed immediately to the public good.[19]

Preprints rapidly disseminated crucial data, but they also raised the issue of avoiding nonsense that led readers astray or hogged attention. In January 2020, a preprint by Indian scientists on bioRxiv pointed to supposedly "uncanny" similarities between the Covid virus and the HIV. Fuelling conspiracy theories about genetic engineering, it was widely discussed on Twitter by news outlets. Within 48 hours, the preprint had received over 90 critical comments and was retracted.[20] Postpublication review had demonstrated its chops. Information was both promptly disseminated and quickly reviewed.

Other instances have been more ambiguous. In September 2020, a researcher who had fled China posted an article on a preprint site claiming that the Covid virus had been created in a lab.[21] The report was subjected to warnings on the site and harsh criticisms elsewhere. Some were published in a journal set up to combat scientific fraud and misinformation.[22] Nonetheless, the preprint drew much attention, including over a million views and three-quarters of a million downloads by March 2021. Picked up by social media, the article's author did the rounds of the morning television shows, caught up in the politicization of China's role in the pandemic's origins.[23]

Peer review reports can be interesting works of scholarship in their own right. Perhaps they should be opened up alongside the content they evaluate. True, such detail may interest only a few. Yet, as always in digitality, space and storage are largely costless, therefore irrelevant considerations. If it already exists, it might as well be preserved. Also up for grabs is whether peer review should remain blinded, keeping at least the reviewers' identity anonymous. Would revealing identities afflict peer review with the same punch-pulling pusillanimity that has come to plague book reviewing? How genuine can criticism be in an increasingly collaborative academic world, with everyone reliant on colleagues and peers for constant evaluation and review? Or would non-anonymous reviews soothe vindictive spirits, forcing reviewers to temper their words and address actual problems rather than just venting spleens? Conclusions are unclear, except that few academics favor revealing reviewers' identities.[24]

Anonymous peer review allows competitors to throw spanners in each others' works. Once again, this is not an issue for the humanities, where prizes for priority are paltry and scholars rarely work on precisely the same problem. But among the sciences, it is not uncommon for anonymous reviewers asked to evaluate papers by competing colleagues to suggest extensive further work before publication, thus hobbling other teams in their race to the goal. Such were the problems tackled with the inauguration of *eLife*, an open journal established in 2012 by Max Planck, Wellcome, and Howard Hughes. Choosing only active scientists who reviewed under their own names, it hoped to avoid the inherited system's malaise. In the meantime, this approach has become widely adopted as a new gold standard by *Nature* and *Science*, among others.

The Marriage of Reader and Content

Conventional publication puts author and reader in touch through methods both targeted and imprecise. The supply side includes advertising, reviews, citations in others' work, lectures, book tours, and other means of getting the word out. Readers, in turn, seek material of interest via reviews, bibliographies, asking around, and searching the web. In effect, the blind seek the sightless. Only through hard work, perseverance, and luck can one hope to make contact. With digitality and its ever more sophisticated search engines, finding pertinent content has become easier. As content is digitized and tagged, it becomes searchable and findable. AbeBooks has made tracking down obscure used books the work of seconds. Dating apps help those seeking specialized erotic fulfillment or complicated emotional satisfaction. So, too, are curiosity and thirst for knowledge more easily slaked by digitality's ability to pinpoint where to look.

Conventional publishers work on a supply *and* demand model. They hawk their wares as customers seek their choices. In the market, publishers face an almost impossible situation, vastly more difficult than for other sellers. In 2020, the US offered 43 new car models and some 260 existing ones to choose among.[25] Before the Great Recession, Americans bought a new car 13 times a lifetime; now the number is about 9.[26] Over the average car-buying lifespan, consumers thus choose among some 300 products once every five years or so. When shopping for food weekly, over a year, they select an average of 260 different items from among the 36,000 found in a typical supermarket.[27]

Books are much more of a crapshoot. In the US alone, 300,000 new books appear annually. Most are not the kind stocked even in large bookstores, much less piled on the front tables. Nonetheless, the choices are overwhelming. In 2014, Amazon had 23 million distinct paperbacks for sale (many more if you count hardbacks and other media, but that raises the likelihood of duplication).[28] The average reader in the US gets through a dozen books a year, the median reader, four.[29] Even assuming that those are all purchased, the sheer pickiness of the selection in the book market compared to supermarkets, not to mention cars and other consumer goods, is staggering. Books involve four choices among 23 million possibilities annually, compared to 260 food items out of 36,000.

And that is ignoring the three million scientific articles published annually. A decade ago, under cosmology (a subfield of astrophysics, itself a subfield of physics, which in turn is a significantly smaller field than chemistry or medicine), the Smithsonian/NASA Astrophysics Data System listed five times as many articles as Netflix has films.[30]

That reader and book ever hook up is little short of miraculous. Perhaps many readers are stuck in what amount to bad literary marriages to the wrong content. Some may be reading Dan Brown when they would be happier with Ken Follett, or they are slogging through Thomas Piketty when a little dalliance with A. B. Atkinson would brighten their lives. From this dilemma springs the infrastructure of choice-making that guides readers. What Tinder and Grindr do for sexual selection, the literary dating services supply for readers—from Oprah to Frederic Raphael, from *Reader's Digest* to the *TLS*.

Publishers' marketing is one aspect of this, too, seeking to alert potential readers to something of interest. Amplification is one role publishers claim to play, but as a rule, it does not work.[31] If everyone in an auditorium stands, no one sees any better than when seated. If all content is amplified, the overall sound level rises, but nothing in particular is heard. And even if the publishers do make themselves noticed, they are so conflicted that no one takes them seriously. Blurbs on book covers must be the most devalued form of speech in the democratic world, perhaps barring letters of recommendation. That is tacitly admitted by how they are banished from the paperback edition in favor of—highly edited—excerpts from reviews. Marketing is less of an issue for periodicals. Journal publishers enter the market only infrequently—when subscriptions come up for renewal or new subscribers sign on. Book publishers, in contrast, enter the market with each new volume, incessantly sounding their claxons and clamoring for attention.

But with digitality, the hunt for perfect content changes. Once material is posted, sophisticated search engines and translation software, aided by ever-better techniques of discoverability, help bring reader and content together efficiently and reliably. We move from matchmakers to dating apps. Rather than readers and works hoping improbably to connect in the dark, grazers will now suss out the tender shoots in the field, honing in on the most delectable.

In digitality, certain inheritances from the old world where physical volumes competed for attention fall away.[32] Book covers and dust jackets may soon be remnants of the past. For centuries, books were published without stiff covers, in the expectation that buyers would bind them to match their library's furnishing. For generations, French books from Gallimard and other houses were issued in stark, elegant, and uniform covers. The Pléiade editions are equally constant—the cream of French literature and thought, uniformly leather-bound on bible paper.

The care devoted to book covers today reveals an increasingly commodified product vying for consumers' attention, much like cereals in the supermarket. The digital world returns us to the Gallimard tradition. Search engines skip the covers and deliver us directly to the title page or, even better, the passage we seek. The fuss about layout, margins, typeface, and other accouterments of the printed page will be left behind as e-readers tailor the page to personal preference. Not only will we bind our books to suit us, we will typeset them. Authors will instead fret over metadata, permanent identifiers, and discoverability, ensuring their message gets out efficiently. Having become electronic files, books will be less and less physical artifacts.

Filtering and Searching: How to Find What We Seek

Information scarcity is no longer our problem. We are awash in data. Scholars are reading more, paying each work less attention as they run faster just to stay in place on the content treadmill.[33] The new challenge is to tame, control, and use the hyper-quantities that threaten to overwhelm our comprehension. Despite more information, our time and attention remain unchanged. How do we find data pertinent to our purpose? Two basic strategies tackle information surfeit: filtering and searching.

Filtering allows others to determine the most useful information; searching permits us to pinpoint data that concern us. Recommendation is a subset of filtering: suggestions of potential interest made by others. Recommendation is becoming systematized and automated. At the moment, it still remains more annoying than helpful, as our past online purchases chase us around the internet, begging for an encore. More sophisticated recommendations use our viewing, reading, or listening choices to prompt tips for further similar pleasures. In the future, suggestions will likely improve. The algorithms are getting to know us better than anyone. A decade ago, Target analyzed shoppers' choices to identify pregnancies, even able to calculate due dates.[34] Yet, even without that degree of prediction, the algorithms know better than we do what is out there, and they can more accurately satisfy our yearnings by connecting us with actually possible choices.[35]

Some argue that filtering is the main act of managing content surfeit. The question is merely when to apply it—before or after dissemination? Publish, then filter, not filter, then publish—that is the new mantra.[36] While this sounds attractive, it presumes that someone is willing to do the filtering. Clay Shirky has suggested an analogy with dinner party conversations: No one would demand that prandial comments be screened before spoken—though we all remember occasions when that might have been advisable.[37] Conversations and publications are not equivalent. We require more thought of one than the other. Can we say the same of blogs, tweets, and other online communication—more formal than dinner party conversation, less than conventional publication?

Filtering alone does not put us in touch with the material we seek. It assumes that content is arrayed from good to bad, with our goal being to remove the mediocre. That is one way of taming content superfluity, proceeding along a hierarchy of evaluation. Searching is another activity altogether. When readers seek information on a topic, they hope for high-quality results. But that is secondary to locating material on their subject in the first place. Searching separates not good from bad but pertinent from irrelevant. At the first pass, pertinence or relevance require no judgment of quality. That may come later but is not the primary concern.

Searching should also be distinguished from browsing. Browsing assumes an initial selection made by others, whether in a journal on a certain subject or an arrangement in a library or bookstore by theme. Within that preliminary sorting, would-be consumers then skim to make a secondary cut. While adequate for a simpler era with fewer choices, browsing is decreasingly useful. Most readers of online articles arrive directly at their destination, guided by a search engine, rather than navigating from the journal homepage, let alone the publisher's.[38] That may explain why the range of articles cited has tended to narrow, as researchers less frequently chance across fortuitous adjacent works while browsing.[39] Tunnel vision is the outcome. Yet, it does not explain why browsing cannot just as well happen on screen as with a journal issue in hand or standing before a shelf of books. Nor does it explain whether the lowered friction costs of clicking through to references in footnotes does not vastly expand the relevant literature readers are led to through online works.

Searching for pertinent material is necessary, however large or small the total amount of information. We are swamped regardless. Filtering may give the comforting illusion of separating wheat from chaff, delivering only the good, but the quantities remain unmanageable. "There are enough peer reviewed articles to read without having those that have not been," as one researcher put the argument against preprint repositories.[40] That is the delusion—that sticking to peer-reviewed articles allows us to surmount the sheer volume even of those.

Recall the old joke about experts who know more and more about less and less until they know everything about nothing. Meanwhile, the generalists know less and less about more and more until they know nothing about everything. Review is less necessary the narrower the field tilled. There, readers more quickly become experts themselves, no longer reliant on others' guidance. It is the generalists who most need pointers to navigate through expansive landscapes of the unknown. Not all scholars are equally dependent upon review, though the overall quantities of information in even small fields keep the specialists busy.

Why review at all? In and of itself, review adds little value. Most basically, it calls attention to something deserving that might otherwise escape notice. Among many works on similar topics, more sophisticated reviewing suggests what we should read first, saving time. Given overwhelming and growing amounts of information, our consumption can never be exhaustive. If authors continue writing while we read, even immortals will never get around to everything. Selecting where to spend our limited attention will always be necessary.

Review itself generates more content, compounding the problem. It explains where a work fits in the historiography, weighs its faults and virtues, suggests improvements, and counsels for or against reading it. A review often satisfies readers, who save the time needed for the work itself. Other times, the review devours attention that could have been devoted to the underlying work. A numerical rating system, Michelin stars for books, requiring just a glance, would sometimes be preferable. But fundamentally, the point of a review is to act as a guide for the hunter, bringing us within striking distance of prey, allowing us the satisfaction of a kill without the bother of the stalk.

Curation is similar. The highlights of an artistic genre, a choice of the best works on a subject, of primary documents illustrating an event—whatever the selection may be, it is pulled together to spare us having to duplicate the curator's efforts. Whether an edited volume, a museum exhibition, or a greatest-hits compilation, curation takes us down a shortcut. If anything, curation might be considered the overarching principle, with reviewing a subsidiary strategy.[41]

The curation accomplished by peer review is but one instance of filtration. The publishers' selection is the first step of a larger sorting process. It is followed after release by press reviews, prizes, edited collections, and other means of calling attention to the best of insurmountable output.

Readers have long paid for guidance through abundance. Reviewers have been with us almost since books first arrived. Many scholars extensively read the meta-content—*NYRB*, *LRB*, *TLS*, and the journals in their field. Nor are the digesters spring chickens. Eighteenth-century publishers issued volumes selecting nuggets from the press, such as *The Gentleman's Magazine* and *Harper's New Monthly Magazine*.[42] German journals of the period provided abstracts of the newest scientific literature.[43] *Reader's Digest* and *CliffsNotes* (now issued by Wiley, one of the most profitable scientific publishers) have been at work for decades. *Blinkist* and *getAbstract* are more modern versions, along with the *Browser* and *Sensemaker*. Scholarly versions include the *Faculty of 1000* (*F1000*) site, which used to rate biology and medicine papers via postpublication review.[44] *Mathematical Reviews* has been evaluating articles since 1940, when it took over a similar function from the *Zentralblatt für Mathematik*, which shunned work by Jews under the Nazi regime.[45]

Even more overtly curatorial are overlay journals. They select from unreviewed content posted on the web. The JMIRx journals (launched in late 2019), for example, curate content posted in medicine, biology, and psychology preprint repositories. Editors find articles, make offers to authors, and consider self-nominations. They add a layer of peer review and typesetting and publish the results in *PubMedCentral*.[46] *Discrete Analysis*, a mathematics overlay journal, links to papers posted on arXiv, indicating that they "have been peer reviewed and judged to be of suitable standard."[47] Overlay journals need not create a new gathering of data unless they want to raise the level of an article's editing or presentation. They can just point readers to already-posted content that has passed muster. That makes them largely indistinguishable from the guides for readers mentioned above.

Filtering allows experts a say over what gets channeled our way. Searching, in contrast, puts us at the mercy of the algorithms, but at least we control what we are looking for and act as the last-instance sorters. However impressive, today's search engines are a pale fore-shadowing of what they must become if we are to tame content superfluity.

Even more crucial, content must be searchable, findable, and reachable. Gone are the days when the vast resources of JSTOR, HeinOnline, and other journal databases were dark to the search engines. At least their content now shows up, even if it still hides behind paywalls. Tagging and making content discoverable have become among dissemination's most important tasks.

Unaffiliated scholars outside the university bubble are frustrated to discover articles they must read but cannot access. Worse, the cost structure of academic papers mocks those who have no choice but to pay retail. For listeners and watchers, Apple prices its songs reasonably, Amazon, its downloads. Not the academic publishers. A review of a book in an OUP journal can cost more than the book itself.[48] Such market tone-deafness says much about why publishing is in a pickle. If they instead instituted reasonable prices and func-tioning micropayment systems, publishers might even be able to move their content instead of suckling at the teat of library budgets.

Such incompetence also explains why Sci-Hub, Z-Library, and other pirate sites (guerilla or black open access) enjoy massive fol-lowings. Sci-Hub has become a darling of the movement.[49] It is now the largest open-access academic resource in the world. After just six years, it hosted 67 million papers, two-thirds of all published research, available to anyone.[50] It violates every conceivable copy-right law and continues only thanks to its location somewhere in Kazakhstan, supported by Russia to poke a stick in the West's eye.

However, Sci-Hub has recently come under attack. Litigation is ongoing in the High Court of New Delhi, and Virgin Media has begun blocking access to it in the UK.[51] Good manners require reg-istering a polite harumph of disapproval of this blackest form of open access. Yet, it is hard to avoid seeing Sci-Hub's success as the publishers reaping what they have sowed. The pirate sites' users are not just scholars denied legitimate access but also professors and students at reputable and connected institutions who find them more convenient than their own libraries' often labyrinthine digital collections.[52] While China is the largest downloader from Sci-Hub, the US is number two.[53] Publishers' inflated fees and cumbersome procedures keep the pirate sites in clover.

The perfect search engine will one day provide a universal index. It will include every word in every work and a means of identifying and locating every image. Granted, it may not pick up concepts that are not expressed in particular terms nor necessarily collect synonyms under a common heading. Strictly speaking, it will be more a concordance than a subject index.[54] But realistically, indexes compiled by hand rarely do that either. And it will solve the problem of languages, such as Chinese, that cannot be ordered alphabetically, therefore indexed only imperfectly.

Anyone who has compiled an index knows that names, places, facts, and specific substantives are easier to include than vaguer concepts and ideas. In Václav Havel's play *The Memorandum*, a new language, Ptydepe, is invented to add precision and avoid homonyms, words that sound alike. One consequence is a proliferation of extremely specific terms for concepts that might resemble each other in natural language. Such a tongue would be an indexer's delight, at the very least sparing us the need for tens of thousands of Wikipedia disambiguation pages. In its absence, we must rely on more sophisticated searching. As that improves and content is better tagged, search engines will do our bidding more dexterously. Fine-tuning for results by language, format, provenance, or dates will become child's play.

We have touched on Michael McCormick's ability to wrest from Widener library's otherwise mute tomes evidence of trade between the Arab world and Europe in the eighth and ninth centuries. In the late 1990s, it took him and his students a week of shoe leather. Once Widener's contents are fully searchable, a similar investigation should be a matter of hours and turn up evidence further down the long tail. That will make Widener less a library and more a database. We are almost there. Google Books has digitized a Widener-sized chunk of content. Only copyright law and the publishers' veto hinder its being put to full use.

As the mega-journals approximate smaller versions of a future global bulletin board, they suffer the tension between filtering and searching. With size no longer a constraint, specialization serves no purpose. Journals or edited volumes focused on particular subjects acted as a preliminary filter. Editors did not have to evaluate submissions outside their remit. The narrower the topic, the more manageable their workload. With active searching rather than passive filtering, however, such needs fall away.

While the mega-journals may foreshadow what is to come, they suffer teething problems of their own. *SpringerPlus* was perhaps the closest mega-journals have come to the global bulletin board, publishing indiscriminately across a Noah's ark of different fields. In the meantime, Springer has shut it, concluding that both humanistic and technical scholars prefer journals more tailored to their subjects.[55] So long as specialized and omnivorous venues coexist, the former will have a leg up. Only when specialization confers no advantage in channeling attention will narrowly focused journals go the way of the Victrola. Journal specialization is, as noted, just a first approximation of indexing and searching. For books, the same holds for tables of content and indexes. Improved search engines will end such crude filtering. Indeed, at the logical extreme, neither books nor articles will need titles.

As content is searched across a massive accumulation like Google Books, the works become less important than the whole. The engine delivers the results, and it matters little precisely whence they stem. The source of a fact or an idea remains important to understanding its context and possibly its validity. A danger in this brave new world of commodified memes will be failing to understand what is meant when the search engine delivers a disembodied snippet of text. Were Irish children really to be eaten, or was Jonathan Swift being ironic? When first developed in the sixteenth and seventeenth centuries, indexes were attacked as diverting readers from the entire work to mere excerpts. Swift coined "index learning" as a term of contempt. Some authors refused to compile indexes lest readers shirk plowing through the entire text.[56]

Books and articles are composed of smaller units, whether assertions, facts, ideas, or memes. What search engines bring us are less broad ideas—by their nature hard to identify, localize, and trace—than compact, discrete units of meaning, some factual, some conceptual, some argumentative or rhetorical. The search algorithms handle "Who was the best-known constitutional lawyer in nineteenth-century Argentina?" better than "How do constitutional differ from civil rights?"

Under the search engine's dispassionate gaze, works will decompose into their constituent memes. Once digitized and searchable, every text's identity dissolves into the mass of all content. Precisely to which conventional work—book, chapter, article, poem, or blog—the search engines deliver us will be less important than its content. Authors working with the omni-searchable mass of global content will pick and choose with little concern for immediate provenance. As Kevin Kelly said about Google Books, "Once text is digital, books seep out of their bindings and weave themselves together." Digitally combined, books will merge into the "collective intelligence of a library." Together, all books become one massive tome, "a single liquid fabric of interconnected works and ideas."[57]

Those who worry that this bodes ill for understanding ideas in their context may be heartened that few such predictions have yet materialized. A decade ago, a company named Citia was in the business of dissolving books into their component memes, the better for users to reconnect and use them as they saw fit. Today, Citia has become a corporate communications software firm.[58] Perhaps more comforting still: such decomposition has occurred since the subject index was first invented in the early thirteenth century. Robert Grosseteste's *Tabula distinctionum* collected references to subjects (that God exists) across the Bible, the Church Fathers, pagan authors, and Arabic writers.[59] Insofar as the effects are bad, we have long suffered them.

What epistemological effects will search engines have? Delivering facts more readily than ideas, will they focus the future's clever minds more empirically? Theory is a means of spanning the gap between facts. It connects them into causal narratives that explain why this, and not that. The fewer the facts at hand, the broader the gulf theories must bridge, the more explanatory work they must perform. Conversely, the more data points we have, the less arching and ambitious theory can be—at least if it aims both to have causal power and account for myriad facts.[60] Easy availability of endless data, our ability to slide ever further down the long tail—will that sap the appeal of grand theory? Will future theories, strapped ever-tighter to ever more granular factual underpinnings, necessarily be less ambitious? Two points define a line. That is simple, powerful, and appealing—but also based on de minimis data. The best we can hope for from a wealth of data, in contrast, is that it clusters, indicating a trend. If we are lucky, it suggests the likelihood of one possible explanation. Being dogmatic is harder as data multiplies.

Evaluating, Not Publishing, Is the Goal

One solution for open dissemination is a global bulletin board, a vast repository where everything is first posted. The mega-journals have already moved in this direction. The networks and consortia of repositories are close behind—organizations such as OpenAIRE in Europe or LAReferencia in Latin America. Because digitality removes size constraints, subject specialization is unnecessary.

Selection takes place after publication, not before. Any topic is welcome.

Posting and publication should be distinguished. Posted, everything can be read in typescript. After this, improvements can be added depending on customer demand, author wishes, or whatever motivates a closer scrutiny of a text's claims or a jazzing-up of its presentation. More important than finding the grain in the chaff is locating what interests us amid the irrelevant. With a global bulletin board, getting words before readers will no longer be the problem. We will have achieved peak dissemination as a steady state.

In a deafening cacophony of content, how do we decide where to start?[61] The more focused and precise our interests, the smaller the problem. For scholars homed in on a microtopic, the concern is more finding information than judging which to begin with. Those in pursuit of broad issues most need evaluative aid. Peer review in its traditional prepublication sense is but a partial answer. While helpful, nor are postpublication guidance and curation a full solution. The horizons of evaluation must expand. So far, reviewing has followed the Michelin guide model, with experts sampling the wares. A more Zagat-like approach might be equally useful, where everyday consumers pool crowd wisdom. The disadvantages are obvious—amateur reviewers, including bloviators and ranters. If anonymized, will the reviewers' worst instincts well forth? If anyone can evaluate and comment, who reviews the reviewers? But if we insist on expertise, where will we find enough?

Nonetheless, review by the vox populi may have its role. Aggregated and averaged, with outliers lopped off and extremes smoothed, this approach may prove useful, much as stock market movements convey information. As some works go viral, up-voted by readers, the Zagat approach may unearth sleepers overlooked by the mandarins. Conversely, Reddit-style voting may also deliver a comedownance to the overinflated reputations of eminent but now complacent authors.

All this presumes that works are read and rated. How likely is that? Publishers claim that peer review is their most important contribution. The distinction between publication and self-publication hinges largely on such vetting. Self-publishing a book on Amazon can be done very inexpensively, so if getting the word out were the only goal, this would be an obvious route. Yet, what self-publication lacks is a major element of the academic prestige economy.

Before Amazon, authors who self-published did so at so-called vanity presses. Such houses were paid to issue whatever came over the transom. No one who could squeeze their manuscript past the lions guarding the gate at any conventional publisher would have gone this route. Yet, in the nineteenth century, authors still commonly bore the costs and risks of dissemination, akin to self-publishing. Henry David Thoreau convinced his publisher, Ticknor & Fields, to assume the costs of his second book, *Walden*. That took some persuasion, given that his first, *A Week on the Concord and Merrimack Rivers*, had done so poorly that he stored 600 unwanted copies in his attic until he could sell them back to the publisher.[62]

One hurdle open-access publishers contend with is the public's confusion of them with vanity presses. The new houses' claim to scholarly integrity is based on peer review. That, in turn, justifies the higher costs they incur. Yet, in the meantime, the stigma attached to self-publishing has faded. As seen, self-published editions now dwarf conventional books in the US. No more than a stream of selfies is vain and preening is self-publication considered self-regarding. After all, only a small fraction of works emerge from university or other academic presses, having run the gauntlet of peer review. Most conventionally published books do not undergo much prepublication scrutiny. That adds to the reasons why post facto review is crucial.

Jumping through the hoops of peer review is just the first barrier to surmount—the admission ticket for the cosmic raffle of attention gathering. Anointed by its publisher, the work emerges onto the field of battle that is the marketplace of prestige. Even in scholarly publishing, most vetting occurs later. The reviews, prizes, fellowships, sabbaticals, grants, conferences, invited talks, and other emoluments that the scholarly world bestows on its favorites all follow publication. The priority of postpublication review is much less of a change than peer review's defenders would have us believe.

But is work reviewed after release? Hume knew that a scholar's nightmare is not to be criticized, but ignored. As in a marriage gone bad, even anger is better than the cold shoulder. Scientists rely on work being noticed. Priority is crucial for reputations, prestige, and prizes. The first to discover something enters the history books, others remain also-rans. Priority can be asserted retrospectively against a late-comer who managed to be noticed first, but being seen as first through the door is far better. The gentlemanly accommodation between Darwin and Alfred Russel Wallace was unusual, including a joint paper to the Linnaean Society in 1858. It contrasted with Darwin's conflict with Richard Owen.[63] Establishing priority by posting a manuscript is a great advantage that explains why scientists have readily taken to prepublication repositories. Curiously, scholars also worry that papers in preprint repositories will be plagiarized, even as they cement their priority.[64]

Establishing priority is crucial for each researcher's career but less for a field's overall progress. Contrary to what Romanticism's individual genius theory of creativity would have us believe, intellectual progress is a collective endeavor. Advances happen independently of any one researcher. If professor X is run over by a bus, colleague Y—working on adjacent issues—would soon arrive at similar conclusions anyway. That is apparent as science becomes more collective, carried forward by large teams. No scholar is irreplaceable.

It is revealed most clearly where trivial necessity clamors for attention—where the market demands quick and easy solutions to mundane problems. Once cars had been equipped with tires early in the twentieth century, exchanging them quickly and easily became pressing. Largely simultaneously, seven different people invented demountable rims for this purpose.[65] The race to the patent office was determinative. Advances in treating osteoarthritis of the knee have arrived in close, almost photo-finish, succession.[66] This holds more broadly, too. In disciplines drilling away at nature's coalface, many investigators are about to make the same breakthrough at any given moment.[67] Newton and Leibniz arrived independently and proximately at calculus. Three teams of two physicists each published papers within weeks of each other in 1964 showing how particle carriers of force, such as photons, could gain mass—part of the work that eventually identified the Higgs boson.[68]

The correspondence between research and reality is less direct in the humanities and social sciences. The fruits of their work are less breakthroughs in understanding something "out there" and more a subjective interpretation of human-centered events that are themselves reciprocally influenced by how they are understood and, in any case, open to legitimately divergent understandings. Yet, broadly the same overarching functionalist logic as in the sciences holds. Creators work within epistemic bubbles that influence what topics seem important and which conceptual tools are useful.

During the 1970s, Saul Kripke was not alone in working on concepts of identity and essential characteristics across different circumstances. Ruth Markus and Alvin Plantinga did too. But when Kripke coined the term "rigid designator" to specify something that holds across all possible worlds, the need to assert priority was less pressing than in the natural sciences—as suggested by his relaxed approach to publishing. Neither patents nor prizes are promised those quickest to publish. Yet scholars here are keen to be associated with breakthrough concepts. "Prisoner's dilemma," "performative utterance," "excluded middle," "inferiority complex," "conspicuous consumption," "creative destruction"—all are seminal ideas attributable to specific thinkers who have expanded our horizons by crafting intellectual tools.

As in the sciences, thought here, too, moves with the herd. As melody and harmony dissolved, at some point, something like John Cage's *4'33"* would have been written. And indeed, Cage was not alone in proposing silence as the best response to music's travails.[69] Yet, it is best not to overstate such claims. The songwriter George M. Cohan, asked by a Senate committee how he came to write "Over There," answered, "It was just a bugle call. If I had not written it Thursday, someone else would have written it Friday. In other words, it had to be written."[70] That was nonsense. Some other song would have been written, and no doubt was. It would have been in much the same style, but it would not have been exactly that one.

That Cohan was exaggerating is the entire premise of copyright law. Authors can monopolize their particular expressions of creativity precisely because they are singular and unique. That distinguishes copyright from patents. A similarly extended hammerlock on ideas is forbidden since it would freeze creativity. Patents are granted only briefly because they monopolize ideas that could have occurred as well to others. Therefore, they can belong only temporarily to the person who first happens to think of them, or at least to register them. Individual expressions, in contrast, can belong to authors for much longer because they are specific and thus less important than a general concept. You can monopolize "My Funny Valentine," but copyrighting jazz would bring civilization to a screeching halt.

Postpublication Review

It is all well and good to recognize the flaws of conventional peer review, acknowledging that postpublication scrutiny is more important. That still leaves the question of whether it takes place enough to be useful.

Posting largely everything that meets minimum quality standards, allowing it to be evaluated subsequently, if ever, in effect already occurs in the mega-journals. *PLOS One* accepts manuscripts that meet certain technical criteria of presentation, language, and methodology.[71] It specifically does not ask about a manuscript's significance. Most submissions vault this hurdle. *PLOS One* and other mega-journals accept between 50% and 70% of submissions. These rates are only somewhat higher than for conventionally peer-reviewed journals, except the most prestigious, and are comparable to those of more specialized open periodicals.[72]

Vast quantities of research thus issue forth. For a while, *PLOS One* was the world's largest journal. Such outpourings are then left to readers to evaluate, sort, and use.[73] Review follows publication. Users determine the work's value, not the publishers. *PLOS One* and other mega-journals are thus arguably as much repositories as journals. Other journals are more overtly curatorial. In 2021, *eLife* began publishing only articles already posted as preprints, issuing the reviews along with the main text. As an overlay journal, that made *eLife* less of a publisher and more of a referee and certifier of content.[74]

Whether filtering or searching, we need better means of getting to pertinent information. It is worth distinguishing among varying levels and qualities of information. Not everything has to be read. Some research seeks to confirm or replicate already-discovered results. It is valuable if it does, and even more if it does not, calling accepted conclusions into question. Though such outcomes are useful for the interested, they do not need to be sorted and filtered for most readers.

Techniques for attention-signaling can be external to the content but also built into the text itself. Harnessing typological conventions, we can distinguish crucial from skimmable and skippable material. We signal passages needing *careful* attention with italics—sometimes just a word or phrase, occasionally a sentence or two.

Capitalization serves a similar function in phone texts, as President Trump reminded us daily. Inexplicably, quotation marks have taken on a similar use for emphasis on signage. The difficulty of italicizing in e-mails is a daily frustration for many, who resort to *bracketing* important words in asterisks and the like. In the nineteenth century, German books sported multiple levels of attention-signaling. Text to be emphasized could be italicized but also double-spaced with extra room between each letter, l i k e   t h i s. Oddly, that made reading harder, since the eye grasps the word less easily if letters are spread out. Perhaps, therefore, this convention has not survived. For extra whammy, German authors also combined italicizing and double-spacing.

That amplified text. Conversely, other conventions indicate second-order content. Foot or endnotes customarily provide the source of ideas or quotations, but often they take on a life of their own as a counterpoint to the text above the page's Plimsoll line. Sometimes they are as interesting as the main content. As mentioned, legal scholarship revels in extensive footnotes. They are often used to hash out historiographical or methodological issues that are insufficiently captivating to deserve the foreground. Novels have played with footnotes as a narrative device: *Sartor Resartus*, *Peter Pan*, *Pale Fire*, *Ficciones*, *Tom Jones*, *Tristam Shandy*, *Finnegan's Wake*, and many others.[75]

Here, too, German publishers of the nineteenth century were inventive. Their books had extensive swaths of text—easily half—indented to indicate supplementary material to read for further enlightenment but dispensable for following the argument's thrust. E-books open up new possibilities for such high- or low-lighting of text. Nor are the author's decisions the only ones. Readers, too, could supply pointers on what was worth attention or not.

Chapter 24 of the third book of *Tristam Shandy* is a reversed meta-use of such techniques. The narrator claims to have excised the novel's best chapter so as not to cast the rest in its shade. Also possible are all manner of annotation—by authors, editors, or readers. Institutionalizing such text hierarchies would be useful. They would help navigate works, supplying readers pointers on how and where to delve to their level of interest. In effect, they enlist the author's help in skimming. Books suitably signposted for rapid reading would not need shorter, article-length versions for wider consumption.

We need a ranking of content in terms of its claims on our attention. Readers should be equal participants. We could take a leaf from Michelin guides—not the red ones for restaurants and hotels, but the green city and regional ones. Their tripartite hierarchy (interesting, worth a detour, worth a trip), suitably modified, could be expanded. Reviewers and readers would contribute their two cents' worth. Reddit's ("the front page of the internet") system of up- and down-voting postings might be a model. The best content, evaluated by different groups of participants, percolates to the top. Wikipedia and Slashdot also enlist participant reviewers, with trust and influence built up by their performance.[76] The Chinese repository, Sciencepaper Online, reviews articles, with readers assigning stars. These are then considered in evaluating academic performance.[77]

Postpublication review takes time and resources. As more works issue forth in a new low-filtering environment, even greater efforts will be needed. In the UK, research funds are allotted after a quinquennial research assessment ranks university departments. In 2008, its costs were £12 million directly and another £47 million for universities to prepare.[78] That itself would pay for a good chunk of research. The assessment establishes each field's pecking order but does not even buy the general reader a list of the best academic works. In any case, given such costs, why pay both for pre- and postpublication evaluation?

How much content is reviewed after publication? If post-facto review is to be a viable alternative, it has to take place. True, prepublication reviews are the opinions of only a few readers, and editors may not always know of the best experts. But at least works are being drawn through some kind of comb. For postpublication review, there is no guarantee. Once content has been posted/published, no one can promise it will be usefully commented on or even read. In 2013, the NIH launched a pilot service to elicit comments on the 22 million articles in the PubMed database. When only 6,000 drew any attention, the project folded in 2018.[79] The vast majority of *PLOS One*'s articles remain uncommented-on.[80]

What percentage of content should elicit reactions for postpublication review to be considered a success? Many writings were reviewed before publication in the old system—even those we do not know of because they never appeared. But in the brave new world of global research participation and ever more authors and output, 100% review is unlikely. We cannot all be authors and reviewers, too. Hyperprolific researchers overburden the system. Perhaps a horse trade needs to be negotiated. The amount anyone may publish could depend on how much of others' content they also review. Tyler Cowen suggests capping researchers' output, requiring them to review instead, thus supposedly improving the quality of a reduced quantity.[81]

10

Too Much Content?

Compared to other ancient civilizations, Athens had a high literacy rate—most well-born males in the city, tapering off rapidly elsewhere and among other groups.[1] But even for those who could read, there was not much to read.[2] How different our predicament!

We produce ever more content. Material to read is no longer our lack, the time to do so is. The real expense of content is not its price but the opportunity cost of what we could be doing otherwise.[3] "Science that is not seen does not exist" is the motto of RedALyC, a large Latin American open-access portal.[4] Being published is not the same as being seen, much less read. We now fight more about attention than publication. Many lament the surfeit of content, wishing to return to an allegedly simpler and sparser past. Few consider that data have grown faster than content. That suggests a need for more, not fewer, articles.[5]

What does too much content mean? Do the oceans have too much water? The question is nonsensical except within some constraint—for fishing, shipping, recreation, CO_2 absorption, or whatever. If every reader is expected to be aware of—never mind reading—each word of the growing mass of content, then we have an impassable dilemma. But if there is some division of labor, and not everyone reads everything, then things look different. With a global production of 2.2 million books and 3 million articles, we put out some 200 billion words annually.[6] They clamor for attention from some five billion potentially reading pairs of eyes.[7] Ignoring newspapers, blogs, magazines, and the like, some forty new words annually await each reader.

That seems surmountable. Yet, averages are misleading—no one consumes one. Like lemmings, we cluster. In the US, the ten bestselling books in 2019 were bought 12 million times in print editions.[8] Though they represented but 1/30,000[th] of all published volumes that year, they accounted for 1/50th of total print book sales of 640 million units.[9] If readers' attention—not just buyers' discretionary dollars—was similarly concentrated, we would have 100 million readers globally poring over 73 books in any given year. Such focus on rare works reveals the power-law distribution of attention—that much content will be read by only a few, most by none. The long tail grows ever longer the more content we have. Finding and selecting what to read are as important as actually consuming it.

Keep in mind that words multiply, but so do readers. Researchers and writers are also readers, so an expansion of the audience is baked into an increase in authorship. As education widens and improves, readership mounts, too. The interested public is larger now than ever. How broadly readership is corralled varies among fields. In theoretical physics, authors and readers are largely the same people. But readers outnumber authors where practitioners and researchers overlap only tangentially, such as in medicine or engineering.[10] A sampling of articles in *Pediatrics*, for example, was read on average 14,700 times over their lifetimes.[11] Open access itself promises to attract a larger audience. It stands to reason that, as barriers fall, more consumers will be tempted to sample the wares. Journals that open up enjoy a bounce in readership.[12] Still, increased downloads do not always translate into more citations.[13] And in any case, the advantage is less than might have been expected if suddenly the candy store flung open its doors.

Open articles are more often cited than those locked behind pay-walls, although, surprisingly, the advantage is modest, some 7% or 8% more. This reading uplift may be thanks to earlier publication than for printed versions. Moreover, the benefit may be greatest for the oldest and most prominent journals. In contrast, lesser-known periodicals suffer from the increased competition for attention allowed by open access, their viewings declining as they open up.[14] Sales of paper versions of digitized open books have also increased between 5% and 8%.[15] A study of Swiss monographs found no effect on sales but a large upturn in views.[16] A Dutch study revealed no effect on either buys or citations but increased online usage.[17]

Meanwhile, another analysis has registered whopping increases—seven times the downloads, ten times more mentions, and 50% more citations. But this was an in-house investigation by Springer of its own open books compared to its non-open works, so possibly it was not entirely impartial.[18] It stands to reason that the long tail of obscure content would—once digitized—benefit most from being discoverable. As measured over the twentieth century in all fields except the humanities, ever fewer articles go wholly uncited, and citations are dispersed over a larger group of them.[19]

Readers are not aimless. They seek what interests them, and the task is guiding them to pertinent material. The content avalanche is partly channelled as some fields organize their best output in a few core journals located at the pinnacle of attention. In less centralized subjects, such as history, that effect is weaker. Here, attention is frag-mented into hundreds of national, temporal, methodological, and other subfields, each issuing work across a welter of outlets. But such fields are not those suffering from an overpowering flow of content.

Information abundance is also tamed by ongoing distillation. Textbooks and other secondary works mediate between the coal-face and consumers. Once-canonical texts fade to become part of the intellectual background noise. In fields that study physical real-ity directly, the upsides of intermediation win outright. What does a medical student gain by reading outdated physiologists? Great books courses in the humanities, in contrast, assume that renewed contact with classic formative texts repays the effort. Disputes here are over which works to include and how to limit an expanding canon to something manageable.

Without necessarily having read Plato, Marx, Weber, or Freud, most university graduates have a vague sense of what they argued, thanks to endless summaries and recapitulations in secondary works. Sometime in the future, everyone other than a few hardcore originalists will agree that the caravan has moved on. Even figures of this stature will have become of primarily historical interest. In the long run, even the greatest thinkers live on only in their distillation.

Too much content? If so, in what sense? From the earliest libraries, readers have complained of too much. Seneca the Younger, Stoic philosopher of the first century CE, condemned large libraries. What was the point of having so many books that no one could read even their titles in a lifetime?[20] Printing worsened matters. In 1525, Erasmus complained of a wave of new books that distracted attention from worthier works of antiquity.[21] In 1996, Umberto Eco echoed the lament, presumably tongue firmly in cheek. There were too many books, and he was hoping for some relief as would-be authors instead channeled their efforts through the then-novel medium of e-mail.[22] Fat chance. Books have continued to proliferate, e-mails even more. And no one would ever complain about a surfeit of content who had ever set foot in a bookstore in the old East Bloc, with its selection of Marxist-Leninist classics, manly proletarian novels, and paeons to overfulfilled five-year plans.

Storage and Memory

With digitality, the cost of storage diminishes dramatically. Already 25 years ago—eons in digital lifespans—we were on the cusp of sufficient capacity to save everything—every printed page or writing, film, photo, TV and radio program, music recording, and phone call.[23] Since then, social media and the web have added massively to content, but storage has expanded even more.

Kryder's law is the correlate to Moore's on the increasing power of semiconductors, and predicts a continuing exponential drop in storage costs.[24] The measure at the turn of the century was tera-bytes. Today, 20 years later, it is zettabytes, a trillion times larger. The equivalents of digital storage devices that those of a certain age remember paying hundreds of dollars for—whirring, blinking, chunky, crashing bits of kit—are now given away as advertising gimmicks on keychains.

The information we need is probably already out there, possibly multiple times, but if we cannot locate it, it might as well not exist. It is silly, however, to reinvent wheels that merely need to be found. That strikes social scientists as a truism. Yet, for natural scientists, who study the same reality as past colleagues, it may be more effi-cient to probe nature anew than to determine whether anyone has previously made similar observations. Descartes put his finger on the problem. Books mixed knowledge haphazardly with dross. Bet-ter, therefore, to go straight to the coalface, mining reality oneself.[25] But for scholars who regard even past errors as interesting, scrub-bing away inherited accretions is profoundly wrong, even in quest of renewal and cultural rebirth.

As more information is stored, duplicative innovation becomes likelier. Yet, with each iteration salted away and with search tools available, subsequent inventors, discoverers, or formulators should be better able to find antecedents before committing redundancy. We can glimpse a world where, if someone somewhere has ever known something, the rest of us can as well, and wheels are never reinvented.

Data surfeit also raises the problem of misinformation. More data are available, but much is bunk. The problem is, as the old joke about advertising goes, it is unclear which part is dreck. No one who has read the readers' comments at the bottom of online articles in even reputable newspapers ever regains their full faith in humanity. The world is full of creeps, jerks, fantasists, knuckle-draggers, the delusional, the very, very angry, and the just plain stupid. For those high-functioning enough to both surf and type, the internet has provided a forum for the first time in human history. The global id is not a pretty sight.

We have touched on the cultural consequences of vast available content and the danger of future creators being discouraged or seeing their role as reusing existing materials rather than creating *ab ovo*. Does too much information undermine our ability to act, vitiating decisiveness in the face of innumerable demands on our attention? Are we becoming a culture of archivists?

Memory and storage are distinct. One affects our psyches directly and unavoidably. The other—external to us—can be tapped as we wish, without obligation. Our collective store of cultural knowledge has been accumulating from before humans invented writing. Oral traditions were no more durable than their carriers. We know of them only insofar as they were committed to some more permanent medium, whether by the scribes who immortalized Homer or the brothers Grimm for Germanic fairy tales. Writing massively expanded our collective cultural storage, as did printing. Not until the digital did we again take such a radical leap. The in-between technologies, such as microfilm and microfiche, were but minor expansions, although enthusiasts at the time thought they might make entire libraries available to the world.[26]

A transactive memory system has multiple people recall information collectively, distributing responsibilities for different aspects. The internet has become our partner in such respects. Psychologists distinguish a feeling-of-knowing something that is actively in our memories from a feeling-of-findability, a sense of how readily we can locate information.[27] As we increasingly rely on the internet as surrogate memory, we become part of a larger intermind.[28]

Whether that is memory or storage need not detain us. Recall Michael McCormick's account of finding evidence of Arab coins in medieval Europe. His hunch that the information was somewhere in Widener paid off. And he lauded previous librarians' foresight in supplying subscriptions to arcane Belgian numismatic journals. That was a hymn of praise to old-fashioned libraries, uninformed by the web's possibilities. Today, with Google Books largely online, we enjoy the assurance that information is out there and must only be located.

Storage presents a problem only in the physical world when we run out of space. Few garages are actually used to shelter cars from the elements. Along with attics and cellars, they store stuff. Only when we reach capacity is there an issue. In digitality, however, space is no longer scarce. Attics have become infinitely expandable. We are hardly conscious of what is stored or even that it is being kept. We live our lives psychologically unencumbered by considerations that, as a society, we have become data packrats. We do not seem paralyzed by too much information. Indeed, one could argue that the more we store, the less we have to remember, the less we are weighted down.

Socrates railed against writing as vitiating true culture. In the *Phaedrus*, he argued that writing will atrophy humans' memories. Relying on writing—marks made by others, external to ourselves—will banish learning from our minds. Plato thought that knowledge from mere reading without contact with a teacher was not true understanding.[29] And indeed, psychologists have documented an offloading effect of computer memory and the internet. Information known to be stored is more likely to be forgotten.[30] And rightly so! What is the point of externalizing data, whether writing or uploading, if not to free our minds for other tasks?

Nietzsche may have been correct that too much memory immobilizes us. But storage spares us the effort of recalling trivialities. Who today remembers phone numbers, all nicely stored on our devices, with our intimates on speed dial? How long has it been since most adults performed long division without benefit of a calculator? Evolutionarily we have outsourced much of our digestive function to fermentation and fire, processes external to ourselves that allow us to absorb nutrients higher up the food chain. And we share such activities with the gut biome we acquire as a symbiotic helpmate to tackle the world more efficiently. Without such shortcuts, humans would be like ruminants, spending our days laboriously digesting plants. Philosophers now discuss distributed cognition as a form of knowing—not just remembering—performed by collectivities that are otherwise bereft of the psychological unity of individuals that normally explains how humans understand.[31]

Writing expanded our mental range. It allowed us to outsource what we now regard as the triviality of committing to memory. Culturally, we became dependent on parchment and paper. Despite some destructions and book burnings, written documents were more capacious and robust than the memories of bards and minstrels.

Digital storage takes us further along a road we have been traveling for centuries. Much is automatically backed up. Every revision and addition to our writings is retained for those who care to know. We leave wide data trails, allowing our lives to be uncovered retrospectively. This information surfeit is not much of an issue for us, except when we are defending our privacy. It is more one for future historians, faced with an embarrassment of riches and needing to sort the excess. As problems go, there are worse.

Authors vs. Readers

Mega-journals, online repositories, and other gushing founts of little-curated, underreviewed, overprovisioned content provoke unease. Letting down the guard of publisher review has created a supply problem. Vast pools of content magma bubble below the surface. Given an outlet to erupt via digital repositories and other low-barrier media, volcanoes of raw content now spew forth. Their deluge washes out the limpid rivulets of publisher-curated content with a vast torrent of good, bad, and indifferent verbiage. A flood of junk science and other would-be knowledge inundates us.[32] As with money, bad knowledge drives out the good. That seems to be the fear.

In this scenario, authors have become the reader's enemy. Best-selling, well-paid writers, the beneficiaries of their publishers' careful curation and promotion, may suffer from a muddying of the waters as new content rushes in to compete for the audience's strained attention spans. Most self-published books are in genre fiction. Whether that detracts from established authors in these niches is unclear.

For academic authors, however, the incentives are different. High-volume, low-selection publishing on the model of *PLOS One* and repositories such as arXiv have been criticized as good for authors but bad for readers.[33] Publishers serve readers—so goes the assumption here—by filtering out low-quality work that would otherwise distract the oversupplied consumer from the best.[34]

Academic authors are more interested in publishing than selling their work. In academe, sales are unimportant. They can be measured only with books and are irrelevant for journal articles. What matters in academia are impact, audience, and citation. Most readers of scholarly literature borrow, not buy. If hiring, promotion, and funding depend on not just publications' quality but also their quantity, some scholars may publish as much as possible. New means of dissemination that issue material without the barriers of peer review may tempt them to empty their desk drawers and fill the repositories.

Online, low-obstacle publishing may reduce the pressure to self-select and self-curate content, sinking authors' shame thresholds.

In the current system, only the need to await results discourages authors from submitting their manuscripts to the most prestigious journals. That burdens these periodicals. *Nature* receives over ten thousand manuscripts annually.[35] In effect, they ration access by time, as manuscripts await review. Money could be added via submission fees paid in addition to publication charges. Authors would be encouraged to think twice before submitting, and selective journals with the heaviest loads would be compensated, removing one argument for high publishing charges.[36]

Compared to the old system of review and filtering, does a larger percentage of all content today see the light of publication than earlier? Some argue that digitality and self-publication allow almost everything ever written to emerge. The total number of published works is therefore increasing.[37] That holds for the self-published books that are merely reproductions of public-domain material. New volumes may issue, but not new titles. But this logic of current surfeit works only on the assumption that in the old system, a rejected manuscript was withdrawn from circulation altogether, never to see the light. That is far from clear.

Although particular publishers and journals may have been selective, the system as a whole was not. If works were resubmitted until they found an outlet, individual selectivity was compatible with overall ecumenicity. In the legacy system, publishers were arrayed along a cascade of prestige. Works rejected by one journal or publisher were usually resubmitted to another, eventually finding their resting place in the hierarchy.

A stream of submissions used to inundate publishers, with rejected manuscripts receiving multiple reviews until they finally came to rest. Did a larger percentage of manuscripts than now remain unpublished, even after running the gauntlet? What happened to manuscripts submitted to any given publisher? Was there market clearance of the slush pile? No single publisher could know, but studies often take them at their word, that rejected manuscripts just vanished back into authors' drawers.[38] Publishers' assurance that their particular rejection settled matters once and for all speaks to their vanity.

With conventional journals, was selection so rigorous that many manuscripts never appeared in any venue? Without a universal register of submissions to which the published outcome can be compared, we cannot know. One study in 2001 reported that slightly more than half of initially rejected manuscripts were ultimately published elsewhere. But this examined editors who had looked to see whether manuscripts they had spurned were eventually issued, therefore likely to be an underestimate.[39] Of manuscripts not accepted by the *Journal of Clinical Investigation*, 85% later emerged elsewhere.[40] Similar statistics can be multiplied at will.[41] One observer was only slightly exaggerating in his conclusion that "if a paper is submitted once, it will ultimately be published, some day in some journal."[42]

Of manuscripts in bioRxiv, a prepublication repository intended as a forum to improve works before formal submission, a third remains unprinted in conventional journals.[43] In arXiv, the physics preprint repository, 64% of articles posted also appeared in journals indexed in Web of Science. This varied from a high of 80% in condensed-matter physics to a low of 20% in computer science, where conference proceedings and their posting are the preferred means of information exchange—in other words, where formal publication is not the aim.[44] Only a small fraction of content, then, is likely to remain in the author's bottom drawer. Has this changed in the era of mega-journals, repositories, and predatory periodicals? Would it further change with a global bulletin board? Even if every manuscript, however often rejected, was posted in the ether, it seems unlikely to increase the amount of disseminated content dramatically.

We also know that much scientific work results in no publication at all. Over 40% of research work in medicine is not issued as articles.[45] That is independent of digitality or open access. Nor is there reason to think that more formerly unpublished work now appears in open repositories. But it does raise the question of whether, with lowered barriers to dissemination, a backlog of work would now emerge in print. Negative results spurned by conventional journals with space constraints might be more likely to appear. Most of the "grey literature" of government studies, reports from nonprofits, preliminary research results, project websites, data archives, and the like were previously never formally published, but could now find an appropriate lodging in online repositories.[46]

Some university systems consider, or even emphasize, the quantity of publication. In China, the number of papers indexed in certain databases is often the basis of advancement.[47] If hiring, promotion, and funding rest with bureaucrats unversed in the fields they administer, quantitative metrics paper over their inability to make qualitative distinctions.[48] Such incentives can be perverse. Indisputably, rubbish has been published. Evidence from predatory journals in China indicates that articles can be ghost-written and plagiarized, and sometimes they are mashups of others' works.[49] Authorship and whole papers can be bought.[50] Since scientists in China earn more than doctors and lawyers, and rewards for publishing in top journals reach deep into six figures, the pressures are intense.[51] In such a system, more sophisticated quantifiable metrics would be an improvement. The h-index, for example, allows a more nuanced view of quality than just the number of works published.[52]

Nor does China stand alone in such respects. Melbourne Business School pays faculty bonuses of $A15,000 for articles published in one of the *Financial Times'* roster of quality journals.[53] When Australia started promoting scholars according to publication quantity, they issued more but worse papers.[54] In Serbia, it was considered a desirable reform of long-entrenched cronyism in academic advancement to require a specified number of articles in impact-factored journals for promotion instead. Alas, the new system was gamed by periodicals that convinced Thompson Reuters to index them while still publishing whatever dreck came over the transom, so long as publication fees were paid.[55]

In the Czech Republic, a preternaturally productive young scholar, Wadim Strielkowski, gamed the system with 60 articles and 17 monographs, all issued by dubious publishers over a quick three years.[56] South Africa's government pays universities a handsome subsidy for every article published in journals indexed in SSCI or SCI.[57] Once a 2010 law required them to meet productivity thresholds for promotion, academics in Italy began citing their own work assiduously to inflate impact factors.[58] Yet, that rule had been a well-intentioned attempt to combat cronyism and nepotism. In well-regarded Western universities, students in three-year life sciences doctoral programs are expected to publish two first-authored articles. Much salami-slicing of research projects is motivated by such requirements. A dean of biological sciences at a UK university detailed how faculty candidates had been chosen solely for the number of their publications, the quality of the journals, their h-index, and other purely quantitative indicators. After reforms, candidates submitted three articles that were actually read by the hiring committee.[59]

Such misincentives are stronger when there are fewer barriers to publication. But ultimately, less-restrictive dissemination is how the problem is expressed, not its source. The incentives arise from universities rewarding quantity. Unless thus prompted, why would anyone, except incurable graphomaniacs, issue their merest scribblings? Arguably, the open-access fora, even the mega-journals with their cheaper fees, impose a greater barrier to the free flow of bilge than subscription periodicals. Conventional outlets require review, but as we have seen with the *Social Text* scandal and others, that is not always an obstacle.

With gold access, at least the perpetrator of arrant nonsense has to pay. Indeed, one could imagine a reverse auction where mega-journals imposed some review and charged fees that rose as the apparent quality of submissions declined. It would be much like the marriage market in simpler times, which was cleared by offering higher dowries for women who found fewer takers.[60] Or like scholarships for clever students, with full-freight tuition for the less so. Admitted on merit, scholarship students at Oxbridge once wore special gowns proclaiming their distinction. If the variable fees charged for each article were made known, this would create in one fell swoop a publicized ranking system, an economic disincentive for unloading sub-par content, and a means of making mediocre but insistent authors subsidize costs.

To expect the dissemination system to throttle the motor of hyperpublication seems misguided. Nothing in digitality or open access requires universities to abandon their own criteria of merit. Even if they do not actually read and evaluate their researchers' publications and instead rely on postpublication metrics, such indicators—used sensibly—should separate wheat and chaff.

Overpublication?

Critics of open access often assume that scholarly careers are driven by quantity as much as quality.[61] Perhaps there is a grain of truth to this in some systems, such as the Chinese, that aspire to a larger presence on the global stage, have not yet arrived at maturity, and cannot be taken as characteristic. And possibly it is an issue in prolific fields where no one can reasonably keep up with their colleagues' output. The quantitative metrics mean more in hyperactive areas. Whether the articles whose quality the metrics supposedly measure are subscription or open access is irrelevant. But they allow hiring, promotion, and funding decisions without reading the material.

Yet, there persists a broader assumption behind such worries about excess content. Some think there are simply too many publications.[62] Others see a more subtle but equally insidious variant of the reward for quantity we have found in some institutions. This is attributed to a neoliberal quantification of intellectual metrics, a Fordist emphasis on measurable output. Neoliberal university systems pressure scholars to publish more than earlier and more than they want to.[63] The implication is that the aim is not better and more quality but has spun off into a cycle of pointless publication.[64]

A nostalgia for a vanished world of gentlemanly leisure pervades such accounts of our current malaise. It is much like the sepia-tinted view of past parenting practices. Cultural nostalgists often long for the early postwar era when intact nuclear families allowed children to be raised by loving stay-at-home mothers. Instead, we now have harried two-career couples, ordering take-out as they quarrel over whose turn it is to pick up junior from daycare. In fact, the unjaundiced eye of social science surveys reveals that parents spend more time today with their offspring, despite the prevalence of working mothers and heavier workloads for all.[65] In the good old days, mothers skimped on cookie baking to play tennis. Today, we work harder at parenting as well as our jobs.

We have less time for hobbies (inane enthusiasms that once passed the idle hours) and snoozing on Saturday mornings. Perhaps that is modernity's curse. But it is no more obviously a decline than is the modern academic's productivity compared to the patrician leisure, the life of reading and doing nothing with the knowledge gained other than teaching a few entitled undergraduates, which used to characterize university faculty. Sure, young academics at top universities have to publish more than their forebearers.[66] That is what upping the game means. Undergraduates, too, have to amass better records to get into these institutions. Bankers also work harder than their two-martini lunch predecessors. Nor has medicine been resting on its laurels. Name a profession where harder work is not the norm. Increased productivity hardly seems worth a remark, much less complaint. Lest we attribute this solely to capitalism and neoliberalism, keep firmly in mind that Soviet five-year plans—innocent of market forces—were relentlessly overfulfilled by hard-working Stakhanovites.

Do scholars overpublish? In the humanities and social sciences, the issue simply does not exist. Scholars publish a book at most every several years, the vast majority never more than one, max two, over their careers. Insofar as they write articles at all, perhaps one every year or so. The main fault here is that humanities articles are sometimes derivative of books, duplicating information scheduled to appear as chapters. The hard sciences and some of the social sciences, in contrast, may have a problem. We have touched on hypertrophied authorship, both the pile-on of multiple authors in the scrum and individuals' preternatural prolificacy. Scientists may issue more publishable units than before. Some observers claim that they achieve this by morcellizing output, salami-slicing projects into more and shorter pieces.[67]

Insofar as it occurs, salami-slicing research into multiple publications suits personnel decisions that reward quantity and the publishers who issue it. But it increases the work of reviewers. Not only do they have more articles to read, but they must also consider the entire nimbus of manuscripts surrounding the one in question to rule out unwarranted duplication.[68] Unfortunately for peer reviewers and librarians who shoulder the burdens of hyperpublication, multiple articles generate higher overall attention metrics. Citations increase when projects are published in many papers, not least because authors cannot resist the temptation to cite themselves.[69] Unfortunately for readers, the sweet spot for maximizing citations appears to be both many and larger articles.[70]

Some observers have suggested limiting how many works should be permitted researchers annually. Following the slow food movement's lead, they think that reflective, snail's-pace scholarship would enhance quality.[71] And some funders have sought to calm the supposedly roiled waters of publication by restricting the number of articles included on applications.

Debates on overpublication must be conducted within each discipline. Outsiders cannot judge whether prolixity is a problem. Publication differs widely among fields. Books play no role in some, articles little in others. And articles serve different functions. At one end, we have statements of much thought and work in fields such as philosophy.[72] Decades hence, the best will still be read. Conversely, in the life sciences and medicine, articles are often just short reports to establish priority and keep colleagues abreast of results. These outpourings may seem overwhelming to philosophers, but each piece is correspondingly ephemeral, not intended to be read even a few months hence as new results emerge and the caravan moves on.

Some fields internalize the review process, taking time to present ideas at talks and seminars, soliciting feedback before publication. Others externalize it, publishing quickly and awaiting responses. We would not want to confuse speed or quantity with quality. But neither should we assume that any increase in publication tempo or output necessarily indicates a decrease in worth. Sometimes more is more.

The output of academic content has increased in line with the growing number of scholars globally. That is not the result of open access and would have held in the old subscription system as well. The effect of mega-journals and online repositories will hit readers less than it will affect other, existing journals. Readers will have to grapple with the overall increase in content however it is delivered. But the immediate consequence will be to heighten competition at the lesser ranks of the publishing food chain. *PLOS One* and other mega-journals do not compete with top-ranked periodicals. Instead, they compete for content with lower-placed journals, which offer less as substitutes for the new outlets. That may portend a shake-out in the industry. Still, it leaves the average reader no worse off and arguably better served by the new open alternatives to yesterday's lesser subscription journals.

On the other hand, we have a different problem if mega-journals and repositories are encouraging more and worse work that earlier would not have been written, would not have been submitted, or would have been rejected by even the least-discerning conventional journal. Is output growing per capita, more for each of the increasing numbers of scholars? Only then would it be true that mega-journals and open access have diluted the quality of published research. Only then could one plausibly argue that open access encourages a downward trend whereby "every paper authored would be published, regardless of its quality."[73] How true is this compared to subscription journals?

More to the point, even if more content per capita is published today, even if some is mediocre, and even if that would formerly never have seen the light—is this necessarily a bad outcome? There is no book so bad, said Pliny the Younger's uncle, that some good cannot be wrung from it.[74] Many assumptions behind these questions need unpacking. Is there a large backlog of unpublished material that can now be issued in the repositories? If so, is this material unpublished because it is mediocre? Or because the established publication channels are swamped and unable to process it? Because the authors cannot afford publication charges or surmount other obstacles? Because established subscription journals apply evaluation criteria that exclude scholars from certain institutions, backgrounds, or countries? Because other nonscholarly obstacles hinder some researchers from issuing their findings?

We need to know two things. Compared to the era of conventional publishing and subscription journals, are there extra publications per capita that see the light with a switch to low-barrier dissemination? Or is the undeniable increase in academic publishing of recent years due to new authors entering the field as universities expand and once-excluded nations join the global research endeavor? If the former, then open access may be a factor. If the latter, not so much. The growth of worldwide research is a welcome development and, in any event, is not due to easier publication.

Globally, there were six million researchers a decade ago, more recently between seven and eight million. Of these, about 20% are repeat authors.[75] These numbers have grown much. In the US, engineers and scientists expanded tenfold from 0.26% of the labor force early in the last century to 2.5% in 1970. Mathematicians and information technologists increased 500-fold over half a century. In 2008, knowledge-based professionals made up 20% to 30% of the labor force in developed nations.[76] More researchers mean more research. China's output of scientific articles has increased 20-fold, from 6,000 in 1990 to 123,000 in 2011. By 2011, Chinese scientists published two-thirds as much as their US colleagues, including only articles indexed by Thomson Reuters. Between 2008 and 2014, the Chinese share of all scientific articles doubled from 10% to 20%.[77] China produces the second largest number of papers, after the US. But scientists (including engineers) make up 0.4% of the labor force in China, compared to 3.1% in the US.[78] The Chinese supply of content thus has ample headroom to expand before it justifies suspicions that more research is diluting standards.

Compared to half a century ago, most of the enhanced amount of content produced today comes from more researchers, not more output per head. That content is increasingly salami-sliced, subdivided into more and smaller articles, is something of a myth. More work is today coauthored. Dividing papers by the growing ranks of coauthors reveals a stable or even declining real output per head.[79] Other studies confirm that per capita research publication has been broadly constant over the past century.[80]

But let the devil have his say. Would it matter if we had proportionally more content today and each researcher authored more than earlier colleagues? Take the question a step further. What if this surplus content is also more mediocre than in the past. Why is that a problem? Once we have more works than we can ever hope to read, selection becomes a necessity. As mentioned, Seneca the Younger in the first century CE complained about that. And once sorting is required, it matters little how much is classified as dross for any given act of choosing. We already have more than we can read. *How* much more is irrelevant.

The per capita output of books ranges widely among nations. Even the measures are sometimes wonky. The British pride themselves on having the highest rates, but that is a statistical artifact.[81] UK and US publishers have long agreed on a monopolistic division of the market.[82] Books in English were issued exclusively in their respective spheres by UK and US presses. The Americans got the Philippines and sometimes Canada, the British, some 70 nations, once from the Empire and many later from the Commonwealth. UK books-in-print numbers are inflated by counting the UK editions of US books. If the Austrians required every German book sold there to be issued in a local edition, as the UK does for US books and vice versa, Austria would be the per capita publishing powerhouse of the world. Something similar must hold for Canada, not to mention Australia and New Zealand.

Iceland publishes more books per inhabitant than anyone. That is unsurprising for so small a country (population 357,000) with its own language. Even if it issued only a phone book, dictionary, thesaurus, and an encyclopedia, it would be ahead of the game. But, in fact, Iceland sports a vibrant publishing industry, all the more impressive for its dollhouse size. Per capita, Iceland publishes 238 times as many books as Kenya. Even compared to the Germans—bibliophiles who invented the medium—it issues two and a half times as many books, and almost four times compared to the Swedes.[83] So are the Icelanders overprovided with content, or are the Swedes deprived?

Where is the downside to as much information as possible, even if it is not all equally good? A similar discussion breaks out every time university admissions are expanded. Only a tiny fraction of 20-year-olds attended tertiary education in the old elitist system; today, one-third of the cohort does. The nature of universities has changed accordingly. Colleges can take less preparation for granted; they have had to broaden standards and to remediate. But besides a few gnarly classics dons, would anyone want to return to the old system?

Granted, we are becoming more credentialized. The BA that in 1890 would have guaranteed a job at the State Department is now an entry-level qualification to steaming lattés at Starbucks. But what of the advantages of having flight attendants noddingly acquainted with the concept of orientalism or IT support staff who can distinguish a mean from a median? Lucky the society able to allow so many such education! Much the same holds for content superfluity. Even if the average BA today no longer reads Latin, the overall cohort of 20-year-olds is better trained than a century ago. Even if not every work is comparable to yesterday's best, and even if some is shoddy, the quality, quantity, and usefulness of content today are overall better.

MA theses are generally neither published nor even archived anywhere. They end up tucked into corners of authors' attics or hard disks. If they were uploaded to depositories instead, the bulk of the world's knowledge would not change. Though currently largely invisible, MA theses are out there, and, once uploaded, they would become more useful. Of course, not every MA thesis is worth wide distribution or readership, but some are. The world would not be worse off if MA theses were suddenly searchable and readable, any more than it is with information overload, even if it is not all equally good. As the saying goes, there is no such thing as bad weather, only unsuitable clothing. There is no such thing as too much information, only inadequate search engines.

Indisputably, we have more information than ever. Is it too much? Even serious studies, not just grumpy old dons, complain about "overly abundant scholarly information."[84] What does too much mean? As the selection tools improve, surfeit should fade as an issue. Sophisticated search engines will tame the content we choose from, allowing us to focus. In any case, it is churlish to complain of excess. The question is, would the world be better off with less?

Economists and psychologists point out that too much choice can provoke anxiety, confusion, and bad decisions.[85] *Free to Choose*, Milton and Rose Friedman's paean to individual liberty, became *Free to Lose*, John Roemer's cautionary tale on the perils of unbridled markets. That is psychology, not epistemology. It holds for the supermarket, not the hardware store. Perhaps we needlessly fret over what to put in our mouths, anoint our skin with, or wash our hair in. But who believes it is better to have fewer tools to repair with, fewer medicines to treat with, fewer concepts to analyze with? Only rarely is surfeit an annoyance. And the obvious bears restating: mediocre, misleading, and mendacious stuff already bloats the web. Enormous quantities of bilge wash through the internet's portals. Open access, in contrast, allows a presence also for the good, the scholarly, the footnoted, the researched, and the reviewed. Again, sometimes more is indeed more.

Even the minimally vetted content posted in repositories, awaiting its readership and critics after the fact, comes with guarantees of quality that the web's bloviations lack. First, even mediocre scientific articles serve a purpose. The long tail is lengthy indeed. Who is to say that not everything finds its spot? Since dissemination costs little, nothing is lost by launching everything and seeing what arrives onshore. Because authors pay for gold access, arrant nonsense must surmount a built-in barrier. Who would front fees to float something they did not think was worth the electrons that fire the pixels that make it legible—or whatever is the digital version of "the paper it is printed on"? The idea that scholars busy themselves churning out garbage to pad their CVs, paying to clog the ether and hog attention, is wildly exaggerated.

We are afraid of being buried in junk science. But where would it come from? Who are these people with the time and funds to run labs producing bad research? You can do it once, but then your reputation suffers. Even at the dawn of digital distribution, Paul Ginsparg, founder of arXiv, argued that the very act of distributing content widely encourages authors to self-regulate. Researchers are keen to ensure that their posted content not embarrass them before a now-magnified audience.[86]

Yes, digitality has unleashed content. Self-published books supply an avalanche of new material that would not otherwise have seen the light. Most are fiction of various genres, hard to compare with academic work. Scholars write to probe and reveal the truth but also to attract notice and advance careers. For each of these motives—especially pursuing truth—they must toe certain lines. Regardless of how they publish, academics write within a framework of evaluation they have internalized, whose criteria they work toward. Unless their work meets scholarly standards, it does them no good.

"Without peer review, we are nothing but well-paid bloggers," one cynical observer of his fellow academics notes.[87] That is fundamentally wrong. Authors who do not follow their discipline's epistemological precepts even when not policed by formal peer review are not scholars. Nor would their work enjoy renown, or their careers receive advancement. In the broader sense of judgment leveled by colleagues, review is omnipresent in academia's panopticon, not just at the instance of passing through the needle's eye of formal evaluation for publication.

In the days of prepublication review, presses were not swamped with hopeless submissions. That books full of rubbish were only rarely published probably says as much about the quality of the intake as about any heroic acts of selection by editors. It is unlikely that only editorial evaluation spared readers inundation by printed bilge. The worst enemies editors face down are mediocrity, over-specialization, and tedious prose. Few authors would have bothered writing a submittable manuscript of nonsense. Why should that have changed?

Just because something is easy to bring out does not mean it is simple to produce. Yes, there are "books" for sale on Amazon consisting of cut-and-pasted Wikipedia content. No, the world is not improved by their presence. But these are like snake oil flogged to rubes, signs of an immature consumer market. The answer is not to forbid snakes or oil, but some combination of education and regulation. Eventually, such misuse will be relegated to the future's equivalent of magazine back pages or late-night TV ads.

Admittedly, plagiarism is easier to commit when only cut and paste are required, not even wielding pen and ink. Nor is plagiarism a crime, but merely a moral blemish. Moreover, certain aesthetic theories validate it as an element of derivative creativity.[88] But plagiarism is also easily exposed by the same technologies that facilitate it. Search engines tuned to such purposes routinely scrutinize undergraduate essays for tell-tale signs of duplication. Colleges hammer home to students that there is no excuse for committing plagiarism just because it can be done.[89]

It is a cultural curiosity that central Europe extravagantly valorizes the doctoral degree. In Germany, most universities are regarded as broadly equivalent in stature, whatever the reality. Ambitious politicians cannot burnish their CVs by attending the equivalent of Oxbridge or the Ivy League. Instead, they must scale the ranks, adding a postgraduate diploma. The outcome has been a rash of plagiarized doctoral dissertations in central Europe.[90] Entire websites are now devoted to scouring German politicians' dissertations for duplicity.[91]

In contrast, a doctoral degree is more a liability than an asset among aspiring politicians in the Anglosphere. US senators and congresspeople sport professional degrees galore, but rarely PhDs.[92] With a doctorate in history, Newt Gingrich was a recent exception. Even less credentialled are politicians in Britain. Most MPs (90%) have no more than a BA, often in liberal arts subjects that would not obviously qualify them to run a modern industrialized economy.[93]

In the academic world, plagiarism is not a serious issue. Scholars are socialized into producing verifiable work. Their reputations depend on convincing their peers of its worth. Especially in the sciences, research and its results are costly and complicated. Long before the point of review, whether before or after publication, the system discourages malarkey. The suspicion that legions of scholars are churning out substandard or even fallacious work, hoping to flog it to an unsuspecting public, is bunk.

Conclusion
Good Enough—Open Access
Meets the Real World

Open access began with a flourish of utopian promise: Every scrap of human knowledge and creativity will be available to everyone anywhere at no upfront cost. Digitality has catapulted the Gutenberg revolution skyward, allowing virtually costless publication of the last copy. It will also eventually drop the costs of producing the first copy, making dissemination more efficient. Everyone can churn out almost professional output at their desks. The distinct roles of author, editor, publisher, and bookseller can collapse into one. Consumers seemingly perch on the cusp of a wondrous new age of intellectual riches.

Open access is a noble cause with true believers. Unfortunately, that cuts two ways. Fervent champions fuel the passions that drive the movement. But framing the cause in Manichean terms alienates potential supporters and drives moderates away. Enormous amounts have been written about open access. Little comes from those whom the movement is intended to benefit, whether researchers or readers. Most issues from librarians, IT specialists, and other denizens of the academic nimbus emergent in library and information science, complete with specialized practitioners, obscure jargon, and an inordinate fondness for acronyms.[1] The "open-access community" is not those for whom the new system is supposedly being created—neither those who supply the content, nor those who are to consume it. Although a broad movement intent on spreading knowledge, open access has paradoxically professionalized itself by sheer quantity. Mastering the debate has become a full-time job.

With lofty ambition comes the likelihood of disappointment. However admirable open access's highest goals are, achieving them has stumbled over several obstacles. The costs and complications of dissemination have been underestimated. Publishers play a more important role than fervent advocates may have realized. Do-it-yourself technologies are good but not perfect. The expense of producing camera-ready copy is greater than anticipated, at least if one is aiming for something more than rough typescript.

In such discussions, the third rail has been the content that creators produce for profit. Authors who make a living from their work have protested what they see as attempts to deprive them of their livelihood. Bereft of a persuasive moral argument against them, open accessors have instead argued the virtues of sharing and the gift economy. Of course, many create and share their output for sheer joy without expecting compensation. And the logic of networks amplifies and enhances work that has been made accessible.[2] But it has proven naïve to expect all intellectual productivity to follow the heart-warming example of barn raisings.

True, many authors are otherwise employed and paid for their work. Why do they need a second bite of the apple? But even this unassailable logic leaves major issues unaddressed. University and other researchers who as salaried employees arguably perform work for hire have not easily been persuaded to drop their claims. Authors hoping to break through to an audience beyond the university are loath to abandon their chance at popularity. Many writers of serious nonfiction are not salaried and seek to live from their work. The case for asking them to open it is unclear. Many humanities fields study creators who are not salaried—writers, composers, artists, choreographers, filmmakers. Even if humanities scholars' content was made available, they would still face subscriptions, paywalls, and the retail price of works they need to study.

In the most difficult position are those creators (novelists, poets, composers, journalists, and sometimes filmmakers) who in another era would have remained freelancers but today work for universities or other institutions. Should their output be considered work for hire? Or are their salaries strictly for teaching, not also creating? If so, should their wages be lower than for their more academic colleagues, or their teaching heavier? Even their students' work is caught in such dilemmas. Work-in-progress novels, for example, are submitted for academic credit in creative writing programs. When they are posted on university websites, sometimes they are pilfered for sale as Amazon self-published works.[3]

But the elephant in the room is the commercial scientific publishing establishment. Having struck gold in research library budgets, it has no intention of relinquishing its gains. It has sunk roots ever deeper into the research world by organizing and managing raw data as well as finished output. More to the point, it has recognized that gold access is not a threat so long as publishing fees are comparable to subscriptions. That insight allowed it to support open access in the guise it champions. In this, it has met little resistance from either scientists or their funders. Yes, funders have often mandated open access. But the gold variant, where they pick up the costs, meets few objections. At $290,000 in research funding per article, a publishing fee of $3,000 is nothing to get riled up about.[4]

The gold route leaves problems unsolved. More content can be read by anyone—undeniably a major gain. But there remains the unaffordable cost of scientific output for libraries. What had been subscription fees became publishing charges. Unless funders are willing to pay at both ends, something has to give. Read-and-publish arrangements bring in libraries directly as payers of article fees. That continues their role in subsidizing a publishing industry that could not otherwise sell its wares. Academic libraries have long been the customers of last resort. But as research globalizes and nations such as China and India come online, the gold-plated Elsevier-style model becomes unaffordable. The appeal of so-called predatory journals for Third World scholars testifies to the failure of the legacy commercial publishers.

New access barriers exclude authors who cannot afford publishing fees. Those shut out by gold paywalls are both scholars from the developing world and humanities and social science researchers in industrialized nations. These groups face two alternatives. They can continue the fight for an ideal form of open access that is less costly and applies to all scholarly content. That will require some combination of copyright reform to pare down durations and efforts to pry loose the commercial publishers' stranglehold on scientific dissemination. For those who judge this an unlikely outcome in the foreseeable future, the alternative is to create other means of open publishing workable for those excluded from the gold system. An ecosystem of new journals and presses has emerged to serve such needs. Authors keen to see them succeed can help by submitting their best work and reading others'.

The fundamental problem open access faces is worth restating. Copyright has become bloated, prey to the rent-seeking academic publishing industry. If it could be returned to the shorter duration of its original formulation, the spoils would be smaller and less worth fighting over. It is lamentable, for example, that publishers can segment the market to sell libraries e-books at higher prices than they charge individual consumers. In effect, they seek to be paid per read, not per book—much as if heavily used family cars were to cost more than if owned by bachelors. Legislators dazzled into submission by the publishing industry's success in portraying itself as defender of creativity and cultural patrimony bear much responsibility. Copyright reform, shortening durations, would go far to solve the problem. But not all the way.

Even if reformed copyright were to speed up content's through-put, filling the public domain more rapidly, curtailing publishers' profits, and streamlining costs, a larger problem would remain. Asking consumers to pay no longer works if we hope to access the entire world's growing content. Digitality makes it possible for everyone to read everything. In the analog world, national collections were the best that could be hoped for, massive agglomerations of cellulose to which expectant readers pilgrimaged. Now we can anticipate a global library on the internet. But that will be impossible so long as readers pay for content. No institution can afford everything, and none could organize it, even with the requisite money. Only if the producers underwrite not only the much greater costs of research and writing—as they already do for scholarship—but also the dissemination of their work, can it be shared worldwide. Whether it is gold or diamond or some other collectivized form of financing is irrelevant—suppliers must pay.

Work for Hire

It is worth pondering why work for hire remains so controversial. The moral logic of open access is that most academic authors have been paid for their research work via salaries. Its fruits therefore belong to the taxpaying public. The relationship is not formally work for hire, but its ethical equivalent. In the European regimes that enshrine moral rights as copyright's centerpiece, the idea of treating creators as salaried employees is practically sacrilegious. The Romantic idiom still resounds strongly here. Authors create freely according to their own will, beholden to no one. It is inconceivable, therefore, that their work be owned by someone else, much less attributed to them, least of all a corporation.

Yet, work for hire responds to two realities. Much work is done by authors hired for the task. And much is collaborative, with the attendant difficulties of assigning sole attribution to any one author. That someone could be credited for creating an airliner or hydro dam—much less paid a cut of the proceeds—seems implausible. Why experiments at CERN, with their hundreds of co-workers, should be different needs a robust argument. The results of collider experiments are duly credited to the scientists who conceive and perform them in a manner Boeing engineers could never hope for. Is that not sufficient? Hollywood's collaborative mega-projects have developed an ecosystem of credit and attribution. Most of their collaborators are salaried, with salary understood to include an element of profit-sharing for the top dogs.

Why should work for hire not apply equally in universities, as it does in corporate research? Science faculties already run along such lines: their researchers have no illusions of being Romantic creators. Salaries are the bulk of their compensation, and they nurture no anticipation of royalties, residuals, or other payments. Fields that produce patentable breakthroughs are the exception. The rules here for profit-sharing are clear and broadly accepted. Humanities faculty, however, still harbor fond dreams attracting a wide audience and its rewards. That fuels their resistance to open access and the cold water it pours on the likelihood of being rewarded as *artistes*.

Universities have carved out a legal niche for themselves. Professors are exempt from work for hire, at least in the US. Work for hire is widely used in America for corporations, while in Europe, it is less common anywhere. The "academic exception" in common law allows professors and other research staff to retain rights to their works, despite having been paid to produce them.[5] Harvard's policy, for example, concedes copyright, and any associated revenues, to its faculty authors, although hedging this about with the inscrutable proviso that, when deciding on publication, it expects them to "make arrangements that best serve the public interest." Yet, having assured faculty that it protects "the traditional rights of scholars with respect to the products of their intellectual endeavors," it ominously goes on to caution that "Where the University takes ownership or control over scholarly works, the University shall consult with authors on plans for publication." And where the project has been especially reliant on university resources, the policy appeals for royalty sharing. Moreover, works created as part of employment by non-teaching staff are regarded as for hire, with the university the owner.[6]

Universities have only rarely sought to impose work for hire on their faculty. The University of Chicago once creamed off proceeds from lectures or books above a low minimum, assuming that its salaries covered faculty's work. That had been abandoned by 1950.[7] The University of Florida's employment contract requires faculty to assign it copyright in their works.[8] These are exceptions.

However hands-off universities may be on copyright, they carefully specify the division of spoils for patents. Until 1980, US federal agencies sponsoring scientific research were encouraged to take ownership of the results or at least to ensure they entered the public domain. After that, tactics changed. With US research and industrial preeminence challenged by Germany and Japan, authorities wanted to put discoveries to work. To ensure findings were actively exploited, they were transferred to those who could best use them. The Bayh-Dole Act in 1980 encouraged universities to own and monetize their patents, although paid for by federal funds.[9] Unexploited basic research benefitted no one. Better to make the knowledge sweat, even if others reaped the profit.[10]

In the sciences, faculty and universities have worked out arrangements for exploiting research findings. Professional schools, business and law especially, have achieved something similar by apportioning working time to cap outside employment. The sticking point remains with the humanities and social sciences, where the stakes are lowest. Faculty here are the most dependent on their employers, with the fewest outside opportunities. Only rarely do these professors derive significant income from extramural lecturing or writing. Yet, humanities faculty pen their articles and books and develop their courses with university support. Without research grants, sabbatical funding, summers off, libraries, teaching and research assistants, media support staff, and other university infrastructure, they would accomplish less.

Something like work for hire could be formally implemented for faculty, recognizing that they are paid ultimately by taxpayers. With work for hire in place, attacks on open access from within academia would lose their sting. Comparing itself to Hollywood, academia could—counterintuitively—take heart. Naturally, the university world resists such suggestions. Professors still fancy themselves more akin to Romantic artistes than Hollywood's scriptwriters. But that is an increasingly archaic view. Academics are paid salaries for their research. They should be recognized by attribution and the integrity right, allowing them to decide their works' final form. But why should they have a monopoly of dissemination?

Like universities, the film industry has a serious insider/outsider problem. Many marginally employed hangers-on lack the perks of full membership. But for those inside the bubble, Hollywood is a unionized redoubt of good pay and generous benefits. Occasionally, screenwriters or others go on strike. But Hollywood has some of the strongest unions in the country, the envy of other industries, and employee-friendly contracts.

Academe remains ensnared in traditional copyright, but not because it is smaller or less significant than the entertainment industry. However popular Hollywood's product, however well-paid its top auteurs and moguls, the university world is orders of magnitude larger. American colleges and universities employ ten times as many people as the motion picture and recording industries, and their income is at least five times as large.[11] Of course, what distinguishes the two sectors is Hollywood's profitability, while taxes finance the university world. Government employees, who also work for the taxpayer, are subject to work for hire. US civil servants may be paid for their intellectual output only if it is unrelated to their official duties.[12] How different are they from university researchers?[13]

Academic work for hire would raise some complications, mostly trivial. How should multiple authors from different institutions be handled? Or authors who switch employers after or during a work's gestation? Would it be unconstitutional if work for hire turned out to discourage faculty productivity and thus the progress of science that copyright is constitutionally mandated to stimulate?[14]

The biggest sticking point remains academic freedom. Nobody disputes that scholars should have liberty from their paymasters to research, teach, and publish as they see fit. Allowing the public access to academic research does not mean giving it a hand on the tiller. Any hint that the university could guide, much less control, its faculty's work must be ruled out categorically. The point of university work for hire is not to grab a cut of largely nonexistent profits, much less to demand a say over the work. It is not even to specify where, when, or how the work appears—except for requiring open access. Instead, the goal is to prevent scholarly work from being hijacked by third-party commercial distributors, especially those that resell it to universities. The university aims to vouchsafe the public's access.

The professoriate has only tangential interests in being read widely. The public does not determine the main conditions of its employment. Even the royalties wider readership promises pale compared to the intramural criteria of advancement, promotion, and research funding. Public recognition will never trump peer acknowledgment; indeed, it may undermine it. Work for hire applied to the professoriate would allow universities to justify requiring open access for academic work. Work for hire removes whatever presumption copyright law introduced that scholarly authors produce a commodity whose sale supplies their livelihood.

Copyright law turned authors into tradespeople, producing, owning, and selling their goods. Those bohemian artistes in the attic were—economically speaking—like shopkeepers. They might slave away inspired by Athena, but their livelihood came from flogging their wares. That helps explain why copyright's noncommercial elements, above all moral rights, sat so uneasily with the economic claims that were its focus. Moral rights were a vestige of the idea that authors produced for a higher purpose and were tied to their work by connections deeper than mere economic exploitation.

From this vantage, open access demanded nonsense of bohemians: though small producers, you must give away the fruit of your labors. Work for hire applied to academics resolves this apparent incongruity by making explicit that many authors are employees, not independent producers. It fits with broader currents of routinizing employment relations in academia, such as graduate students unionizing to be treated like other white-collar employees.

In other words, open access does not ask the professoriate for sacrifices or to labor only for the love of it. Whatever the moral argument for open access, academic authors are not assumed to live by their work.[15] Their work is also a vocation, not only an avocation. They should be motivated by truth-seeking and are rewarded in the prestige economy of academic recognition. But in economic terms, they have already been paid. Their results are therefore to be made available. This clarification by work for hire of university researchers' status ignores amateurs and the irregularly employed. But at least it explains why employee authors do not expect to sustain themselves from the retail market in intellectual property, and why they should not even aspire to the few remaining perks that derive from their pretend status as independent authors, such as advances and royalties.

Work for hire applied to universities would thus be among the rules that distinguish scholarship's mercenary motives from those of pure learning and truth-seeking. It would be akin to the rules restricting faculty with professional qualifications from practicing their vocations too assiduously at the expense of scholarship.

Having already been paid for, work for hire would be pursued only for its intrinsic merits and rewards internal to the academy. Money beyond salary is removed from the equation. The Romantic view of copyright straddled a contradiction between treating authors' output as both the fruit of a higher calling and a marketable commodity. Work for hire eliminates that internal inconsistency.

Whatever the specifics in employment law of treating academics as hired labor, universities are free to structure their incentives to nudge faculty in this direction. In the UK, centralized research funding allows the government to leverage scholars into compliance. In the decentralized US system, that is less likely. But even here, universities can employ, promote, and tenure based on content, not publication venue. They can give priority or special consideration to open works or refuse to count research that is not accessibly published. They can reward efforts at the postpublication review that will become increasingly needed in the new system. Evaluative work could itself become part of promotion reviews. Retired faculty could occupy useful niches during their career sunsets as evaluators, much as many discover an aptitude for book reviews.

Many universities already require posting faculty work in repositories. Others have gone further, making it part of hiring and promotion. In 2013, the Higher Education Funding Council for England began requiring research outputs to be open-access for submission to future Research Excellence Framework evaluations, which determine funding for academic departments.[16] The University of Liège now evaluates and promotes based only on materials in its open-access repository.[17]

A Hundred Flowers Blooming

Making work for hire the default position for regularly employed academics solves only some problems. Above all, it leaves aside authors without institutional affiliation. In the eighteenth and nineteenth centuries, before higher education and research institutionalized, more scholarly work was done by researchers who—though technically amateurs, in not being salaried careerists—were nonetheless among the great minds of their time: Joseph Priestly, Benjamin Franklin, Michael Faraday, Charles Darwin, Francis Galton, and perhaps Gregor Mendel, whose upkeep was provided by his Augustinian monastery at Brunn. Our era leaves little conceptual space for amateur figures in scholarship, any more than in sports.[18] Classified as independent scholars, they are usually thought of as those who, for whatever reasons, did not seek or obtain conventional university positions. Unsurprisingly, many are women: Jane Jacobs, Hannah Arendt, Susan Sontag.

Nor does work for hire help pay for output from the Global South or from the humanities in the developed world. The likelihood of rolling back copyright's distended terms to shrink the problem of locked-up content is small. The disseminators and freelance authors have little reason to mount that barricade. Nor should we count on the scientific publishers giving up their foothold in gold access. Only a small fraction of funders' budgets pays for publication, so expecting them to throw in their lot with nonscience authors also seems implausible.

A more realistic prospect is to build open-access systems for those unserved by the scientific publishers. Latin America has solved the problem for its authors. A global bulletin board of some sort might be one step, allowing rudimentary access to everything, with further dissemination of works that justify extra investment. In the meantime, efforts abound to provide alternatives to gold publishing, which are needed for scholars without funding. It is here that savings wrung from a deft application of digital technologies to dissemination could do most good.

Open journals already exist in abundance. The main directory lists 17,000, with 12,000 collecting no publishing fees.[19] Naturally, these are neither the biggest nor most prestigious outlets. They are spring chicken periodicals. Nothing is gained by bellyaching that reputation does not arrive instantaneously. *Nature* did not command an audience with its first issue. With time, the best of these diamond open access journals will acquire patina and prestige. Scholars eager to make them competitive should submit their best work, encouraging their peers to do the same.

According to Lotka's law, 60% of authors make one contribution to their field, only 15% more than that.[20] A minority of authors are the source of disproportionate content.[21] This power-law distribution appears to hold for the digital age, too, at least as measured by contributions to one journal.[22] Only in subjects where many are credited, such as high-energy physics, might one expect countervailing tendencies.[23]

High-publication fields require tidy sums—say 80 articles a year at $3,000 a pop. The problem is less pressing elsewhere. Sticking with books, if the average scholar publishes one or two monographs over a career, is it unreasonable for at least the most senior and best-paid among them to front some of the publishing charges under their own steam? Amortized over 30 years, the expense does not seem back-breaking. Police are often required to buy their uniforms, but they are also given allowances to defray costs. While many police are uniformed, not all scholars publish, so targeting resources would be useful.

Surveyed on what they would be willing to contribute, scholars have not been helpful. One study revealed they could accept paying publishing charges of $649.[24] Another produced even less realistic results: 55% were willing to pay nothing, 30% less than $100, and 30% less than $500.[25] On the other hand, the tax code distinguishes independent contractors from employees by asking whether they provide their own tools and supplies. Analogously, if the professoriate performs work for hire, it should not be expected to defray publication costs.

Monies will be needed to help underfunded scholars meet publication fees. Having required accessibility of articles, UK Research and Innovation, the body responsible for government funding in Britain, moved on to books in 2021. It required books, chapters, and edited collections to be accessible within 12 months of publication, either in the version of record or the author's accepted manuscript, ideally with CC BY licensing, and it also announced funds to help pay for this.[26] Wellcome moved in this direction earlier, in 2013.[27] More such efforts are needed.

From the demand side, open-access periodicals and book publishers are multiplying. An archipelago of new independent presses caters to the humanities and social sciences. Some began as early as the 1980s and 1990s, predating scientists' efforts in the same direction.[28] The numbers are small but growing. As of 2022, the most comprehensive directory of open-access books listed some 50,000 titles, representing perhaps three-quarters of all accessible volumes.[29] As of 2012, new open university presses in Australia had published more books than traditional ones in conventional formats.[30] By 2015, the Australian National University Press had published over 650 open books.[31]

In the UK, dominated for centuries by Oxford University Press and Cambridge University Press, new university publishers have arisen to specialize in open access: University College London, Huddersfield, Westminster, and Leeds, Sheffield, and York, united as White Rose.[32] Cambridge and Oxford themselves now issue accessible editions.[33] In the US, Lever Press is a joint effort by some 60 small liberal arts colleges.[34] Some university presses have open-access series—UC, MIT, and Johns Hopkins. Intech Open claims to be the world's leading open-access publisher, with over 5,000 titles.[35]

OpenEdition, a French house, allows free viewing but charges for PDF versions.[36] Open Humanities Press and Open Book Publishers are other accessible presses, as are Punctum, Ubiquity, and Open

Library of the Humanities.[37] German versions include Language Science Press, KIT Scientific Publishing (Karlsruhe Institute for Technology), and Göttingen University Press. Stockholm and Lund University Presses are Swedish variants.[38] Selling print-on-demand editions next to free online ones brings in 40% of Open Book Publisher's income. Open Library of Humanities and others employ a subscription model, with libraries paying production costs upfront, making books freely available for all.[39]

Libraries have entered the fray, too, becoming publishers in their own right.[40] A quarter of all American university presses report to their university's chief librarian.[41] Cornell University library runs arXiv. When almost anyone anywhere can store digital content, libraries realize they will need to make themselves useful in ways other than as repositories for a local audience of printed cellulose stored in house.[42]

Many of these ventures are precarious and boot-strapped. Most of the journals are small. Less than half the book publishers (40%) break even, a quarter run at a loss, and almost a third do not even know their financial status. Most rely on volunteer labor, most run with less than one full-time staff person, and 70% ring up less than $10,000 in annual costs, half less than $1,000. Sometimes they just give up the ghost and vanish—176 of them in the century's first two decades. And for the still-surviving, archiving and preserving are inconsistent at best.[43] There is a long way still to go.

By reclaiming a role in dissemination rather than focusing on research and writing and leaving the broadcast task to commercial houses, scholarly publishers have revived a lost tradition. Small-scale diamond or green presses and journals would (have to) be run by researchers and universities themselves, much as when academic societies issued the main periodicals in their fields.[44] One wrinkle has been the tendency of new open university presses to cater to their own faculty. As with UCL Press, that gives the locals a means to meet funders' requirements for accessible publications. But the message it sends about quality is ambiguous. If faculty shun their local press, is that because it is mediocre? Or would a list made up entirely of its own professors' works suggest a lowering of standards?[45] Either way, insofar as open access helps us move away from the prestige signals sent by the legacy publishers' catalogs, it should matter less.

Efforts to promote open publication must be encouraged. Major press outlets could review open books more prominently. Over the past decade, far less than 1% of the books reviewed in the *London Review of Books* have been open-access works, even fewer in the *Los Angeles Review of Books*.[46] Hoping to sprinkle a bit of stardust on the first cohort of its Luminos series, the University of California Press took out a full-page ad in the *New York Review of Books*. Yet, the lack of coverage is not necessarily due to ingrained hostility. Open works are unlikely to be the kind of trade books most often reviewed in popular outlets. The authors of scholarly monographs are more interested in evaluation by professional periodicals. Not many open books have been published yet, and the reviews have been broadly in line with their presence. Most of the open presses are new, and their contacts with the pertinent editors are only just forming. Having said that, imagine the pleasure of one day reading a review and then promptly downloading the book.

Senior scholars should show the way. Though young scholars in industrialized nations are doubtless more digitally adept than their elders, they are still sufficiently in thrall to the established prestige hierarchy that they publish less in open journals than their peers from the Global South.[47] The tenured professoriate owes a duty here. Unshackled from the prestige treadmill, they lose nothing by issuing their work accessibly. Lionel Gossman, a distinguished professor of literature at Princeton, was an admirable exemplar, publishing several works with Open Books.[48] So, too, has been Jan Ziolkowski, professor of medieval Latin at Harvard, whose six-volume work, *The Juggler of Notre Dame*, is freely available.[49] John Braithwaite, professor of criminology at the Australian National University, has published six open books with his institution's press, including an 800-page doorstopper on *Macrocriminology and Freedom*.[50] The legal theorist Peter Drahos's *Regulatory Theory* has been whatever one calls an open-access bestseller.[51] Peter Miller's *How the World Changed Social Media* (UCL Press 2016) has been downloaded over 600,000 times.[52]

Like environmentalism, open access has become a cause that few dare attack outright. Many bow ritually in its direction without much follow-up. Openwash is the result. Universities have tweaked agreements with the databases to allow contributing alumni continued access to JSTOR and other perks of the digital paradise they enjoyed as students before being ejected into the bleak world on the far side of the paywall. Publishers' hybrid journals allow them to claim open-access bona fides while conducting business as usual. So does openwrapping, their clever swaddling of accessible content in layers of proprietary (and useful) services—indexing, discoverability, tools for classroom use, data analytics—for which they then charge.[53] When Cambridge University Press negotiates read-and-publish agreements with US university libraries, the polite fiction that the press is nonprofit helps sugar-coat the deal, compared to negotiating with the commercial behemoths.[54] None of this goes to the core of the issue.

The Way Forward

The stakes of open access are crucial. A solution is possible. The monies needed to make all past and future scholarly work available to anyone anywhere are already present in the library system. They just need repurposing. Everyone can have the library of Alexandria on their tablets. It is no longer a technical or physical impossibility. It is not even a financial issue. The obstacles are legal.

The mass of nonscholarly content requires other approaches. Work produced by freelancers that retains market appeal will have to be paid for. Streaming services provide broad, if not open, access. That may be as much as can be achieved for many media. Most books and articles lose any harvestable value soon after publication. If courts and publishers leave controlled digital lending intact, that may provide an acceptable solution for much content. Though not ideal, reading on screen is certainly preferable to books enmired on the shelves of a few research libraries. Most authors do not manage to live from selling their works. Suppose they can be persuaded that the greater attention possible via open access is more valuable than a few dollars in royalties. They will perhaps throw in their lot with salaried university researchers.

The aspirations for open access are so fervent, the goals so noble, that the cause is tempted by hyperbole. That is both a strength and a weakness. The best is the enemy of the good. Nowhere is that truer than for open access. Good enough is the best we can hope for.

Acknowledgments

As befits a book about distributing and sharing knowledge, I have debts to settle.

Once again, Michael Kellogg lightened my burdens, dredging up information far and wide. So, too, did Jacob Glazer, who appeared out of the blue and kindly and very competently volunteered to hone his research skills on topics of use to me. Ross Mounce, a true expert in the field, supplied insights, corrections, and guidance, for which I am grateful.

Peter Mandler and Ian Baldwin gave the manuscript a thorough reading, with lots of useful suggestions and cautions the outcome. So did Lisbet Rausing, several times. Christoph Conrad, Carol Mandel, Andy Redman, Niko Pfund, William Pike, Peter Mancall, Lisa Bitel, and Simon Chaplin supplied particulars to dispel my ignorance. Richard Fisher kindly added me to the distribution list of his extremely informative monthly newsletter.

Tony Marx and Tony Ageh of the New York Public Library have discussed the issues here with me many times, not to mention showing what can be done in practical terms through an institution that uniquely combines scholarly heft as one of the world's greatest research collections with the street cred of the largest public library system anywhere. I have learned much from the examples set by Brewster Kahle and Carl Malamud.

In 2005, just starting the research that led to an earlier book on the history of copyright, I knew very little about open access. Nonetheless, Anjana Shrivastava took a reckless gamble and enlisted me as the respondent to a talk in Berlin by Larry Lessig, then the dominant figure in the field. Only days before the event did I learn that a Lessig talk was also a multimedia spectacle. Any hopes of keeping the audience in its seats for my comments required rising to the occasion. After a crash course in Powerpoint and a Google trawl for images, something visual came together. Larry has, in the meantime, moved on to other subjects, while I have finally arrived at the point where I could do a decent job of responding. My thanks to Anjana for having prompted me to become the expert that I was then touted as.

Some of the ideas here were first presented in "Why Are Universities Open Access Laggards?" *Bulletin of the German Historical Institute,* 63 (2018). Many thanks to the organizers of that talk at the German Historical Institute in Washington and the resulting article. Peter Kaufman of MIT persuaded me that an article could become a book. For that confidence, I am very grateful.

Notes

Introduction

1. Bryce Huebner et al., "Making an Author in Radically Collaborative Research," in Thomas Boyer-Kassem et al., eds., *Scientific Collaboration and Collective Knowledge* (Oxford 2018) 101.

2. Stephen G. Nichols and Abby Smith, *The Evidence in Hand: Report of the Task Force on the Artifact in Library Collections* (Council on Library and Information Resources, November 2001) 30, https://www.clir.org/pubs/reports/pub103/.

Chapter 1

1. C. Armstrong et al., eds., *Access to Knowledge in Africa: The Role of Copyright* (Claremont SA 2010) 335.

2. Charlotte Hess and Elinor Ostrom, "Introduction: An Overview of the Knowledge Commons," in Hess and Ostrom, eds., *Understanding Knowledge as a Commons* (Cambridge MA 2007) 11–13.

3. In the case of porn, its share of the web varies from 10% to 30%, depending on whom you ask: Michael Castleman, "Dueling Statistics: How Much of the Internet Is Porn?" *Psychology Today* (3 November 2016), https://www.psychologytoday.com/gb/blog/all-about-sex/201611/dueling-statistics-how-much-the-internet-is-porn.

4. "Scientific and Technical Journal Articles," World Bank, https://data.worldbank.org/indicator/IP.JRN.ARTC.SC.

5. JSTOR article numbers from https://constellate.org/builder/?provider=jstor&start=1800&end=2021&doc_type=article.

6. Benoît Godin, "The Most Cherished Indicator: Gross Domestic Expenditures on R&D (GERD)," Project on the History and Sociology of S&T Statistics: Working Paper No. 22 (Montreal, Canadian Science and Innovation Indicators Consortium, 2003) 5, http://www.csiic.ca/PDF/Godin_22.pdf; Steven P. Dehmer et al., "Reshuffling the Global R&D Deck, 1980–2050," *PLOS One*, 14, 3 (2019), https://www.ncbi.nlm.nih.gov/pmc/articles/PMC6440631/; World Bank: Data; Research and Development Expenditure (% of GDP), https://data.worldbank.org/indicator/GB.XPD.RSDV.GD.ZS.

7. Lutz Bornmann and Rüdiger Mutz, "Growth Rates of Modern Science: A Bibliometric Analysis Based on the Number of Publications and Cited References," arXiv (8 May 2014), https://arxiv.org/abs/1402.4578.

8. Roberto Bolli, "Reflections on the Irreproducibility of Scientific Papers," *Circulation Research*, 117, 8 (2015), https://www.ahajournals.org/doi/epub/10.1161/CIRCRESAHA.115.307496.

9. Philip Mirowski, "The Future(s) of Open Science," *Social Studies of Science*, 48, 2 (2018) 179–180, https://journals.sagepub.com/doi/full/10.1177/0306312718772086.

10. An attempt to account in Roger E. Bohn and James E. Short, "How Much Information? 2009: Report on American Consumers," Global Information Industry Center, University of California, San Diego (December 2009), https://www.researchgate.net/publication/242562463_How_Much_Information_2009_Report_on_American_Consumers.

11. James Stayer, "The Anabaptist Revolt and Political and Religious Power," in Benjamin W. Redekop and Calvin W. Redekop, eds., *Power, Authority, and the Anabaptist Tradition* (Baltimore 2001) 50.

12. Claus-Peter Clasen, "Medieval Heresies in the Reformation," *Church History*, 32, 4 (1963) 393, 404; Leonard W. Levy, *Treason against God: A History of the Offense of Blasphemy* (New York 1981) 245; Gershom Scholem, *Sabbatai Ṣevi: The Mystical Messiah: 1626–1676*, 2nd ed. (Princeton 1975) 628; Elisheva Carlebach, *The Pursuit of Heresy: Rabbi Moses Hagiz and the Sabbatian Controversies* (New York 1990) 9, 184.

13. Ann Margaret Doyle, *Social Equality in Education: France and England, 1789–1939* (Cham 2018) 109; Terry Wrigley, "Curriculum Change in English Schools: Educating Working-Class Children," *Social and Education History*, 3, 3 (2014) 212.

14. Vito Tanzi and Ludger Schuknecht, *Public Spending in the Twentieth Century* (Cambridge 2000) 34.

15. R. D. Anderson, *European Universities from the Enlightenment to 1914* (Oxford 2004) 11.

16. Thomas D. Snyder, ed., *120 Years of American Education: A Statistical Portrait* (Washington DC 1993) table 24. Similar statistics for percentages of the whole population in "Percentage of the U.S. Population Who Have Completed Four Years of College or More from 1940 to 2020, by Gender," *Statista*, https://www.statista.com/statistics/184272/educational-attainment-of-college-diploma-or-higher-by-gender/.

17. Peter Mandler, *The Crisis of the Meritocracy: Britain's Transition to Mass Education since the Second World War* (Oxford 2020) 2–3.

18. Eric Klinenberg, *Palaces for the People: How Social Infrastructure Can Help Fight Inequality, Polarization, and the Decline of Civic Life* (New York 2018).

19. Michael Kevane and William A. Sundstrom, "The Development of Public Libraries in the United States, 1870–1930: A Quantitative Assessment," Santa Clara University, *Scholar Commons* (2014) 1, https://scholarcommons.scu.edu/cgi/viewcontent.cgi?article=1039&context=econ; Wayne A. Wiegand, *Part of Our Lives: A People's History of the American Public Library* (New York 2015) 1, 2.

20. Thomas Ralf, ed., *Deutschland in Daten* (Bonn 2015) 162.

21. Svend Dahl, *History of the Book* (New York 1958) 68.

22. "Historic Trends in Book Production," *AI Impacts* (7 February 2020) fig. 3, https://aiimpacts.org/historic-trends-in-book-production/; Jeremiah E. Dittmar, "Information Technology and Economic Change: The Impact of the Printing Press," *Quarterly Journal of Economics*, 126, 3 (2011) 1133.

23. James F. English, *The Economy of Prestige: Prizes, Awards, and the Circulation of Cultural Value* (Cambridge MA 2005) 19.

24. Peter Baldwin, *The Copyright Wars* (Princeton 2014) 119, 323.

25. Peter Suber, "Knowledge as a Public Good," *SPARC Open Access Newsletter*, 139 (2009), http://legacy.earlham.edu/~peters/fos/newsletter/11-02-09.htm.

26. Paul J. Heald, "The Demand for Out-of-Print Works and Their (Un)Availability in Alternative Markets," *Illinois Public Law and Legal Theory Research Papers Series*, No. 14–31, fig. 1, https://papers.ssrn.com/sol3/papers.cfm?abstract_id=2409118.

27. Alliance of Independent Authors, "Facts and Figures about Self Publishing: The Impact and Influence of Indie Authors," *ALLi Blog* (22 June 2020), https://selfpublishingadvice.org/facts-and-figures-about-self-publishing-the-impact-and-influence-of-indie-authors/.

28. Hugh Trevor-Roper, *The European Witch-Craze of the Sixteenth and Seventeenth Centuries and Other Essays* (New York 1967) 101–102.

29. Seren Boyd, "Pushing Back: Tackling the Anti-vax Movement," *BMA* (11 January 2021), https://www.bma.org.uk/news-and-opinion/pushing-back-tackling-the-anti-vax-movement.

30. King's College, Policy Institute, "Covid Conspiracies and Confusions: The Impact on Compliance with the UK's Lockdown Rules and the Link with Social Media Use," (18 June 2020), https://www.kcl.ac.uk/policy-institute/assets/covid-conspiracies-and-confusions.pdf.

31. William Eamon, "From the Secrets of Nature to Public Knowledge," in David C. Lindberg and Robert S. Westman, eds., *Reappraisals of the Scientific Revolution* (Cambridge 1990) 346.

32. Orla Higgins et al., "A Literature Review on Health Information-seeking Behaviour on the Web," European Centre for Disease Prevention and Control (October 2011) 8, https://www.ecdc.europa.eu/en/publications-data/literature-review-health-information-seeking-behaviour-web-health-consumer-and.

33. Examples in Peter Suber, *Open Access* (Cambridge MA 2012) 203. If anything, open access might help the situation of freely available but ill-digested information

by supplying it from the horse's mouth, the professional literature, rather than via a detour through journalists' often unhelpful hands.

34. Sharon Swee-Lin Tan and Nadee Goonawardene, "Internet Health Information Seeking and the Patient-Physician Relationship," *Journal of Medical Internet Research*, 19, 1 (2017), https://www.jmir.org/2017/1/e9/.

35. Richard Wrangham, *The Goodness Paradox: The Strange Relationship between Virtue and Violence in Human Evolution* (New York 2019) 20 and *passim*.

36. Johan Grolle, "Those Who Obeyed the Rules Were Favored by Evolution," *Spiegel* (22 March 2019), https://www.spiegel.de/international/interview-with-anthropologist-richard-wrangham-a-1259252.html.

37. Joseph Henrich, *The Secret of Our Success: How Culture Is Driving Human Evolution, Domesticating Our Species, and Making Us Smarter* (Princeton 2017) ch. 11 and *passim*.

38. Nicholas A. Christakis and James H. Fowler, *Connected: The Surprising Power of Our Social Networks and How They Shape Our Lives* (New York 2009).

39. Joseph Henrich, *The WEIRDest People in the World: How the West Became Psychologically Peculiar and Particularly Prosperous* (New York 2020) 448–452.

40. Joel Mokyr, *The Gifts of Athena: Historical Origins of the Knowledge Economy* (Princeton 2002) 74–75.

41. Robert Barnes, "Cloistered Bookworms in the Chicken-Coop of the Muses: The Ancient Library of Alexandria," in Roy MacLeod, ed., *The Library of Alexandria* (London 2010) 63–65.

42. Ian F. McNeely and Lisa Wolverton, *Reinventing Knowledge: From Alexandria to the Internet* (New York 2009) 21.

43. 3.5 million books × 200 pages × 400 words.

44. Michael McCormick, "Research and Teaching: Making Connections in Widener Library," *Harvard Magazine* (1997), https://www.harvardmagazine.com/sites/default/files/html/1997/05/scholars.mccormick.html.

45. G. R. Hardy, "S. Ramanujan, F.R.S.," *Nature*, 105, 2642 (1920) 495.

46. Eric J. Hobsbawm, "From West European to World Science: Seventeenth–Twentieth Centuries," in Peter Hanns Reill and Balázs A. Szelényi, eds., *Cores, Peripheries, and Globalization: Essays in Honor of Ivan T. Berend* (Budapest 2011) 262.

47. B. Zorina Khan, *The Democratization of Invention: Patents and Copyrights in American Economic Development, 1790–1920* (Cambridge 2005) chs. 8, 9; Meredith L. McGill, *American Literature and the Culture of Reprinting, 1834–1853* (Philadelphia 2003).

48. Jeremy Farrar with Anjana Ahuja, *Spike: The Virus vs the People: The Inside Story* (London 2021) 24–31; Michael A. Johansson et al., "Preprints: An Underutilized Mechanism to Accelerate Outbreak Science," *PLOS Medicine* (3 April 2018), https://journals.plos.org/plosmedicine/article?id=10.1371/journal.pmed.1002549; Peter Baldwin, *Fighting the First Wave: Why the Coronavirus Was Tackled So Differently across the Globe* (Cambridge 2020) 14–15.

49. Holly Else, "How a Torrent of COVID Science Changed Research Publishing—In Seven Charts," *Nature* (16 December 2020), https://www.nature.com/articles/d41586-020-03564-y.

50. Vannevar Bush, "As We May Think," *Atlantic* (July 1945), https://www.theatlantic.com/magazine/archive/1945/07/as-we-may-think/303881/.

51. Andy Clark and David Chalmers, "The Extended Mind," *Analysis*, 58, 1 (1998); Andy Clark, *Supersizing the Mind: Embodiment, Action, and Cognitive Extension* (Oxford 2008).

52. Roger Clarke, "Information Wants to be Free . . ." http://www.rogerclarke.com/II/IWtbF.html.

53. Alain M. Schoenenberger, "Are Higher Education and Academic Research a Public Good or a Public Responsibility? A Review of the Economic Literature," in Luc Weber and Sjur Bergan, eds., *The Public Responsibility for Higher Education and Research* (Council of Europe, Strasbourg 2005) 66–67, https://rm.coe.int/the-public-responsibility-for-higher-education-and-research/168075ddd0.

54. 63% in the US, 66% in Germany, 79% in Japan, figures from 2018: OECD. Stat, Gross Domestic Expenditure on R&D by Sector of Performance and Source of Funds; Sector: Total Intramural; Source of Funds: Business Enterprise Sector Divided by Total Funding; Measure: PPP Dollars—Current prices, US Dollar, Millions. https://stats.oecd.org/Index.aspx?DataSetCode=GERD_SOF.

55. Department for Business, Innovation, and Skills, *What Is the Relationship Between Public and Private Investment in Science, Research, and Innovation?* (April 2015) 7, https://assets.publishing.service.gov.uk/government/uploads/system/uploads/attachment_data/file/438763/bis-15-340-relationship-between-public-and-private-investment-in-R-D.pdf.

56. Wesley M. Cohen et al., "Protecting Their Intellectual Assets: Appropriability Conditions and Why US Manufacturing Firms Patent (Or Not)," National Bureau of Economic Research Working Paper No. 7552 (2000).

57. Michael Strevens, "Scientific Sharing, Communism, and the Social Contract," in Boyer-Kassem et al., eds., *Scientific Collaboration and Collective Knowledge*, 3.

58. Krzysztof Trzciński, "Citizenship in Europe: The Main Stages of Development of the Idea and Institution," *Studies in European Affairs*, 1 (2021) 13, http://cejsh.icm.edu.pl/cejsh/element/bwmeta1.element.ojs-doi-10_33067_SE_1_2021_1; Andrew T. Young, "How the City Air Made Us Free: The Self-Governing Medieval City and the Bourgeois Revaluation," *Journal of Private Enterprise*, 32, 4 (2017).

59. Generally, see Susan C. Lawrence, *Privacy and the Past: Research, Law, Archives, Ethics* (New Brunswick 2016).

60. Laura M. Beskow, "Lessons from HeLa Cells: The Ethics and Policy of Biospecimens," *Annual Review of Genomics and Human Genetics*, 17 (2016), https://www.annualreviews.org/doi/10.1146/annurev-genom-083115-022536?url_ver=Z39.88-2003&rfr_id=ori%3Arid%3Acrossref.org&rfr_dat=cr_pub%3Dpubmed.

61. Ian Vincent McGonigle, "Patenting Nature or Protecting Culture? Ethnopharmacology and Indigenous Intellectual Property Rights," *Journal of Law and the Biosciences* (6 February 2016) 223, https://academic.oup.com/jlb/article/3/1/217/1751287.

62. Howard Wolinsky, "Ancient DNA and Contemporary Politics," *EMBO Reports*, 20, 12 (2019), https://www.embopress.org/doi/full/10.15252/embr.201949507; Jessica Bardill, "Native American DNA: Ethical, Legal, and Social Implications of an Evolving Concept," *Annual Review of Anthropology*, 43 (2014).

63. Daniel Jütte, *The Age of Secrecy: Jews, Christians, and the Economy of Secrets, 1400–1800* (New Haven 2015).

64. Paul A. David, "From Keeping 'Nature's Secrets' to the Institutionalization of 'Open Science'," in Rishab Aiyer Ghosh, ed., *Code: Collaborative Ownership and the Digital Economy* (Cambridge MA 2005) 94.

65. Jana Bacevic and Chris Muellerleile, "The Moral Economy of Open Access," *European Journal of Social Theory*, 21, 2 (2018) 175.

66. "How Much Does Your Country Invest in R&D?" UNESCO Institute for Statistics, http://uis.unesco.org/apps/visualisations/research-and-development-spending/.

67. Mu-Hsuan Huang and Mei-Jhen Huang, "An Analysis of Global Research Funding from Subject Field and Funding Agencies Perspectives in the G9 Countries," *Scientometrics* (2018) table 5, https://dl.acm.org/doi/abs/10.1007/s11192-018-2677-y.

68. Godfrey Oswald, ed., *Library World Records*, 3rd ed. (Jefferson NC 2017) 17, 19, https://books.google.co.uk/books?hl=en&lr=&id=G4owDwAAQBAJ&oi=fnd&pg=PP1&dq=world+%22largest+libraries%22&ots=WEFE21BUfB&sig=74hB718P84QKiZseD-GwNBEhyE4&redir_esc=y#v=onepage&q=world%20%22largest%20libraries%22&f=false.

69. Suber, *Open Access*, 30.

70. WIPO, *World Intellectual Property Indicators 2019*, calculated from figures on 205–206.

71. WIPO, *World Intellectual Property Indicators 2019*, 15.

72. Fran M. Collyer, "Global Patterns in the Publishing of Academic Knowledge: Global North, Global South," *Current Sociology*, 66, 1 (2018) 58.

73. Alexander Gerschenkron, *Economic Backwardness in Historical Perspective* (Cambridge MA 1962).

74. Index Mundi, https://www.indexmundi.com/g/r.aspx?v=4010; Hannah Ritchie and Max Roser, "Technology Adoption," *Our World in Data* (2019), "Technology Adoption in US Households," https://ourworldindata.org/technology-adoption#citation.

75. US authors were invited to the UK by their British publishers in hopes of securing local copyright for their works: Katie McGettigan, "When American Literature Came to Grove Terrace NW5," *Kentishtowner* (13 May 2021), https://www.kentishtowner.co.uk/2021/05/13/american-literature-came-grove-terrace/.

76. Adolf Fleischmann, "Die Berner Übereinkunft zum Schutze des Urheberrechts," *UFITA*, 103 (1986) 50.

77. Baldwin, *Copyright Wars*, 277.

78. In 2018, China filed almost three times as many patents as the US. WIPO, *World Intellectual Property Indicators 2019*, 7.

79. Timothy Bazzle, "Pharmacy of the Developing World: Reconciling Intellectual Property Rights in India with the Right to Health: TRIPS, India's Patent System, and Essential Medicines," *Georgetown Journal of International Law*, 42, 3 (2011).

80. Armstrong et al., eds., *Access to Knowledge in Africa*, 318–320, 326.

81. Arguments summarized in Martin Paul Eve, *Open Access and the Humanities* (Cambridge 2014) 62–67, https://doi.org/10.1017/CBO9781316161012; Philip Mirowski, "What Is 'Open Science' Open To?" (February 2014), https://www.academia.edu/11571042/What_is_Open_Science?auto=download; Bacevic and Muellerleile, "Moral Economy of Open Access," 179; David Golumbia, "Marxism and Open Access in the Humanities: Turning Academic Labor against Itself," *Workplace*, 28 (2016) 75.

82. Nathaniel Tkacz, *Wikipedia and the Politics of Openness* (Chicago 2015).

83. Samuel A. Moore, "A Genealogy of Open Access: Negotiations between Openness and Access to Research," *Revue Française des Sciences de l'information et de la communication*, 11 (2017), https://journals.openedition.org/rfsic/3220.

84. Nicholas Kulish, "Direct Democracy, 2.0," *New York Times* (6 May 2012); Richard Barbrook and Andy Cameron, "The Californian Ideology," *Mute*, 1, 3 (1995), https://www.metamute.org/editorial/articles/californian-ideology.

85. Examples in Leslie Chan et al., eds., *Contextualizing Openness: Situating Open Science* (Ottawa 2019), https://www.idrc.ca/en/book/contextualizing-openness-situating-open-science.

86. Thomas Maier, *Masters of Sex: The Life and Times of William Masters and Virginia Johnson, the Couple Who Taught America How to Love* (New York 2009) 175.

Chapter 2

1. David Blank, "'Our Fellow Shakespeare': A Contemporary Classic in the Early Modern University," *Review of English Studies*, 71, 301 (2020); Devoney Looser, *The Making of Jane Austen* (Baltimore 2017) 4.

2. Martin Hägglund, *This Life: Secular Faith and Spiritual Freedom* (New York 2020).

3. Friedrich Nietzsche, *The Use and Abuse of History*.

4. Washington Irving, "The Mutability of Literature," in his *The Sketch Book* (New York n.d.).

5. Hugo Reinert and Erik S. Reinert, "Creative Destruction in Economics: Nietzsche, Sombart, Schumpeter," in Jürgen G. Backhaus and Wolfgang Dreschler, eds., *Friedrich Nietzsche (1844–1900)* (New York 2006).

6. "How Many Melodies Are There in the Universe?" Everything2.com, https://everything2.com/title/How+many+melodies+are+there+in+the+universe%253F; https://plus.maths.org/content/how-many-melodies-are-there.

7. All the Music LLC, http://allthemusic.info/.

8. Dean Keith Simonton, "Thematic Fame and Melodic Originality in Classical Music: A Multivariate Computer-content Analysis," *Journal of Personality*, 48, 2 (1980) 216; Dean Keith Simonton, "The Decline and Fall of Musical Art: What Happened to Classical Composers?" *Empirical Studies of the Arts*, 27, 2 (2009) 210–212.

9. Grosso modo the argument of Colin Martindale, *The Clockwork Muse: The Predictability of Artistic Change* (New York 1990).

10. Ed Simon, "Stories in Formaldehyde: The Strange Pleasures of Taxonomizing Plot," *The Millions* (2 October 2020), https://themillions.com/2020/10/stories-in-formaldehyde-the-strange-pleasures-of-taxonomizing-plot.html.

11. Pamela Samuelson, "Reconceptualizing Copyright's Merger Doctrine," *Journal of the Copyright Society of the USA*, 63, 3 (2016).

12. Joseph M. Santiago, "The Blurred Lines of Copyright Law: Setting a New Standard for Copyright Infringement in Music," *Brooklyn Law Review*, 83, 1 (2017).

13. Constance Malpas and Brian Lavoie, "Strength in Numbers: The Research Libraries UK (RLUK) Collective Collection," *OCLC Research* (2016) 19, https://www.oclc.org/content/dam/research/publications/2016/oclcresearch-strength-in-numbers-rluk-collective-collection-2016.pdf.

14. William M. Landes and Richard A. Posner, "Indefinitely Renewable Copyright," *University of Chicago Law Review*, 70 (2003) 474.

15. James Shackell, "'Most of Australia's Literary Heritage Is Out of Print:' The Fight to Rescue a Nation's Lost Books," *Guardian* (23 June 2021), https://www.theguardian.com/books/2021/jun/24/most-of-australias-literary-heritage-is-out-of-print-the-fight-to-rescue-a-nations-lost-books.

16. *Gowers Review of Intellectual Property* (December 2006) 52–53, https://assets.publishing.service.gov.uk/government/uploads/system/uploads/attachment_data/file/228849/0118404830.pdf.

17. Only 13% of copyrights registered between 1923 and 1942 in the US were renewed. Rebecca Giblin, "A New Copyright Bargain: Reclaiming Lost Culture and Getting Authors Paid," *Columbia Journal of Law & the Arts*, 41, 3 (2018) 375.

18. Richard Schiff, "Originality," in Schiff and Robert Nelson, eds., *Critical Terms for Art History* (2nd ed.; Chicago 2003) 145–149; Edward Earle, "The Effect of Romanticism on the 19th Century Development of Copyright Law," *Intellectual Property Journal*, 6 (1991) 275–276.

19. Walter Bappert, *Wege zum Urheberrecht: Die geschichtliche Entwicklung des Urheberrechtsgedankens* (Frankfurt 1962) 20–22.

20. John Willinsky, *The Intellectual Properties of Learning: A Prehistory from Saint Jerome to John Locke* (Chicago 2018) 34.

21. Nick Groom, "Unoriginal Genius: Plagiarism and the Construction of 'Romantic' Authorship," in Lionel Bently et al., eds., *Copyright and Piracy* (Cambridge 2010) 274–275; Carla Hesse, "The Rise of Intellectual Property, 700 BC–AD 2000: An Idea in the Balance," *Daedalus*, 131, 2 (2002) 26–30.

22. Martha Woodmansee, *The Author, Art, and the Market: Rereading the History of Aesthetics* (New York 1994) 35–40.

23. Alan Bradshaw and Morris B. Holbrook, "Remembering Chet: Theorizing the Mythology of the Self-Destructive Bohemian Artist as Self-Producer and Self-Consumer in the Market for Romanticism," *Marketing Theory*, 7, 2 (2007).

24. Honoré de Balzac, "Pro Aris et Focis: Lettre adressée aux écrivains du XIXe siècle," *Revue de Paris*, ns 11 (1834) 63.

25. Simon Schaffer, "Scientific Discoveries and the End of Natural Philosophy," *Social Studies of Science*, 16 (1986).

26. Thomas Nickles, "Enlightenment versus Romantic Models of Creativity in Science—and Beyond," *Creativity Research Journal*, 7 (1994) 278.

27. Marx, *The German Ideology*, part IA.

28. Michael Nielsen, *Reinventing Discovery: The New Era of Networked Science* (Princeton 2012).

29. Howard Bloom, "Who's Smarter: Chimps, Baboons or Bacteria? The Power of Group IQ," in Mark Tovey, ed., *Collective Intelligence* (Oakton 2008) 251–253; Stefan Wuchty et al., "The Increasing Dominance of Teams in Production of Knowledge," *Science*, 316 (2007) 1036–1039; Richard M. Shiffrin et al., "Scientific Progress despite Irreproducibility: A Seeming Paradox," *Proceedings of the National Academy of Science*, 115, 11 (2018) 2633–2635.

30. Steven Shapin, *A Social History of Truth: Civility and Science in Seventeenth-Century England* (Chicago 1994) ch 8.

31. Simon Fuller and James O'Sullivan, "Structure over Style: Collaborative Authorship and the Revival of Literary Capitalism," *Digital Humanities Quarterly*, 11, 1 (2017).

32. David W. Shapiro et al., "The Contributions of Authors to Multiauthored Biomedical Research Papers," *Journal of the American Medical Association*, 271, 6 (1994) 438.

33. William J. Broad, "The Publishing Game: Getting More for Less," *Science*, 211 (1981) 1137; LSE Public Policy Group, "Maximizing the Impacts of Your Research: A Handbook for Social Scientists," Consultation Draft 3 (14 April 2011) 114, https://blogs.lse.ac.uk/impactofsocialsciences/files/2018/06/Handbook-PDF-for-the-LSE-impact-blog-April-2011.pdf.

34. Hans-Jürgen Quadbeck-Seeger, ed., *World Records in Chemistry* (Weinheim 1999) 135.

35. ATLAS Collaboration Phys. Lett. B 716, 1–29 (2012). See https://www.nature.com/news/physics-paper-sets-record-with-more-than-5-000-authors-1.17567.

36. G. Aad et al., "Combined Measurement of the Higgs Boson Mass in *pp* Collisions at $\sqrt{s}$ = 7 and 8 TeV with the ATLAS and CMS Experiments," *Physical Review Letters*, 114, 191803 (2015).

37. Producers Guild of America, "Code of Credits," https://www.producersguild.org/page/coc_tmp_2.

38. "What Do 'Best Boy' and 'Dolly Grip' Mean?" *Reel Rundown* (20 April 2016), https://reelrundown.com/film-industry/What-is-a-Best-Boy-Film-Terminology-and-Movie-Terms.

39. Stephen Follows, "How Many People Work on a Hollywood Film?" (21 February 2014), https://stephenfollows.com/how-many-people-work-on-a-hollywood-film/.

40. Vijaysree Venkatraman, "Conventions of Scientific Authorship," *Science* (16 April 2010), https://www.sciencemag.org/careers/2010/04/conventions-scientific-authorship#.

41. "CRediT—Contributor Roles Taxonomy," *Casrai*, https://casrai.org/credit/; Alex Holcombe, "Farewell Authors, Hello Contributors," *Nature* (5 July 2019), https://www.nature.com/articles/d41586-019-02084-8.

42. English, *Economy of Prestige*.

43. John Tebbel, "The Book Business in the US," in David Daiches and Anthony Thorlby, eds., *The Modern World* (London 1976) iii, 533; Paul W. Kingston et al., "The Columbia Economic Survey of American Authors: A Summary of Findings," Center for Social Sciences, Columbia University (1981) 14.

44. Christine Larson, "The Profession of Author in the 21st Century," *Authors Guild* (2019) 4, 17–18, https://www.authorsguild.org/industry-advocacy/authors-guild-issues-report-exploring-the-factors-leading-to-the-decline-of-the-writing-profession/.

45. Alexander Busch, "The Vicissitudes of the *Privatdozent*," *Minerva*, 1, 3 (1963) 319.

46. Robert Wicks, *Schopenhauer* (Malden 2008) 8.

47. Forty per million in 1835, 507 in 2010: Claude Diebolt, *Die langfristige Entwicklung des Schulsystems in Deutschland im 19. und 20. Jahrhundert* (2005), C.3. Anzahl der Lehrer in Deutschland (1835–1940), Deutschland, Professoren an den Universitäten. 1997 [2005]. Gesis, histat: Historische Statistik, https://histat.gesis.org/histat/de/table/details/F19F3B6F210A682349F308D8618F1D0C#tabelle. (1835–1940), Deutschland, Professoren an den Universitäten, 1997 [2005]; Statistisches Bundesamt, H201—Hochschulstatistik, Professoren nach Geschlecht, Insgesamt, Excel file provided by Statistisches Bundesamt.

48. "Number of Faculty Members in Humanities and Other Fields," American Academy of Arts and Sciences, https://www.amacad.org/humanities-indicators/workforce/number-faculty-members-humanities-and-other-fields.

49. What is known as "guaranteed author's money," some $25,000 annually until the recipient turns 70, which has replaced a slightly more generous system of "state artist's salary." My thanks to Aris Fioretos for this information.

50. John L. Campbell and Ove K. Pedersen, *The National Origins of Policy Ideas: Knowledge Regimes in the United States, France, Germany, and Denmark* (Princeton 2014) 51, 104–105.

51. HSBC Global Research, "Survey of Funders Supports the Benign Open Access Outcome Priced into Shares" (11 February 2013) 5, https://www.research.hsbc.com/midas/Res/RDV?ao=20&key=RxArFbnG1P&n=360010.PDF%20.

52. "Research and Development Expenditure (% of GDP)," World Bank, https://data.worldbank.org/indicator/GB.XPD.RSDV.GD.ZS?end=2019&start=1996&view=chart.

53. European Commission, Directorate-General for Research and Innovation, *Future of Scholarly Publishing and Scholarly Communication* (January 2019) 21, https://op.europa.eu/en/publication-detail/-/publication/464477b3-2559-11e9-8d04-01aa75ed71a1.

54. Robert Anderson, *British Universities Past and Present* (London 2006) 5, 37.

55. Anderson, *European Universities*, 9.

56. Anderson, *European Universities*, 61–62.

57. Baldwin, *Copyright Wars*, 217–20.

58. Drummond Rennie et al., "When Authorship Fails: A Proposal to Make Contributors Accountable," *Journal of the American Medical Association*, 278, 7 (1997), https://jamanetwork.com/journals/jama/article-abstract/417997.

59. Peter Galison, "The Collective Author," in Mario Biagioli and Peter Galison, eds., *Scientific Authorship: Credit and Intellectual Property in Science* (New York 2002) 328–329.

60. Bryce Huebner, *Macrocognition: A Theory of Distributed Minds and Collective Intentionality* (Oxford 2014).

Chapter 3

1. Monika Dommann, *Authors and Apparatus: A Media History of Copyright* (Ithaca 2019) 100–103.

2. Alandis Kyle Brassel, "Confused, Frustrated, and Exhausted: Solving the U.S. Digital First Sale Doctrine Problem through the International Lens," *Vanderbilt Journal of Transnational Law*, 48, 1 (2015) 254.

3. Geoffrey A. Fowler, "Want to Borrow that E-book from the Library? Sorry, Amazon Won't Let You," *Washington Post* (10 March 2021).

4. Rebecca Klar, "Amazon under Pressure to Lift Ban on E-book Library Sales," *The Hill* (2 December 2020), https://thehill.com/business-a-lobbying/528280-amazon-under-pressure-to-lift-ban-on-e-book-library-sales.

5. Andrew Albanese, "Amazon Publishing, DPLA Ink Deal to Lend E-books in Libraries," *Publishers Weekly* (18 May 2021), https://www.publishersweekly.com/pw/by-topic/industry-news/libraries/article/86399-amazon-publishing-dpla-ink-deal-to-lend-digital-content-in-libraries.html.

6. David R. Hansen and Kyle K. Courtney, "A White Paper on Controlled Digital Lending of Library Books," (2018), https://controlleddigitallending.org/whitepaper.

7. *Capitol Records LLC v. ReDigi Inc.*, 934 F. Supp. 2d 640 (S.D.N.Y. 2013).

8. Its story in Deanna Marcum and Roger C. Schonfeld, *Along Came Google: A History of Library Digitization* (Princeton 2021).

9. James Somers, "Torching the Modern-Day Library of Alexandria," *Atlantic* (20 April 2017).

10. The British Library's "Private Case Collection" forms part of Gale Cengage's "Archives of Sexuality & Gender, Part III" which Gale licenses to other libraries, https://www.bl.uk/press-releases/2019/february/private-case-collection-launched.

11. Its history in Roger C. Schonfeld, *JSTOR: A History* (Princeton 2003).

12. https://about.jstor.org/oa-and-free/.

13. https://case.law/.

14. McKinsey Global Institute, "Digital America: A Tale of the Haves and the Have-Mores" (1 December 2015), https://www.mckinsey.com/industries/technology -media-and-telecommunications/our-insights/digital-america-a-tale-of-the-haves -and-have-mores.

15. ProQuest had the exclusive right to license its Early English Books Online (EEBO) "Phase 2" texts to new customers, or to users outside the original Phase 2 partnership. This restriction ended on January 1, 2021, thus opening it to readers in general, https://textcreationpartnership.org/tcp-texts/eebo-tcp-early-english-books -online/. Thanks to Ross Mounce for this.

16. Mario Biagioli, "Rights or Rewards? Changing Frameworks of Scientific Authorship," in Biagioli and Galison, eds., *Scientific Authorship*, 256–257.

17. William E. Savage and Anthony J. Olejniczak, "More Journal Articles and Fewer Books: Publication Practices in the Social Sciences in the 2010's," *PLOS One* (3 February 2022), https://journals.plos.org/plosone/article?id=10.1371/journal .pone.0263410.

18. HSBC Global Research, "Going for Gold: Open Access Risks Are Diminishing for Reed Elsevier and Informa" (31 August 2012) 18, https://www.research.hsbc .com/midas/Res/RDV?p=pdf&key=ZMbgS0Q5vv&n=341184.PDF.

19. An example: Mary Poovey, *A History of the Modern Fact: Problems of Knowledge in the Sciences of Wealth and Society* (Chicago 1998).

20. Marilyn Deegan, *The Academic Book of the Future Project Report: A Report to the AHRC and the British Library* (June 2017) 40–41, https://academicbookfuture.org /end-of-project-reports-2/.

21. Anthony F. J. van Raan, "On Growth, Ageing, and Fractal Differentiation of Science," *Scientometrics*, 47, 2 (2000) 350; Bornmann and Mutz, "Growth Rates of Modern Science," 10.

22. David Worlock, "After Content: Scholarly Communications After Articles?" *DavidWorlock.Com* (19 November 2021), https://www.davidworlock.com/2021/11 /after-content-scholarly-communications-after-articles/.

23. Daniele Fanelli and Vincent Larivière, "Researchers' Individual Publication Rate Has Not Increased in a Century," *PLOS One* (9 March 2016) 5, https://journals .plos.org/plosone/article?id=10.1371/journal.pone.0149504.

24. John P. A. Ioannidis et al., "The Scientists Who Publish a Paper Every Five Days," *Nature*, 561 (2018) 167–169, https://www.nature.com/articles/d41586-018 -06185-8.

25. Christopher Anderson, "Writer's Cramp," *Nature*, 355 (1992) 101, https:// www.nature.com/articles/355101a0.pdf.

26. Jack Grove, "Restrict Researchers to One Paper a Year, Says UCL Professor," *Times Higher Education* (28 November 2019).

27. The 2019 version: http://www.icmje.org/icmje-recommendations.pdf.

28. Shapiro et al., "Contributions of Authors to Multiauthored Biomedical Research Papers," 441.

29. Ioannidis et al., "Scientists Who Publish a Paper Every Five Days," 167–169.

30. Arnold S. Jacobs, "An Analysis of Section 16 of the Securities Exchange Act of 1934," *New York Law School Law Review*, 32 (1987) is 492 pages long.

31. Stephen Bainbridge, "Law Review Word Limits Go Unenforced . . . at Least at Harvard and Yale" (15 October 2013), https://www.professorbainbridge.com /professorbainbridgecom/2013/10/law-review-word-limits-go-unenforced-at-least -at-harvard-and-yale.html.

32. Gerhard A. Ritter, "Entstehung und Entwicklung des Sozialstaates in vergleichender Perspektive," *Historische Zeitschrift*, 243, 1 (1986) is almost half the length of his subsequent book *Der Sozialstaat: Entstehung und Entwicklung im internationalen Vergleich* (Munich 1989). Tomáš Lackner and Richard A. B. Leschen, "A Monograph of the Australopacific Saprininae (Coleoptera, Histeridae)," *ZooKeys*, 689 (2017), https://zookeys.pensoft.net/article/12021/ is book length.

33. Oxford University Press's *Very Short Introduction* series is among the best known, strictly limited to 30,000 words, and is at some 750 titles and counting.

34. Cited in Arthur Austin, "Footnote Skulduggery and Other Bad Habits," *University of Miami Law Review*, 44 (1990) 1009; Joan Ames Magat, "Bottomheavy: Legal Footnotes," *Journal of Legal Education*, 60, 1 (2010) 70.

35. Lori McPherson, "Law Review Articles Have Too Many Footnotes," *Journal of Legal Education*, 68, 2 (2019).

36. Anne-Wil K. Harzing and Ron van der Wal, "Google Scholar as a New Source for Citation Analysis," *Ethics in Science and Environmental Politics*, 8 (2008) 64.

37. "Highly Cited Researchers (h > 100) According to Their Google Scholar Citations Public Profiles," https://www.webometrics.info/en/hlargerthan100. That was the case when this was consulted early in 2021. A year later, the first nonscientist was Stiglitz at 34. Amartya Sen followed at 64. The list now includes only living authors, explaining the disappearance of past greats, except that the first humanist is Theodor Adorno at 349, apparently an oversight.

38. Lawprofblawg and Darren Bush, "Law Reviews, Citation Counts, and Twitter (Oh my!): Behind the Curtains of the Law Professor's Search for Meaning," *Loyola University Chicago Law Journal*, 50 (2018) 333.

39. Katherine W. McCain, "Obliteration by Incorporation," in Blaise Cronin and Cassidy R. Sugimoto, eds., *Beyond Bibliometrics: Harnessing Multidimensional Indicators of Scholarly Impact* (Cambridge MA 2014). This footnote commits that crime, since the idea comes originally from Robert Merton. But this also ignores the converse issue, that in some fields, such as history, the act of finding an obscure work that is then cited (what we call research) obliges subsequent scholars to cite the intermediary work as well, giving credit for the finding, too, not just pretending that their erudition extended to the original source.

40. Fred R. Shapiro and Michelle Pearse, "The Most Cited Law Review Articles of All Time," *Michigan Law Review*, 110 (2012) 1485.

41. As pointed out by Hirsch himself, after whom the index is named: J. E. Hirsch, "An Index to Quantify an Individual's Scientific Research Output," *Proceedings of the National Academy of Sciences*, 102, 46 (2005) 16571.

42. Differences among fields are explored in A.W. Harzing, and S. Alakangas, "Google Scholar, Scopus, and the Web of Science: A Longitudinal and Cross-Disciplinary Comparison," *Scientometrics*, 106, 2 (2016).

43. Stephen Bosch et al., "Deal or No Deal: Periodicals Price Survey 2019," *Library Journal* (4 April 2019) table 3, https://www.libraryjournal.com/?detailStory =Deal-or-No-Deal-Periodicals-Price-Survey-2019.

44. Mu-Hsuan Huang and Mei-Jhen Huang, "An Analysis of Global Research Funding from Subject Field and Funding Agencies Perspectives in the G9 Countries," *Scientometrics* (2018) table 4, https://dl.acm.org/doi/abs/10.1007/s11192-018 -2677-y.

45. HSBC Global Research, "Reed Elsevier" (30 April 2012) 25, https://www .research.hsbc.com/midas/Res/RDV?p=pdf&key=0gdqbAbXzv&n=328354.PDF.

46. Burcu Yucesoy et al., "Success in Books: A Big Data Approach to Bestsellers," *EPJ Data Science*, 7, 7 (2018) 3, https://link.springer.com/article/10.1140/epjds /s13688-018-0135-y#Fig3.

47. Fei Shu et al., "Is It Such a Big Deal? On the Cost of Journal Use in the Digital Era," *College and Research Libraries*, 79, 6 (2018) 1, https://crl.acrl.org/index.php/crl /rt/printerFriendly/16829/18997.

48. Neil Beagrie, "Preservation, Trust, and Continuing Access for e-Journals," 6–7, DPC Technology Watch Reports, https://www.dpconline.org/docs/technology -watch-reports/924-dpctw13-04/file.

49. John Willinsky, *The Access Principle: The Case for Open Access to Research and Scholarship* (Cambridge MA 2006) ch. 4.

50. John J. Regazzi, *Scholarly Communications: A History from Content as King to Content as Kingmaker* (Lanham 2015) 10.

51. John B. Thompson, *Books in the Digital Age: The Transformation of Academic and Higher Education Publishing in Britain and the United States* (Cambridge 2005) 101.

52. Vincent Larivière et al., "The Oligopoly of Academic Publishers in the Digital Era," *PLOS One* (10 June 2015), https://doi.org/10.1371/journal.pone.0127502.

53. Greg Tananbaum, "Of Wolves and Boys: The Scholarly Communication Crisis," *Learned Publishing*, 16 (2003) 286, https://onlinelibrary.wiley.com/doi/epdf/10.1087/095315103322422035.

54. S. C. Bradford, "Sources of Information on Specific Subjects," *British Journal of Engineering*, 137 (1934), available at https://www.tandfonline.com/doi/abs/10.1300/J105v01n03_06.

55. https://openstax.org/.

56. MIT OpenCourseWare: https://ocw.mit.edu/courses/online-textbooks/. See also https://fredonia.libguides.com/oer/textbooks.

57. Open Syllabus, OER Metrics, https://oer.opensyllabus.org/?category=Top%20Titles&.

58. "Consumer Expenditure on Educational Books in the United States from 1999 to 2020," https://www.statista.com/statistics/192867/consumer-expenditures-on-educational-books-in-the-us-since-1999/.

59. "Student Spending on Course Material in the United States from the Academic Years 2007/08 to 2019/20," https://www.statista.com/statistics/592371/student-spending-course-material-usa/.

60. Stephen Buranyi, "Is the Staggeringly Profitable Business of Scientific Publishing Bad for Science?" *Guardian* (27 June 2017), https://www.theguardian.com/science/2017/jun/27/profitable-business-scientific-publishing-bad-for-science.

61. Richard Edwards and David Shulenberger, "The High Cost of Scholarly Journals (and What to Do about It)," *KU ScholarWorks*, 2, https://kuscholarworks.ku.edu/bitstream/handle/1808/12546/Highe%20Cost%20of%20Scholarly%20-%20Change.pdf.

62. Association of Research Libraries, *ALR Statistics, 2003–04*, Graph 4, http://www.libqual.org/documents/admin/2012/ARL_Stats/2004-05arlstats.pdf. More recent continuing bad news in Rachael Pells, "Top Universities' Journal Subscriptions 'Average £4 Million.'" *Times Higher Education* (12 June 2018), https://www.timeshighereducation.com/news/top-universities-journal-subscriptions-average-4-million-pounds.

63. Fei Shu et al., "Is It Such a Big Deal?" fig. 2; Tananbaum, "Of Wolves and Boys," 285.

64. John W. Houghton, "Crisis and Transition: The Economics of Scholarly Communication," *Learned Publishing*, 14 (2001) 168, https://onlinelibrary.wiley.com/doi/epdf/10.1087/095315101750240412.

65. Donald A. Barclay, "Academic Print Books Are Dying," *Conversation* (10 November 2015), https://theconversation.com/academic-print-books-are-dying-whats-the-future-46248.

66. Chandra Prabha and John E. Ogden, "Recent Trends in Academic Library Materials Expenditures," *Library Trends*, 42, 3 (1994) fig. 2; *Trends in the Finances of UK Higher Education Libraries: 1999–2009*, 14–15, http://www.rin.ac.uk/system/files/attachments/library_trends_report_screen.pdf.

67. https://www.elsevier.com/books-and-journals/journal-pricing/print-price -list.

68. Thanks to Ian Baldwin for this caution.

69. Stephen Bosch et al., "Deal or No Deal: Periodicals Price Survey 2019," *Library Journal* (4 April 2019) table 3, https://www.libraryjournal.com/?detailStory =Deal-or-No-Deal-Periodicals-Price-Survey-2019.

70. Peter Mandler, "Open Access: A Perspective from the Humanities," *Insights*, 27, 2 (2014), http://doi.org/10.1629/2048-7754.89.

71. Mary Waltham, "The Future of Scholarly Journals Publishing among Social Science and Humanities Associations," *Journal of Scholarly Publishing*, 41, 3 (2010) 264–265, accessible version at https://www.marywaltham.com/JSPfulltextarticle April2010.pdf.

72. Joseph Esposito, "Why Elsevier is a Library's Best Friend," *Scholarly Kitchen* (9 January 2018), https://scholarlykitchen.sspnet.org/2018/01/09/50692/.

73. Shu et al., "Is It Such a Big Deal?" fig. 3.

74. Rob Johnson et al., *The STM Report: An Overview of Scientific and Scholarly Publishing* (5th ed.; 2018) 6, 76, https://www.stm-assoc.org/2018_10_04_STM_Report _2018.pdf.

75. HSBC Global Research, "Going for Gold," 14.

76. Ann M. Blair, *Too Much to Know: Managing Scholarly Information before the Modern Age* (New Haven 2010) 18.

77. https://scoap3.org/.

78. https://www.openlibhums.org/.

79. Richard Poynder, "Open Access: 'Information Wants to Be Free'?" *Open and Shut?* (2 December 2020) 82, https://poynder.blogspot.com/2020/12/open-access -information-wants-to-be-free.html.

80. Peter Gruss, president of the Max Planck Society, quoted in Ralf Schimmer et al., "Disrupting the Subscription Journals' Business Model for the Necessary Large-scale Transformation to Open Access," Max Planck Digital Library Open Access Policy White Paper (28 April 2015) 4, https://pure.mpg.de/rest/items/item _2148961_7/component/file_2149096/content.

81. David Shulenberger, "Substituting Article Processing Charges for Subscriptions: The Cure Is Worse than the Disease," Association of Research Libraries (20 July 2016), https://www.arl.org/wp-content/uploads/2018/09/substituting-apcs-for -subscriptions-20july2016.pdf.

82. Mellon Foundation, *Pay It Forward: Investigating a Sustainable Model of Open Access Article Processing Charges for Large North American Research Institutions* (University of California Libraries, 30 June 2016), 87, 89, https://escholarship.org/uc /item/8326n305.

83. Abel L. Packer, "The SciElo Open Access: A Gold Way from the South," *Canadian Journal of Higher Education*, 39, 3 (2009) 123, https://journals.sfu.ca/cjhe/index.php/cjhe/article/view/479/504.

84. Valerie Spezi et al., "Open-access Mega-journals: The Future of Scholarly Communication or Academic Dumping Ground?" *Journal of Documentation*, 73, 2 (2017) 273, https://www.emerald.com/insight/content/doi/10.1108/JD-06-2016-0082/full/html.

85. "Springer Nature Announces Gold Open Access Options for Nature Journals from January 2021," Springer Nature Group (24 November 2020), https://group.springernature.com/gb/group/media/press-releases/springer-nature-announces-gold-oa-options-for-nature-journals/18614608.

86. Stephen Bosch et al., "Deal or No Deal: Periodicals Price Survey 2019," *Library Journal* (4 April 2019) table 3, https://www.libraryjournal.com/?detailStory=Deal-or-No-Deal-Periodicals-Price-Survey-2019.

87. Mark McGurl, *Everything and Less: The Novel in the Age of Amazon* (London 2021) 35.

88. Rebecca Darley et al., *Open Access Journals in Humanities and Social Science: A British Academy Research Report* (British Academy 2014) 7–8, https://www.thebritishacademy.ac.uk/publications/open-access-journals-humanities-and-social-science/. This underestimates the half-lives of humanities articles by perhaps 50% since it counts only downloads from publishers' sites, not also JSTOR, source of half of such downloads. Personal communication from Peter Mandler.

89. House of Commons Business, Innovation and Skills Committee, *Open Access: Fifth Report of Session 2013–14* (10 September 2013) i, 14–15, https://publications.parliament.uk/pa/cm201314/cmselect/cmbis/99/99.pdf.

90. Mellon Foundation, *Pay It Forward*, 7.

91. University of California, Office of Scholarly Communications, "An Introductory Guide to the UC Model Transformative Agreement," https://osc.universityofcalifornia.edu/uc-publisher-relationships/resources-for-negotiating-with-publishers/negotiating-with-scholarly-journal-publishers-a-toolkit/an-introductory-guide-to-the-uc-model-transformative-agreement/.

92. Gemma Hersh, "Working towards a Transition to Open Access," *Elsevier* (26 September 2017), https://www.elsevier.com/connect/working-towards-a-transition-to-open-access; Poynder, "Open Access: 'Information Wants to Be Free'?" 34.

93. Anna McKie, "'Location-specific' Blocks on Journal Access Could be OA 'Interim Solution'," *Times Higher Education* (8 November 2019), https://www.timeshighereducation.com/news/location-specific-blocks-journal-access-could-be-oa-interim-solution.

94. Jason Potts et al., "A Journal Is a Club: A New Economic Model for Scholarly Publishing," *Prometheus*, 35, 1 (2017) 78, https://www.tandfonline.com/doi/full/10.1080/08109028.2017.1386949.

95. Brian Resnick, "The World Just Redefined the Kilogram," *Vox* (16 November 2018), https://www.vox.com/science-and-health/2018/11/14/18072368/kilogram -kibble-redefine-weight-science; Bureau International des Poids et Mesures, "Resolution 1 of the 17th CGPM (1983)," https://www.bipm.org/en/CGPM/db/17/1/.

96. https://www.crossref.org/services/crossmark/.

97. Jean-Claude Guédon, "Open Access: Toward the Internet of the Mind," 31, https://www.budapestopenaccessinitiative.org/boai15/Untitleddocument.docx.

98. https://f1000research.com/; Johnson et al., *STM Report*, 18.

99. Jean-Claude Guédon, *Open Access Scholarly Publishing Association* (9 December 2020), https://oaspa.org/open-post-the-rise-of-immediate-green-oa-undermines -progress/#comment-15016.

100. Even the first version deposited is largely indistinguishable from the version of record: Martin Klein et al., "Comparing Published Scientific Journal Articles to their Pre-print Versions," *International Journal on Digital Libraries* (18 January 2018), https://link.springer.com/article/10.1007/s00799-018-0234-1. Similar results in Jessica K. Polka et al., "Preprints in Motion: Tracking Changes between Posting and Journal Publication," bioRxiv (20 February 2021), https://www.biorxiv.org /content/10.1101/2021.02.20.432090v1.

101. For example: Jane Winters, "Giving with One Click, Taking with the Other: E-legal Deposit, Web Archives and Researcher Access," in Paul Gooding and Melissa Terras, eds., *Electronic Legal Deposit: Shaping the Library Collections of the Future* (London 2020), the preprint version at https://sas-space.sas.ac.uk/9439/1 /Giving%20with%20one%20click%2C%20taking%20with%20the%20other.pdf.

102. Consider the three depository versions of an article by Sergei Dubovsky, "The QCD β-Function on the String Worldsheet," arXiv, https://arxiv.org/abs /1807.00254. The second one corresponds to the published version, at *Physical Review D* (21 December 2018), https://journals.aps.org/prd/abstract/10.1103 /PhysRevD.98.114025#fulltext. But the third one, from 5 June 2019, has moved on. Thanks to Ross Mounce for this example.

103. Kathleen Shearer, "Correcting the Record: The Critical Role of OA Repositories in Open Access and Open Science," *OASPA News* (11 December 2020), https:// oaspa.org/guest-post-correcting-the-record-the-critical-role-of-oa-repositories-in -open-access-and-open-science/.

104. Blair, *Too Much to Know*, 39.

105. Amazon's Quantum Ledger Database is an example of non-blockchain technology with a central authority that simplifies things, rather than having to embody the entire record-keeping and verifying function in the act of recording: https://aws.amazon.com/qldb/.

106. Baldwin, *Fighting the First Wave*, 21.

107. Deborah Cohen and Peter Mandler, "Silent Changes to *The History Manifesto*," *Deborah Cohen* (23 March 2013), http://www.deborahacohen.com/ profile/?q=content/silent-changes-history-manifesto.

Chapter 4

1. Budapest Open Access Initiative, 14 February 2002, https://www.budapestopenaccessinitiative.org/read.

2. Henry Ansgar Kelly, "Inquisitorial Due Process and the Status of Secret Crimes," in Stanley Chodorow, ed., *Proceedings of the Eighth International Congress of Medieval Canon Law* (Vatican City 1992) 419–420.

3. Marion Renault, "An Elixir From the French Alps, Frozen in Time," *New York Times* (17 December 2020).

4. Jütte, *Age of Secrecy*, 22.

5. Rowan Jacobsen, "Life, New and Improved," *Scientific American*, 325, 1 (2021) 29.

6. Alejandro Barredo Arrieta et al., "Explainable Artificial Intelligence (XAI): Concepts, Taxonomies, Opportunities and Challenges toward Responsible AI," *Information Fusion*, 58 (2020).

7. "Proposal for a Regulation of the European Parliament and of the Council Laying Down Harmonised Rules on Artificial Intelligence (Artificial Intelligence Act) and Amending Certain Union Legislative Acts," COM/2021/206 final, *EUR-Lex*, https://eur-lex.europa.eu/legal-content/EN/TXT/?qid=1623335154975&uri=CELEX%3A52021PC0206.

8. Thomas H. Davenport and Keith W. Dreyer, "AI Will Change Radiology, but It Won't Replace Radiologists," *Harvard Business Review* (27 March 2018), https://hbr.org/2018/03/ai-will-change-radiology-but-it-wont-replace-radiologists.

9. Yilun Wang and Michal Kosinski, "Deep Neural Networks Are More Accurate than Humans at Detecting Sexual Orientation from Facial Images," *Journal of Personality and Social Psychology*, 114, 2 (2018), https://doi.apa.org/doiLanding?doi=10.1037%2Fspspa0000098.

10. John Leuner, "A Replication Study: Machine Learning Models Are Capable of Predicting Sexual Orientation From Facial Images," (Masters thesis, University of Pretoria, November 2018), https://arxiv.org/pdf/1902.10739.pdf.

11. Eamon, "From the Secrets of Nature to Public Knowledge," 334.

12. Paul A. David, "From Keeping 'Nature's Secrets' to the Institutionalization of 'Open Science,'" in Rishab Aiyer Ghosh, ed., *Code: Collaborative Ownership and the Digital Economy* (Cambridge MA 2005) 90.

13. Richard R. John, *Spreading the News: The American Postal System from Franklin to Morse* (Cambridge MA 1995) 37.

14. Robert Darnton, *The Forbidden Best-Sellers of Pre-Revolutionary France* (New York 1996); Darnton, *The Literary Underground of the Old Regime* (Cambridge MA 1985).

15. Mokyr, *Gifts of Athena*, 44.

16. Eric S. Raymond, "The Cathedral and the Bazaar," http://www.catb.org/~esr/writings/cathedral-bazaar/cathedral-bazaar/ar01s04.html; Richard Campbell, "When

Open Source Came to Microsoft," *CODE Magazine* (2020), https://www.codemag
.com/Article/2009041/When-Open-Source-Came-to-Microsoft.

17. Peter B. Kaufman, *The New Enlightenment and the Fight to Free Knowledge* (New
York 2021) ch. 3.

18. Stig Fredrikson, "How I Helped Alexandr Solzhenitsyn Smuggle His Nobel
Lecture from the USSR," *Nobel Prize*, https://www.nobelprize.org/prizes/literature
/1970/solzhenitsyn/article/.

19. William A. Bone, "The Centenary of the Friction Match," *Nature* (2 April
1927) 495, https://www.nature.com/articles/119495a0.pdf.

20. Rodney Stark, *For the Glory of God: How Monotheism Led to Reformations, Science, Witch-Hunts, and the End of Slavery* (Princeton 2003) 77; A. N. Wilson, *Tolstoy*
(London 1988) 237, 425, 493–495.

21. Isabel Hofmeyr (2013) *Gandhi's Printing Press* (Cambridge MA 2013) 2–3, 29,
67; Shyamkrishna Balganesh, "Gandhi and Copyright Pragmatism," *California Law
Review*, 101 (2013) 1709, otherwise https://papers.ssrn.com/sol3/papers.cfm?abstract
_id=2233063#.

22. https://commons.wikimedia.org/wiki/File:Gandhi-Home-Rule-First-Edition
-1909.jpg. Thanks to Ross Mounce for this.

23. *Congressional Record*, House (7 October 1988) 24336; US Constitution, art. I,
§8, cl. 8.

24. Baldwin, *Copyright Wars*, 4.

25. Cecil C. Kuhne III, "The Steadily Shrinking Public Domain: Inefficiencies
of Existing Copyright Law in the Modern Technology Age," *Loyola Law Review*, 50
(2004) 560.

26. Albert N. Greco, "Academic Libraries and the Economics of Scholarly Publishing in the Twenty-First Century," *Journal of Scholarly Publishing*, 47, 1 (2015) 3.

27. Yu Zie et al., "China's Rise as a Major Contributor to Science and Technology," *Proceedings of the National Academy of Sciences*, 111, 26 (2014) 9437, https://
www.pnas.org/content/111/26/9437#xref-ref-1-1. Less exuberant figures in Chuanyi
Wang and Qiang Zha, "Measuring Systemic Diversity of Chinese Universities," *Quality & Quantity*, 52 (2018) 1340, https://link.springer.com/article/10.1007/s11135
-017-0524-5.

28. Xiaotian Chen, "Scholarly Journals' Publication Frequency and Number of
Articles in 2018–2019: A Study of SCI, SSCI, CSCD, and CSSCI Journals," *Publications*
(8 September 2019), https://www.mdpi.com/2304-6775/7/3/58.

29. Samuel Moore et al., "'Excellence R Us:' University Research and the Fetishi-
sation of Excellence," *Palgrave Communications* (19 January 2017), https://www
.nature.com/articles/palcomms2016105.

30. An unpleasant example in Philip G. Altbach and Hans de Wit, "Too Much
Academic Research Is Being Published," *University World News* (7 September 2018),
https://www.universityworldnews.com/post.php?story=20180905095203579.

31. Lisong Liu, "Return Migration and Selective Citizenship: A Study of Returning Chinese Professional Migrants from the United States," *Journal of Asian American Studies*, 15, 1 (2012) 37, https://doi.org/10.1353/jaas.2012.0007.

32. Brian Lavoie et al., "Anatomy of Aggregate Collections: An Example of Google Print for Libraries," *D-Lib Magazine*, 11, 9 (2005) fig. 5, http://www.dlib.org/dlib/september05/lavoie/09lavoie.html.

33. Brian F. Lavoie and Roger C. Schonfeld, "Books without Boundaries: A Brief Tour of the System-wide Print Book Collection," *Journal of Electronic Publishing*, 9, 2 (2006), https://quod.lib.umich.edu/j/jep/3336451.0009.208?view=text;rgn=main.

34. Rick Anderson, "How Important Are Library Sales to the University Press? One Case Study," *Scholarly Kitchen* (23 June 2014), https://scholarlykitchen.sspnet.org/2014/06/23/how-important-are-library-sales-to-the-university-press-one-case-study/.

35. Joseph J. Esposito and Karen Barch, *Monograph Output of American University Presses, 2009–2013: A Report Prepared for the Andrew W. Mellon Foundation* (10 February 2017) 23, https://3spxpi1radr22mzge33bla91-wpengine.netdna-ssl.com/wp-content/uploads/2017/02/Monograph-Output-of-University-Presses.pdf.

36. Lisa Rose-Wiles, "Are Print Books Dead? An Investigation of Book Circulation at a Mid-sized Academic Library," Seton Hall University eRepository (2013) 12, https://scholarship.shu.edu/cgi/viewcontent.cgi?article=1057&context=lib_pub.

37. Chelsea Follett and Andrea Vacchiano, "A Reminder of How Far Transatlantic Travel Has Come," *HumanProgress* (2 August 2018), https://www.humanprogress.org/a-reminder-of-how-far-transatlantic-travel-has-come/#:~:text=First%2C%20consider%20the%20cost.,approximately%202%20million%20Spanish%20maravedis.

38. "What Is The Most Expensive Object Ever Built?" *ZidBits* (6 November 2010), https://zidbits.com/?p=19.

39. 77 million days of labor or $445 million at the current Egyptian minimum daily rate ($5.73/day) or ca $1 billion of construction costs by a modern firm per pyramid. Ed Davey, "What Is the Most Expensive Object on Earth?" *BBC* (29 April 2016), https://www.bbc.co.uk/news/magazine-36160368.

40. Michael Gibbons et al., *The New Production of Knowledge: The Dynamics of Science and Research in Contemporary Societies* (London 1994) 11.

41. John Preston, *Fall: The Mystery of Robert Maxwell* (np 2020) 24–26.

42. Gordon Graham, "The Journals Crisis: Origins and Resolution," *Serials*, 4, 2 (1991) 20; Robert W. Cahn, "The Origins of Pergamon Press: Rosbaud and Maxwell," *European Review*, 2, 1 (1994).

43. Preston, *Fall*, 30–31.

44. Hebe Vessuri et al., "Excellence or Quality? Impact of the Current Competition Regime on Science and Scientific Publishing in Latin America and its Implications for Development," *Current Sociology*, 62, 5 (2014) 648.

45. Brian Cox, "The Pergamon Phenomenon, 1951–1991," *Learned Publishing*, 15, 4 (2002) 278.

46. Aileen Fyfe et al., "Untangling Academic Publishing: A History of the Relationship between Commercial Interests, Academic Prestige and the Circulation of Research," (May 2017) 17, https://zenodo.org/record/546100#.YKJDGKhKia8.

47. "Expenditure Trends in ARL University Libraries, 1998–2018," https://www.arl.org/wp-content/uploads/2019/10/expenditure-trends.pdf.

48. Mark Rambler, "Do It Yourself? A New Solution to the Journals Crisis," *Journal of Electronic Publishing*, 4, 3 (1999), https://quod.lib.umich.edu/cgi/t/text/idx/j/jep/3336451.0004.306/--do-it-yourself-a-new-solution-to-the-journals-crisis?rgn=main;view=fulltext.

49. Glenn S. McGuigan and Robert D. Russell, "The Business of Academic Publishing: A Strategic Analysis of the Academic Journal Publishing Industry and Its Impact on the Future of Scholarly Publishing," *Electronic Journal of Academic and Special Librarianship*, 9 (2008) 1–11, https://digitalcommons.unl.edu/ejasljournal/105/.

50. Johnson et al., *STM Report*, 19.

51. Buranyi "Is the Staggeringly Profitable Business of Scientific Publishing Bad for Science?"

52. RELX, "Results for the Year to 31 December 2020" (11 February 2021), https://www.relx.com/~/media/Files/R/RELX-Group/documents/press-releases/2021/results-2020-pressrelease.pdf.

53. Robert-Jan Smits and Rachael Pells, *Plan S for Shock* (London 2022) 120, https://www.ubiquitypress.com/site/books/m/10.5334/bcq/

54. Bo-Christer Björk, "Why Is Access to the Scholarly Journal Literature So Expensive?" *Portal*, 21, 2 (2021), https://preprint.press.jhu.edu/portal/sites/ajm/files/21.2editorial.pdf.

55. Jörg Albrecht, "Forscher, hört die Signale," *Frankfurter Allgemeine Zeitung* (17 June 2012) 54.

56. Clay Shirky, *Here Comes Everybody: The Power of Organizing without Organizations* (New York 2008).

57. Moore, "Genealogy of Open Access."

58. Irving, "Art of Book-Making," 65.

59. Jane Hugo and Linda Newell (1991) "*New Horizons in Adult Education*: The First Five Years (1987–1991)," *Public-Access Computer Systems Review*, 2, 1 (1991), https://hdl.handle.net/10657/5149. Having been bought by Wiley, the journal later disappeared behind a paywall. Tonette S. Rocco, "Turning a Corner: The Future of *New Horizons in Adult Education and Human Resource Development*," *New Horizons in Adult Education and Human Resource Development* (30 January 2013) 1–2, https://doi.org/10.1002/nha.20001.

60. Samuel A. Moore, "Revisiting 'the 1990s Debutante:' Scholar-led Publishing and the Pre-history of the Open Access Movement," *Journal of the Society for Information Science and Technology*, 71, 7 (2020).

61. Budapest Open Access Initiative. More detail on the history of such declarations: Jorge Machado, "Open Data and Open Science," in Sarita Albagli et al., *Open Science, Open Issues* (Brasilia 2015) 192–196, https://www.researchgate.net/publication/303963675_Open_Science_open_issues.

62. Bethesda Statement on Open Access Publishing (20 June 2003), https://web.archive.org/web/20120311105112/http://www.earlham.edu/~peters/fos/bethesda.htm.

63. Berlin Declaration on Open Access to Knowledge in the Sciences and Humanities (23 October 2003), https://openaccess.mpg.de/Berlin-Declaration.

64. Mission Statement at the Berlin 11 Open Access Conference of the Max Planck Society (20 November 2013), https://openaccess.mpg.de/mission-statement_en.

65. John Unsworth and Eyal Amiran, "Postmodern Culture: Publishing in the Electronic Medium," *Public-Access Computer Systems Review*, 2, 1 (1991) 74–75, http://mural.uv.es/diades/arby3.htm.

66. Nancy Gusack and Clifford A. Lynch, "The TULIP Project," *Library Hi Tech*, 13, 4 (1995).

67. Richard E. Lucier and Peter Brantley, "The Red Sage Project: An Experimental Digital Journal Library for the Health Sciences," *D-Lib Magazine* (August 1995), https://www.dlib.org/dlib/august95/lucier/08lucier.html.

68. Waltham, "Future of Scholarly Journals Publishing among Social Science and Humanities Associations."

69. Rita Gardner, "Open Access and Learned Societies," in Nigel Vincent and Chris Wickham, eds., *Debating Open Access* (London 2013) 18, https://www.thebritishacademy.ac.uk/publications/debating-open-access/.

70. Guédon, "Open Access: Toward the Internet of the Mind," 9.

71. Bethesda Statement on Open Access Publishing.

72. Open Knowledge Foundation, "Open Definition," version 2.1, Compilation, 2.1.5, https://opendefinition.org/od/2.1/en/.

73. Guédon, "Open Access: Toward the Internet of the Mind," 10.

74. Carlos A. Sierra, "Elite Journals and the Defeat of Science," (21 March 2017), http://www.bgc-jena.mpg.de/~csierra/blog/2017/03/21/rejectNature/.

75. HSBC Global Research, "Going for Gold," 12.

76. HSBC Global Research, "Going for Gold," 9.

77. Roger C. Schonfeld, "The Supercontinent of Scholarly Publishing?" *Scholarly Kitchen* (3 May 2018), https://scholarlykitchen.sspnet.org/2018/05/03/supercontinent-scholarly-publishing/; Bo-Christer Björk, "Gold, Green, and Black Open Access," *Learned Publishing* (7 February 2017), https://onlinelibrary.wiley.com/doi/10.1002/leap.1096.

78. "Springer Nature Announces Gold Open Access Options for Nature Journals from January 2021," Springer Nature Group (24 November 2020), https://group.springernature.com/gb/group/media/press-releases/springer-nature-announces-gold-oa-options-for-nature-journals/18614608.

79. Bethesda Statement on Open Access Publishing.

80. Schimmer et al., "Disrupting the Subscription Journals' Business Model," 1.

81. *Accessibility, Sustainability, Excellence: How to Expand Access to Research Publications* (June 2012), https://www.sconul.ac.uk/sites/default/files/documents/finch -report-final.pdf.

82. House of Commons Business, Innovation and Skills Committee, *Open Access: Fifth Report of Session 2013–14*, i, 11–12.

83. Stephen Curry, "We Need to Talk about Open Access," *Reciprocal Space* (24 November 2012), http://occamstypewriter.org/scurry/2012/11/24/we-need-to-talk -about-open-access/.

84. *Accessibility, Sustainability, Excellence*, 7–8, 17.

85. Fyfe et al., "Untangling Academic Publishing," 16.

86. https://www.coalition-s.org/; "Science Without Publication Paywalls, a Preamble to: cOAlition S for the Realisation of Full and Immediate Open Access," https://www.coalition-s.org/wp-content/uploads/cOAlitionS_Preamble.pdf.

87. Shina Caroline Lynn Kamerlin et al., "Journal Open Access and Plan S: Solving Problems or Shifting Burdens?" *Development and Change* (29 January 2021), https://onlinelibrary.wiley.com/doi/full/10.1111/dech.12635.

88. "Reaction of Researchers to Plan S: Too Far, Too Risky," https://sites.google. com/view/plansopenletter/home.

89. Eduardo Aguado López and Arianna Becerril García, "Latin America's Longstanding Open Access Ecosystem Could Be Undermined by Proposals from the Global North," *LSE* (6 November 2019), https://blogs.lse.ac.uk/latamcaribbean /2019/11/06/latin-americas-longstanding-open-access-ecosystem-could-be -undermined-by-proposals-from-the-global-north/.

90. "Plan S Rights Retention Strategy," https://www.coalition-s.org/rights -retention-strategy/.

91. Holly Else, "A Guide to Plan S: The Open-access Initiative Shaking up Science Publishing," *Nature* (8 April 2021), https://www.nature.com/articles/d41586 -021-00883-6.

92. Smits and Pells, *Plan S for Shock*, 75, 85.

93. "NIH Public Access Policy Details," https://publicaccess.nih.gov/policy.htm.

94. Darley et al., *Open Access Journals in Humanities and Social Science*, 13; Guédon, "Open Access: Toward the Internet of the Mind," 20.

95. https://www.gatesfoundation.org/about/policies-and-resources/open-access -policy; https://www.hhmi.org/news/hhmi-announces-open-access-publishing-policy.

96. https://wellcome.org/grant-funding/guidance/open-access-guidance /open-access-policy.

97. Geoffrey Crossick, "Monographs and Open Access: A Report to HEFCE," (January 2015) 60–61, https://dera.ioe.ac.uk/21921/1/2014_monographs.pdf.

98. OAPEN-CH, *The Impact of Open Access on Scientific Monographs in Switzerland* (Swiss National Science Foundation; Bern, 2018) 13, https://www.snf.ch /SiteCollectionDocuments/OAPEN-CH_schlussbericht_en.pdf.

99. "About DASH," https://dash.harvard.edu/pages/About.

100. A list of university open access policies: Berkman Klein Center, "Policies of the Kind Recommended in the Guide," https://cyber.harvard.edu/hoap/Additional_resources#Policies_of_the_kind_recommended_in_the_guid.

101. https://hal.archives-ouvertes.fr/?lang=en; http://roar.eprints.org/view/geoname/geoname=5F2=5FDE.html; http://roar.eprints.org/.

102. Chris Wickham, "Open Access in the UK and the International Environment: The View from Humanities and Social Science," in Vincent and Wickham, eds., *Debating Open Access*, 46–48.

103. Thompson, *Books in the Digital Age*.

104. https://www.repository.cam.ac.uk/.

105. UK Research and Innovation, "UKRI Open Access Policy," (6 August 2021) Annex 1, https://www.ukri.org/publications/ukri-open-access-policy/.

106. *Accessibility, Sustainability, Excellence*, 34–35; HSBC Global Research, "Going for Gold," 23.

107. European Commission, *Future of Scholarly Publishing and Scholarly Communication*, 21. That meshes reasonably with the €7.6 billion estimate by the Max Planck Society a few years earlier: Schimmer et al., "Disrupting the Subscription Journals' Business Model," 5.

108. Johnson et al., *STM Report*, 24.

109. https://knowledgeunlatched.org/.

110. Michael Jubb, *Academic Books and their Future: A Report to the AHRC and the British Library* (June 2017) 192, https://academicbookfuture.org/end-of-project-reports-2/.

111. Marcel Knöchelmann, "Knowledge Unlatched, Failed Transparency, and the Commercialisation of Open Access Book Publishing," *LSE* (3 October 2018), https://blogs.lse.ac.uk/impactofsocialsciences/2018/10/03/knowledge-unlatched-failed-transparency-and-the-commercialisation-of-open-access-book-publishing/; "The Enclosure of Scholarly Infrastructures, Open Access Books and the Necessity of Community," *ScholarLed* (5 June 2019), https://blog.scholarled.org/open-research-library/.

112. "Wiley Acquires Open Access Innovator Knowledge Unlatched," *Knowledge Unlatched* (2 December 2020), https://knowledgeunlatched.org/2021/12/wiley-acquires-oa-innovator-ku/.

113. https://www.openmonographs.org/.

114. MIT: https://direct.mit.edu/books/pages/direct-to-open; Michigan: https://blog.press.umich.edu/2021/05/u-m-press-fund-to-mission-model-aims-to-expand-open-access-monograph-publishing/; Central European University: https://ceup.openingthefuture.net/.

115. Suzanne Smalley "MIT Press to Release Many Spring Titles Open Access," *Inside Higher Ed* (14 December 2021), https://www.insidehighered.com/news/2021/12/14/mit-press-plans-release-much-spring-slate-open-access#.YbmVJlc2f3c.twitter.

116. https://unglue.it/.

117. Izabella Penier et al., *COPIM: Revenue Models for Open Access Monographs 2020*, 17, https://zenodo.org/record/4455511#.YR4uHI5Ki_A.

118. https://www.berghahnjournals.com/page/577.

119. Bo-Christer Björk, "Have the 'Mega-journals' Reached the Limits to Growth?" *PeerJ* (26 May 2015), https://peerj.com/articles/981/.

120. https://plos.org/resources/community-action-publishing/; Jeffrey Brainard, "New PLOS Pricing Test Could Signal End of Scientists Paying to Publish Free Papers," *Science* (15 October 2020), https://www.sciencemag.org/news/2020/10 /new-plos-pricing-test-could-signal-end-scientists-paying-publish-free-papers.

121. https://doaj.org/.

122. Jeroen Bosman et al., *The Open Access Diamond Journals Study: Findings* (9 March 2021) 30, https://zenodo.org/record/4558704.

123. Aaron Swartz, "Guerilla Open Access Manifesto" (July 2008), https:// archive.org/details/GuerillaOpenAccessManifesto/page/n1/mode/2up.

124. Sérgio Amadeu da Silveira, "Aaron Swartz and the Battles for Freedom of Knowledge," *Sur*, 18 (2013) 11–12, https://sur.conectas.org/en/aaron-swartz-battles -freedom-knowledge/. A similar case: Samantha Murphy, "'Guerilla Activist' Releases 18,000 Scientific Papers," *MIT Technology Review* (22 July 2011), https:// www.technologyreview.com/2011/07/22/192838/guerilla-activist-releases-18000 -scientific-papers/.

125. Austin C. Murnane, "Faith and Martyrdom: The Tragedy of Aaron Swartz," *Fordham Intellectual Property, Media, and Entertainment Law Journal*, 24 (2014) 1109–1110.

126. Kaufman, *New Enlightenment*, 22–26.

127. "The Cost of Knowledge," http://thecostofknowledge.com/.

128. Nisha Gaind, "Huge US University Cancels Subscription with Elsevier," *Nature*, 567 (7 March 2019) 15.

129. "UC Terminates Subscriptions with World's Largest Scientific Publisher in Push for Open Access to Publicly Funded Research," University of California Press Room (28 February 2019), https://www.universityofcalifornia.edu/press-room /uc-terminates-subscriptions-worlds-largest-scientific-publisher-push-open-access -publicly.

130. "Elsevier Transformative Open Access Agreement," University of California, Office of Scholarly Communication, https://osc.universityofcalifornia.edu/uc -publisher-relationships/elsevier-oa-agreement/.

131. Lisa Janicke-Hinchliffe, "Transformative Agreements: A Primer," *Scholarly Kitchen* (23 April 2019), https://scholarlykitchen.sspnet.org/2019/04/23/ transformative-agreements/.

132. Richard Poynder, "Plan S: What Strategy Now for the Global South?" *Open and Shut* (15 February 2019) 9, https://poynder.blogspot.com/2019/02/plan-s-what -strategy-now-for-global.html.

133. "Jisc, UK Institutions and Wiley Agree Ground-breaking Deal," *Jisc News* (2 March 2020), https://www.jisc.ac.uk/news/jisc-uk-institutions-and-wiley-agree-ground -breaking-deal-02-feb-2020.

134. Roger C. Schonfeld, "Read and Publish: Is It Good for the Academy?" *Scholarly Kitchen* (4 September 2018), https://scholarlykitchen.sspnet.org/2018/09/04 /read-publish-good-academy/.

135. Shaun Yon-Seng Khoo, "Article Processing Charge Hyperinflation and Price Insensitivity: An Open Access Sequel to the Serials Crisis," *LIBER Quarterly*, 29, 1 (2019), https://www.liberquarterly.eu/article/10.18352/lq.10280/.

136. "Four Concerns About the New UC-Elsevier Deal," *The Taper* (19 March 2021), http://thetaper.library.virginia.edu/2021/03/19/four-concerns-about-the-new -uc-elsevier-deal.html.

137. University of California, Office of Scholarly Communications, "Introductory Guide to the UC Model Transformative Agreement."

138. The indifference to the overall price libraries were willing to pay is made clear here: Jeffrey MacKie-Mason, "Supporting OA2020: Changing the Journal Funding Model to Pre-payment Doesn't Increase Publisher Market Power," *madLibbing* (23 October 2016), https://madlibbing.berkeley.edu/supporting-oa2020-changing -the-journal-funding-model-to-pre-payment-doesnt-increase-publisher-market -power/.

139. Poynder, "Open Access: 'Information Wants to Be Free'?" 78–79.

140. Latin America receives 20% of Spanish book production, sends only 2% of its. Julieta Lionetti, "Asymmetry in the Spanish Book World: Spain vs. Latin America," *Publishing Perspectives* (8 March 2012), https://publishingperspectives.com /2012/03/asymmetry-in-the-spanish-book-world-spain-vs-latin-america/.

141. Valerie Miles, "Publishing in Spain and Latin America," 19th International Rights Directors Meeting, Frankfurt Book Fair 2005, https://www.academia .edu/5276532/Publishing_in_Spain_and_Latin_America.

142. Agencia Chilena ISBN, *Informe Estadístico 2019*, 48; CERLALC, *El espacio iberoamericano del libro 2018*, table 12, 14, 16, https://cerlalc.org/publicaciones /el-espacio-iberoamericano-del-libro/.

143. Fran M. Collyer, "Global Patterns in the Publishing of Academic Knowledge: Global North, Global South," *Current Sociology*, 66, 1 (2018) 66.

144. Sandra Miguel et al., "Open Access and Scopus: A New Approach to Scientific Visibility From the Standpoint of Access," *Journal of the American Society for Information Science and Technology* (11 April 2011) fig. 8, https://onlinelibrary.wiley .com/doi/abs/10.1002/asi.21532.

145. Bosman et al., *Open Access Diamond Journals Study*, figs. 11, 12.

146. Juan Pablo Alperin, "The Public Impact of Latin America's Approach to Open Access," (Dissertation, Stanford 2015), 1.

147. https://www.scielo.org/.

148. Abel L. Packer et al., *SciELO: 15 Years of Open Access* (UNESCO, Paris 2014) 15, http://old.scielo.org/local/File/book.pdf.

149. Alperin, "Public Impact of Latin America's Approach to Open Access," 12.

150. Its history in Packer, "SciElo Open Access: A Gold Way from the South."

151. Witold Kieńć, "Authors from the Periphery Countries Choose Open Access More Often," *Learned Publishing* (30 January 2017), https://onlinelibrary.wiley.com/doi/full/10.1002/leap.1093.

152. https://www.redalyc.org/; https://www.clacso.org/; http://amelica.org/index.php/en/home/; https://www.latindex.org/latindex/inicio; http://www.lareferencia.info/es/.

153. A much disputed post on this, originally by Jeffrey Beal in 2015, is now found here, for some reason supposedly authored by Stef Brezgov: "Is SciELO a Publication Favela?" *ScholarlyOA* (28 May 2019), https://scholarlyoa.com/is-scielo-a-publication-favela/.

154. https://clarivate.libguides.com/webofscienceplatform/scielo;   Phill   Jones, "Defending Regional Excellence in Research or Why Beall is Wrong About SciELO," *Scholarly Kitchen* (10 August 2015), https://scholarlykitchen.sspnet.org/2015/08/10/defending-regional-excellence-in-research-or-why-beall-is-wrong-about-scielo/.

155. Rogerio Meneghini and Abel L. Packer, "Is There Science beyond English?" *EMBO Reports*, 8, 2 (2007) 115, https://www.embopress.org/doi/full/10.1038/sj.embor.7400906.

156. Luis Reyes-Galindo, "On SciELO and RedALyC," Cardiff University Blogs, Sociology of Science and Open Access (5 August 2015), https://blogs.cardiff.ac.uk/luisreyes/on-scielo-and-redalyc/.

157. Pierre Mounier, "'Publication Favela' or Bibliodiversity? Open Access Publishing Viewed from a European Perspective," *Learned Publishing* (6 September 2018), https://onlinelibrary.wiley.com/doi/full/10.1002/leap.1194.

158. Abel L. Packer, "The Pasts, Presents, and Futures of SciELO," in Martin Paul Eve and Jonathan Gray, eds., *Reassembling Scholarly Communications: Histories, Infrastructures, and Global Politics of Open Access* (Cambridge MA 2020) fig. 21.2, https://direct.mit.edu/books/book/4933/Reassembling-Scholarly-CommunicationsHistories.

159. https://clarivate.libguides.com/webofscienceplatform/scielo.

160. López and García, "Latin America's Longstanding Open Access Ecosystem Could Be Undermined"; Hebe Vessuri et al., "Excellence or Quality? Impact of the Current Competition Regime on Science and Scientific Publishing in Latin America and Its Implications for Development," *Current Sociology*, 62, 5 (2014) 657–658.

161. Arianna Becerril-García and Eduardo Aguado-López, "The End of a Centralized Open Access Project and the Beginning of a Community-Based Sustainable Infrastructure for Latin America: Redalyc.org after Fifteen Years," *HAL* (18 June 2018), https://hal.archives-ouvertes.fr/hal-01816693.

Chapter 5

1. Françoise Rousseau-Hans et al., "Les pratiques de publications et d'accès ouvert des chercheurs français en 2019," *HAL* (25 June 2020) 32, 76, 37, https://hal-cea.archives-ouvertes.fr/cea-02450324v2/document.

2. "Higher Education Staff Statistics: UK, 2018/19," (23 January 2020), HESA, https://www.hesa.ac.uk/news/23-01-2020/sb256-higher-education-staff-statistics.

3. In Egypt: https://en.wikipedia.org/wiki/Egyptian_Knowledge_Bank; and Uruguay: https://foco.timbo.org.uy/home.

4. Smriti Mallapaty, "India Pushes Bold 'One Nation, One Subscription' Journal-access Plan," *Nature* (3 September 2020), https://www.nature.com/articles/d41586-020-02708-4.

5. Jean-Claude Guédon, "Mixing and Matching the Green and Gold Roads to Open Access—Take Two," *Serials Review*, 34, 1 (2008) 46, http://eprints.rclis.org/11791/.

6. HSBC Global Research, "Reed Elsevier," 24.

7. Jill Lepore, "The New Economy of Letters," *Chronicle of Higher Education* (3 September 2013).

8. Paul Ginsparg, "First Steps towards Electronic Research Communication," *Computers in Physics*, 8, 4 (1994) 395.

9. Robin Osborne, "Why Open Access Makes No Sense," in Vincent and Wickham, eds., *Debating Open Access*.

10. Universities are increasingly allowing access to alumni, at least for a while. In the US this is sometimes linked to joining an alumni association and being dunned for contributions.

11. Jennifer Howard, "JSTOR Tests Free, Read-Only Access to Some Articles," *Chronicle of Higher Education* (13 January 2012), https://www.chronicle.com/blogs/wiredcampus/jstor-tests-free-read-only-access-to-some-articles?cid=gen_sign_in.

12. ElHassan ElSabry, "Unaffiliated Researchers: A Preliminary Study," *Challenges* (2017), 5, https://www.mdpi.com/2078-1547/8/2/20.

13. https://www.deepdyve.com/. Other examples of such vendors include Proquest Udini, ReadCube Access, and RightFind.

14. Alperin, "Public Impact of Latin America's Approach to Open Access," 49–51.

15. Abraham Miller-Rushing et al., "The History of Public Participation in Ecological Research," *Frontiers in Ecology*, 10, 6 (2012), https://www.researchgate.net/publication/262093387_The_history_of_public_participation_in_ecological_research; Rick Bonney et al., "Next Steps for Citizen Science," *Science*, 343 (2014), https://www.researchgate.net/publication/261186507_Next_Steps_for_Citizen_Science; Bruno J. Strasser and Muki Haklay, "Citizen Science: Expertise, Demokratie und öffentliche Partizipation," Swiss Science Council, 2018, https://www.swir.ch/images/stories/pdf/de/Policy_Analysis_SSC_1_2018_Citizen_Science_WEB.pdf.

16. British special advisors and civil servants fear trouble if their work computers reveal that they have visited Sci-Hub or Z-Library in search of material they have no other access to.

17. To be fair, only 10% of scholars surveyed in 2010 agreed with the idea that the general public did not benefit from open access to academic research. Suenje Dallmeier-Tiessen et al., "Highlights from the SOAP Project Survey: What Scientists Think about Open Access Publishing," arXiv (28 January 2011) 6, https://arxiv.org/abs/1101.5260.

18. Quoted in Jean-Claude Guédon, "The 'Green' and 'Gold' Roads to Open Access: The Case for Mixing and Matching," *Serials Review*, 30, 4 (2004) 327, http://eprints.rclis.org/5860/.

19. Alesia Zuccala, "Open Access and Civic Scientific Information Literacy," *Information Research*, 15, 1 (2010) 5, http://informationr.net/ir/15-1/paper426.html.

20. Kamerlin et al., "Journal Open Access and Plan S."

21. Suber, *Open Access*, 17.

22. Samuel A. Moore, "Open Access, Plan S and 'Radically Liberatory' Forms of Academic Freedom," *Development and Change* (29 January 2021), https://onlineli brary.wiley.com/doi/10.1111/dech.12640; "Signatories Publish Statement on Rights Retention Strategy," *STM* (3 February 2021), https://www.stm-assoc.org/rightsreten tionstrategy/. And a riposte: "COAlition S Response to the STM Statement: The Rights Retention Strategy Restores Long-standing Academic Freedoms," *Plan S* (3 February 2021), https://www.coalition-s.org/blog/the-rights-retention-strategy-restores -long-standing-academic-freedoms/.

23. Rick Anderson "Open Access, Academic Freedom, and the Spectrum of Coercive Power," *Scholarly Kitchen* (5 November 2018), https://scholarlykitchen.sspnet .org/2018/11/05/open-access-academic-freedom-and-the-spectrum-of-coercive -power/; Lynn Kamerlin et al., "Response to Plan S from Academic Researchers: Unethical, Too Risky!" *For Better Science* (11 September 2018), https://forbetter-science.com/2018/09/11/response-to-plan-s-from-academic-researchers-unethical -too-risky/.

24. Rick Anderson, "Open Access and Academic Freedom: Teasing Out Some Important Nuances," *Development and Change* (2021) 8, https://onlinelibrary.wiley .com/doi/epdf/10.1111/dech.12636#.YBrmwHFD7Tk.twitter.

25. Paul Fussell, *Class: A Guide through the American Status System* (New York 1983) 166.

26. Patricia E. Campbell, "University Inventions Reconsidered: Debunking the Myth of University Ownership," *William & Mary Business Law Review*, 11 (2019) 79.

27. Vaclav Smil, *Enriching the Earth: Fritz Haber, Carl Bosch, and the Transformation of World Food Production* (Cambridge MA 2001) 74–77 and *passim*.

28. Corynne McSherry, *Who Owns Academic Work? Battling for Control of Intellectual Property* (Cambridge MA 2001) 147.

29. J. H. Reichman, "Computer Programs as Applied Scientific Know-How: Implication of Copyright Protection for Commercialized University Research," *Vanderbilt Law Review*, 42 (1989) 647–648.

30. Harvard University, Office of Technology Development, "Statement of Policy in Regard to Intellectual Property (IP Policy)," https://otd.harvard.edu /faculty-inventors/resources/policies-and-procedures/statement-of-policy-in-regard -to-intellectual-property/#inventions-and-patents.

31. In fact, this is usually wiped out by the ban on receiving any earned income for activities performed during their government service, except for book royalties, which do not count as earned income. US Office of Government Ethics, "Book Deals Involving Government Employees," (6 March 2008) pt 2, https://www.oge .gov/web/oge.nsf/News+Releases/7A40ADA00743E87D852585BA005BECD7/$FILE /DO-08-006%20(1)__.pdf.

32. Ashley Packard, "Copyright or Copy Wrong? An Analysis of University Claims to Faculty Work," *Communication Law and Policy*, 7 (2002) 276, 295.

33. Thompson, *Books in the Digital Age*, 215.

34. Tim Wu, "How Professors Help Rip Off Students," *New York Times* (11 December 2019).

35. Richard Read, "A $280 College Textbook Busts Budgets, but Harvard Author Gregory Mankiw Defends Royalties," *Oregonian* (19 January 2019), https://www .oregonlive.com/education/2015/02/a_280_college_textbook_busts_b.html.

36. Medicine being the reverse. Brian Lavoie and Lorcan Dempsey, "Beyond 1923: Characteristics of Potentially In-copyright Print Books in Library Collections," in Lorcan Dempsey et al., eds., *Understanding the Collective Collection: Towards a System-Wide Perspective on Library Print Collections* (OCLC Research; Dublin OH 2013) table 6.

37. https://books.google.com/ngrams.

38. Franco Moretti, *Distant Reading* (London 2013).

39. Tim McCormick, "From Monograph to Multigraph: The Distributed Book," *LSE* (17 January 2013), https://blogs.lse.ac.uk/impactofsocialsciences/2013/01/17 /from-monograph-to-multigraph-the-distributed-book/.

40. Peter Suber, "Gratis and Libre Open Access," *SPARC*, https://sparcopen.org /our-work/gratis-and-libre-open-access/.

41. Bryan L. Frye, "Plagiarism Is Not a Crime," *Duquesne Law Review*, 54 (2016) 147–148.

42. During the copyright term, similar removal from the market is possible in nations without moral rights: R. Anthony Reese, "The First Sale Doctrine in the Era of Digital Networks," *Boston College Law Review*, 44 (2003) 595–596, https://papers .ssrn.com/sol3/papers.cfm?abstract_id=463620.

43. https://creativecommons.org/licenses/by/4.0/.

44. Mandler, "Open Access: A Perspective from the Humanities"; Wellcome Trust, "The Suitability of the CC-BY Licence for Research Publications in the

Humanities and Social Sciences (HSS)," http://docplayer.net/29379-The-suitability
-of-the-cc-by-licence-for-research-publications-in-the.html.

45. An extreme example in Robert Dingwall, "Why Open Access is Good News for Neo-Nazis," *Social Science Space* (17 October 2012), https://www.socialscienc-espace.com/2012/10/why-open-access-is-good-news-for-neo-nazis/.

46. For example: James Emmott, "On Academic Integrity and the Right to Copy," *Journal of Victorian Culture*, 18, 4 (2013).

47. C.W. Schadt, "A Rant on Strawberries, Open Access Licenses, and the Reuse of Published Papers," *C.W. Schadt/ORNL-UTK Microbial Ecology Lab (2* July 2013), https://schadtlab.wordpress.com/2013/07/02/a-rant-on-strawberries-open-access -licenses-and-the-reuse-of-published-papers/; Rosie Redfield, "When Is it Ethical to Re-publish Open-access Scholarly Articles?" *RRResearch* (20 July 2013), http:// rrresearch.fieldofscience.com/2013/07/apple-academic-press-predatory.html.

48. Martin Paul Eve, "OA Books Being Reprinted under CC BY License," *Open Access*, https://eve.gd/2021/03/02/oa-books-being-reprinted-under-cc-by-license/.

49. Paul Klimpel, *Free Knowledge Based on Creative Commons Licenses*, 10, https://commons.wikimedia.org/wiki/File:Free_Knowledge_thanks_to_Creative _Commons_Licenses.pdf.

50. Jane Secker et al., *Understanding the CLA License to UK Higher Education* (Universities UK et al., July 2019) 6, https://ukcopyrightliteracy.files.wordpress .com/2019/07/cnac-research-project-report-final-with-logos-1.pdf.

51. Crossick, "Monographs and Open Access," 48.

52. Opinions sampled in Andy Nobes and Sian Harris, "Open Access in Devel-oping Countries—Attitudes and Experiences of Researchers," *Zenodo* (30 September 2019), table 10, https://zenodo.org/record/3464868#.YMY4o_lKia-.

53. Richard Poynder, "Open Access: Could Defeat be Snatched from the Jaws of Victory?" *Open and Shut* (18 November 2019) 68–69, https://poynder.blogspot .com/2019/11/open-access-could-defeat-be-snatched.html.

54. Eduardo Aguado-López and Arianna Becerril-Garcia, "North vs South—Are Open Access Models in Conflict?" *University World News* (5 October 2019), https:// www.universityworldnews.com/post.php?story=20191001143012482.

55. David Nimmer, "The Moral Imperative against Academic Plagiarism," *DePaul Law Review*, 54, 1 (2004) 76.

56. Sherry Turkle, *The Empathy Diaries* (New York 2021) 321.

57. Björk, "Why Is Access to the Scholarly Journal Literature So Expensive?"

58. Peter Suber, "Thinking about Prestige, Quality, and Open Access," *SPARC Open Access Newsletter*, 125 (2008), https://dash.harvard.edu/handle/1/4322577.

59. Martin Paul Eve and Ernesto Priego, "Who Is Actually Harmed by Predatory Publishers?" *TripleC*, 15, 2 (2017), https://www.triple-c.at/index.php/tripleC/article /view/867.

60. Eelco Ferwerda et al., *A Landscape Study on Open Access and Monographs* (October 2017) 84, https://zenodo.org/record/815932#.YLdc16hKia8.

61. John B. Thompson, *Book Wars: The Digital Revolution in Publishing* (Cambridge 2021) 146.

62. John B. Thompson, *Merchants of Culture: The Publishing Business in the Twenty-First Century* (2nd ed.; New York 2012) 91.

63. Karl Miller, "Harry and the Pot of Gold," *Raritan*, 20, 3 (2001) 132, https:// search.proquest.com/docview/203900537/fulltextPDF/44D833B2EFD4498BPQ /1?accountid=14512.

64. Elliott Green, "What Are the Most-cited Publications in the Social Sciences (According to Google Scholar)?" *LSE* (12 May 2016), https://blogs.lse.ac.uk /impactofsocialsciences/2016/05/12/what-are-the-most-cited-publications-in-the -social-sciences-according-to-google-scholar/.

65. Though there is a bookstore in Tokyo that sells only one book at a time. https://www.indy100.com/offbeat/this-japanese-bookshop-only-sells-one-book -at-a-time-7287071.

66. Crossick, "Monographs and Open Access," 37.

67. Chen, "Scholarly Journals' Publication Frequency and Number of Articles in 2018–2019," 3.

68. Jop de Vrieze, "Open-access Journal Editors Resign after Alleged Pressure to Publish Mediocre Papers," *Science* (4 September 2018), https://www.sciencemag .org/news/2018/09/open-access-editors-resign-after-alleged-pressure-publish -mediocre-papers; Martin Enserink, "Open-access Publisher Sacks 31 Editors amid Fierce Row over Independence," *Science* (20 May 2015), https://www.sciencemag .org/news/2015/05/open-access-publisher-sacks-31-editors-amid-fierce-row-over -independence.

69. https://www.journalguide.com/journals/plos-medicine.

70. HSBC Global Research, "Going for Gold," 24.

71. Jan Velterop, "On the Dangers of SciHub and Hybrid Journals," *SciELO in Perspective* (22 March 2016), https://blog.scielo.org/en/2016/03/22/on-the-dangers -of-scihub-and-hybrid-journals/#.YK-iIahKia8.

72. Lindsay Waters, "Rescue Tenure from the Tyranny of the Monograph," *Chronicle of Higher Education* (20 April 2001), https://www.chronicle.com/article /rescue-tenure-from-the-tyranny-of-the-monograph/?cid2=gen_login_refresh&cid =gen_sign_in; Deegan, *Academic Book of the Future Project Report*, 42.

73. More on specialization: Jones, "Defending Regional Excellence in Research."

74. Themes I have discussed in Peter Baldwin, "Betting on Vetting: Evaluation, not Publication, Should Be Academe's New Priority," *Chronicle of Higher Education* (17 February 2014).

75. Mirowski, "Future(s) of Open Science," 183–184.

76. Neal S. Young et al., "Why Current Publication Practices May Distort Science," *PLOS Medicine*, 5, 10 (2008), https://journals.plos.org/plosmedicine/article /comment?id=10.1371/annotation/b70a4689-cf09-4db6-a97b-8608b87e629e. Similar arguments in Hebe Vessuri et al., "Excellence or Quality? Impact of the Current

Competition Regime on Science and Scientific Publishing in Latin America and Its Implications for Development," *Current Sociology*, 62, 5 (2014) 649.

77. Mark Carden, "Time is Money: Why Scholarly Communication Can't Be Free," *Digital Science* (10 February 2015), https://www.digital-science.com/blog /guest/time-is-money-why-scholarly-communication-cant-be-free/.

78. HSBC Global Research, "Survey of Funders Supports the Benign Open Access Outcome Priced into Shares," 11.

79. Johnson et al., *STM Report*, 47.

80. HSBC Global Research, "Reed Elsevier," 21.

81. David Crotty, "The 'Burden' of Peer Review," *Scholarly Kitchen* (31 August 2010), https://scholarlykitchen.sspnet.org/2010/08/31/the-burden-of-peer-review/; Julia Wallace, "PEER: Final Report," (ECP-2007-DILI-537003, 1 September 2008–31 May 2012) 10, http://www.peerproject.eu/fileadmin/media/reports/20120618_PEER _Final_public_report_D9-13.pdf.

82. Ferwerda et al., *Landscape Study on Open Access*, 54.

83. To judge from the use of the English word, and a complaint from a mathematician over the use of the Anglicism, in Rousseau-Hans et al., "Les pratiques de publications et d'accès ouvert," 33.

84. Surveyed in Richard Smith, "Classical Peer Review: An Empty Gun," *Breast Cancer Research*, 12 (2010), https://breast-cancer-research.biomedcentral.com /articles/10.1186/bcr2742; Richard Smith, "Peer Review: A Flawed Process at the Heart of Science and Journals," *Journal of the Royal Society of Medicine*, 99, 4 (2006), https://www.ncbi.nlm.nih.gov/pmc/articles/PMC1420798/.

85. Lutz Bornmann, "Scientific Peer Review: An Analysis of the Peer Review Process from the Perspective of Sociology of Science Theories," *Human Architecture: Journal of the Sociology of Self-Knowledge*, 6, 2 (2008), https://www.researchgate.net /publication/254693844_Scientific_Peer_Review_An_Analysis_of_the_Peer_Review _Process_from_the_Perspective_of_Sociology_of_Science_Theories.

86. Joel Williamson, "Wounds Not Scars: Lynching, the National Conscience, and the American Historian," and the accompanying reports, *Journal of American History*, 83, 4 (1997). Discussed in Peter Loewenberg, "The Historian's Self-Reflection and American Racism," *Journal of the American Psychoanalytic Association*, 69, 2 (2021).

87. Examples in David F. Horrobin, "The Philosophical Basis of Peer Review and the Suppression of Innovation," *Journal of the American Medical Association*, 263, 10 (1990) 1440, https://jamanetwork.com/journals/jama/article-abstract/380984; José Luis Ricón, "Peer Rejection in Science," *Nintil* (2 December 2020), https://nintil .com/discoveries-ignored; Juan Miguel Campanario, "Consolation for the Scientist: Sometimes It Is Hard to Publish Papers That Are Later Highly-Cited," *Social Studies of Science*, 23 (1993) 343–346.

88. Juan Miguel Campanario, "Rejecting and Resisting Nobel Class Discoveries: Accounts by Nobel Laureates," *Scientometrics*, 81, 2 (2009).

89. Stuart Macdonald and Jaqueline Kam, "Aardvark et Al: Quality Journals and Gamesmanship in Management Studies," *Journal of Information Science*, 33, 6 (2007) 706.

90. Kathleen Fitzpatrick, *Planned Obsolescence: Publishing, Technology, and the Future of the Academy* (New York 2011) 24–28.

91. Ofer H. Azar, "Rejections and the Importance of First Response Times," *International Journal of Social Economics*, 31, 3 (2004) 259.

92. "How We Found 15 Million Hours of Lost Time," *Rubriq Blog* (3 June 2013), https://rubriqblog.wordpress.com/2013/06/03/how-we-found-15-million-hours -of-lost-time/.

93. Phil Davis, "Cascading Peer-Review: The Future of Open Access?" *Scholarly Kitchen* (12 October 2010), https://scholarlykitchen.sspnet.org/2010/10/12 /cascading-peer-review-future-of-open-access/; Amy Bourke-Waite, "Innovations in Scholarly Peer Review at Nature Publishing Group and Palgrave Macmillan," *UKSG Insights*, 28, 2 (2015), https://insights.uksg.org/articles/10.1629/uksg.243/.

94. Michael Clarke, "Game of Papers: eLife, BMC, PLoS and EMBO Announce New Peer Review Consortium," *Scholarly Kitchen* (15 July 2013), https:// scholarlykitchen.sspnet.org/2013/07/15/game-of-papers-elife-bmc-plos-and-embo -announce-new-peer-review-consortium/.

95. Bo-Christer Björk and Paul Catani, "Peer Review in Megajournals Compared with Traditional Scholarly Journals: Does It Make a Difference?" *Learned Publishing*, 29, 1 (2016), https://onlinelibrary.wiley.com/doi/full/10.1002/leap.1007.

96. David J. Solomon, "A Survey of Authors Publishing in Four Megajournals," *PeerJ* (22 April 2014) 6, https://peerj.com/articles/365/.

97. Spezi et al., "Open-access Mega-journals," 271.

98. Michèle Lamont, *How Professors Think: Inside the Curious World of Academic Judgement* (Cambridge MA 2009) 8.

99. Rousseau-Hans et al., "Les pratiques de publications et d'accès ouvert," 50.

100. An overview in Yves Gingras, *Bibliometrics and Research Evaluation* (Cambridge MA 2016).

101. Mario Biagioli, "Fraud by Numbers: Metrics and the New Academic Misconduct," *Los Angeles Book Review* (7 September 2020), https://lareviewofbooks.org /article/fraud-by-numbers-metrics-and-the-new-academic-misconduct/.

102. Macdonald and Kam, "Aardvark et Al," 707.

103. Allen W. Wilhite and Eric A. Fong, "Coercive Citation in Academic Publishing," *Science*, 335 (3 February 2012), https://science.sciencemag.org/content /335/6068/542.full.

104. LSE Public Policy Group, "Maximizing the Impacts of Your Research: A Handbook for Social Scientists," 110.

105. Yves Gingras and Mahdi Khelfaoui, "Why the h-index Is a Bogus Measure of Academic Impact," *Conversation* (8 July 2020), https://theconversation.com/why -the-h-index-is-a-bogus-measure-of-academic-impact-141684.

106. Richard Van Noorden and Dalmeet Singh Chawla, "Hundreds of Extreme Self-citing Scientists Revealed in New Database," *Nature* (19 August 2019), https://www.nature.com/articles/d41586-019-02479-7.

107. Stéphane Baldi, "Normative versus Social Constructivist Processes in the Allocation of Citations," *American Sociological Review*, 63, 6 (1998) 841.

108. LSE Public Policy Group, "Maximizing the Impacts of Your Research," 25.

109. Michael J. Moravcsik and Poovanalingam Murugesan, "Some Results on the Quality and Function of Citations," *Social Studies of Science*, 5, 1 (1975) 91.

110. A defense of drawing conclusions about articles from the journals where they are published: Ludo Waltman and Vincent A. Traag, "Use of the Journal Impact Factor for Assessing Individual Articles Need Not Be Statistically Wrong," *F1000 Research* (14 May 2020), https://f1000research.com/articles/9-366.

111. Diana Hicks et al., "Bibliometrics: The Leiden Manifesto for Research Metrics," *Nature* (22 April 2015), https://www.nature.com/news/bibliometrics-the-leiden-manifesto-for-research-metrics-1.17351.

112. LSE Public Policy Group, "Maximizing the Impacts of Your Research," 25.

113. Jennifer Lin, "Altmetrics Gaming: Beast Within or Without?" in Mario Biagioli and Alexandra Lippman, eds., *Gaming the Metrics: Misconduct and Manipulation in Academic Research* (Cambridge MA 2020).

114. Johan Bollen et al., "A Principal Component Analysis of 39 Scientific Impact Measures," *PLOS One* (29 June 2009), https://journals.plos.org/plosone/article?id=10.1371/journal.pone.0006022#.

115. Ross Mounce, "Open Access and Altmetrics: Distinct but Complementary," *Bulletin of the American Society for Information Science and Technology* (15 April 2013), https://asistdl.onlinelibrary.wiley.com/doi/10.1002/bult.2013.1720390406; Kent Anderson, "All the News That Fits: What's Really Driving Altmetric's Top 100 Articles List?" *Scholarly Kitchen* (13 December 2017), https://scholarlykitchen.sspnet.org/2017/12/13/news-fits-whats-really-driving-altmetrics-top-100-articles-list/.

116. Bethesda Statement on Open Access Publishing.

117. https://sfdora.org/read/. A similar emphasis on marrying qualitative to quantitative evaluation in Hicks et al., "Bibliometrics: The Leiden Manifesto for Research Metrics."

118. Chris Woolston, "Impact Factor Abandoned by Dutch University in Hiring and Promotion Decisions," *Nature* (25 June 2021), https://www.nature.com/articles/d41586-021-01759-5.

119. Haakon Gjerløw, "Peer Review, DORA, and Science," *PRIO Blogs* (25 September 2020), https://blogs.prio.org/2020/09/peer-review-dora-and-science/.

120. Shulenberger, "Substituting Article Processing Charges for Subscriptions."

121. HSBC Global Research, "Survey of Funders Supports the Benign Open Access Outcome Priced into Shares," 6.

122. HSBC Global Research, "Going for Gold," 25.

123. Richard Poynder, "PLoS ONE, Open Access, and the Future of Scholarly Publishing," *Open and Shut?* (7 March 2011) 27, https://richardpoynder.co.uk/PLoS_ONE.pdf.

124. David Mazieres and Eddie Kohler, "Get Me Off Your Fucking Mailing List," http://www.scs.stanford.edu/~dm/home/papers/remove.pdf; Joseph Stromberg, "'Get Me Off Your Fucking Mailing List' Is an Actual Science Paper Accepted by a Journal," *Vox* (21 November 2014), https://www.vox.com/2014/11/21/7259207/scientific-paper-scam.

125. Robert Phiddian, "Are Parody and Deconstruction Secretly the Same Thing?" *New Literary History*, 28, 4 (1997) 683.

126. Brian Lloyd, "Ern Malley and His Rivals," *Australian Literary Studies*, 20, 1 (2001).

127. Alan D. Sokal, "Transgressing the Boundaries: Towards a Transformative Hermeneutics of Quantum Gravity," *Social Text*, 46/47 (1996).

128. "SCIgen: An Automatic CS Paper Generator," https://pdos.csail.mit.edu/archive/scigen/.

129. Cyril Labbé, "Ike Antkare: One of the Great Stars in the Scientific Firmament," Les rapports de recherche du Laboratoire d'Informatique de Grenoble, *HAL* (17 August 2016), https://hal.archives-ouvertes.fr/hal-01354123.

130. John Bohannon, "US Charges Journal Publisher with Misleading Authors," *Science* (7 October 2016), https://science.sciencemag.org/content/354/6308/23.summary; Jeffrey Brainard, "U.S. Judge Rules Deceptive Publisher Should Pay $50 Million in Damages," *Science* (3 April 2019), https://www.sciencemag.org/news/2019/04/us-judge-rules-deceptive-publisher-should-pay-501-million-damages.

131. Jeffrey Beall, "Criteria for Determining Predatory Open-Access Publishers" (1 January 2015), https://web.archive.org/web/20161130184313/https://scholarlyoa.files.wordpress.com/2015/01/criteria-2015.pdf.

132. "Beall's List of Predatory Publishers 2017," https://web.archive.org/web/20170103170903/https:/scholarlyoa.com/. Threatened with defamation suits by publishers he had included, Beall closed his list in 2017.

133. Cenyu Shen and Bo-Christer Björk, "'Predatory' Open Access: A Longitudinal Study of Article Volumes and Market Characteristics," *BMC Medicine* (1 October 2015), https://bmcmedicine.biomedcentral.com/articles/10.1186/s12916-015-0469-2; Chen, "Scholarly Journals' Publication Frequency and Number of Articles in 2018–2019."

134. WIPO, *The Global Publishing Industry in 2018* (Geneva 2018) 26.

135. Mohammad Salehi et al., "Publishing in Predatory Open Access Journals: Authors' Perspectives," *Learned Publishing*, 33 (2020).

136. WIPO, *Global Publishing Industry in 2018*, 26.

137. Rick Anderson, "Why Should We Worry about Predatory Journals? Here's One Reason," *Cabells* (3 March 2020), https://blog.cabells.com/2020/03/03/guest-post-why-should-we-worry-about-predatory-journals-heres-one-reason/.

138. Kień, "Authors from the Periphery Countries Choose Open Access More Often."

139. Simon Wakeling et al., "Open-Access Mega-Journals: A Bibliometric Profile," PLOS One (18 November 2016) table 4, https://journals.plos.org/plosone/article?id=10.1371/journal.pone.0165359.

140. Kień, "Authors from the Periphery Countries Choose Open Access More Often."

141. Juliet Nabyonga-Orem et al., "Article Processing Charges Are Stalling the Progress of African Researchers," BJM Global Health, 5, 9 (2020), https://gh.bmj.com/content/5/9/e003650#xref-ref-2-1.

142. Nobes and Harris, "Open Access in Developing Countries," table 8.

143. Dallmeier-Tiessen et al., "Highlights from the SOAP Project Survey," 9. Non-payers were much higher in the HSS, lowest in the life sciences.

144. International Labour Organization, ILOSTAT, Statistics on Wages, Data, Mean nominal monthly earnings of employees by sex and economic activity, https://ilostat.ilo.org/topics/wages/#.

145. Nabyonga-Orem et al., "Article Processing Charges Are Stalling the Progress of African Researchers."

146. David J. Solomon and Bo-Christer Björk, "Publication Fees in Open Access Publishing: Sources of Funding and Factors Influencing Choice of Journal," Journal of the American Society for Information Science and Technology (24 October 2011) table 5, https://onlinelibrary.wiley.com/doi/abs/10.1002/asi.21660. A more recent survey found that 60% of Global South authors paid the APC themselves: Nobes and Harris, "Open Access in Developing Countries."

147. Predatory journals' average publishing charges were $178 in one study, $100 in another, compared to anything from $1,000 to $9,000 for gold open-access journals. Shen and Björk, "'Predatory' Open Access"; Larissa Shamsheer et al., "Potential Predatory and Legitimate Biomedical Journals: Can You Tell the Difference?" BMC Medicine (16 March 2017), https://bmcmedicine.biomedcentral.com/articles/10.1186/s12916-017-0785-9.

148. D. Mills and K. Inouye, "Problematizing 'Predatory Publishing': A Systematic Review of Factors Shaping Publishing Motives, Decisions, and Experiences," Learned Publishing (23 August 2020), https://onlinelibrary.wiley.com/doi/full/10.1002/leap.1325; Songqing Lin, "Why Serious Academic Fraud Occurs in China," Learned Publishing, 26, 1 (2013), https://www.researchgate.net/publication/274869749_Why_serious_academic_fraud_occurs_in_China; Ayokunle Olumuyiwa Omobowale et al., "Peripheral Scholarship and the Context of Foreign Paid Publishing in Nigeria," Current Sociology, 62, 5 (2014) 667.

149. Chen, "Scholarly Journals' Publication Frequency and Number of Articles in 2018–2019."

150. Songqing Lin and Lijuan Zhan, "Trash Journals in China," Learned Publishing, 27, 2 (2014) 151, https://onlinelibrary.wiley.com/doi/abs/10.1087/20140208.

151. Reggie Raju et al., "Predatory Publishing from the Global South Perspective," in Punctum Books, ed., *Predatory Publishing* (Coventry 2018), https://www.google.com/url?client=internal-element-cse&cx=partner-pub-9759840060944682:1306350668&q=https://hcommons.org/deposits/download/hc:19828/CONTENT/predatory-publishing.pdf/&sa=U&ved=2ahUKEwihjqPfo8v2AhWcgnIEHUb_BYMQFnoECAQQAQ&usg=AOvVaw1XGbR82czGAQJJWarZ8XYG.

152. Shen and Björk, "'Predatory' Open Access."

153. Alliance of Independent Authors, "Facts and Figures about Self Publishing."

Chapter 6

1. "Data Centres and Data Transmission Networks," IEA Tracking Report (June 2020), https://www.iea.org/reports/data-centres-and-data-transmission-networks.

2. Frederick G. Kilgour, *Evolution of the Book* (Oxford 1998) 26.

3. Caleb Everett, *Numbers and the Making of Us: Counting and the Course of Human Cultures* (Cambridge MA 2017) 243. Unless we accept the Berekhat Ram figure from 230,000 years ago as symbolic: Genevieve von Petzinger, *The First Signs: Unlocking the Mysteries of the World's Oldest Symbols* (New York 2016) 35.

4. Jeff Rothenberg, *Avoiding Technological Quicksand: Finding a Viable Technical Foundation for Digital Preservation*, Council on Library and Information Resources (Washington DC 1999) 2, https://www.clir.org/pubs/reports/rothenberg/.

5. Arch Mission Foundation, https://www.archmission.org/.

6. Ernie Smith, "Why the PDF Is Secretly the World's Most Important File Format," *Vice* (3 May 2018), https://www.vice.com/en/article/pam43n/why-the-pdf-is-secretly-the-worlds-most-important-file-format.

7. "Number of Independent Bookstores in the United States from 2009 to 2020," https://www.statista.com/statistics/282808/number-of-independent-bookstores-in-the-us/. The growth to 4,100 in 2020 is probably a fluke of some sort.

8. "Book Store Sales in the United States from 1992 to 2020," https://www.statista.com/statistics/197710/annual-book-store-sales-in-the-us-since-1992/.

9. Laurel Wickersham Salisbury, "It's Not That Easy: Artist Resale Royalty Rights and the ART Act," *Center for Art Law* (1 July 2019), https://itsartlaw.org/2019/07/01/its-not-that-easy-artist-resale-royalty-rights-and-the-art-act/#_ftn3.

10. "A Giant Leap . . . Backwards," *Readers First* (6 July 2018), http://www.readersfirst.org/news/2018/7/6/a-giant-leap-backwards.

11. Digital Economy Act 2017, https://www.legislation.gov.uk/ukpga/2017/30/section/31/enacted.

12. Campaign to Investigate the Academic Book Market, https://academicebookinvestigation.org/.

13. Rob Green, "Know Your Rights: The Key to eBook Access," *CILIP* (29 June 2021), https://www.cilip.org.uk/news/571553/Know-your-rights-the-key-to-eBook-access.htm; "Campaign to Investigate the Academic Ebook Market."

14. "IFLA Statement on Controlled Digital Lending" (May 2021), International Federation of Library Associations, https://www.ifla.org/publications/node/93954.

15. Andrew Albanese, "Maryland Library E-book Bill Becomes Law," *Publishers Weekly* (1 June 2021), https://www.publishersweekly.com/pw/by-topic/industry -news/libraries/article/86528-maryland-library-e-book-bill-becomes-law.html; Andrew Albanese, "New York Legislature Passes Library E-book Bill," *Publishers Weekly* (11 June 2021), https://www.publishersweekly.com/pw/by-topic/industry -news/libraries/article/86637-new-york-legislature-passes-library-e-book-bill.html. The NY bill was vetoed by the governor in December 2021. Andrew Albanese, "Hochul Vetoes New York's Library E-book Bill," *Publishers Weekly* (30 December 2021), https://www.publishersweekly.com/pw/by-topic/digital/copyright/article /88205-hochul-vetoes-new-york-s-library-e-book-bill.html.

16. "AAP Sues Maryland over E-Lending Law," *Authors Alliance* (10 December 2021), https://www.authorsalliance.org/2021/12/10/update-aap-sues-maryland-over -e-lending-law/.

17. Peter M. Routhier, "U.S. Congress Investigates Publisher Restrictions on Library E-Books," *Internet Archive Blogs* (24 September 2021), http://blog.archive .org/2021/09/24/u-s-congress-investigates-publisher-restrictions-on-library-e -books/; "Wyden, Eshoo Press Big Five Publishers on Costly, Overly Restrictive E-Book Contracts with Libraries," US Senate, Committee on Finance (23 September 2021), https://www.finance.senate.gov/chairmans-news/wyden-eshoo-press-big-five -publishers-on-costly-overly-restrictive-e-book-contracts-with-libraries.

18. C174/15 Vereniging Opebare Bibliotheken vs Stichting Leenrecht, http:// curia.europa.eu/juris/liste.jsf?num=C-174/15 or https://eur-lex.europa.eu/legal -content/en/TXT/?uri=CELEX:62015CJ0174.

19. Rebecca Giblin et al., "Available, but Not Accessible? Investigating Publishers' E-lending Licensing Practices," *InformationResearch*, 24, 3 (2019), http:// informationr.net/ir/24-3/paper837.html.

20. Daniel A. Gross, "The Surprisingly Big Business of Library E-Books," *New Yorker* (2 Sepember 2021), https://www.newyorker.com/news/annals-of -communications/an-app-called-libby-and-the-surprisingly-big-business-of-library -e-books.

21. Andrew Albanese, "Penguin Random House Changes Library E-book Lending Terms," *Publishers Weekly* (4 September 2018), https://www.publishersweekly .com/pw/by-topic/industry-news/libraries/article/77904-penguin-random-house -changes-its-library-e-book-terms.html.

22. Secker et al., *Understanding the CLA License to UK Higher Education*, fig. 8.

23. *Report of the Commission on the Future of the UC Berkeley Library* (October 2013) 6, https://academic-senate.berkeley.edu/sites/default/files/final_cfucbl_report _10.16.13_0.pdf.

24. Thanks to Tony Ageh for discussions on this point.

25. Constance Malpas, "Subsidence and Uplift: The Library Landscape," in Dempsey et al., eds., *Understanding the Collective Collection*, figs. 2, 3.

26. Michael Levine-Clark et al., "Uniqueness and Collection Overlap in Academic Libraries," *Proceedings of the Charleston Library Conference* (2009), https://docs.lib.purdue.edu/cgi/viewcontent.cgi?article=1037&context=charleston.

27. Constance Malpas and Brian Lavoie, "Right-scaling Stewardship: A Multi-scale Perspective on Cooperative Print Management," *OCLC Research* (March 2014), fig. 3, https://www.oclc.org/content/dam/research/publications/library/2014/oclcresearch-cooperative-print-management-2014.pdf.

28. Malpas and Lavoie, "Strength in Numbers," 28.

29. Lavoie et al., "Anatomy of Aggregate Collections," fig. 2. This may have been high since it counted book manifestations, not just titles as such, ie each individual edition of books with many such.

30. Lorcan Dempsey, "Libraries and the Long Tail," *D-Lib Magazine*, 12, 4 (2006), http://www.dlib.org/dlib/april06/dempsey/04dempsey.html.

31. Dempsey, "Libraries and the Long Tail."

32. Brian Lavoie et al., "Reflections on Collective Collections," *College and Research Libraries*, 81, 6 (2020) fig. 2, 4, https://crl.acrl.org/index.php/crl/article/viewFile/24618/32425.

33. Brian Lavoie et al., "Print Management at 'Mega-scale': A Regional Perspective on Print Book Collections in North America," in Dempsey et al., eds., *Understanding the Collective Collection*, 173.

34. Lavoie et al., "Reflections on Collective Collections," 993.

35. Malpas and Lavoie, "Right-scaling Stewardship," tables 2, 3.

36. Malpas and Lavoie, "Strength in Numbers," 16.

37. Lavoie and Schonfeld, "Books without Boundaries."

38. Lavoie et al., "Print Management at 'Mega-scale,'" 183.

39. Lavoie et al., "Print Management at 'Mega-scale,'" 163.

40. Richard Wellen, "Open Access, Megajournals, and MOOCs: On the Political Economy of Academic Unbundling," *SAGE Open* (2013) 4, https://journals.sagepub.com/doi/full/10.1177/2158244013507271.

41. "An Interview with Frances Pinter," *Knowledge Unlatched*, http://www.knowledgeunlatched.org/2013/01/an-interview-with-frances-pinter/.

42. Malpas and Lavoie, "Right-scaling Stewardship," 8.

43. Schonfeld, "Supercontinent of Scholarly Publishing?"

44. Roger C. Schonfeld, "In Latest Sign of Its Resurgence, Clarivate Acquires Kopernio," *Scholarly Kitchen* (10 April 2018), https://scholarlykitchen.sspnet.org/2018/04/10/clarivate-acquires-kopernio/.

45. Nicholson Baker, *Double Fold: Libraries and the Assault on Paper* (New York 2001).

46. Nichols and Smith, *Evidence in Hand*, 12–14.

47. Bosman et al., *Open Access Diamond Journals Study*, 8.

48. Fitzpatrick, *Planned Obsolescence*, 148–150.

49. "LOCKSS, CLOCKSS, and Portico: Potential Digital Archive Solutions for Rutgers," Rutgers Staff Resources (30 January 2007), https://www.libraries.rutgers .edu/rul/staff/collection_dev/reports/lockss-clockss-portico.shtml.

50. Beagrie, "Preservation, Trust, and Continuing Access for e-Journals," 8.

51. "LOCKSS GLN Keepers Reports" (18 January 2021), https://reports.lockss. org/keepers/; https://clockss.org/about/; "Titles and Collections," https://www .portico.org/coverage/titles/.

52. Winters, "Giving with One Click, Taking with the Other."

53. Paul Gooding and Melissa Terras, "'An Ark to Save Learning from Deluge'?: Reconceptualising Legal Deposit after the Digital Turn," in Gooding and Terras, eds., *Electronic Legal Deposit*.

54. Will Manley, "The Manley Arts: One-Tenth of One Percent," *Booklist* (1 November 1999).

55. Alan Sica, "Sociogenesis Versus Psychogenesis: The Unique Sociology of Norbert Elias," *Mid-American Review of Sociology*, 9, 1 (1984) 50.

56. Steven Marcus, *The Other Victorians: A Study of Sexuality and Pornography in Mid-Nineteenth-Century England* (New York 1964) xv.

57. Robert Darnton, *Literary Underground of the Old Regime*, vi.

58. Dahlia Remler, "Are 90% of Academic Papers Really Never Cited?" *DahliaRemler* (9 April 2014), https://dahliaremler.com/2014/04/09/are-90-of-academic -papers-really-never-cited-searching-citations-about-academic-citations-reveals-the -good-the-bad-and-the-ugly/.

59. Rose-Wiles, "Are Print Books Dead?" 5.

60. Michael Lesk, "How Much Information Is There in the World?" https://lesk. com/mlesk/ksg97/ksg.html.

61. Thompson, *Book Wars*, 417–418.

62. Cliff Guren et al., *COVID-19 and Book Publishing: Impacts and Insights for 2021* (5 January 2021), https://thefutureofpublishing.com/2021/01/covid-19-and -book-publishing-impacts-and-insights-for-2021/.

63. Rüdiger Wischenbart, *Global 50: The World Ranking of the Publishing Industry 2020*, 20–22, https://www.wischenbart.com/upload/Global50-Publishing-Ranking -2020_ScreenOpt.pdf; Rebecca Marston, "People 'Rediscovering Books' as Lockdown Sales Jump," *BBC* (27 October 2020), https://www.bbc.co.uk/news/business -54703164; Mark Sweney, "Harry Potter Publisher Says Covid Is Weaving Magic over Book Sales," *Guardian* (27 October 2020), https://www.theguardian.com/business /2020/oct/27/harry-potter-publisher-covid-bloomsbury-book-sales-lockdown.

64. John Sherer, "Making OA Monographs More Discoverable, Usable, and Sustainable," *Longleaf Services* (12 August 2020), https://longleafservices.org/blog /the-sustainable-history-monograph-pilot/.

65. "Book Sales Volume in France from 2010 to 2018," *Statista*, https://www .statista.com/statistics/420733/book-sales-france/; "Marketed Production of Books

in France from 2010 to 2019," *Statista*, https://www.statista.com/statistics/420120 /commercialized-production-of-books-france/.

66. Associazione Italiana Editori, *Report on Publishing in Italy: Highlights 2018*, 4, https://www.aie.it/Portals/_default/Skede/Allegati/Skeda105-4263-2018.10.22 /Highlights_2018_DEF_digitale.pdf?IDUNI=pavjmaj34x0vmvd1w4v42lqy8441.

67. CERLALC, *El espacio iberoamericano del libro 2018*, 27, 33.

68. Esposito and Barch, *Monograph Output of American University Presses*; "Trends in Academic Books Published in the Humanities and Other Fields," American Academy of Arts and Sciences, Humanities Indicators, IV-37a, https://www.amacad.org/ humanities-indicators/funding-and-research/trends-academic-books-published -humanities-and-other.

69. Crossick, "Monographs and Open Access," 21.

70. Calculated from the figures in Wischenbart, *Global* 50, 25–27, 10–11.

71. "Number of New Titles and Editions Published in the United States from 2002 to 2013, by Type," *Statista*, https://www.statista.com/statistics/248345/number -of-titles-published-in-the-us-by-type/.

72. "Print Isn't Dead, Says Bowker's Annual Book Production Report," *Bowker* (18 May 2011), http://www.bowker.com/news/2011/290243111.html. This report is no longer available on the web.

73. Bowker, *Self-Publishing in the United States, 2013–2018*, https://media2 .proquest.com/documents/bowker-selfpublishing-report2019.pdf.

74. Thompson, *Book Wars*, 259.

75. "Number of Self-published Books in the United States from 2008 to 2018, by Format," *Statista*, https://www.statista.com/statistics/249036/number-of-self -published-books-in-the-us-by-format/. Similar figures here: Bowker, "Self-Publishing in the United States, 2013–2018: Print and Ebooks," (2019) 5, 6, https:// actualitte.com/PDF/autopublication%20etats%20unis%20chiffres%20bowker.pdf.

76. "Largest Self-publishing Companies in the United States in 2018, by Numbers of Titles Published," *Statista*, https://www.statista.com/statistics/249043/largest -self-publishing-companies-in-the-us-by-number-of-titles-published/.

77. Alliance of Independent Authors, "Facts and Figures about Self Publishing."

78. Andrew Albanese, "BiblioBazaar: How a Company Produces 272,930 Books A Year," *Publishers Weekly* (15 April 2010), https://www.publishersweekly.com/pw /by-topic/industry-news/publisher-news/article/42850-bibliobazaar-how-a -company-produces-272-930-books-a-year.html.

79. "Print Isn't Dead, Says Bowker's Annual Book Production Report." This report is no longer available, but the figures are partly reproduced in Michael Kelley, "Bowker Declares Print Isn't Dead," *Library Journal* (18 May 2011), https://www .libraryjournal.com/?detailStory=bowker-declares-print-isnt-dead.

80. Rebecca J. Rosen, "The Missing 20th Century: How Copyright Protection Makes Books Vanish," *Atlantic* (30 March 2012), https://www.theatlantic.com /technology/archive/2012/03/the-missing-20th-century-how-copyright-protection -makes-books-vanish/255282/.

81. WIPO, *Global Publishing Industry in 2018*, table 6.

82. Agencia Chilena ISBN, *Informe Estadístico 2019*, 22.

83. CERLALC, *El espacio iberoamericano del libro 2018*, 63.

84. Hector Tobar, "Self-published E-books Rife with Illicit Erotica, Survey Finds," *Los Angeles Times* (21 October 2013); McGurl, *Everything and Less*, 53, 153.

85. "Smashwords Survey 2017," 28, https://blog.smashwords.com/2017/06 /smashwords-survey-2017.html. Similar data at "Which Self-Published Genres Sell The Most Books? Self-Publishing Relief Has The Answer!" (19 August 2015), https:// selfpublishingrelief.com/self-published-genres-sell-most/.

86. Edward R. Robertson, "Self-Publishing's Share of the Kindle Market by Genre," http://edwardwrobertson.com/self-publishing/self-publishings-share-of-the -kindle-market-by-genre/.

87. Adam Rowe, "How Indie Genre Fiction Ebooks Are Thriving Online," *Forbes* (13 January 2018), https://www.forbes.com/sites/adamrowe1/2018/01/13 /how-indie-genre-fiction-ebooks-are-thriving-online/?sh=77e35b3311fa.

88. WIPO, *Global Publishing Industry in 2018*, table 5; "Breakdown of Book Pub- lisher Sales Volume in France from 2010 to 2018, by Segment," *Statista*, https:// www.statista.com/statistics/420905/book-publishers-sales-volumeby-genre-france/; Associazione Italiana Editori, *Report on Publishing in Italy: Highlights 2018*, 4; CER- LALC, *El espacio iberoamericano del libro 2018*, table 31.

89. Lavoie and Dempsey, "Beyond 1923," 64.

90. Charlie Tyson, "A Publisher of One's Own," *Inside Higher Ed* (17 July 2014), https://www.insidehighered.com/news/2014/07/17/self-publishing-option-academics -periphery.

Chapter 7

1. Background in Joe Karaganis, ed., *Shadow Libraries: Access to Knowledge in Global Higher Education* (Cambridge MA 2018), https://direct.mit.edu/books /book/3600/Shadow-LibrariesAccess-to-Knowledge-in-Global.

2. "NYU's Arabic Collections Online Usage Jumps 700% in March," http://www .nyu.edu/about/news-publications/news/2020/april/nyu-s-arabic-collections-online -usage-jumps-700--in-march.html.

3. With 20% in the public domain and 10% in copyright and commercially available. Thompson, *Merchants of Culture*, 362.

4. US Copyright Office, *Orphan Works and Mass Digitization* (June 2015) 36–38, https://www.copyright.gov/orphan/reports/orphan-works2015.pdf.

5. David Hansen, "Digitizing Orphan Works: Legal Strategies to Reduce Risks for Open Access to Copyrighted Orphan Works," *Harvard Library* (August 2016) ii, https://dash.harvard.edu/handle/1/27840430.

6. James Boyle, "A Copyright Black Hole Swallows Our Culture," *Financial Times* (7 September 2009).

7. Elisabeth Niggemann et al., *The New Renaissance: Report of the "Comité des Sages" on Bringing Europe's Cultural Heritage Online* (European Commission; Brussels 2011) 15, https://op.europa.eu/en/publication-detail/-/publication/79a38a23-e7d9 -4452-b9b0-1f84502e68c5. Though, admittedly, the committee also insisted on an opportunity for cultural institutions to digitize works whose rights-holders did not exploit them (p. 26).

8. US Copyright Office, *Report on Orphan Works* (January 2006) 8–9, https:// www.copyright.gov/orphan/orphan-report-full.pdf; US Copyright Office, *Orphan Works and Mass Digitization*, 7; *Gowers Review of Intellectual Property*, 71–72.

9. "Directive 2012/28/EU of the European Parliament and of the Council of 25 October 2012 on Certain Permitted Uses of Orphan Works," *Official Journal of the European Union*, L 299/5 (27 October 2012), https://eur-lex.europa.eu/legal-content/ EN/TXT/PDF/?uri=CELEX:32012L0028&from=EN.

10. https://www.orphanworkslicensing.service.gov.uk/view-register.

11. Michelle M. Wu, "Building a Collaborative Digital Collection: A Necessary Evolution in Libraries," *Law Library Journal*, 103 (2011).

12. And equivalent rules abroad. Alexander B. Pope, "A Second Look at First Sale: An International Look at U.S. Copyright Exhaustion," *Journal of Intellectual Property Law* 19, 1 (2011) 216–223.

13. Michelle M. Wu, "Collaborative Academic Library Digital Collections Post-Cambridge University Press, HathiTrust and Google Decisions on Fair Use," *Journal of Copyright in Education and Librarianship*, 1, 1 (2016) 2, 17, https://www.jcel-pub .org/article/view/5921/5345.

14. Hansen and Courtney, "White Paper on Controlled Digital Lending of Library Books."

15. Timothy B. Lee, "University Libraries Offer Online 'Lending' of Scanned In-copyright Books," *Ars Technica* (7 April 2020), https://arstechnica.com/tech-policy /2020/04/university-libraries-offer-online-lending-of-scanned-in-copyright-books/.

16. https://blog.archive.org/national-emergency-library/.

17. Sherer, "Making OA Monographs More Discoverable;" "Hachette v. Internet Archive: Internet Archive's Memorandum for Summary Judgment," (7 July 2022) 27, https://www.eff.org/document/hachette-v-internet-archive-internet-archives -memorandum-summary-judgment.

18. *Hachette Book Group Inc v. Internet Archive* 1:20-cv-04160, US District Court, S.D. New York, https://www.courtlistener.com/docket/17211300/hachette-book-group-inc-v-internet-archive/; Stephen Beemsterboer, "Fahrenheit 2020: Torching the Internet's Library of Alexandria at the Height of a Global Pandemic," *Journal of Law, Technology, & Policy*, 2 (2021), https://papers.ssrn.com/sol3/papers.cfm?abstract _id=4037768.

19. Boston Library Consortium, "Consortial CDL: Implementing Controlled Digital Lending as a Mechanism for Interlibrary Loan," (September 2021), https:// blc.org/CDLforILL.

20. C174/15 Vereniging Opebare Bibliotheken vs Stichting Leenrecht, http://curia.europa.eu/juris/liste.jsf?num=C-174/15 or https://eur-lex.europa.eu/legal-content/en/TXT/?uri=CELEX:62015CJ0174; Rob Green, "Know Your Rights: The Key to eBook Access," *CILIP* (29 June 2021), https://www.cilip.org.uk/news/571553/Know-your-rights-the-key-to-eBook-access.htm.

21. Digital Economy Act 2017.

22. Jacob Flynn et al., "What Happens When Books Enter the Public Domain? Testing Copyright's Under Use Hypothesis across Australia, New Zealand, the United States and Canada," *UNSW Law Journal*, 42, 4 (2019) 1229; https://www.unswlawjournal.unsw.edu.au/wp-content/uploads/2019/11/3-Flynn-Giblin-and-Petitjean.pdf.

23. Leonid Taycher, "Books of the World, Stand Up and Be Counted! All 129,864,880 of You," *Inside Google Books* (5 August 2010), http://booksearch.blogspot.com/2010/08/books-of-world-stand-up-and-be-counted.html?m=1. This may be an overcount caused by duplicates in Google's metadata: Jon Stokes, "Google's Count of 130 Million Books Is Probably Bunk," *Ars Technica* (9 August 2020), https://arstechnica.com/science/2010/08/googles-count-of-130-million-books-is-probably-bunk/. On the other hand, what is the likelihood that Google consulted much beyond the English-language literature?

24. Malpas and Lavoie, "Strength in Numbers," fig. 2.

25. The underlying report estimated the number of books, not including journals and newspapers, arriving at a range between 59 and 95 million, for a mean of 77 million. Niggemann et al., *New Renaissance*, 38, 116.

26. https://www.worldcat.org/.

27. Lavoie et al., "Reflections on Collective Collections," fig. 4. 128 million in 2013: Lavoie et al., "Print Management at 'Mega-scale,'" 173.

28. Lavoie and Schonfeld, "Books without Boundaries."

29. Lavoie and Schonfeld, "Books without Boundaries."

30. "New Book Titles Published this Year," *Worldometer*, https://www.worldometers.info/books/.

31. E-mail from WorldCat, 17 February 2021.

32. Lavoie and Schonfeld, "Books without Boundaries."

33. Lavoie and Dempsey, "Beyond 1923," 62; Greg Cam and Sean Redmond (8 May 2019), https://twitter.com/GregCram/status/1126153216280989698. Of 170,000 volumes in the HathiTrust published in these years, 51% were in the public domain. Melissa Levine, "Finding the Public Domain: The Copyright Review Management System," *Ithaka S&R* (26 October 2016), https://sr.ithaka.org/publications/finding-the-public-domain/.

34. Thompson, *Book Wars*, 129.

35. Arif E. Jinha, "Article 50 Million: An Estimate of the Number of Scholarly Articles in Existence," *Learned Publishing*, 23, 3 (2010), https://www.researchgate.net/publication/229062236_Article_50_million_An_estimate_of_the_number_of_scholarly_articles_in_existence.

36. The figures vary. Among the highest is 4 to 4.5 million articles annually across the globe, but this includes every book review and conference proceeding as well. Bosman et al., *Open Access Diamond Journals Study*, 30.

37. That correlates reasonably with other estimates from 2018 of 70 million articles. Johnson et al., *STM Report*, 25.

38. Radames J. B. Cordero et al., "Life Science's Average Publishable Unit (APU) Has Increased over the Past Two Decades," *PLOS ONE* (16 June 2016), https://journals.plos.org/plosone/article?id=10.1371/journal.pone.0156983.

39. Niggemann et al., *New Renaissance*, 38, 116, 145.

40. Kalev Leetaru, "Mass Book Digitization: The Deeper Story of Google Books and the Open Content Alliance," *First Monday*, 13, 10 (2008), https://firstmonday .org/ojs/index.php/fm/article/view/2101. Microsoft announced it would digitize books from the British Library at what appeared to be $25/volume. Jonathan Band, "The Google Library Project: Both Sides of the Story," *Plagiary: Cross-disciplinary Studies in Plagiarism, Fabrication, and Falsification* (2006) 13, https://quod.lib.umich .edu/cgi/p/pod/dod-idx/google-library-project-both-sides-of-the-story.pdf?c =plag;idno=5240451.0001.002;format=pdf.

41. Claudia Dale Goldin, "The Economics of Emancipation," *Journal of Economic History*, 33, 1 (1973) 73–74; Peter McPhee, *The French Revolution, 1789–1799* (Oxford 2002) 191.

42. *Punch* (24 April 1847) 178, quoted in Melissa J. Homestead, *American Women Authors and Literary Property, 1822–1869* (Cambridge 2005) 49.

43. Baldwin, *Copyright Wars*, 116.

44. David Matthews, "Is It Time to Nationalise Academic Publishers?" *Times Higher Education* (2 March 2018), https://www.timeshighereducation.com/blog /it-time-nationalise-academic-publishers; Jean-Claude Burgelman, "Scholarly Publishing Needs Regulation," *Research Professional News* (28 January 2021), https:// researchprofessionalnews.com/rr-news-europe-views-of-europe-2021-1-scholarly -publishing-needs-regulation/.

45. Barclay, "Academic Print Books Are Dying."

46. Benedicte Page, "'Group Action Needed to Safeguard the Academic Book', Warns Report," *Bookseller* (12 June 2017), https://www.thebookseller.com/news /group-action-needed-safeguard-academic-book-warns-report-567951.

47. Rupert Gatti and Marc Mierowsky, "Funding Open Access Monographs," *College & Research Libraries News*, 77, 9 (2016) 458, https://crln.acrl.org/index.php /crlnews/article/view/9557/10901.

48. Ferwerda et al., *Landscape Study on Open Access*, 38, 71.

49. Dan Strempel, "Cost of Open Access Book Publishing Goes Under the Microscope," *Simba Information* (10 December 2020), https://www.simbainformation .com/Content/Blog/2020/12/10/Cost-of-Open-Access-Book-Publishing-Goes-Under -the-Microscope. Some publishing charges for journal articles are listed in https:// www.openaccess.cam.ac.uk/publishing-open-access/how-much-do-publishers -charge-open-access.

50. Martin Paul Eve et al., "Cost Estimates of an Open Access Mandate for Monographs in the UK's Third Research Excellence Framework," *UKSG Insights* (8 November 2017), https://insights.uksg.org/articles/10.1629/uksg.392/.

51. Eelco Ferwerda et al., *A Project Exploring Open Access Monograph Publishing in the Netherlands* (OAPEN-NL 2013) 4, https://oapen.fra1.digitaloceanspaces.com /0cdef1a177b6470ea5257240682b38e3.pdf.

52. OAPEN-CH, *Impact of Open Access on Scientific Monographs in Switzerland*, 8.

53. Nancy L. Maron et al., "The Costs of Publishing Monographs," *Ithaka S+R* (5 February 2016), https://sr.ithaka.org/publications/the-costs-of-publishing -monographs/. A more recent study also has figures in excess of charges levied by most open-access publishers: Nancy Maron and Kim Schmelzinger, *The Cost to Publish TOME Monographs* (Association of University Presses 2022), https://hcommons .org/deposits/item/hc:47235/.

54. Noah Moxham and Aileen Fyfe, "The Royal Society and the Prehistory of Peer Review, 1665–1965," *Historical Journal*, 61, 4 (2018) 872, https://www .cambridge.org/core/journals/historical-journal/article/royal-society-and-the -prehistory-of-peer-review-16651965/93B903FD4D6561AA7224C62EE57B0C18 /share/02a909c3ee615bca306491e0feba0b28f6309245.

55. Charles Watkinson, "University Presses and the Impact of COVID-19," *Learned Publishing* (18 January 2021), https://onlinelibrary.wiley.com/doi/full/10.1002 /leap.1352.

56. Richard Fisher, "Guest Post—What Are Academic Book Publishers For? Part 2," *Scholarly Kitchen* (2 September 2020), https://scholarlykitchen.sspnet.org/2020 /09/02/guest-post-what-are-academic-book-publishers-for-part-2/?informz=1.

57. Michael Jubb, *Academic Books and Their Future: A Report to the AHRC and the British Library* (June 2017) 13, 107, https://academicbookfuture.org/end-of-project -reports-2/.

58. Richard Fisher, "Guest Post—What Are Academic Book Publishers For? Part 1," *Scholarly Kitchen* (1 September 2020), https://scholarlykitchen.sspnet.org /2020/09/01/guest-post-what-are-academic-book-publishers-for-part-1/.

59. Sherer, "Making OA Monographs More Discoverable."

60. There were 339,000 new titles published in the US in 2015: International Publishers Association, *Annual Report 2015–16*, table 2, https://www .internationalpublishers.org/images/aa-content/ipa-reports/ipa-annual-report -2015-2016/ipa-annual-report-2015-2016.pdf.

61. Though admittedly 35% in Italy. But since only 3% of Italian books are from the educational sector, something is screwy with the numbers. Similar issues occur with the US numbers of educational volumes sold (only 4.4%). WIPO, *Global Publishing Industry in 2018*, tables 1, 2, 3.

62. Agencia Chilena ISBN, *Informe Estadístico 2019*, 51; CERLALC, *El espacio iberoamericano del libro 2018*, 53.

63. Porter Anderson, "US Market Statistics: The AAP StatShot Annual Report for 2019," *Publishing Perspectives* (31 July 2020), https://publishingperspectives.

com/2020/07/united-states-market-statistics-aap-statshot-annual-report-for-2019/. That is confirmed here: WIPO, *The Global Publishing Industry in 2016*, table A1.

64. Ferwerda et al., *Landscape Study on Open Access*, 82–83.

65. https://aupresses.org/. E-mail from the AUP, 17 February 2021.

66. Thompson, *Books in the Digital* Age, 52.

67. Authored and edited books and editions. Eve et al., "Cost Estimates of an Open Access Mandate for Monographs."

68. Eve et al., "Cost Estimates of an Open Access Mandate for Monographs."

69. Heather Piwowar et al., "The State of OA: A Large-Scale Analysis of the Prevalence and Impact of Open Access Articles," *PeerJ* (2018), https://doi.org/10.7717/peerj.4375. This source puts the total of open-access articles, both gold and diamond, at about a fifth of all articles, but that includes all forms of publications, not just articles: Bosman et al., *Open Access Diamond Journals Study*, 30.

70. European Commission, *Future of Scholarly Publishing and Scholarly Communication*, 30.

71. Johnson et al., *STM Report*, 139.

72. Alberto Martín-Martín et al., "Evidence of Open Access of Scientific Publications in Google Scholar: A Large-scale Analysis," *Journal of Informetrics*, 12 (2018) fig. 6, 4.

73. Numbers from: Institute of Museum and Library Services; Research: Data Collection; Supplementary Tables; Public Library Revenue and Expenses; Table 26. Total collection expenditures of public libraries and percentage distribution of expenditures, by type of expenditure and state: Fiscal year 2012; Total collection expenditures; Total (in thousands), 73, http://www.imls.gov/assets/1/AssetManager/FY2012%20PLS_Tables_21_thru_31A.pdf; Tai Phan et al., *Academic Libraries: 2012: First Look* (National Center for Education Statistics, January 2014) table 9, http://nces.ed.gov/pubs2014/2014038.pdf; Amy Bitterman et al., US Department of Education, *Characteristics of Public Elementary and Secondary School Library Media Centers in the United States: Results From the 2011–12 Schools and Staffing Survey: First Look*, Table 1, Number of public schools that reported having library media centers, by selected school characteristics: 2011–12; Total number of schools; Number of schools with a library media center, 6, http://nces.ed.gov/pubs2013/2013315.pdf; Dave Bogart, ed., *Library and Book Trade Almanac* (60th ed; Medford NJ 2015) 381.

74. Information kindly provided by Outsell, Inc., a California-based research and advisory firm for data, information, and analytics.

75. Phan et al., *Academic Libraries: 2012*, tables 8, 9. The numbers in Albert N. Greco, "Academic Libraries and the Economics of Scholarly Publishing in the Twenty-First Century," *Journal of Scholarly Publishing*, 47, 1 (2015) table 7 are a small fraction of this and include only 785 libraries. The figures do not have much internal consistency—they add up to no more than 50% for various types of library acquisitions.

76. Information kindly provided by Outsell, Inc., a California-based research and advisory firm for data, information, and analytics.

77. £12.4 million in 2013. Eve et al., "Cost Estimates of an Open Access Mandate for Monographs."

78. Phan et al., *Academic Libraries: 2012*, table 9.

79. Schimmer et al., "Disrupting the Subscription Journals' Business Model," 5.

80. Lavoie et al., "Reflections on Collective Collections," fig. 2, 4.

81. Paul N. Courant and Matthew "Buzzy" Nielsen, "On the Cost of Keeping a Book," in Council on Library and Information Resources, *The Idea of Order: Transforming Research Collections for 21st Century Scholarship* (Washington DC 2010) 91, http://www.clir.org/pubs/abstract/pub147abst.html.

82. Phan et al., *Academic Libraries: 2012*, table 8.

83. Phan et al., *Academic Libraries: 2012*, table 9.

84. Cambridge University Press, for example, allows the submitted manuscript of a book to be posted and the published version of one chapter six months after publication: https://www.cambridge.org/core/services/open-access-policies/open-access-books/green-open-access-policy-for-books.

85. Ferwerda et al., *Landscape Study on Open Access*, 28.

86. Holland: Article 25fa of the Copyright Act (Taverne Amendment), but only for university-affiliated researchers and for work done at least partly with Dutch government funding: https://www.openaccess.nl/en/in-the-netherlands/you-share-we-take-care. Belgium: https://openaccess.be/belgian-open-access-legislation/. France: https://www.openaire.eu/france-final-text-of-the-law-for-oa-has-been-adopted.

87. HSBC Global Research, "Going for Gold," 8.

88. "Plan S Rights Retention Strategy," *Plan S*, https://www.coalition-s.org/rights-retention-strategy/; "cOAlition S Response to the STM Statement: The Rights Retention Strategy Restores Long-standing Academic Freedoms," *Plan S* (3 February 2021), https://www.coalition-s.org/blog/the-rights-retention-strategy-restores-long-standing-academic-freedoms/; Lisa Janicke-Hinchliffe, "Explaining the Rights Retention Strategy," *Scholarly Kitchen* (17 February 2021), https://scholarlykitchen.sspnet.org/2021/02/17/rights-retention-strategy/.

89. Robert Kiley and Johan Rooryck, "Guest Post—The Rise of Immediate Green OA Undermines Progress: A Response From cOAlition S," *Open Access Scholarly Publishing Association* (11 December 2020), https://oaspa.org/guest-post-the-rise-of-immediate-green-oa-undermines-progress-a-response-from-coalition-s/.

90. Liz Ferguson et al., "Open Post: The Rise of Immediate Green OA Undermines Progress," *Open Access Scholarly Publishing Association* (4 December 2020), https://oaspa.org/open-post-the-rise-of-immediate-green-oa-undermines-progress/; "Signatories Publish Statement on Rights Retention Strategy," *STM* (3 February 2021), https://www.stm-assoc.org/rightsretentionstrategy/.

91. A story told in Baldwin, *Copyright Wars*.

92. Reed Elsevier, Pearson, Wolters Kluwer, Springer. Wischenbart, *Global* 50, 18. If we count Pearson as an educational rather than scientific publisher, that brings Wiley, a US corporation, into the top five.

93. WIPO, *Global Publishing Industry in 2016*, table A1.

94. Mary Nell Bryant, "English Language Publication and the British Traditional Market Agreement," *Library Quarterly*, 49, 4 (1979); Thompson, *Books in the Digital Age*, 74–75.

95. Poynder, "Open Access: Could Defeat be Snatched from the Jaws of Victory?" 62–63.

96. Mallapaty, "India Pushes Bold 'One Nation, One Subscription' Journal-access Plan"; Amitabh Sinha, "Govt Proposes to Buy Bulk Subscriptions of All Scientific Journals, Provide Free Access to All," *Indian Express* (1 January 2021), https://indianexpress.com/article/india/pune/one-nation-one-subscription-govt-draft-policy-7128799/lite/.

97. Poynder, "Plan S: What Strategy Now for the Global South?" 14.

98. They are tracked at the ESAC Transformative Agreement Registry, https://esac-initiative.org/about/transformative-agreements/agreement-registry/.

99. Though Cambridge University Press has now signed read-and-publish agreements with over 100 US university libraries. Lindsay McKenzie, "Big Read-and-Publish Push Arrives," *Inside Higher Ed* (1 April 2021), https://www.insidehighered.com/news/2021/04/01/cambridge-university-press-strikes-deals-open-access.

100. Lisa Janicke-Hinchliffe, "The Biggest Deal," *Scholarly Kitchen* (16 March 2021), https://scholarlykitchen.sspnet.org/2021/03/16/the-biggest-big-deal/; Danielle Cooper and Oya Y. Rieger, *What's the Big Deal? How Researchers Are Navigating Changes to Journal Access*, Ithaka S&R Research Report (22 June 2021) 7, https://sr.ithaka.org/publications/whats-the-big-deal/. Unbundling arrangements are tracked at https://sparcopen.org/our-work/big-deal-cancellation-tracking/.

101. Roger C. Schonfeld, "To Bundle or Not to Bundle? That Is the Question," *Scholarly Kitchen* (13 April 2020), https://scholarlykitchen.sspnet.org/2020/04/13/bundle-question/.

102. https://unsub.org/.

103. https://home.cern/science/computing/storage; Michelle Starr, "Less Than 1% of Large Hadron Collider Data Ever Gets Looked At," *Science Alert* (6 January 2019), https://www.sciencealert.com/over-99-percent-of-large-hadron-collider-particle-collision-data-is-lost.

104. Melissa Liton, "How Much Data Comes From the IOT?" *Sumo Logic* (7 February 2018), https://www.sumologic.com/blog/iot-data-volume/.

105. Poynder, "Open Access: Could Defeat Be Snatched from the Jaws of Victory?" 9.

106. Alejandro Posada and George Chen, "Inequality in Knowledge Production: The Integration of Academic Infrastructure by Big Publishers," *HAL* (15 June 2018), https://hal.archives-ouvertes.fr/hal-01816707v1.

107. https://eosc-portal.eu/.

108. OECD, "Open Science," https://www.oecd.org/sti/inno/open-science.htm.

109. Johnson et al., *STM Report*, 9.

Chapter 8

1. Lavoie et al., "Print Management at 'Mega-scale,'" fig. 9.

2. Malpas and Lavoie, "Strength in Numbers," 17.

3. Various e-mails from the British Library, February and March 2021.

4. This suggests an unexpectedly high level of English-language publication from other nations since only about a third of the titles are published in the UK, another 14% in the US or Canada. Malpas and Lavoie, "Strength in Numbers," 12–13.

5. E-mail from the Bibliothèque Nationale, 26 February 2021. More on this in Baldwin, *Copyright Wars*, 362.

6. 12% of Widener's 14 million volumes. The French figures are from an e-mail from the Bibliothèque Nationale, 26 February 2021.

7. Using WorldCat's figure of 120 million separate imprints globally. Lavoie, et al., "Print Management at "Mega-scale," 173.. Of course, adjusting for journal publication, the institution would have to be even larger.

8. Library of Congress, "Fiscal 2020 Budget Justification," 7, https://www.loc.gov/static/portals/about/reports-and-budgets/documents/budgets/fy2020.pdf.

9. Figures for how many readers the Library of Congress's twenty reading rooms seat have been impossible to find, but the Bibliothèque Nationale in France seats some 1,800 and the British Library perhaps 1,200. E-mail, Library of Congress, 22 February 2021.

10. https://www.internationales-buero.de/en/unesco.php.

11. John Feather, *Publishing, Piracy, and Politics: An Historical Study of Copyright in Britain* (London 1994) 97–121.

12. 528,000 in 2018 compared to 423,000. "Scientific and Technical Journal Articles," World Bank, https://data.worldbank.org/indicator/IP.JRN.ARTC.SC.

13. Lorraine Estelle et al., "How to Enable Smaller Independent Publishers to Participate in OA Agreements," *Information Power* (8 June 2021) 27, https://wellcome.figshare.com/articles/online_resource/How_to_enable_smaller_independent_publishers_to_participate_in_OA_agreements/14731308/1.

14. *Accessibility, Sustainability, Excellence*, 63; "Written Evidence Submitted by the Russell Group," Commons Select Committees, Business, Innovation and Skills (7 February 2013) 3.2–3.4, https://publications.parliament.uk/pa/cm201213/cmselect/cmbis/writev/openaccess/m76.htm.

15. Hersh, "Working towards a Transition to Open Access"; Poynder, "Open Access: 'Information Wants to Be Free'?" 34; McKie, "'Location-specific' Blocks on Journal Access."

16. https://plos.org/resources/for-institutions/faqs/.

17. López and García, "Latin America's Longstanding Open Access Ecosystem Could Be Undermined."

18. Poynder, "Open Access: Could Defeat be Snatched from the Jaws of Victory?" 67.

19. "SAGE Open Lowers APCs for HSS Researchers" (23 January 2013), https://www.researchinformation.info/news/sage-open-lowers-apcs-hss-researchers?news _id=1089; Solomon, "A Survey of Authors Publishing in Four Megajournals," 8.

20. Suber, *Open Access*, 37; Suber, "Thinking about Prestige, Quality, and Open Access."

21. E. C. Mossner, *The Life of David Hume* (Oxford 1980) 612.

22. Ann Komaromi, "The Material Existence of Soviet Samizdat," *Slavic Review*, 63, 3 (2004) 603.

23. Azar Nafisi, *Reading Lolita in Tehran* (New York 2008) 39.

24. Donald Davidson and Gilbert Harman, eds., *Semantics of Natural Language* (Dordrecht 1972). $251 in hardback, $89 in paper.

25. Kaufman, *New Enlightenment*, 76–77.

26. HSBC Global Research, "Going for Gold," 8.

27. Orau and Rubriq, part of Research Square, are examples: https://www.orau .org/research-reviews-evaluations/index.html; https://www.researchsquare.com/ publishers/editorial-services.

28. Amy Bourke-Waite, "Innovations in Scholarly Peer Review at Nature Publishing Group and Palgrave Macmillan," *UKSG Insights*, 28, 2 (2015), https://insights .uksg.org/articles/10.1629/uksg.243/.

29. Michael Clarke, "An Interview With Keith Collier, Co-Founder of Rubriq," *Scholarly Kitchen* (5 February 2013), https://scholarlykitchen.sspnet.org/2013/02/05 /an-interview-with-keith-collier-co-founder-of-rubriq/.

30. Jason Priem and Bradley M. Hemminger, "Decoupling the Scholarly Journal," *Frontiers in Computational Neuroscience* (5 April 2012), https://www.frontiersin .org/articles/10.3389/fncom.2012.00019/full#B19.

31. My thanks to William Pike, practitioner of these arts, for information and thoughts on this.

32. Matthew McCreary, "7 Common Questions about Self-Publishing on Amazon," *Entrepreneur Europe* (31 October 2019), https://www.entrepreneur.com /article/341595.

33. David Kadavy, "24 Things I Learned Self Publishing 3 Books in Only 6 Months," *The Writing Cooperative* (5 June 2018), https://writingcooperative.com /24-things-i-learned-publishing-3-books-in-only-6-months-1b8f743e9e86.

34. Laura Pepper Wu, "Going Permafree on Amazon: My Reflections after 100,000 Downloads," *30 Day Books* (19 November 2013), https://www.30daybooks .com/going-perma-free-my-reflections-after-100000-downloads-of-my-ebook/.

35. Juris Dilevko and Keren Dali, "The Self-publishing Phenomenon and Libraries," *Library & Information Science Research*, 28 (2006) 210–211.

36. Thompson, *Book Wars*, 226–228.

37. Figures from queries sent the following publications: *London Times*, 830; *New York Review of Books*, 400; *Economist*, 200; *Times Literary Supplement*, 1,500; *London Review of Books*, 300; *New York Times Book Review*, 500. That makes a total of 3,730. Discounting by 20% for duplicate reviews, we get about 3,000 individual titles reviewed in the most prominent Anglophone outlets.

38. Joel Friedlander, "The Trouble with Word Processors," *The Book Designer* (19 January 2010), https://www.thebookdesigner.com/2010/01/the-trouble-with-word -processors/.

39. Stevan Harnad, "Scholarly Skywriting and the Prepublication Continuum of Scientific Inquiry," *Psychological Science*, 1, 6 (1990) 342.

40. Stevan Harnad, "Scholarly Journals at the Crossroads: A Subversive Proposal for Electronic Publishing," (27 June 1994), https://web.archive.org/web /20020414062202/https:/www.arl.org/scomm/subversive/sub01.html.

41. Ginsparg, "First Steps towards Electronic Research Communication," 395.

42. Robert Cameron, "A Universal Citation Database as a Catalyst for Reform in Scholarly Communication," *First Monday*, 2, 4 (1997), https://firstmonday.org/ojs/ index.php/fm/article/view/522/443.

43. Budapest Open Access Initiative.

44. Baldwin, *Copyright Wars*, 366–367.

45. Ferwerda et al., *Landscape Study on Open Access*, 64.

46. https://dissexpress.proquest.com/search.html. ProQuest was bought by Clarivate, the indexers who calculate impact factors through their Web of Science, in December 2021 for $5 billion: https://clarivate.com/clarivate-proquest-acquisition/.

47. https://ethos.bl.uk.

48. "American Historical Association Statement on Policies Regarding the Embargoing of Completed History PhD Dissertations," *Perspectives on History* (22 July 2013), https://www.historians.org/publications-and-directories/perspectives-on -history/summer-2013/american-historical-association-statement-on-policies -regarding-the-embargoing-of-completed-history-phd-dissertations; Scott Jaschik, "Embargoes for Dissertations?" *Inside Higher Ed* (24 July 2013), https://www .insidehighered.com/news/2013/07/24/historians-association-faces-criticism -proposal-embargo-dissertations.

49. Joachim Schöpfel et al., "A French-German Survey of Electronic Theses and Dissertations: Access and Restrictions," *D-Lib Magazine*, 21, 3/4 (2015), https://www .dlib.org/dlib/march15/schopfel/03schopfel.html#n6.

50. "Business Model," https://arxiv.org/about/reports-financials; Poynder, "PloS ONE, Open Access, and the Future of Scholarly Publishing," 11.

51. My thanks to Lukas Richter for this point.

52. 53,000 registered in 2009. Beagrie, "Preservation, Trust, and Continuing Access for e-Journals," 6. A detailed account of the number of journals in Guédon, "Mixing and Matching the Green and Gold Roads to Open Access—Take Two," 43–44, and Michael Mabe, "The Growth and Number of Journals," *Serials*, 16, 2 (2003) 193, https://serials.uksg.org/articles/abstract/10.1629/16191/.

53. Priem and Hemminger, "Decoupling the Scholarly Journal."

54. Dorothy Bishop, "How to Bury Your Academic Writing," *BishopBlog* (26 August 2012), http://deevybee.blogspot.com/2012/08/how-to-bury-your-academic-writing.html.

55. Peter Binfield, "Open Access MegaJournals—Have They Changed Everything?" *Open Access Week* (23 October 2013), https://creativecommons.org.nz/2013/10/open-access-megajournals-have-they-changed-everything/.

56. https://www.scielo.org/.

57. Björk, "Have the 'Mega-journals' Reached the Limits to Growth?"

58. Binfield, "Open Access MegaJournals—Have They Changed Everything?"

59. Björk, "Have the 'Mega-journals' Reached the Limits to Growth?"

60. Wakeling et al., "Open-Access Mega-Journals."

61. "Criteria for Publication," *PLOS One*, https://journals.plos.org/plosone/s/criteria-for-publication.

62. Johnson et al., *STM Report*, 7.

63. Young et al., "Why Current Publication Practices May Distort Science."

64. Binfield, "Open Access MegaJournals—Have They Changed Everything?"

65. Guédon, "'Green' and 'Gold' Roads to Open Access."

Chapter 9

1. Peter Baldwin, *Contagion and the State in Europe, 1830–1930* (Cambridge 2004) 461–462.

2. Phil Pochoda, "The Big One: The Epistemic System Break in Scholarly Monograph Publishing," *New Media & Society*, 15, 3 (2012) 362.

3. Tony Ross-Hellauer et al., "Survey on Open Peer Review: Attitudes and Experience amongst Editors, Authors and Reviewers," *PLOS One*, 12, 12 (2017).

4. David Pontille and Didier Torny, "Peer Review: Readers in the Making of Scholarly Knowledge," in Eve and Gray, eds., *Reassembling Scholarly Communications*, 116.

5. https://mcpress.media-commons.org/plannedobsolescence/author/fitzpatrick/.

6. Timothy Gowers, "The End of an Error? Considering the Alternatives to Formal Peer Review," *Times Literary Supplement* (24 October 2017).

7. Alla Katsnelson, "Microbe Gets Toxic Response," *Nature*, 462, 741 (2010), https://www.nature.com/news/2010/101207/full/468741a.html; Quirin Schiermeier, "Arsenic-loving Bacterium Needs Phosphorus After All," *Nature* (9 July 2012), https://www.nature.com/news/arsenic-loving-bacterium-needs-phosphorus-after-all-1.10971.

8. Ginsparg, "First Steps towards Electronic Research Communication," 390; Alessandro Delfanti and Nico Pitrelli, "Open Science: Revolution or Continuity?" in Albagli et al., *Open Science, Open Issues*, 63.

9. Richard Van Noorden, "Open Access: The True Cost of Science Publishing," *Nature*, 495, 7442 (2013), https://www.nature.com/news/open-access-the-true-cost-of-science-publishing-1.12676.

10. https://scipost.org.

11. Matthew Hutson, "Boycott Highlights AI's Publishing Rebellion," *Science*, 360, 6390 (2018) 699.

12. http://www.ssrn.com/.

13. http://repec.org/.

14. http://www.ncbi.nlm.nih.gov/pmc/.

15. Michael A. Johansson et al., "Preprints: An Underutilized Mechanism to Accelerate Outbreak Science," *PLOS Medicine*, 15, 4 (2018) 3, https://doi.org/10.1371/journal.pmed.1002549.

16. https://en.wikipedia.org/wiki/List_of_academic_journals_by_preprint_policy.

17. Christos Petrou, "Scientific Output in the Year of COVID, An Update," *Scholarly Kitchen* (23 February 2021), https://scholarlykitchen.sspnet.org/2021/02/23/guest-post-scientific-output-in-the-year-of-covid-an-update/.

18. BioRxiv.org is one of the sites.

19. Kai Kupferschmidt, "'A Completely New Culture of Doing Research:' Coronavirus Outbreak Changes how Scientists Communicate," *Science* (26 February 2020), https://www.sciencemag.org/news/2020/02/completely-new-culture-doing-research-coronavirus-outbreak-changes-how-scientists.

20. Kupferschmidt, "Completely New Culture."

21. Li-Meng Yan et al., "Unusual Features of the SARS-CoV-2 Genome Suggesting Sophisticated Laboratory Modification Rather Than Natural Evolution and Delineation of Its Probable Synthetic Route," *Zenodo* (14 September 2020), https://zenodo.org/record/4028830. This was followed the next month with claims that it was a bioweapon. Li-Meng Yan et al., "SARS-CoV-2 Is an Unrestricted Bioweapon: A Truth Revealed through Uncovering a Large-Scale, Organized Scientific Fraud," *Zenodo* (8 October 2020), https://zenodo.org/record/4073131.

22. Takahiko Koyama et al., "Reviews of 'Unusual Features of the SARS-CoV-2 Genome Suggesting Sophisticated Laboratory Modification Rather Than Natural Evolution and Delineation of Its Probable Synthetic Route," *Rapid Reviews: COVID-19* (24 September 2020), https://rapidreviewscovid19.mitpress.mit.edu/pub/78we86rp/release/2.

23. Rob Kuznia et al., "Weird Science: How a 'Shoddy' Bannon-backed Paper on Coronavirus Origins Made its Way to an Audience of Millions," *CNN* (21 October 2020), https://edition.cnn.com/2020/10/21/politics/coronavirus-lab-theory-yan-bannon-invs/index.html; Craig Timberg, "Scientists Said Claims about China Creating the Coronavirus Were Misleading. They Went Viral Anyway," *Washington Post* (12 February 2021).

24. Ross-Hellauer et al., "Survey on Open Peer Review"; Mark Ware, "Peer Review: Benefits, Perceptions, and Alternatives," *PRC Summary Papers*, 4 (2008) 20,

https://ils.unc.edu/courses/2015_fall/inls700_001/Readings/Ware2008-PRCPeer Review.pdf.

25. "Number of New Car Models Offered in the U.S. Market from 2000 to 2020," *Statista*, https://www.statista.com/statistics/200092/total-number-of-car-models-on -the-us-market-since-1990/.

26. Phil LeBeau, "Americans Buying Fewer New Cars in Lifetime," *CNBC* (22 October 2012), https://www.cnbc.com/id/49504504.

27. "Guess How Many Items the Average Grocery Shopper Buys in a Year," *Grocery and Retail News* (23 January 2014), https://couponsinthenews.com/2014/01/23 /guess-how-many-items-the-average-grocery-shopper-buys-in-a-year/.

28. "How Many Books Does Amazon Have for Sale?" *Quora* (4 July 2014), https://www.quora.com/How-many-books-does-Amazon-have-for-sale.

29. Kerri Jarema, "This Is How Many Books the Average American Reads in a Year," *Bustle* (19 April 2018), https://www.bustle.com/p/how-many-books-did-the -average-american-read-in-the-last-year-this-new-study-may-surprise-you-8837851.

30. Michael J. Kurtz and Edwin A. Henneken, "Finding and Recommending Scholarly Articles," in Cronin and Sugimoto, eds., *Beyond Bibliometrics*, 245.

31. Michael Bhaskar, *The Content Machine: Towards a Theory of Publishing from the Printing Press to the Digital Network* (London 2013) 103.

32. Sherer, "Making OA Monographs More Discoverable."

33. Carol Tenopir et al., "Electronic Journals and Changes in Scholarly Article Seeking and Reading Patterns," *Aslib Proceedings*, 61, 1 (2009) 27, https://www .researchgate.net/publication/39728529_Electronic_Journals_and_Changes_in _Scholarly_Article_Seeking_and_Reading_Patterns.

34. Charles Duhigg, "How Companies Learn Your Secrets," *New York Times Magazine* (16 February 2012), https://www.nytimes.com/2012/02/19/magazine /shopping-habits.html.

35. Linyuan Lü et al., "Recommender Systems," arXiv (6 February 2012) 69, https://arxiv.org/abs/1202.1112.

36. Shirky, *Here Comes Everybody*, ch. 4; Charles Leadbeater, *We-Think: Mass Innovation, Not Mass Production* (2nd ed.; London 2009) xxvii.

37. Ziyad Marar, "Creating Scholarly Knowledge in the Digital Age," in Vincent and Wickham, eds., *Debating Open Access*, 84.

38. Johnson et al., *STM Report*, 59.

39. James A. Evans, "Electronic Publication and the Narrowing of Science and Scholarship," *Science*, 321, 5887 (2008).

40. Rousseau-Hans et al., "Les pratiques de publications et d'accès ouvert," 54.

41. Michael Bhaskar, *Curation: The Power of Selection in a World of Excess* (London 2016).

42. Marion B. Smith, "South Carolina and *The Gentleman's Magazine*," *South Carolina Historical Magazine*, 95, 2 (1994); Thomas Lilly, "The National Archive: Harper's New Monthly Magazine and the Civic Responsibilities of a Commercial Literary Periodical, 1850–1853," *American Periodicals*, 15, 2 (2005).

43. Regazzi, *Scholarly Communications*, 80.

44. https://f1000.com/. In January 2020, F1000 was bought by Taylor & Francis, a commercial publisher. It has now been folded into some sort of open-access platform run by Routledge: https://think.f1000.com/routledgeopenresearch/.

45. https://www.ams.org/mr-database.

46. JMIRx journals present themselves as diamond open access, asking no publication fees from authors, but in fact they do extract an article processing charge of $1,000 through various subscription arrangements from member universities and other institutions. "What is JMIRx?" https://support.jmir.org/hc/en-us/articles/360034752692.

47. Tim Gowers, "Discrete Analysis—An arXiv Overlay Journal," *Gower's Weblog*, https://gowers.wordpress.com/2015/09/10/discrete-analysis-an-arxiv-overlay-journal/.

48. $51 for a review of Jessica Goldberg, *Trade and Institutions in the Medieval Mediterranean* in the *English Historical Review*, https://www.jstor.org/stable/24474127, compared to $40.99 for the book on Amazon, pointed out in Katie Phillips, "The Role of Book Reviews in the Academic Book Ecosystem," *Arcadia* (August 2020), https://zenodo.org/record/5533887#.YVc_dZrMK_A.

49. Ian Graber-Stiehl, "Science's Pirate Queen," *Verge* (8 February 2018), https://www.theverge.com/2018/2/8/16985666/alexandra-elbakyan-sci-hub-open-access-science-papers-lawsuit; Bastian Greshake, "Looking into Pandora's Box: The Content of Sci-Hub and its Usage," *F1000 Research* (21 April 2017), https://f1000research.com/articles/6-541/v1.

50. Daniel S. Himmelstein et al., "Sci-Hub Provides Access to Nearly All Scholarly Literature," *eLife* (2018), https://doi.org/10.7554/eLife.32822.

51. Cooper and Rieger, *What's the Big Deal?* 19.

52. John Bohannon, "Who's Downloading Pirated Papers? Everyone," *Science* (28 April 2016), https://www.sciencemag.org/news/2016/04/whos-downloading-pirated-papers-everyone.

53. https://twitter.com/aj_boston/status/1492564765880770560.

54. The distinction arose in the early thirteenth century. Denis Duncan, *Index, A History of the* (London 2021) 51.

55. Steven Inchcoombe and Heinz Weinheimer, "A Few Words on Sound Science, Megajournals, and an Announcement about SpringerPlus," *SpringerOpen Blog* (13 June 2016), http://blogs.springeropen.com/springeropen/2016/06/13/a-few-words-on-sound-science-megajournals-and-an-announcement-about-springerplus/.

56. Blair, *Too Much to Know*, 144.

57. Kevin Kelly, "Scan This Book!" *New York Times Magazine* (14 May 2006). Similar ideas in John Perry Barlow, "A Declaration of the Independence of Cyberspace" (8 February 1996), https://projects.eff.org/~barlow/Declaration-Final.html.

58. Back then, in 2012: Lauren Goode, "Citia Lets You Skip the Boring Stuff in E-books (And Get to the Important Parts)," *All Things D* (30 May 2012), https://

allthingsd.com/20120530/citia-lets-you-skip-the-boring-stuff-in-e-books-and-get-to
-the-important-parts. Today: https://www.citia.co/.

59. Duncan, *Index, A History of the*, 72.

60. Third-wave economics, relying on masses of instant data, is an example. "Enter Third-Wave Economics," *Economist* (23 October 2021).

61. Some preliminary thoughts on this in Baldwin, "Betting on Vetting."

62. Bradley P. Dean and Gary Scharnhorst, "The Contemporary Reception of Walden," *Studies in the American Renaissance* (1990) 294, https://www.jstor.org /stable/30227595.

63. Curtis N. Johnson, "Charles Darwin, Richard Owen, and Natural Selection: A Question of Priority," *Journal of the History of Biology*, 52, 1 (2019), https://pubmed .ncbi.nlm.nih.gov/29725900/.

64. Rousseau-Hans et al., "Les pratiques de publications et d'accès ouvert," 53.

65. *Revision of Copyright Laws: Hearings before the Committee on Patents, House of Representatives (February–April 1936)* (Washington DC 1936) 718–719.

66. James H. Lubowitz et al., "Two of a Kind: Multiple Discovery AKA Simultaneous Invention Is the Rule," *Arthroscopy*, 34, 8 (2018), https://www .arthroscopyjournal.org/action/showPdf?pii=S0749-8063%2818%2930498-5.

67. Wikipedia has a long list of examples through the ages: https://en.wikipedia .org/wiki/List_of_multiple_discoveries.

68. Frank Close, "How the Boson Got Higgs's Name," *Nature*, 465 (2010).

69. https://en.wikipedia.org/wiki/4%E2%80%B233%E2%80%B3#Precursors.

70. *Revision of Copyright Laws: Hearings before the Committee on Patents, House of Representatives (February-April 1936)* 198.

71. PLOS, Criteria for Publication, https://journals.plos.org/plosone/s/criteria -for-publication.

72. Björk, "Have the 'Mega-journals' Reached the Limits to Growth?"; Spezi et al., "Open-access Mega-journals," 270.

73. HSBC Global Research, "Reed Elsevier," 26; Poynder, "PLoS ONE, Open Access, and the Future of Scholarly Publishing," 6.

74. Michael B. Eisen et al., "Peer Review: Implementing a 'Publish, Then Review' Model of Publishing," *eLife* (1 December 2020), https://elifesciences.org /articles/64910.

75. William Denton, "Fictional Footnotes and Indexes," *Miskatonic University Press* (6 January 2021), https://www.miskatonic.org/footnotes.html; Shari Benstock, "At the Margin of Discourse: Footnotes in the Fictional Text," *PMLA*, 98, 2 (1983).

76. Fitzpatrick, *Planned Obsolescence*, 35–37.

77. http://en.paper.edu.cn/; Changping Hu et al., "Exploring a New Model for Preprint Server: A Case Study of CSPO," *Journal of Academic Librarianship*, 36, 3 (2010) 258.

78. Adam Eyre-Walker and Nina Stoletzki, "The Assessment of Science: The Relative Merits of Post-Publication Review, the Impact Factor, and the Number of

Citations," *PLOS Biology*, 11, 10 (2013), https://www.ncbi.nlm.nih.gov/pmc/articles/PMC3792863/.

79. Johnson et al., *STM Report*, 53.

80. A mere 5% ten years ago. David Crotty, "Peer Review May Be Old and Imperfect, but It Still Works," *Scholarly Kitchen* (23 December 2010), https://scholarlykitchen.sspnet.org/2010/12/23/davids-pick-for-2010-peer-review-may-be-old-and-imperfect-but-it-still-works/.

81. Tyler Cowen, "Covid Improved How the World Does Science," *Bloomberg Opinion* (1 January 2021), https://www.bloombergquint.com/business/covid-improved-how-the-world-does-science.

Chapter 10

1. William V. Harris, *Ancient Literacy* (Cambridge MA 1989) ch 4.

2. Hugh Bowden, *Classical Athens and the Delphic Oracle* (Cambridge 2005) 41.

3. McGurl, *Everything and Less*, 136.

4. Alperin, "Public Impact of Latin America's Approach to Open Access," 13.

5. Young et al., "Why Current Publication Practices May Distort Science."

6. 200 pages/book × 400 words/page is 176 billion in books. 5 pages × 1,000 words is 15 billion in articles. Let us say 200 billion words in round numbers.

7. 7.8 billion humans, of whom 74% are over 15 and 86% of them in turn literate, i.e., some 5 billion potential readers.

8. "Best-selling Print Books in the United States in 2020, by Unit Sales," https://www.statista.com/statistics/324911/best-selling-trade-paperback-books-usa/.

9. "U.S. Book Industry—Statistics & Facts" (10 November 2020), https://www.statista.com/topics/1177/book-market/.

10. Johnson et al., *STM Report*, 39.

11. Donald W. King et al., "Measuring Total Reading of Journal Articles," *D-Lib Magazine*, 12, 10 (2006), http://www.dlib.org/dlib/october06/king/10king.html.

12. Lars Wenaas, "Attracting New Users or Business as Usual? A Case Study of Converting Academic Subscription-based Journals to Open Access," *Quantitative Science Studies*, 2, 2 (2021), https://direct.mit.edu/qss/article/2/2/474/97554/Attracting-new-users-or-business-as-usual-A-case.

13. Johnson et al., *STM Report*, 131–32.

14. Nicola De Bellis, *Bibliometrics and Citation Analysis: From the Science Citation Index to Cybermetrics* (Lanham 2009) 294–300; Mark J. McCabe and Christopher M. Snyder, "Identifying the Effect of Open Access on Citations Using a Panel of Science Journals," *Economic Inquiry*, 52, 4 (2014), https://onlinelibrary.wiley.com/doi/abs/10.1111/ecin.12064; Bo-Christer Björk and David Solomon, "Open Access versus Subscription Journals: A Comparison of Scientific Impact," *BMC Medicine* (2012), https://bmcmedicine.biomedcentral.com/articles/10.1186/1741-7015-10-73; Mirjam Curno and Stephanie Oeben, "Scientific Excellence at Scale: Open Access

Journals Have a Clear Citation Advantage over Subscription Journals," *Frontiers Science News* (11 July 2018), https://blog.frontiersin.org/2018/07/11/scientific-excellence-at-scale-open-access-journals-have-a-clear-citation-advantage-over-subscription-journals/.

15. Abhishek Nagaraj and Imke Reimers, "Digitization and the Demand for Physical Works: Evidence from the Google Books Project," *SSRN* (4 March 2019), https://papers.ssrn.com/sol3/papers.cfm?abstract_id=3339524.

16. OAPEN-CH, *Impact of Open Access on Scientific Monographs in Switzerland*, 44–45.

17. Ferwerda et al., *Project Exploring Open Access Monograph Publishing in the Netherlands*, 4.

18. Christina Emery et al., "The OA Effect: How Does Open Access Affect the Usage of Scholarly Books," *Springer Nature* (7 November 2017), https://resource-cms.springernature.com/springer-cms/rest/v1/content/15176744/data/v3.

19. Vincent Larivière and Yves Gingras, "The Decline in the Concentration of Citations, 1900–2007," https://arxiv.org/ftp/arxiv/papers/0809/0809.5250.pdf.

20. Barnes, "Cloistered Bookworms in the Chicken-Coop of the Muses," 70.

21. Quoted in Blair, *Too Much to Know*, 55.

22. Umberto Eco, "Afterword," in Geoffrey Nunberg, ed., *The Future of the Book* (Berkeley 1996) 301.

23. Michael Lesk, "How Much Information Is There in the World?" https://lesk.com/mlesk/ksg97/ksg.html.

24. Chip Walter, "Kryder's Law: The Doubling of Processor Speed Every 18 Months Is a Snail's Pace Compared with Rising Hard-disk Capacity, and Mark Kryder Plans to Squeeze in Even More Bits," *Scientific American* (1 August 2005), https://www.scientificamerican.com/article/kryders-law/. Some cautions on the slowing of this process occur in David S. H. Rosenthal et al., "The Economics of Long-Term Digital Storage" (2012), https://web.stanford.edu/group/lockss/resources/2012-09_The_Economics_of_Long-Term_Digital_Storage.pdf.

25. René Descartes, "Recherche de la verité par la lumière naturelle," Charles Adam and Paul Tannery, *eds., Oeuvres de Descartes* (Paris 1996) 10: 495–532, quoted in Blair, *Too Much to Know*, 5.

26. Dommann, *Authors and Apparatus*, 100–103.

27. Evan R. Risko et al., "On Retrieving Information from External Knowledge Stores: Feeling-of-findability, Feeling-of-knowing, and Internet Search," *Computers in Human Behavior*, 65 (2016).

28. Daniel M. Wegner and Adrian F. Ward, "The Internet Has Become the External Hard Drive for Our Memories," *Scientific American* (1 December 2013), https://www.scientificamerican.com/article/the-internet-has-become-the-external-hard-drive-for-our-memories/; Betsy Sparrow et al., "Google Effects on Memory: Cognitive Consequences of Having Information at Our Fingertips," *Science*, 333 (2011).

29. Plato, *Phaedrus* (trans. Robin Waterfield; Oxford 2002) 69; 274e–275b.

30. Elizabeth J. Marsh and Suparna Rajaram, "The Digital Expansion of the Mind: Implications of Internet Usage for Memory and Cognition," *Journal of Applied Research in Memory and Cognition*, 8 (2019) 6.

31. Huebner, *Macrocognition*, ch. 7.

32. Kenneth L. Carriveau, Jr., "A Brief History of E-Prints and the Opportunities They Open for Science Librarians," *Science & Technology Libraries*, 20, 2/3 (2001) 77.

33. Poynder, "PLoS ONE, Open Access, and the Future of Scholarly Publishing," 14.

34. Stevan Harnad, "British Academy Report on Peer Review and Metrics," *Open Access Archivangelism* (4 September 2007), http://openaccess.eprints.org/index.php?/archives/285-guid.html.

35. E-mail from Springer Nature Group, 3 February 2021.

36. Wellcome Trust, *Costs and Business Models in Scientific Research Publishing* (April 2004) 3, https://wellcome.org/sites/default/files/wtd003184_0.pdf; Stevan Harnad, "No-Fault Peer Review Charges: The Price of Selectivity Need Not Be Access Denied or Delayed," *D-Lib Magazine*, 16, 7/8 (2010), http://www.dlib.org/dlib/july10/harnad/07harnad.html.

37. Thompson, *Book Wars*, 217.

38. Timothy Laquintano, *Mass Authorship and the Rise of Self-Publishing* (Iowa City 2016) 2.

39. Ann C. Weller, *Editorial Peer Review: Its Strengths and Weaknesses* (Medford NJ 2001) 64–65.

40. Campanario, "Consolation for the Scientist," 343.

41. Jaime A. Teixeira da Silva et al., "Establishing Sensible and Practical Guidelines for Desk Rejections," *Science and Engineering Ethics*, 24 (2018) 1352–1353.

42. Jan P. Vandenbroucke, "Can the Quality of Peer Review Be Measured?" *Journal of Clinical Epidemiology*, 47, 7 (1994) 822.

43. Kent R. Anderson, "BioRxiv: Trends and Analysis of Five Years of Preprints," *Learned Publishing*, 33 (2020).

44. Vincent Larivière et al., "ArXiv E-Prints and the Journal of Record: An Analysis of Roles and Relationships," *Journal of the Association for Information Science and Technology*, 65, 6 (2014) 1161.

45. Ruijun Chen et al., "Publication and Reporting of Clinical Trial Results: Cross Sectional Analysis across Academic Medical Centers," *British Medical Journal*, 352 (2016); Christine Schmucker et al., "Extent of Non-Publication in Cohorts of Studies Approved by Research Ethics Committees or Included in Trial Registries," *PLOS One* (23 December 2014).

46. Regazzi, *Scholarly Communications*, 8.

47. Lin, "Why Serious Academic Fraud Occurs in China."

48. Jane Qiu, "Publish or Perish in China," *Nature*, 463 (2010), https://www.nature.com/news/2010/100112/full/463142a.html.

49. Lin and Zhan, "Trash Journals in China," 147.

50. Mara Hvistendahl, "China's Publication Bazaar," *Science*, 342, 6162 (2013), https://science.sciencemag.org/content/342/6162/1035.full.

51. Wei Quan et al., "Publish or Impoverish: An Investigation of the Monetary Reward System of Science in China (1999–2016)," *Aslib Journal of Information Management* (18 September 2017), https://www.emerald.com/insight/content/doi /10.1108/AJIM-01-2017-0014/full/html.

52. One scholar has published 275 articles, of which 150 have not yet been cited and may never be. Nonetheless he has an h-index of 37; that is, 37 articles that have been cited at least 37 times. So this is a better measure of his worth than the bulk of his article numbers. Lin and Zhan, "Trash Journals in China," 152.

53. Macdonald and Kam, "Aardvark et Al," 706.

54. Linda Butler, "Explaining Australia's Increased Share of ISI Publications: The Effects of a Funding Formula Based on Publication Counts," *Research Policy*, 32, 1 (2003), https://www.sciencedirect.com/science/article/abs/pii/S0048733302000070 ?via%3Dihub.

55. Dragan Djuric, "Penetrating the Omerta of Predatory Publishing: The Romanian Connection," *Science and Engineering Ethics*, 21 (2015).

56. Vaclav Stetka, "Battling Predators in Prague: A Case Study of the Rise and Effects of the Predatory Publishing Model," Punctum Books, ed., *Predatory Publishing*, 6–7.

57. Fran M. Collyer, "Global Patterns in the Publishing of Academic Knowledge: Global North, Global South," *Current Sociology*, 66, 1 (2018) 67.

58. Marco Seeber et al., "Self-citations as Strategic Response to the Use of Metrics for Career Decisions," *Research Policy*, 48, 2 (2019).

59. Mark W. J. Ferguson, "Do Judge: Treat Metrics Only as Surrogates," *Nature* (26 October 2016), https://www.nature.com/news/fewer-numbers-better-science -1.20858.

60. An example from the fifteenth century: Diane Owen Hughes, "Sumptuary Law and Social Relations in Renaissance Italy," in John Bossy, ed., *Disputes and Settlements* (Cambridge 1983) 94.

61. Poynder, "PLoS ONE, Open Access, and the Future of Scholarly Publishing," 27.

62. David Nicholas et al., "Peer Review: Still King in the Digital Age," *Learned Publishing*, 28, 1 (2015) 15, https://onlinelibrary.wiley.com/doi/epdf/10.1087/20150104. Even those who make a living from publishing it: Timo Hannay, "Stop the Deluge of Science Research," *Guardian* (5 August 2014), https://www.theguardian.com/higher -education-network/blog/2014/aug/05/why-we-should-publish-less-scientific -research.

63. Eve, *Open Access and the Humanities*, 112; Bacevic and Muellerleile, "Moral Economy of Open Access," 179.

64. Altbach and de Wit, "Too Much Academic Research Is Being Published."

65. Giulia M. Dotti Sani and Judith Treas, "Educational Gradiants in Parents' Child-Care Time across Countries, 1965–2012," *Journal of Marriage and Family*, 78, 4 (2016), https://archive.org/details/sani602561/mode/2up.

66. John Robert Warren, "How Much Do You Have to Publish to Get a Job in a Top Sociology Department? Or to Get Tenure? Trends over a Generation," *Sociological Science* (27 February 2019), https://sociologicalscience.com/articles-v6-7-172/.

67. William J. Broad, "The Publishing Game: Getting More for Less," *Science*, 211 (1981) 1137.

68. "The Cost of Salami Slicing," *Nature Materials*, 4, 1 (2005), https://www .nature.com/articles/nmat1305.

69. Baldi, "Normative versus Social Constructivist Processes in the Allocation of Citations," 841.

70. Lutz Bornmann and Hans-Dieter Daniel, "Multiple Publication of a Single Research Study: Does it Pay?" *Journal of the American Society for Information Science and Technology*, 58, 8 (2007).

71. Uta Frith, "Fast Lane to Slow Science," *Trends in Cognitive Sciences*, 24, 1 (2020), https://www.cell.com/trends/cognitive-sciences/fulltext/S1364-6613(19)30242 -6?_returnURL=https%3A%2F%2Flinkinghub.elsevier.com%2Fretrieve%2Fpii%2FS 1364661319302426%3Fshowall%3Dtrue.

72. J. L. Austin, "Three Ways of Spilling Ink," *Philosophical Review*, 75, 4 (1966), for example.

73. Poynder, "PLoS ONE, Open Access, and the Future of Scholarly Publishing," 28–29.

74. Quoted in Blair, *Too Much to Know*, 18.

75. *Accessibility, Sustainability, Excellence*, 21; Johnson et al., *STM Report*, 25. This tallies broadly with a figure of one million publishing annually. Regazzi, *Scholarly Communications*, 5.

76. Katy Börner, *Atlas of Science: Visualizing What We Know* (Cambridge MA 2010) 4.

77. *UNESCO Science Report: Towards 2030* (Paris 2015) table 1.4, https://en .unesco.org/unescosciencereport.

78. Zie et al., "China's Rise as a Major Contributor to Science and Technology," 9437, 9440.

79. Johnson et al., *STM Report*, 38.

80. Fanelli and Larivière, "Researchers' Individual Publication Rate."

81. Alison Flood, "UK Publishes More Books per Capita Than Any Other Country, Report Shows," *Guardian* (22 October 2014), https://www.theguardian.com /books/2014/oct/22/uk-publishes-more-books-per-capita-million-report.

82. Mary Nell Bryant, "English Language Publication and the British Traditional Market Agreement," *Library Quarterly*, 49, 4 (1979).

83. International Publishers Association, *Annual Report 2015–2016*, table 2, https://www.internationalpublishers.org/images/reports/Annual_Report_2016/IPA _Annual_Report_2015-2016_interactive.pdf.

84. Nicholas et al., "Peer Review: Still King in the Digital Age," 15.

85. Hazel Rose Markus and Barry Schwartz, "Does Choice Mean Freedom and Well-Being?" *Journal of Consumer Research*, 37 (2010); David S. Ackerman et al., "Having Many Choice Options Seems Like a Great Idea, but . . ." *Journal of Marketing Education*, 36, 3 (2014); Frank Schilbach et al., "The Psychological Lives of the Poor," *American Economic Review*, 106, 5 (2016).

86. Ginsparg, "First Steps towards Electronic Research Communication," 394.

87. Gjerløw, "Peer Review, DORA, and Science."

88. Baldwin, *Copyright Wars*, 338.

89. Susan D. Blum, *My Word! Plagiarism and College Culture* (Ithaca 2010).

90. Serbian conditions are similar: Zorana Suvakovic, "Serbia's Degree Mills," *Aljazeera* (25 July 2014), https://www.aljazeera.com/opinions/2014/7/25/serbias -degree-mills. Even Putin apparently plagiarized his way to an advanced degree. Julie Corwin, "Russia: U.S. Academics Charge Putin With Plagiarizing Thesis," *Radio Free Europe* (27 March 2006), https://www.rferl.org/a/1067113.html.

91. https://www.vroniplag.de/.

92. 68% of the House and 77% of the Senate have post-BA degrees. Congressional Research Service, "Membership of the 116th Congress: A Profile" (17 December 2020), 5, https://sgp.fas.org/crs/misc/R45583.pdf. About the same number have PhDs in the UK and US: 25 Representatives and Senators, 21 MPs in 2012: "How Many Sitting UK MPs Who Hold a PhD Degree?" *Student Room*, https://www .thestudentroom.co.uk/showthread.php?t=2204934.

93. Over 40% of MPs have studied politics, English, philosophy, or history. "MPs and Their Degrees: Here's Where and What Our UK Politicians Studied," *Studee* (13 December 2019), https://studee.com/media/mps-and-their-degrees-media/. Only 17% in a recent parliament had STEM degrees. "MPs with Both an Educational and Occupational Background in STEM Are the Most Likely to Demonstrate Engagement with STEM Issues in Parliament," *LSE British Politics and Policy* (9 August 2021), https://blogs.lse.ac.uk/politicsandpolicy/stem-mps-pmbs/. Only 10% have postgraduate qualifications: Rebecca Montacute and Tim Carr, "Parliamentary Privilege: The MPs in 2017," Sutton Trust, *Research Brief*, 18 (2017), https://www.suttontrust.com /wp-content/uploads/2020/01/Parliamentary-privilege-2017_FINAL-1.pdf.

Conclusion

1. Stephen Pinfield et al., *Open Access in Theory and Practice: The Theory-Practice Relationship and Openness* (Milton Park 2021) 176.

2. Yochai Benkler, *The Wealth of Networks: How Social Production Transforms Markets and Freedom* (New Haven 2007).

3. Jennifer Sinor, "One Size Doesn't Fit All in Open Access," *Chronicle of Higher Education* (24 March 2014), https://www.chronicle.com/article/one-size-doesnt-fit -all-in-open-access/?cid=gen_sign_in.

4. HSBC Global Research, "Reed Elsevier," 25.

5. 17 USC Sect 101. McSherry, *Who Owns Academic Work?* ch. 3.

6. Harvard University, Office of Technology Development, "Statement of Policy in Regard to Intellectual Property (IP Policy)," https://otd.harvard.edu/faculty-inventors/resources/policies-and-procedures/statement-of-policy-in-regard-to-intellectual-property/#inventions-and-patents.

7. Todd F. Simon, "Faculty Writings: Are They 'Works Made for Hire' under the 1976 Copyright Act?" *Journal of College and University Law*, 9, 4 (1982–83) 496.

8. Reichman, "Computer Programs as Applied Scientific Know-How," 676.

9. The Stevenson-Wydler Technology Innovation Act and Bayh-Dole Act. Rebecca S. Eisenberg, "Public Research and Private Development: Patents and Technology Transfer in Government-Sponsored Research," *Virginia Law Review*, 82, 8 (1996) 1665.

10. Reichman, "Computer Programs as Applied Scientific Know-How," 645–646; Steven C. Ward, *Neoliberalism and the Global Restructuring of Knowledge and Education* (New York 2012) 92; Malhar N. Kumar, "Ethical Conflicts in Commercialization of University Research in the Post–Bayh–Dole Era," *Ethics & Behavior*, 20, 5 (2010) 325.

11. In 2009, four-year colleges in the US had a staff of 3.7 million. With enrollments of almost 13 million in 2009 and an average tuition of $21,657, that suggests an annual income from this source alone of $280 billion. Added to that were approximately $60 billion in federal and private R&D funding in 2011. In 2013, the motion picture and recording industries employed 388,000 people. The industries' gross intake was $61.2 billion in 2010. Figures from: Institute of Education Sciences Digest of Education Statistics, 2011 Tables and Figures, http://nces.ed.gov/programs/digest/d11/tables/dt11_196.asp; Congressional Research Service memo from Sue Kirchhoff (9 December 2011) at http://www.techdirt.com/articles/20111212/02244817037/congressional-research-service-shows-hollywood-is-thriving.shtml; US Department of Labor, Bureau of Labor Statistics, *Industries at a Glance*; Motion Picture and Sound Recording Industries: NAICS 512; Workforce Statistics: Employment, Unemployment, and Layoffs; Employment, all employees (seasonally adjusted), http://www.bls.gov/iag/tgs/iag512.htm#workforce.

12. US Office of Government Ethics, "Book Deals Involving Government Employees" (6 March 2008) 3, https://www.oge.gov/web/oge.nsf/News+Releases/7A40ADA00743E87D852585BA005BECD7/$FILE/DO-08-006%20(1)__.pdf.

13. Samuel E. Trosow, "Copyright Protection for Federally Funded Research: Necessary Incentive or Double Subsidy?" (7 September 2003) 80, http://publish.uwo.ca/~strosow/Sabo_Bill_Paper.pdf.

14. Pamela A. Kilby, "The Discouragement of Learning: Scholarship Made for Hire," *Journal of College and University Law*, 21, 3 (1994) 474.

15. Bacevic and Muellerleile, "Moral Economy of Open Access," 180.

16. House of Commons Business, Innovation and Skills Committee, *Open Access: Fifth Report of Session 2013–14*, i, 13.

17. Guédon, "Open Access: Toward the Internet of the Mind," 15.

18. Which is why we have books extolling the virtues of amateurship: Andy Merrifield, *The Amateur: The Pleasures of Doing What You Love* (London 2017).

19. https://doaj.org/.

20. Alfred J. Lotka, "The Frequency Distribution of Scientific Productivity," *Journal of the Washington Academy of Sciences*, 12, 16 (1926).

21. On other similar measures: De Bellis, *Bibliometrics and Citation Analysis*, ch. 4. There are between 7 and 8 million researchers, of whom about 20% are repeat authors. Johnson et al., *STM Report*, 25. Similar figures here: Mabe, "Growth and Number of Journals,"193.

22. Ian Rowlands, "Emerald Authorship Data, Lotka's Law and Research Productivity," *AsLib Proceedings*, 57, 1 (2005), https://www.emerald.com/insight/content /doi/10.1108/00012530510579039/full/html?casa_token=fasNnMYJzzsAAAAA :kzTO40e6njqjJf_NIecKnF58lqwkWCRBXXuJ4p-he-ZMCWC5GGWYjC -Gzwt7dc6RXx04W41iDVk7SSDfzK_o_aMge5tW3hFyaRgonF7kY-xuMJ1I-yYo. And see Isaiah T. Arkin, "Science, Music, Literature and the One-hit Wonder Connection," *Research Trends* (March 2011), https://www.researchtrends.com/issue22 -march-2011/science-music-literature-and-the-one-hit-wonder-connection/.

23. H. Kretschmer and R. Rousseau, "Author Inflation Leads to a Breakdown of Lotka's Law," *Journal of the American Society for Information Science and Technology*, 52 8 (2001) 610–614.

24. Solomon and Björk, "Publication Fees in Open Access Publishing," 101.

25. Mellon Foundation, *Pay it Forward*, 29.

26. UK Research and Innovation, "UKRI Open Access Policy" (6 August 2021) Annex 1, https://www.ukri.org/publications/ukri-open-access-policy/.

27. "Wellcome Trust Extends Open Access Policy to Include Scholarly Monographs and Book Chapters" (29 May 2013), https://wellcome.org/press-release /wellcome-trust-extends-open-access-policy-include-scholarly-monographs-and -book.

28. Moore, "Revisiting 'the 1990s Debutante.'"

29. https://www.doabooks.org/; Ferwerda et al., *Landscape Study on Open Access*, 21.

30. Colin Steele, "Open Access in Australia: An Odyssey of Sorts?" *UKSG Insights* 26, 3 (2013) 282–289, http://doi.org/10.1629/2048-7754.91.

31. Roxanne Missingham, "University Presses Decline to Decline: New Models Down Under," *CAUL Publishing* (30 November 2015), https://caullibrarypublishing .wordpress.com/2015/11/30/university-presses-decline-to-decline-new-models -down-under/.

32. Janneke Adema and Graham Stone, *Changing Publishing Ecologies: A Landscape Study of New University Presses and Academic-Led Publishing* (Jisc nd) 8, https:// repository.jisc.ac.uk/6666/1/Changing-publishing-ecologies-report.pdf.

33. https://www.cambridge.org/core/services/open-research/open-access/oa -book-pilot-flip-it-open.

34. https://www.leverpress.org/about.

35. https://www.intechopen.com/.

36. More on European open access publishing: Mounier, "'Publication Favela' or Bibliodiversity?"

37. Some of these are collected together as Scholarled: https://scholarled .org/#overview. Similar is Radical Open Access: http://radicaloa.disruptivemedia .org.uk/.

38. Agata Morka and Rupert Gatti, *Academic Libraries and Open Access Books in Europe* (OPERAS, January 2021) 27, 48, https://copim.pubpub.org/academic -libraries-and-open-access-books-in-europe-a-landscape-study.

39. Adema and Stone, *Changing Publishing Ecologies*, 56.

40. The Library Publishing Coalition, https://librarypublishing.org/.

41. Adema and Stone, *Changing Publishing Ecologies*, 9–10. Or one in six, depending on whom you ask: Anthony Cond, "The University Press and the Academic Book of the Future," in Rebecca E. Lyons and Samantha J. Rayner, eds., *The Academic Book of the Future* (Basingstoke 2016) 47, https://link.springer.com/book/10.1057 %2F9781137595775.

42. Lorcan Dempsey, "Library Collections in the Life of the User: Two Directions," *LIBER Quarterly*, 26, 4 (2016), https://www.liberquarterly.eu/articles/10.18352 /lq.10170/.

43. Bosman et al., *Open Access Diamond Journals Study*, 8, 40, 100, 110.

44. Potts et al., "A Journal Is a Club," 78.

45. London Economics, *Economic Analysis of Business Models for Open Access Monographs: Annex 4 to the Report of the HEFC Monographs and Open Access Project* (January 2015) 16, https://re.ukri.org/documents/hefce-documents/mono-annex-4 -economic-analysis-pdf/.

46. Phillips, "Role of Book Reviews in the Academic Book Ecosystem."

47. Kień, "Authors from the Periphery Countries Choose Open Access More Often"; Johnson et al., *STM Report*, 80.

48. Alessandra Tosi, "Professor Lionel Gossman: In Memoriam," https://blogs .openbookpublishers.com/professor-lionel-gossman-in-memoriam/. My own attempt to set a good example was less successful. Only after coming to an agreement with Princeton University Press to release a recent book in an open-access edition two years after publication did I notice that the press has no such program. After the agreed-upon interval, they sent me a PDF, satisfied that they had kept their end of the bargain. It is now available at https://archive.org/details/BaldwinCopyright CCBYNCND or https://directory.doabooks.org/handle/20.500.12854/44072.

49. https://www.openbookpublishers.com/section/101/1.

50. https://press.anu.edu.au/publications/series/peacebuilding-compared/ macrocriminology-and-freedom.

51. https://press.anu.edu.au/publications/regulatory-theory.

52. https://www.uclpress.co.uk/pages/statistics.

53. "A Not So Direct #OpenEd17 Reflection: Openwrapping," Scott Robison (18 October 2017), http://scottrobison.net/blog/2017/10/18/a-not-so-direct-opened17 -reflection-openwrapping/.

54. Lindsay McKenzie, "Big Read-and-Publish Push Arrives," *Inside Higher Ed* (1 April 2021), https://www.insidehighered.com/news/2021/04/01/cambridge -university-press-strikes-deals-open-access. CUP's handsome profits, bested only by OUP, help finance the university. Though doubtless a worthy cause, that does not make its output cheaper or more available.

Index